Lovesick Ellie 1 is a work of fiction. Names, characters, places, and incidents are the products of the author's imagination or are used fictitiously. Any resemblance to actual events, locales, or persons, living or dead, is entirely coincidental.

A Kodansha Trade Paperback Original

Published in the United States by
Kodansha USA Publishing, LLC, New York.

Publication rights for this English edition arranged through
Kodansha Ltd., Tokyo.

First published in Japan in 2015 by Kodansha Ltd., Tokyo
as *Koiwazurai no Ellie*, volume 1.

ISBN 978-1-64651-317-8

Printed in the United States of America.

9 8 7 6 5 4 3 2 1

Translation: Ursula Ku
Lettering: Allen Berry
Additional Lettering and Layout: Lys Blakeslee
Editing: Sarah Tilson, Vanessa Tenazas
YKS Services LLC/SKY JAPAN, Inc.
Kodansha USA Publishing edition cover design by Matthew Akuginow

Publisher: Kiichiro Sugawara

Director of Publishing Services: Ben Applegate
Associate Director of Operations: Stephen Pakula
Publishing Services Managing Editors: Alanna Ruse, Madison Salters
Production Managers: Emi Lotto, Angela Zurlo

KODANSHA.US

KODANSHA

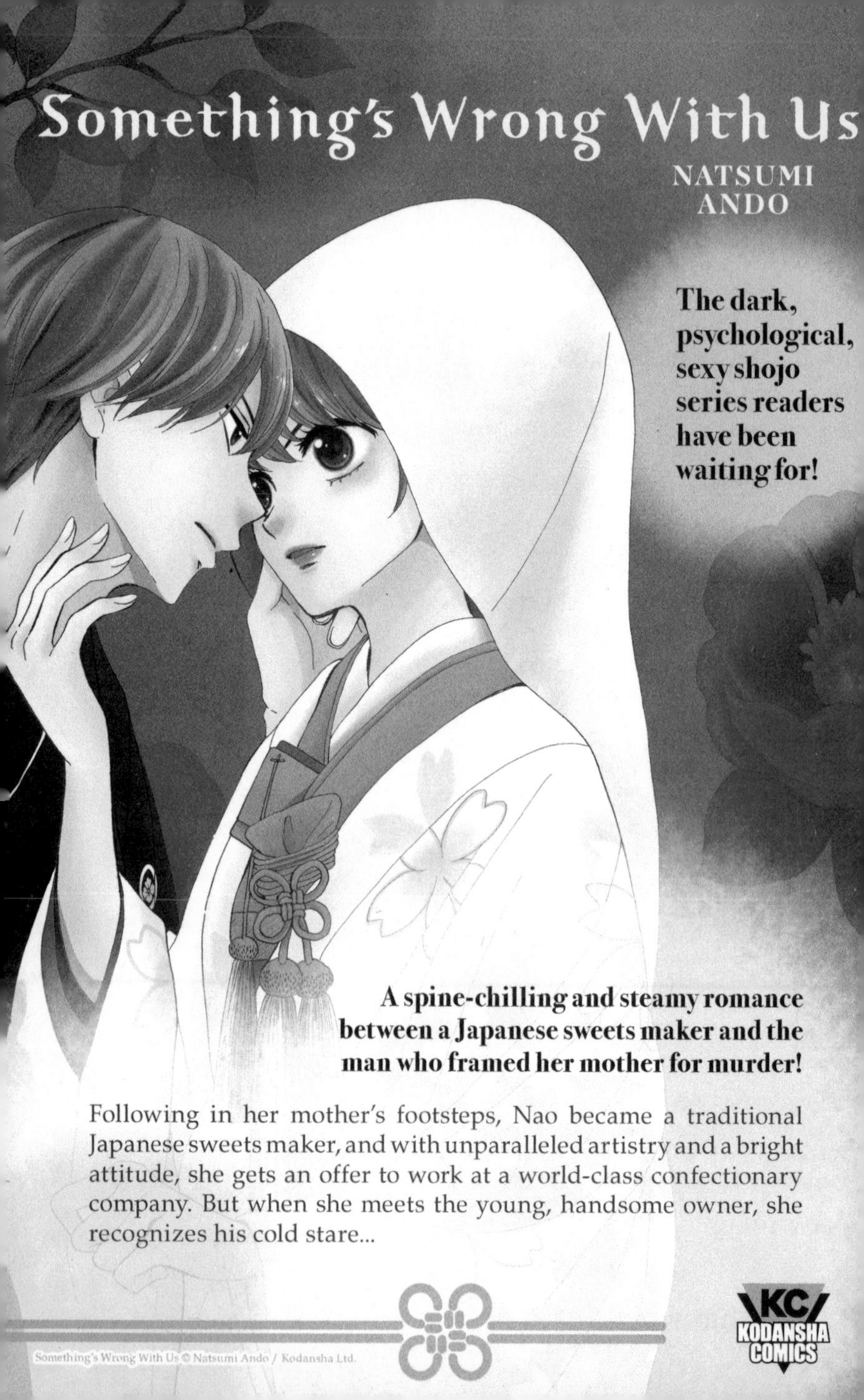
Something's Wrong With Us
NATSUMI ANDO
The dark, psychological, sexy shojo series readers have been waiting for!
A spine-chilling and steamy romance between a Japanese sweets maker and the man who framed her mother for murder!
Following in her mother's footsteps, Nao became a traditional Japanese sweets maker, and with unparalleled artistry and a bright attitude, she gets an offer to work at a world-class confectionary company. But when she meets the young, handsome owner, she recognizes his cold stare...
KC KODANSHA COMICS
Something's Wrong With Us © Natsumi Ando / Kodansha Ltd.

A picture-perfect shojo series from Yoko Nogiri, creator of the hit *That Wolf-Boy is Mine!*

Mako's always had a passion for photography. When she loses someone dear to her, she clings onto her art as a relic of the close relationship she once had... Luckily, her childhood best friend Kei encourages her to come to his high school and join their prestigious photo club. With nothing to lose, Mako grabs her camera and moves into the dorm where Kei and his classmates live. Soon, a fresh take on life, along with a mysterious new muse, begin to come into focus!

LOVE IN FOCUS

Praise for Yoko Nogiri's *That Wolf-Boy is Mine!*

"Emotional squees...will-they-won't-they plot...[and a] pleasantly quick pace."
—Otaku USA Magazine

"A series that is pure shojo sugar—a cute love story about two nice people looking for their places in the world, and finding them with each other." —Anime News Network

A SMART, NEW ROMANTIC COMEDY FOR FANS OF *SHORTCAKE CAKE* AND *TERRACE HOUSE!*

A romance manga starring high school girl Meeko, who learns to live on her own in a boarding house whose living room is home to the odd (but handsome) Matsunaga-san. She begins to adjust to her new life away from her parents, but Meeko soon learns that no matter how far away from home she is, she's still a young girl at heart — especially when she finds herself falling for Matsunaga-san.

THE SWEET SCENT OF LOVE IS IN THE AIR! FOR FANS OF OFFBEAT ROMANCES LIKE *WOTAKOI*

Sweat and Soap © Kintetsu Yamada / Kodansha Ltd.

In an office romance, there's a fine line between sexy and awkward... and that line is where Asako — a woman who sweats copiously — meets Koutarou — a perfume developer who can't get enough of Asako's, er, scent. Don't miss a romcom manga like no other!

The adorable new odd-couple cat comedy manga from the creator of the beloved *Chi's Sweet Home*, in full color!

Sue & Tai-chan

Konami Kanata

Sue is an aging housecat who's looking forward to living out her life in peace... but her plans change when the mischievous black tomcat Tai-chan enters the picture! Hey! Sue never signed up to be a catsitter! *Sue & Tai-chan* is the latest from the reigning meow-narch of cute kitty comics, Konami Kanata.

Young characters and steampunk setting, like *Howl's Moving Castle* and *Battle Angel Alita*

A boy with a talent for machines and a mysterious girl whose wings he's fixed will take you beyond the clouds! In the tradition of the high-flying, resonant adventure stories of Studio Ghibli comes a gorgeous tale about the longing of young hearts for adventure and friendship!

The boys are back, in 400-page hardcovers that are as pretty and badass as they are!

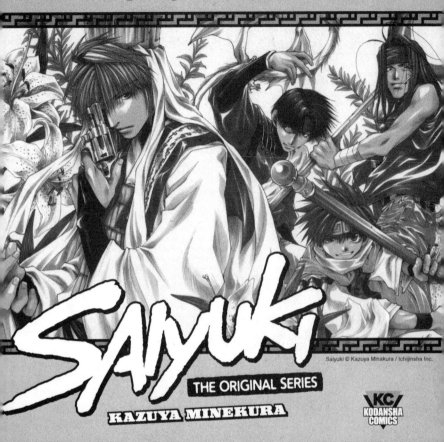

Saiyuki © Kazuya Minekura / Ichijinsha Inc.

SAIYUKI
THE ORIGINAL SERIES
KAZUYA MINEKURA

KC KODANSHA COMICS

"AN EDGY COMIC LOOK AT AN ANCIENT CHINESE TALE." —YALSA

Genjo Sanzo is a Buddhist priest in the city of Togenkyo, which is being ravaged by yokai spirits that have fallen out of balance with the natural order. His superiors send him on a journey far to the west to discover why this is happening and how to stop it. His companions are three yokai with human souls. But this is no day trip — the four will encounter many discoveries and horrors on the way.

FEATURES NEW TRANSLATION, COLOR PAGES, AND BEAUTIFUL WRAPAROUND COVER ART!

The art-deco cyberpunk classic from the creators of *xxxHOLiC* and *Cardcaptor Sakura*!

CLOVER © CLAMP ShigatsuTsuitachi CO.,LTD./Kodansha Ltd

Su was born into a bleak future, where the government keeps tight control over children with magical powers—codenamed "Clovers." With Su being the only "four-leaf" Clover in the world, she has been kept isolated nearly her whole life. Can ex-military agent Kazuhiko deliver her to the happiness she seeks? Experience the complete series in this hardcover edition, which also includes over twenty pages of ravishing color art!

Knight of the ICE

Yayoi Ogawa

Knight of the Ice ©Yayoi Ogawa

SKATING THRILLS AND ICY CHILLS WITH THIS NEW TINGLY ROMANCE SERIES!

A rom-com on ice, perfect for fans of *Princess Jellyfish* and *Wotakoi*. Kokoro is the talk of the figure-skating world, winning trophies and hearts. But little do they know... he's actually a huge nerd! From the beloved creator of *You're My Pet* (*Tramps Like Us*).

Chitose is a serious young woman, working for the health magazine *SASSO*. Or at least, she would be, if she wasn't constantly getting distracted by her childhood friend, international figure skating star Kokoro Kijinami! In the public eye and on the ice, Kokoro is a gallant, flawless knight, but behind his glittery costumes and breathtaking spins lies a secret: He's actually a hopelessly romantic otaku, who can only land his quad jumps when Chitose is on hand to recite a spell from his favorite magical girl anime!

Lovesick Ellie

1

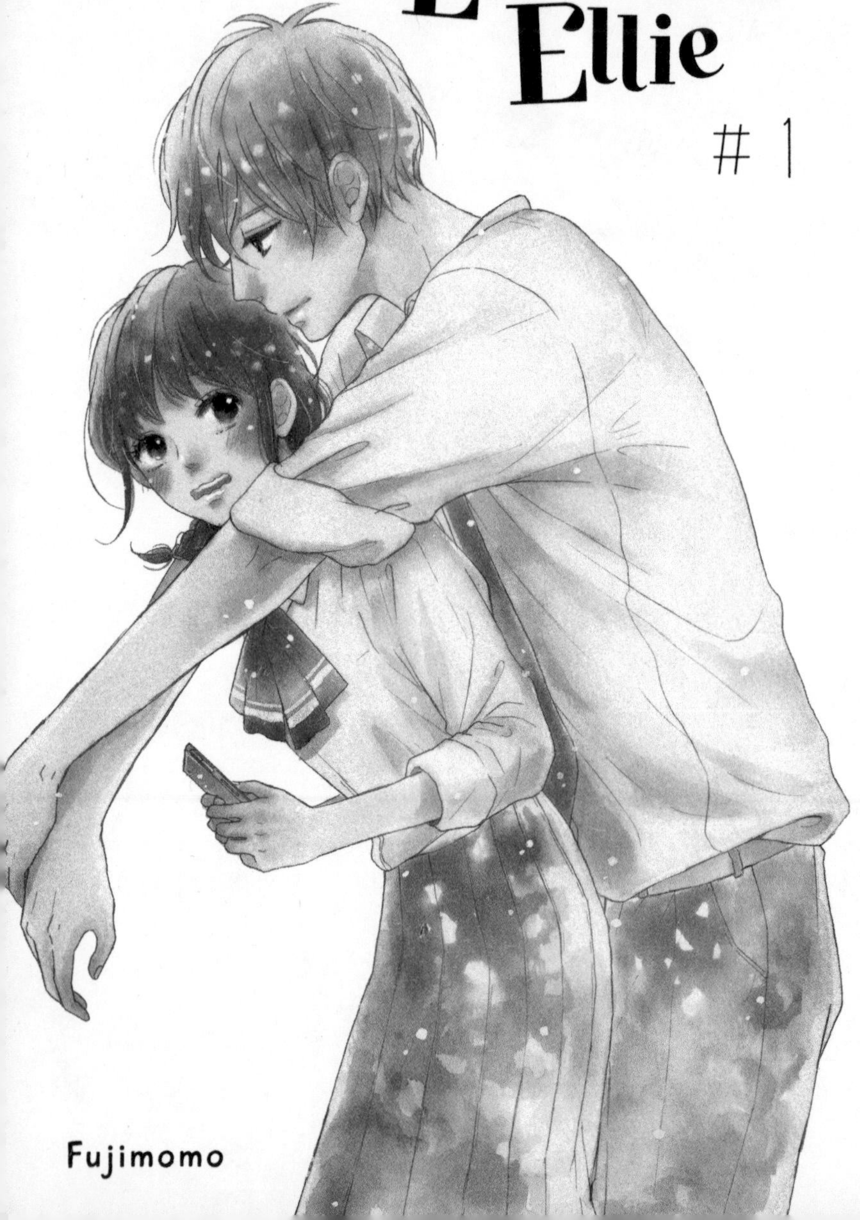

Fujimomo

Lovesick Ellie
contents

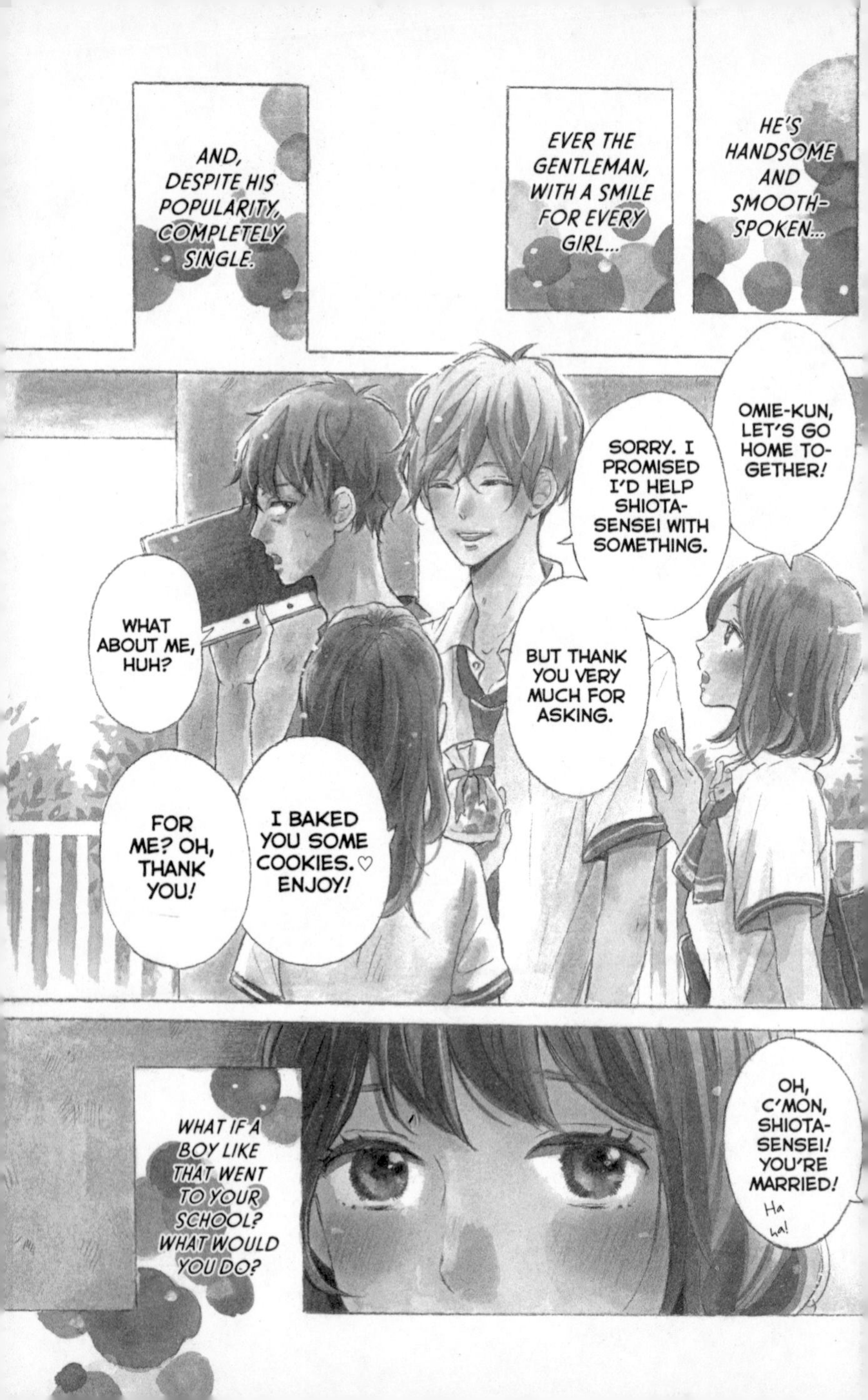
HE'S HANDSOME AND SMOOTH-SPOKEN...
EVER THE GENTLEMAN, WITH A SMILE FOR EVERY GIRL...
AND, DESPITE HIS POPULARITY, COMPLETELY SINGLE.
OMIE-KUN, LET'S GO HOME TO-GETHER!
SORRY. I PROMISED I'D HELP SHIOTA-SENSEI WITH SOMETHING.
BUT THANK YOU VERY MUCH FOR ASKING.
WHAT ABOUT ME, HUH?
I BAKED YOU SOME COOKIES.♡ ENJOY!
FOR ME? OH, THANK YOU!
OH, C'MON, SHIOTA-SENSEI! YOU'RE MARRIED!
Ha ha!
WHAT IF A BOY LIKE THAT WENT TO YOUR SCHOOL? WHAT WOULD YOU DO?

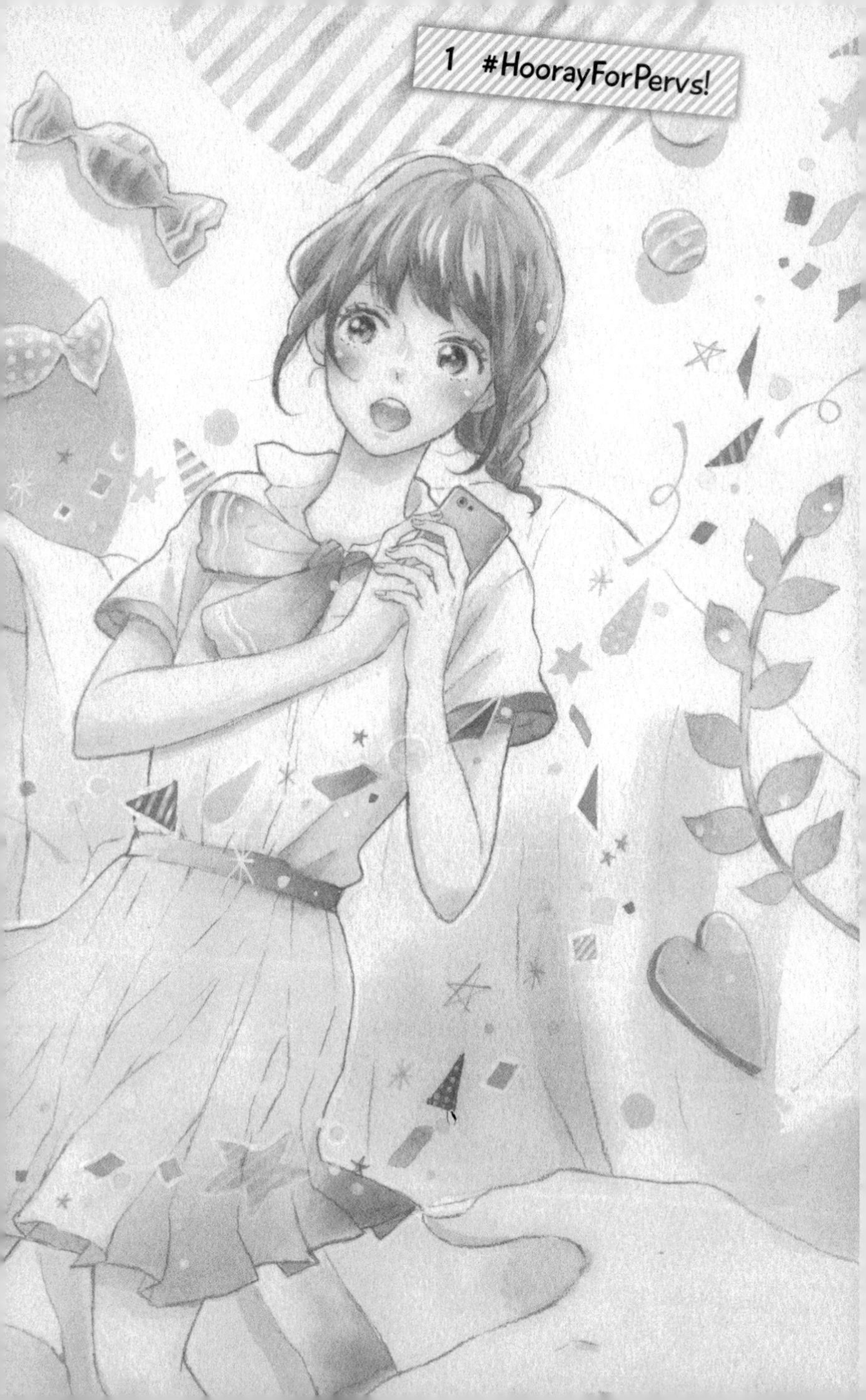
1 #HoorayForPervs!

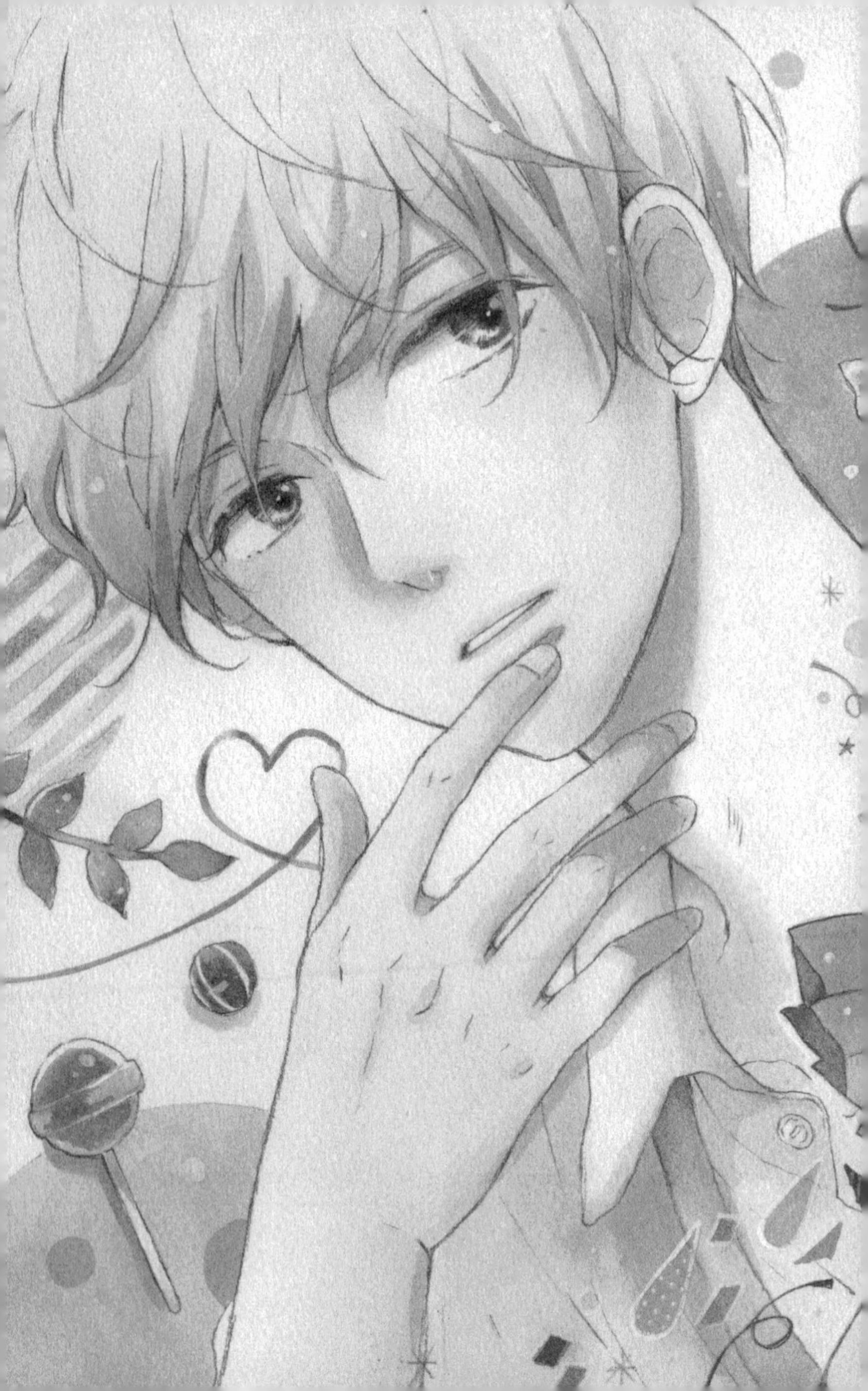

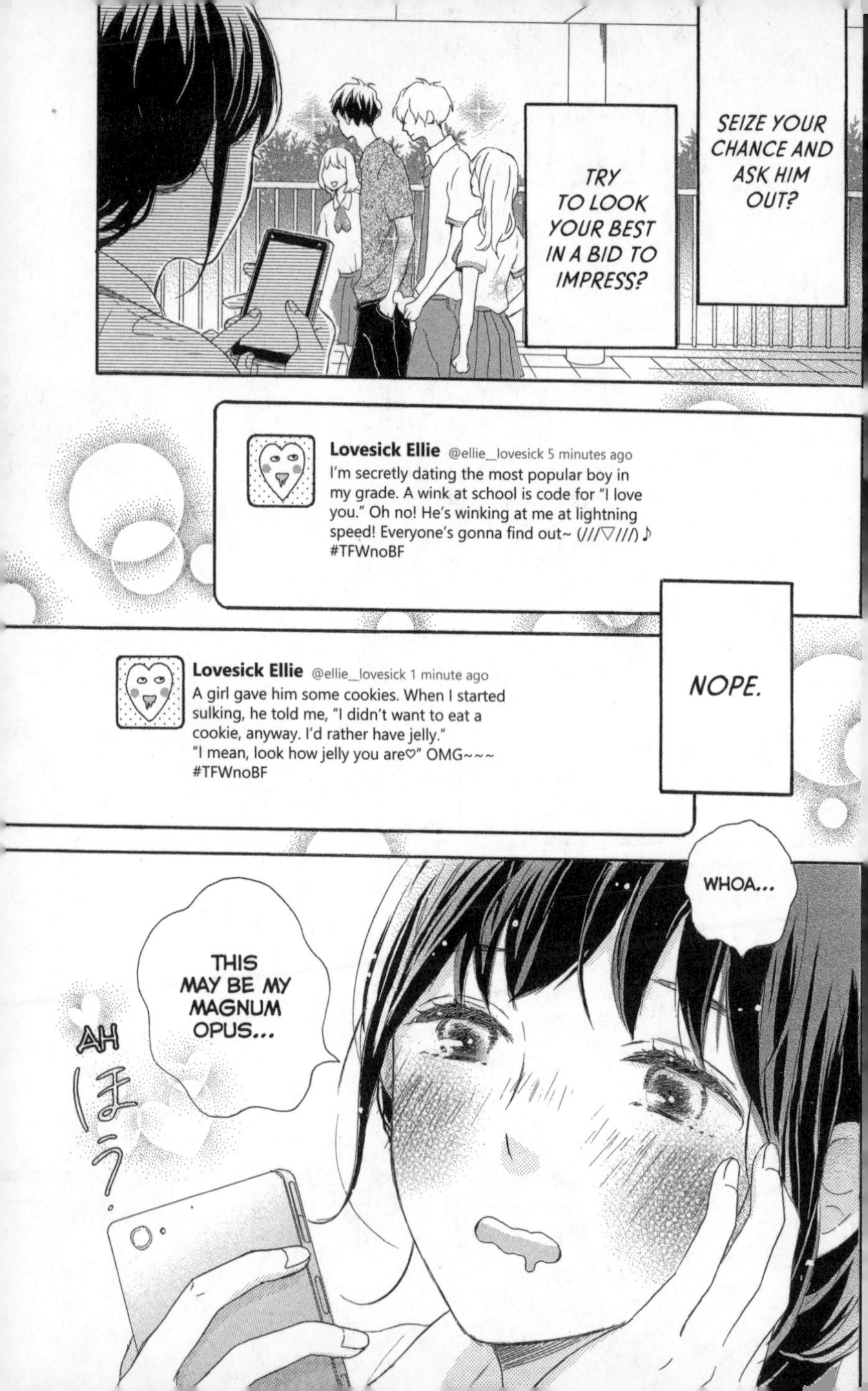

SEIZE YOUR CHANCE AND ASK HIM OUT?
TRY TO LOOK YOUR BEST IN A BID TO IMPRESS?
Lovesick Ellie @ellie__lovesick 5 minutes ago
I'm secretly dating the most popular boy in my grade. A wink at school is code for "I love you." Oh no! He's winking at me at lightning speed! Everyone's gonna find out~ (///▽///)♪
#TFWnoBF
NOPE.
Lovesick Ellie @ellie__lovesick 1 minute ago
A girl gave him some cookies. When I started sulking, he told me, "I didn't want to eat a cookie, anyway. I'd rather have jelly."
"I mean, look how jelly you are♡" OMG~~~
#TFWnoBF
WHOA...
THIS MAY BE MY MAGNUM OPUS...
AH
ほう

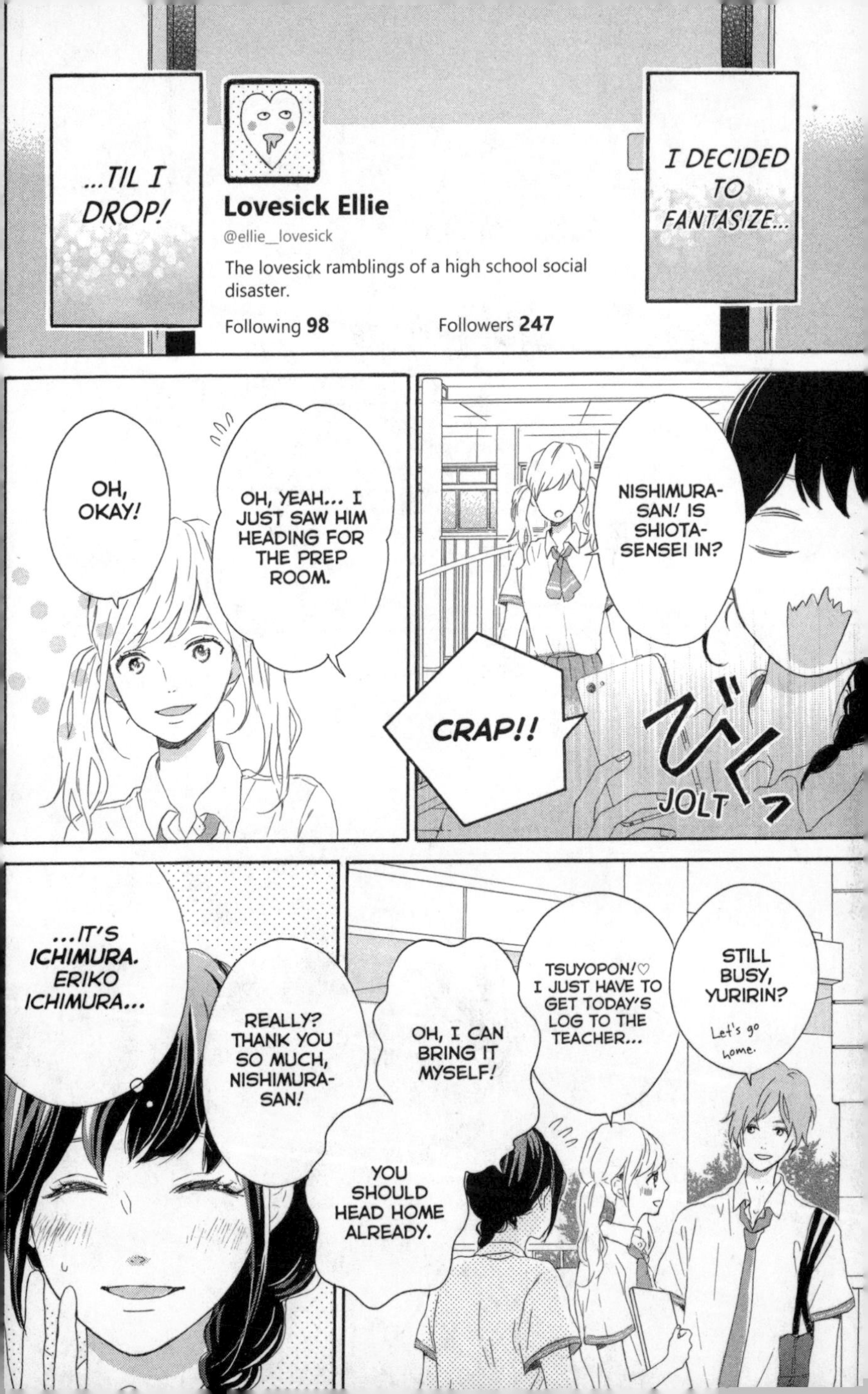
I DECIDED TO FANTASIZE...
Lovesick Ellie
@ellie__lovesick
The lovesick ramblings of a high school social disaster.
Following 98
Followers 247
...TIL I DROP!
NISHIMURA-SAN! IS SHIOTA-SENSEI IN?
びくっ
JOLT
CRAP!!
OH, YEAH... I JUST SAW HIM HEADING FOR THE PREP ROOM.
OH, OKAY!
STILL BUSY, YURIRIN?
Let's go home.
TSUYOPON!♡ I JUST HAVE TO GET TODAY'S LOG TO THE TEACHER...
OH, I CAN BRING IT MYSELF!
YOU SHOULD HEAD HOME ALREADY.
REALLY? THANK YOU SO MUCH, NISHIMURA-SAN!
...IT'S ICHIMURA. ERIKO ICHIMURA...

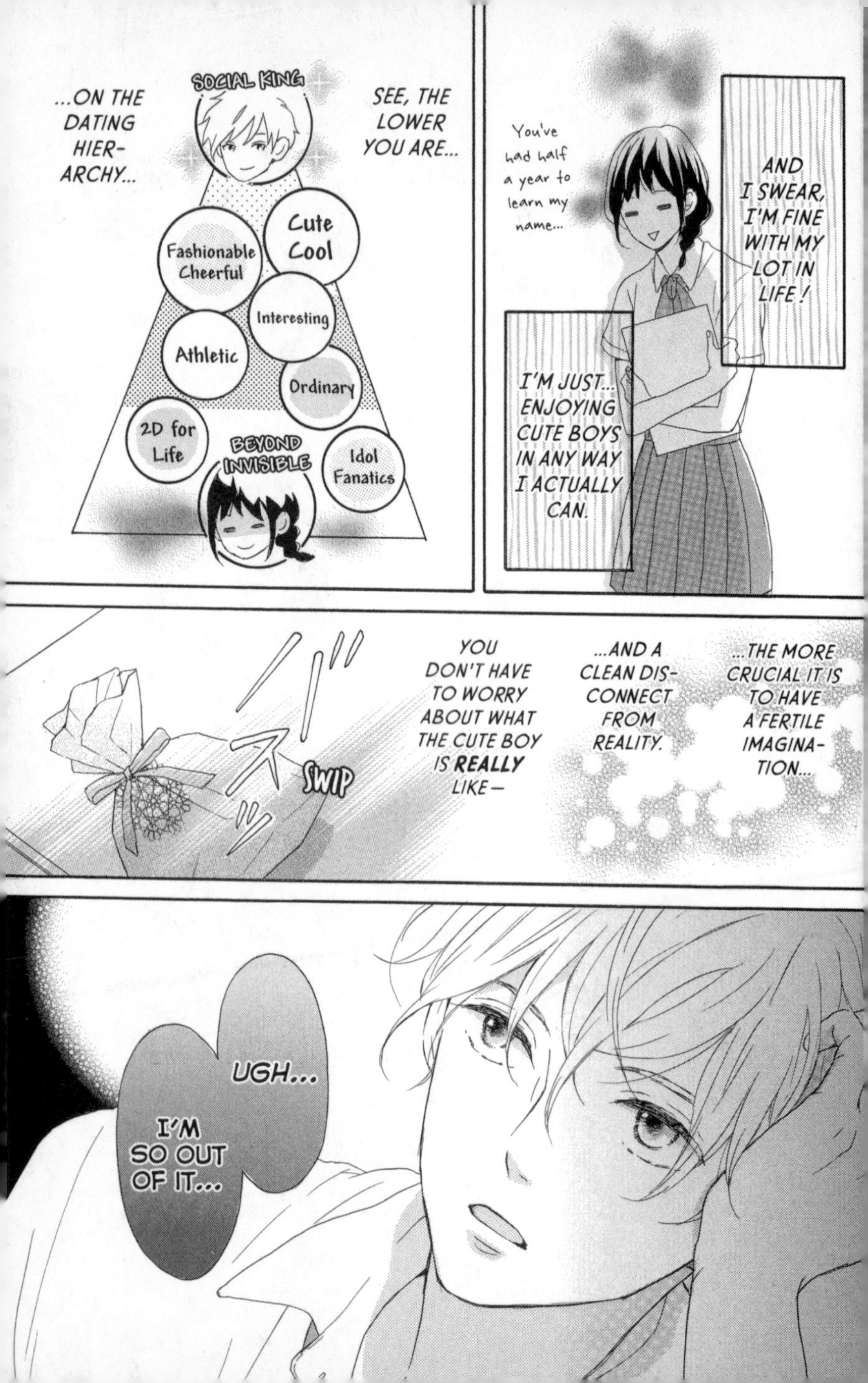

AND I SWEAR, I'M FINE WITH MY LOT IN LIFE!
You've had half a year to learn my name...
I'M JUST... ENJOYING CUTE BOYS IN ANY WAY I ACTUALLY CAN.
SEE, THE LOWER YOU ARE...
...ON THE DATING HIER-ARCHY...
SOCIAL KING
Cute Cool
Fashionable Cheerful
Interesting
Athletic
Ordinary
2D for Life
BEYOND INVISIBLE
Idol Fanatics
...THE MORE CRUCIAL IT IS TO HAVE A FERTILE IMAGINA-TION...
...AND A CLEAN DIS-CONNECT FROM REALITY.
YOU DON'T HAVE TO WORRY ABOUT WHAT THE CUTE BOY IS **REALLY** LIKE—
SWIP
UGH...
I'M SO OUT OF IT...

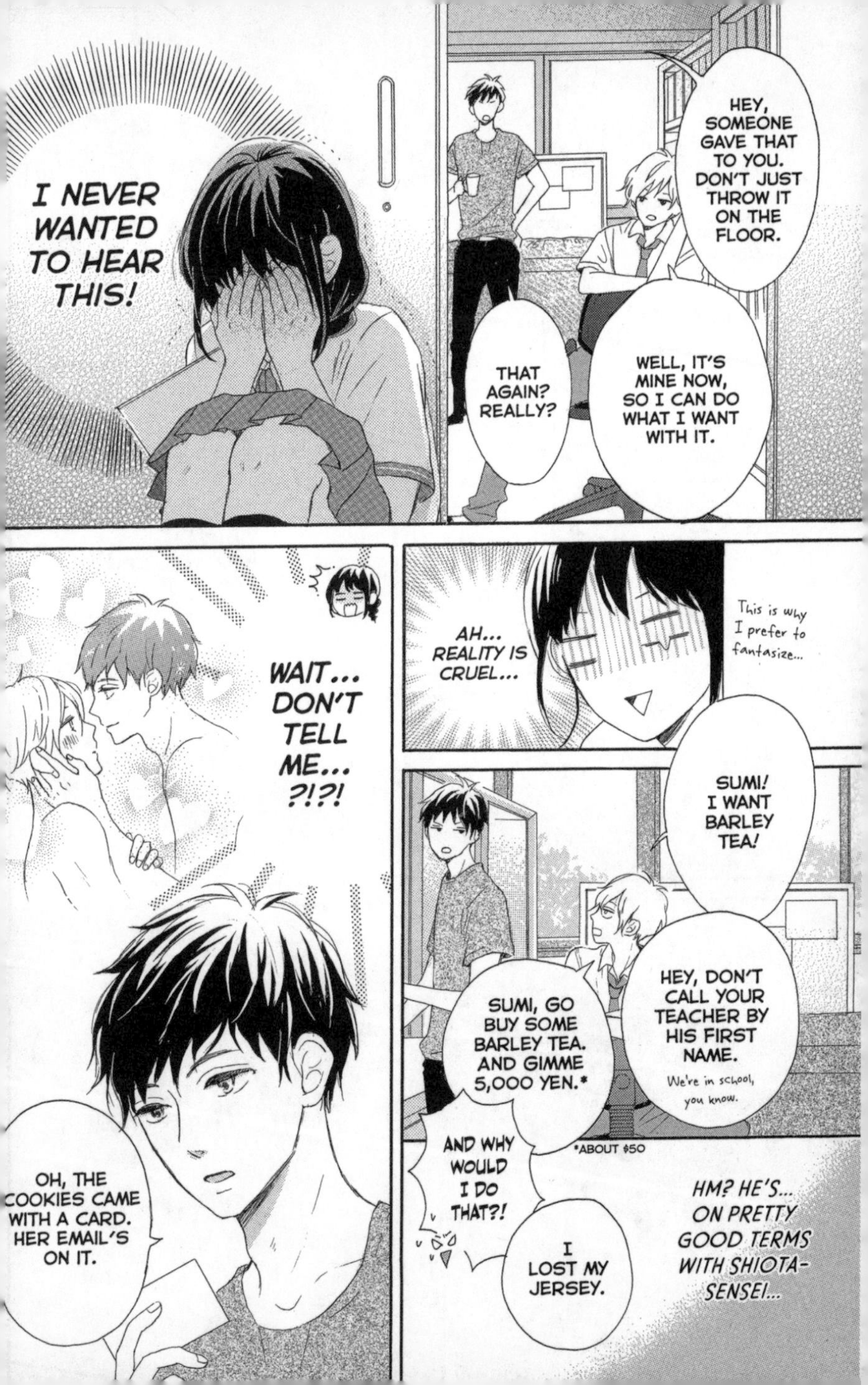
HEY, SOMEONE GAVE THAT TO YOU. DON'T JUST THROW IT ON THE FLOOR.
WELL, IT'S MINE NOW, SO I CAN DO WHAT I WANT WITH IT.
THAT AGAIN? REALLY?
I NEVER WANTED TO HEAR THIS!
This is why I prefer to fantasize...
AH... REALITY IS CRUEL...
SUMI! I WANT BARLEY TEA!
HEY, DON'T CALL YOUR TEACHER BY HIS FIRST NAME.
We're in school, you know.
SUMI, GO BUY SOME BARLEY TEA. AND GIMME 5,000 YEN.*
*ABOUT $50
HM? HE'S... ON PRETTY GOOD TERMS WITH SHIOTA-SENSEI...
AND WHY WOULD I DO THAT?!
I LOST MY JERSEY.
WAIT... DON'T TELL ME... ?!?!
OH, THE COOKIES CAME WITH A CARD. HER EMAIL'S ON IT.

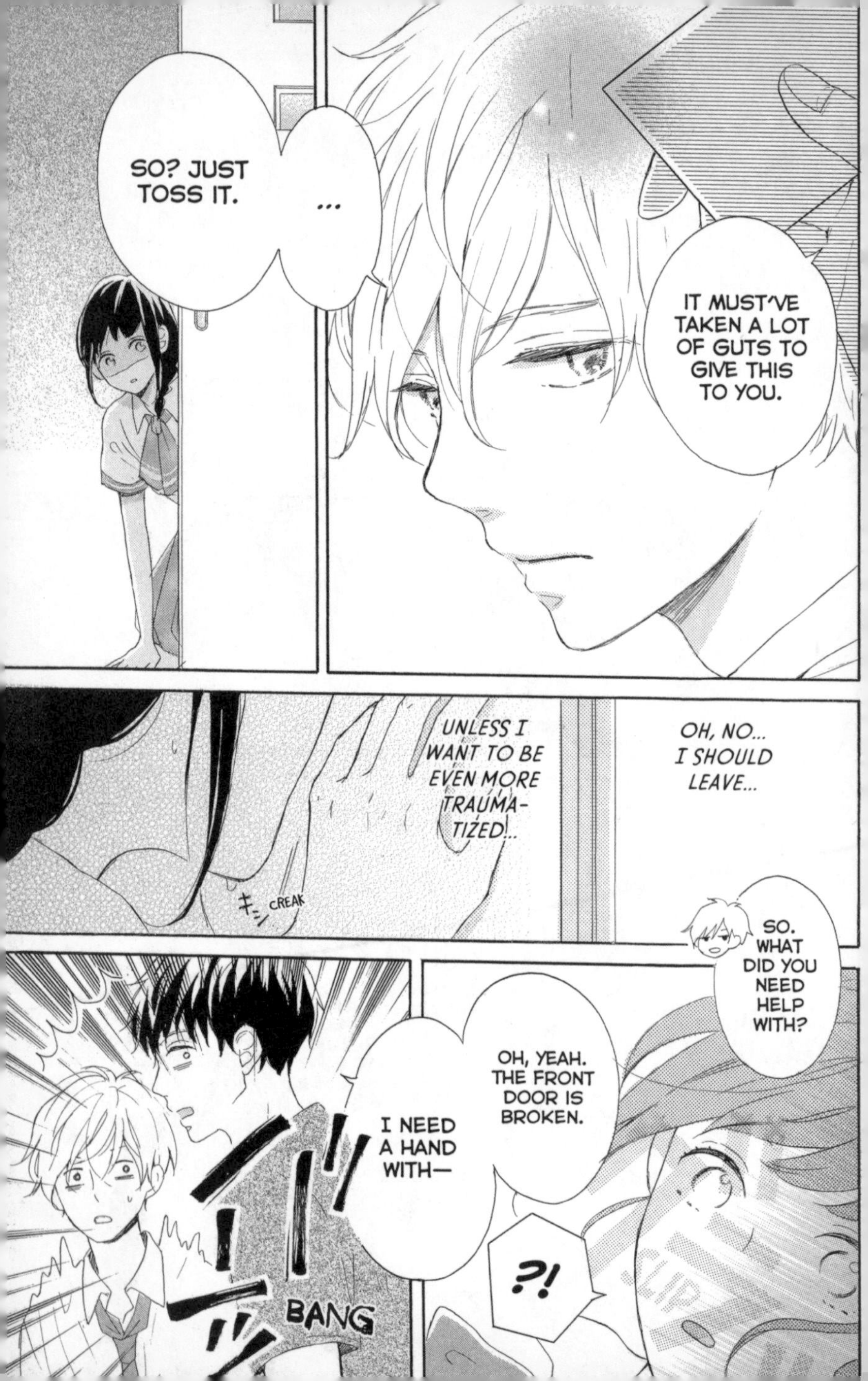
IT MUST'VE TAKEN A LOT OF GUTS TO GIVE THIS TO YOU.
...
SO? JUST TOSS IT.
OH, NO... I SHOULD LEAVE...
UNLESS I WANT TO BE EVEN MORE TRAUMATIZED...
CREAK
SO. WHAT DID YOU NEED HELP WITH?
OH, YEAH. THE FRONT DOOR IS BROKEN.
I NEED A HAND WITH—
?!
BANG

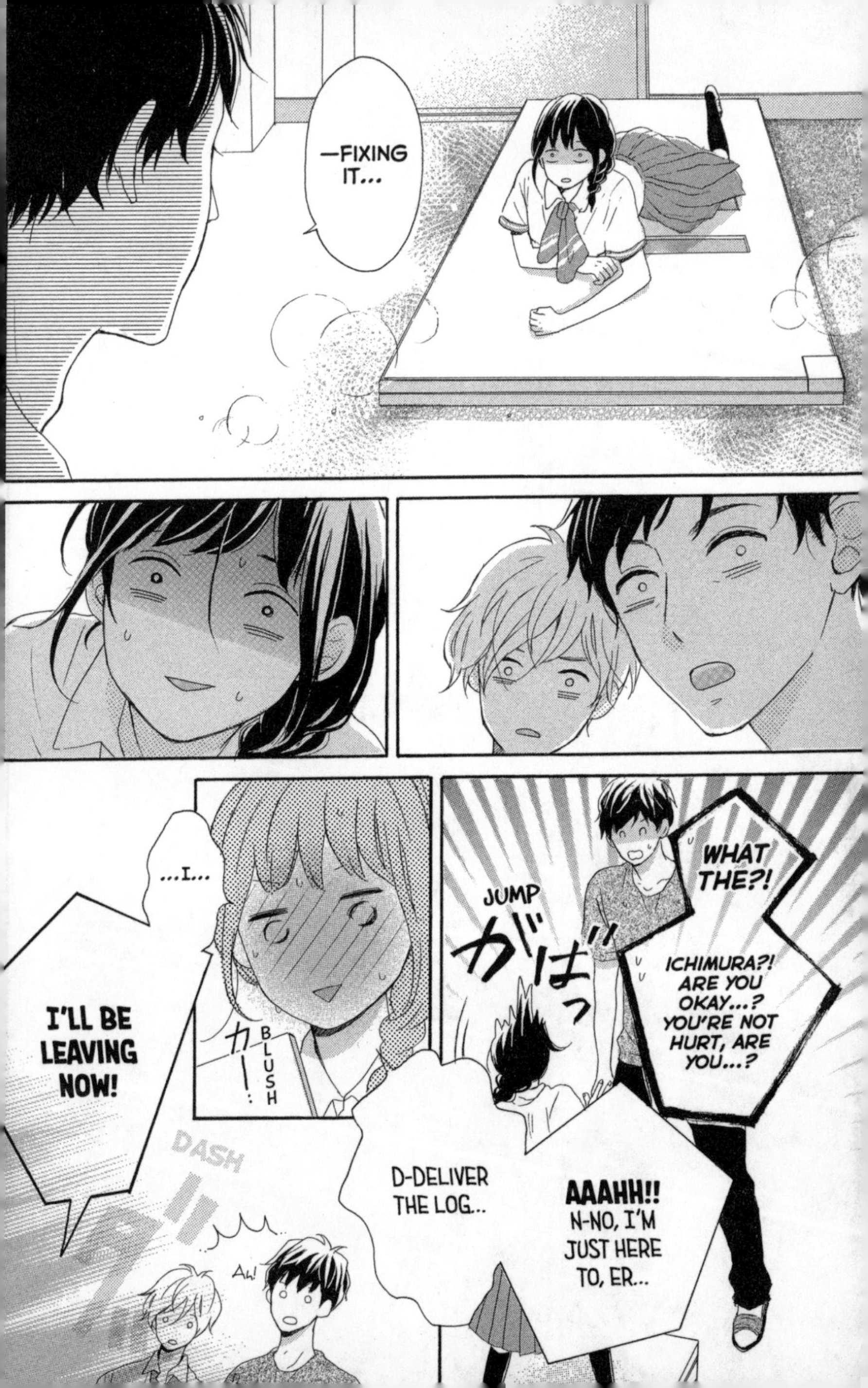
—FIXING IT...
WHAT THE?!
JUMP
がばっ
ICHIMURA?! ARE YOU OKAY...? YOU'RE NOT HURT, ARE YOU...?
AAAHH!! N-NO, I'M JUST HERE TO, ER...
D-DELIVER THE LOG...
...I...
カー
BLUSH
I'LL BE LEAVING NOW!
DASH
Ah!

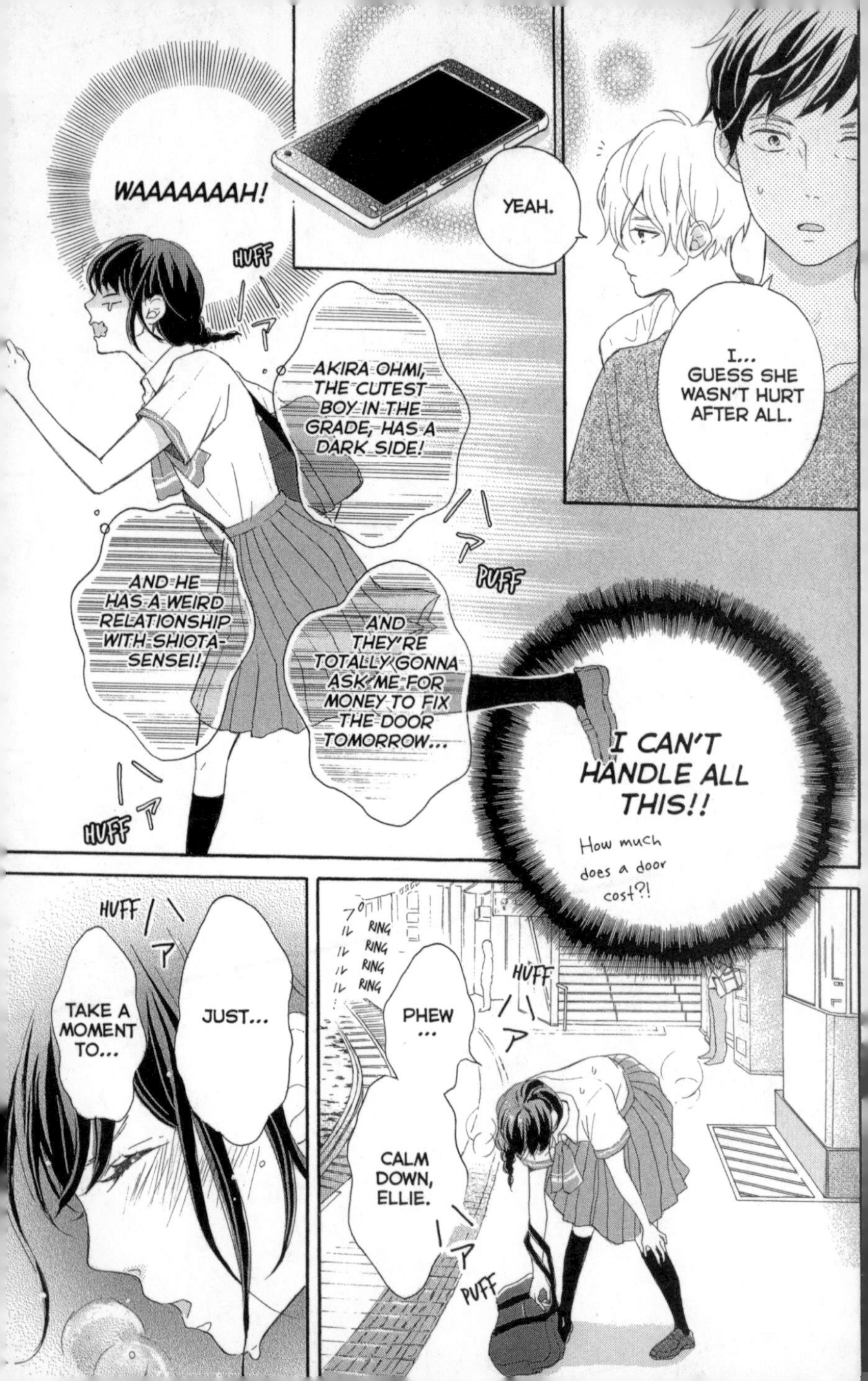
I... GUESS SHE WASN'T HURT AFTER ALL.
YEAH.
I CAN'T HANDLE ALL THIS!!
How much does a door cost?!
WAAAAAAAH!
HUFF
AKIRA OHMI, THE CUTEST BOY IN THE GRADE, HAS A DARK SIDE!
PUFF
AND THEY'RE TOTALLY GONNA ASK ME FOR MONEY TO FIX THE DOOR TOMORROW...
AND HE HAS A WEIRD RELATIONSHIP WITH SHIOTA-SENSEI!
HUFF
RING RING RING RING
HUFF
PHEW...
CALM DOWN, ELLIE.
PUFF
HUFF
JUST...
TAKE A MOMENT TO...

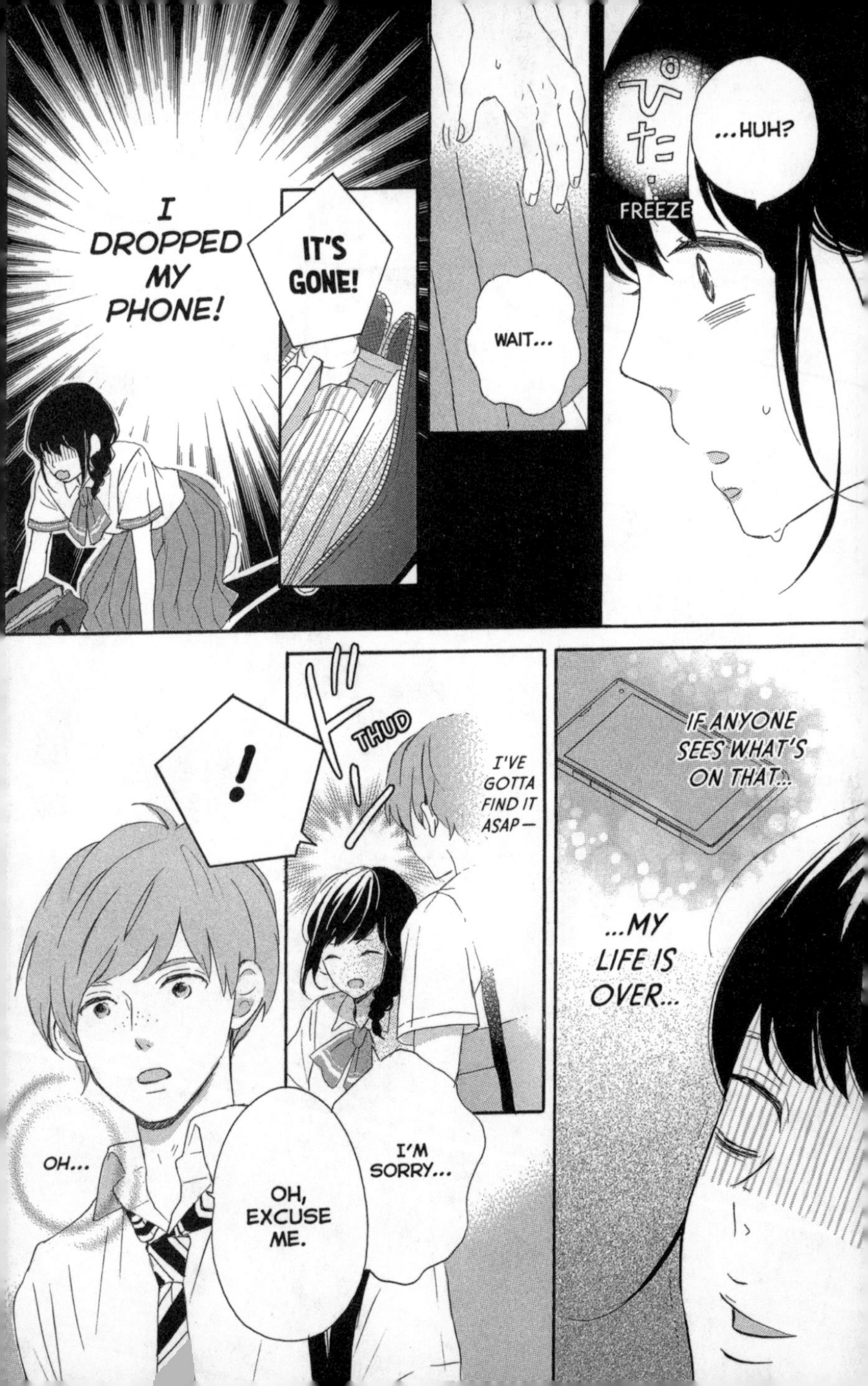
...HUH?
ぴた
FREEZE
WAIT...
IT'S GONE!
I DROPPED MY PHONE!
IF ANYONE SEES WHAT'S ON THAT...
...MY LIFE IS OVER...
THUD
I'VE GOTTA FIND IT ASAP—
I'M SORRY...
!
OH, EXCUSE ME.
OH...

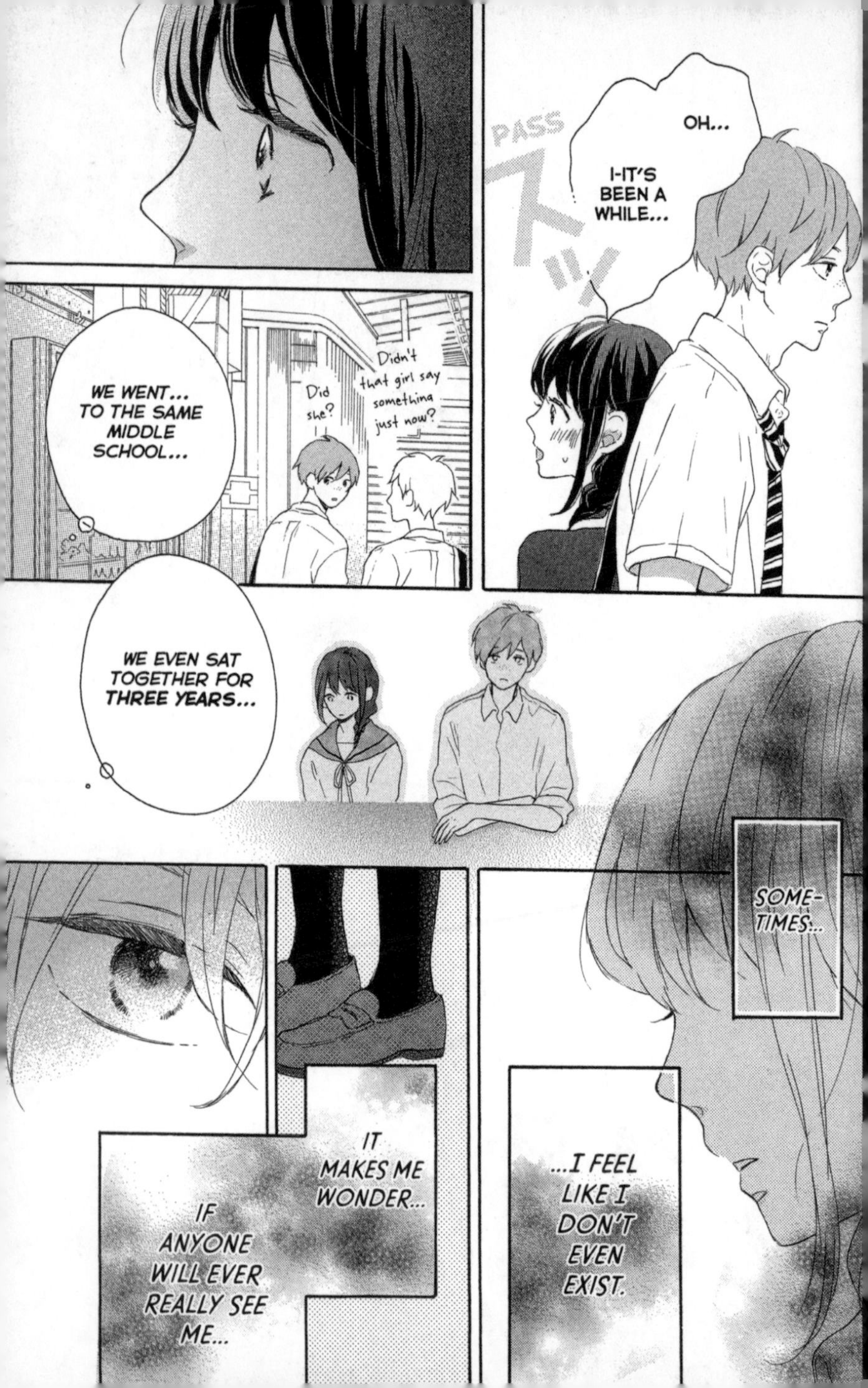
PASS
OH...
I-IT'S BEEN A WHILE...
Didn't that girl say something just now?
Did she?
WE WENT... TO THE SAME MIDDLE SCHOOL...
WE EVEN SAT TOGETHER FOR THREE YEARS...
SOMETIMES...
...I FEEL LIKE I DON'T EVEN EXIST.
IT MAKES ME WONDER...
IF ANYONE WILL EVER REALLY SEE ME...

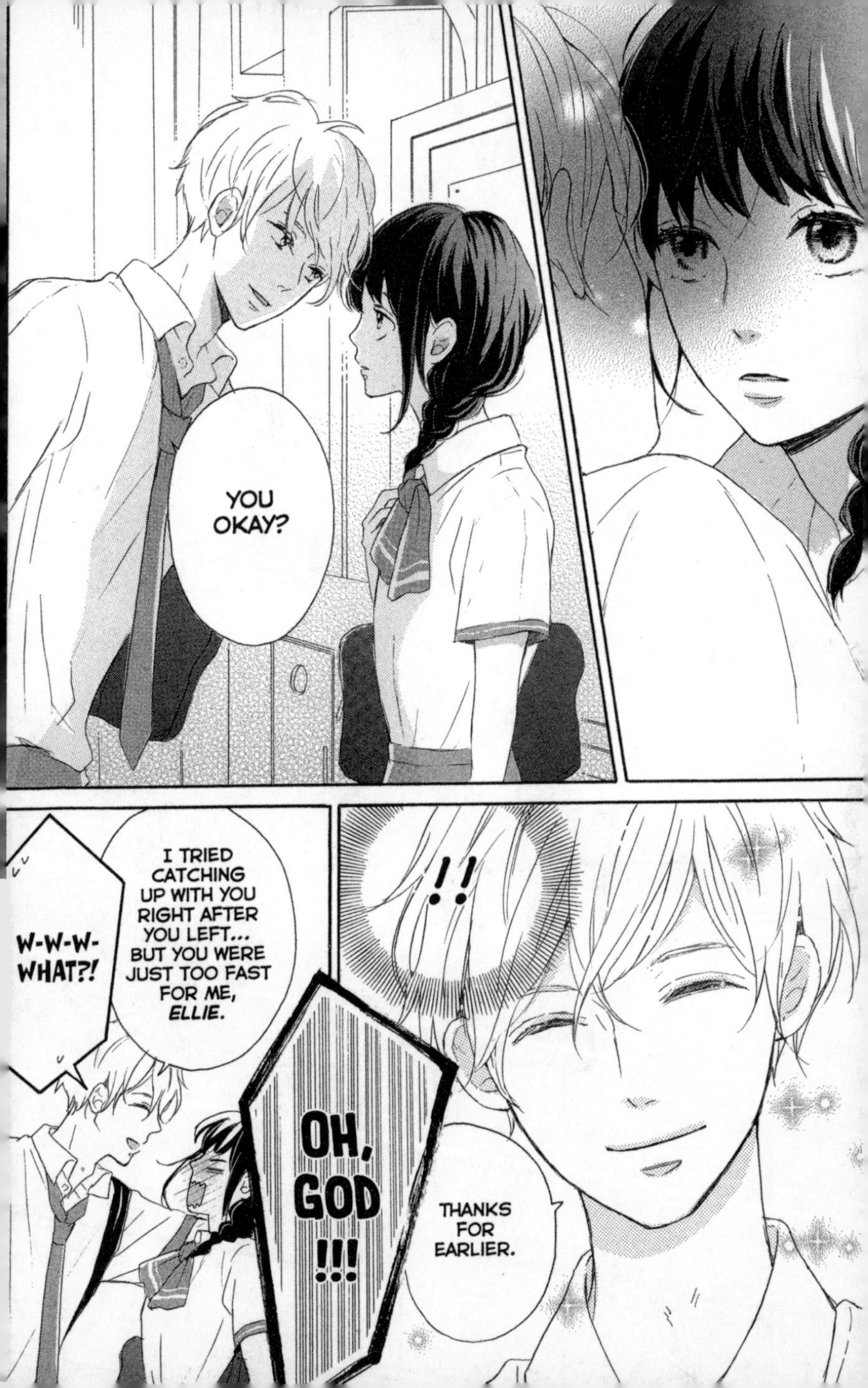
YOU OKAY?
!!
THANKS FOR EARLIER.
I TRIED CATCHING UP WITH YOU RIGHT AFTER YOU LEFT... BUT YOU WERE JUST TOO FAST FOR ME, *ELLIE*.
W-W-W-WHAT?!
OH, GOD!!!

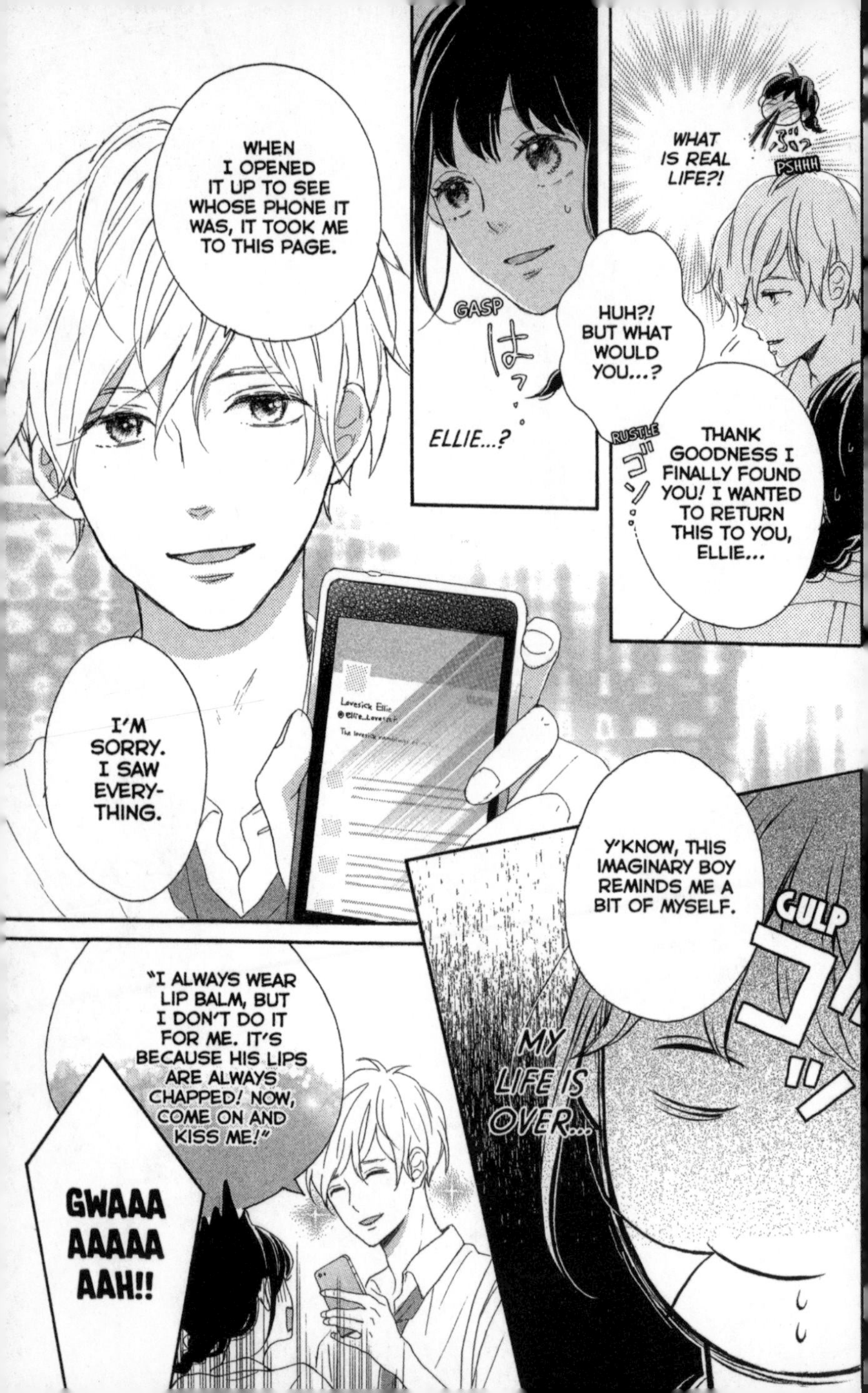
WHAT IS REAL LIFE?!
PSHHH
RUSTLE
THANK GOODNESS I FINALLY FOUND YOU! I WANTED TO RETURN THIS TO YOU, ELLIE...
HUH?! BUT WHAT WOULD YOU...?
GASP
ELLIE...?
WHEN I OPENED IT UP TO SEE WHOSE PHONE IT WAS, IT TOOK ME TO THIS PAGE.
I'M SORRY. I SAW EVERYTHING.
Y'KNOW, THIS IMAGINARY BOY REMINDS ME A BIT OF MYSELF.
GULP
MY LIFE IS OVER...
"I ALWAYS WEAR LIP BALM, BUT I DON'T DO IT FOR ME. IT'S BECAUSE HIS LIPS ARE ALWAYS CHAPPED! NOW, COME ON AND KISS ME!"
GWAAAAAAAAAAH!!

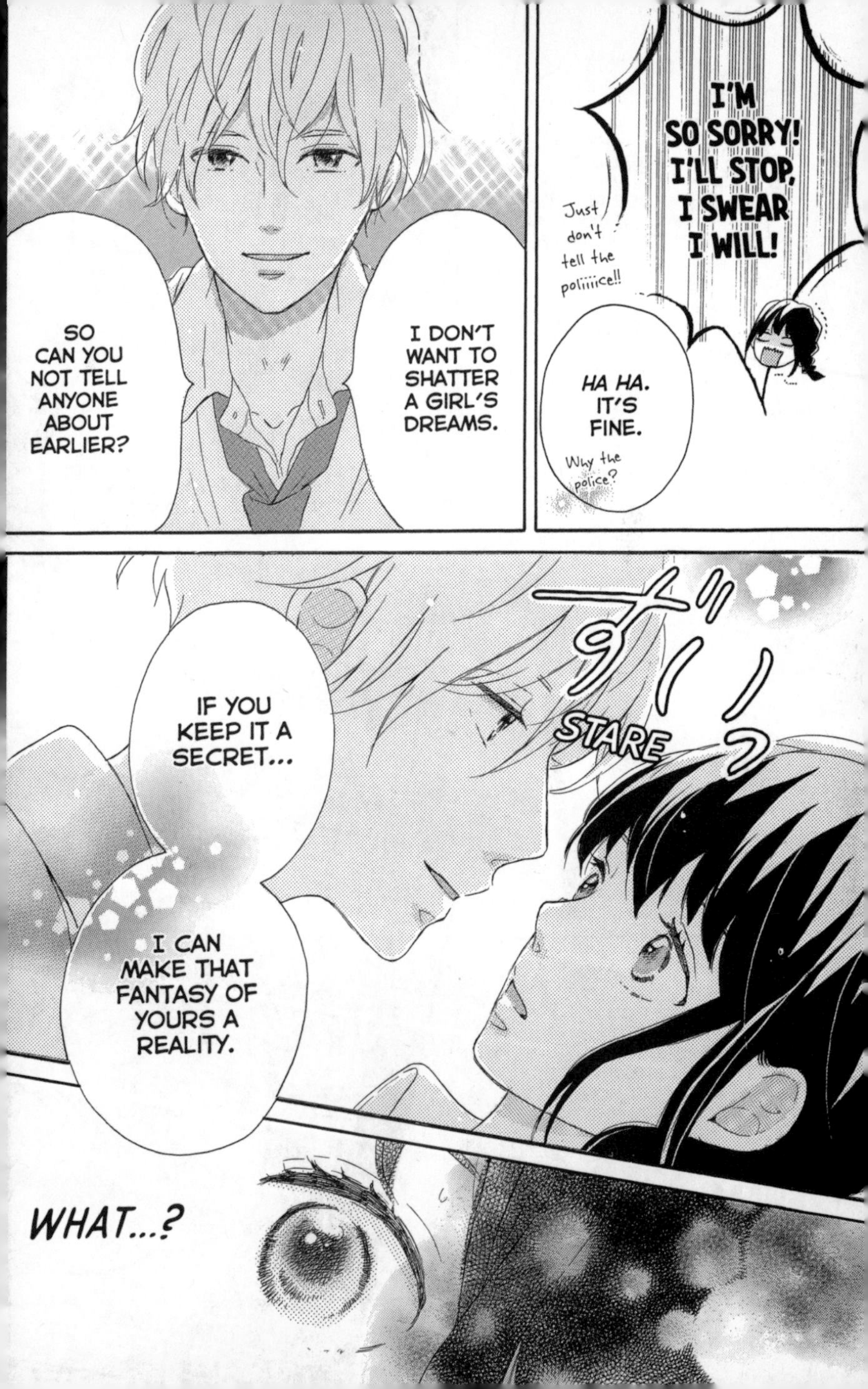
I'M SO SORRY! I'LL STOP, I SWEAR I WILL!
Just don't tell the poliiiice!!
HA HA. IT'S FINE.
Why the police?
I DON'T WANT TO SHATTER A GIRL'S DREAMS.
SO CAN YOU NOT TELL ANYONE ABOUT EARLIER?
STARE
IF YOU KEEP IT A SECRET...
I CAN MAKE THAT FANTASY OF YOURS A REALITY.
WHAT...?

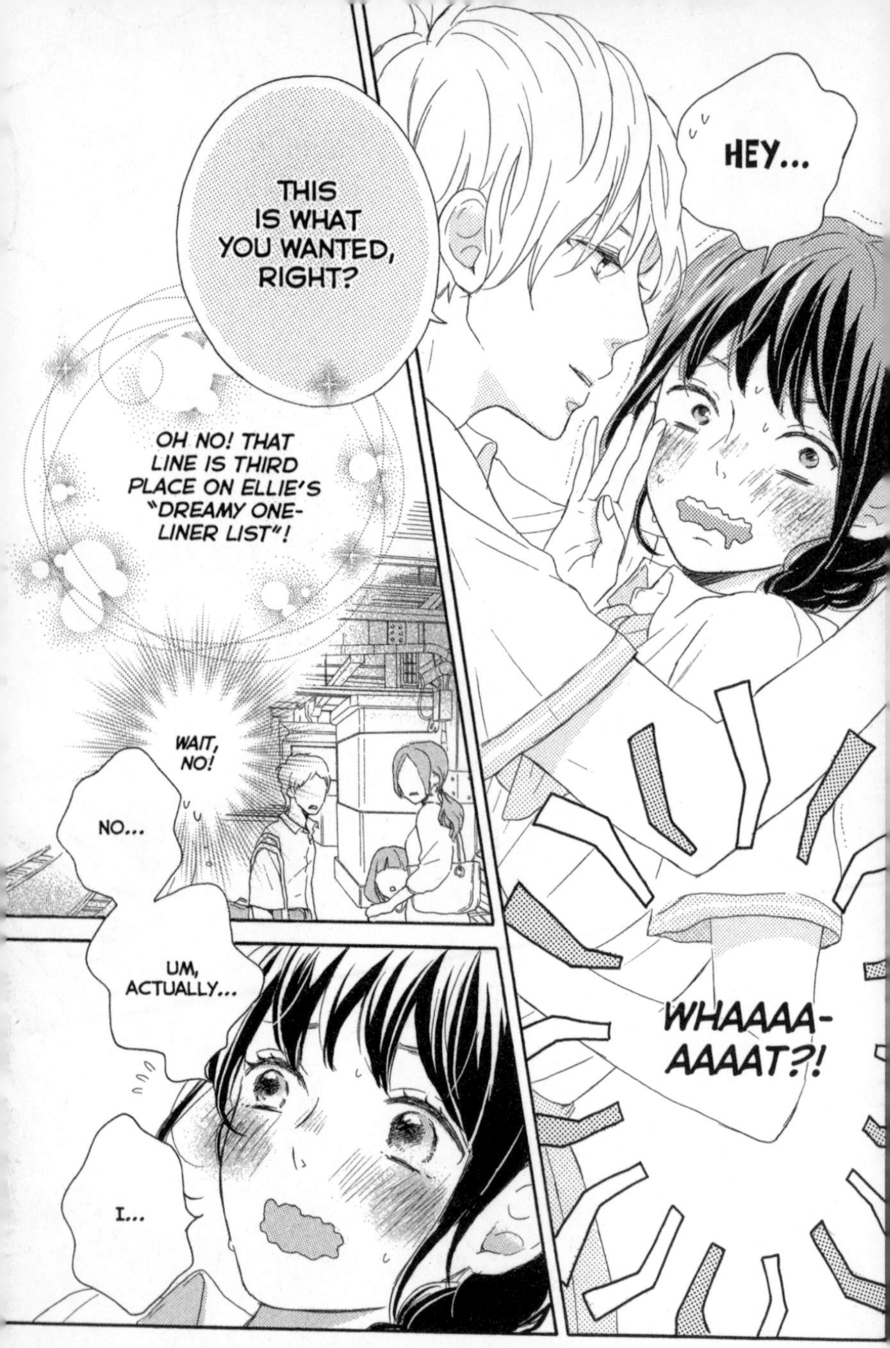
HEY...
THIS IS WHAT YOU WANTED, RIGHT?
WHAAAA-AAAAT?!
OH NO! THAT LINE IS THIRD PLACE ON ELLIE'S "DREAMY ONE-LINER LIST"!
WAIT, NO!
NO...
UM, ACTUALLY...
I...

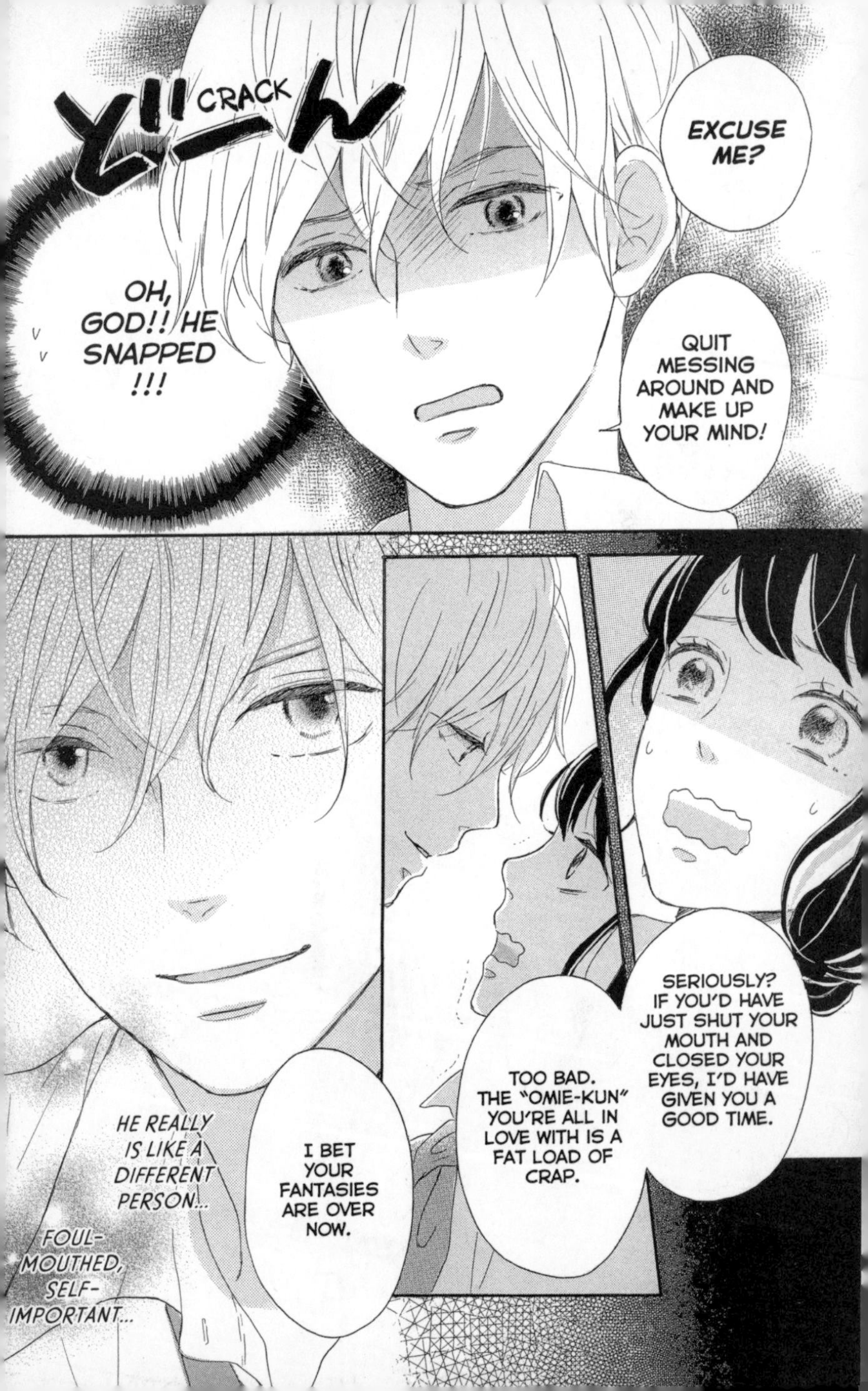
EXCUSE ME?
QUIT MESSING AROUND AND MAKE UP YOUR MIND!
CRACK
OH, GOD!! HE SNAPPED !!!
SERIOUSLY? IF YOU'D HAVE JUST SHUT YOUR MOUTH AND CLOSED YOUR EYES, I'D HAVE GIVEN YOU A GOOD TIME.
TOO BAD. THE "OMIE-KUN" YOU'RE ALL IN LOVE WITH IS A FAT LOAD OF CRAP.
I BET YOUR FANTASIES ARE OVER NOW.
HE REALLY IS LIKE A DIFFERENT PERSON...
FOUL-MOUTHED, SELF-IMPORTANT...

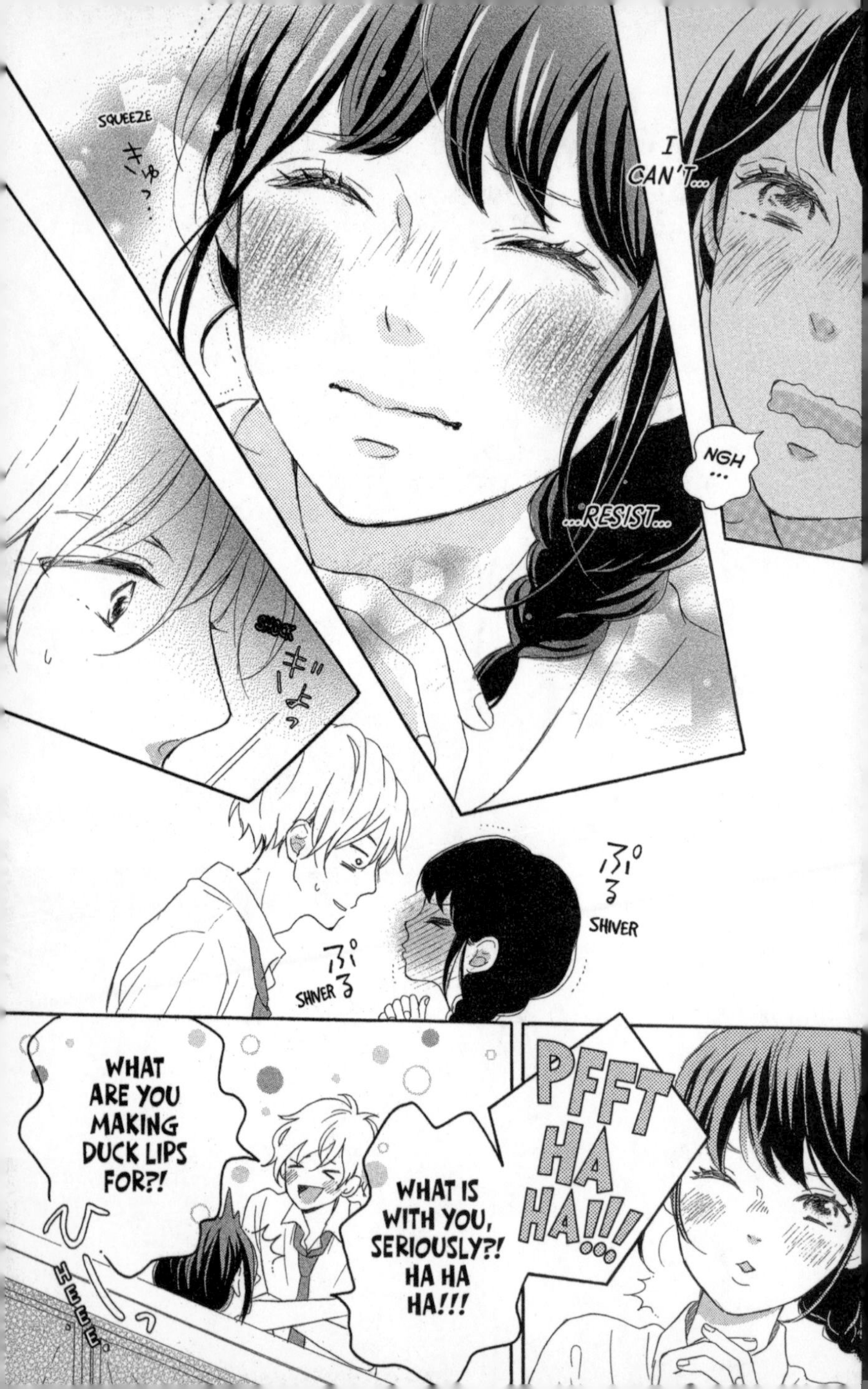
I CAN'T...
NGH...
...RESIST...
SQUEEZE
きゅっ...
SHOCK
ぎょっ
ぷる
SHIVER
ぷる
SHIVER
PFFT HA HA!!!
WHAT IS WITH YOU, SERIOUSLY?! HA HA HA!!!
WHAT ARE YOU MAKING DUCK LIPS FOR?!
HEEEE

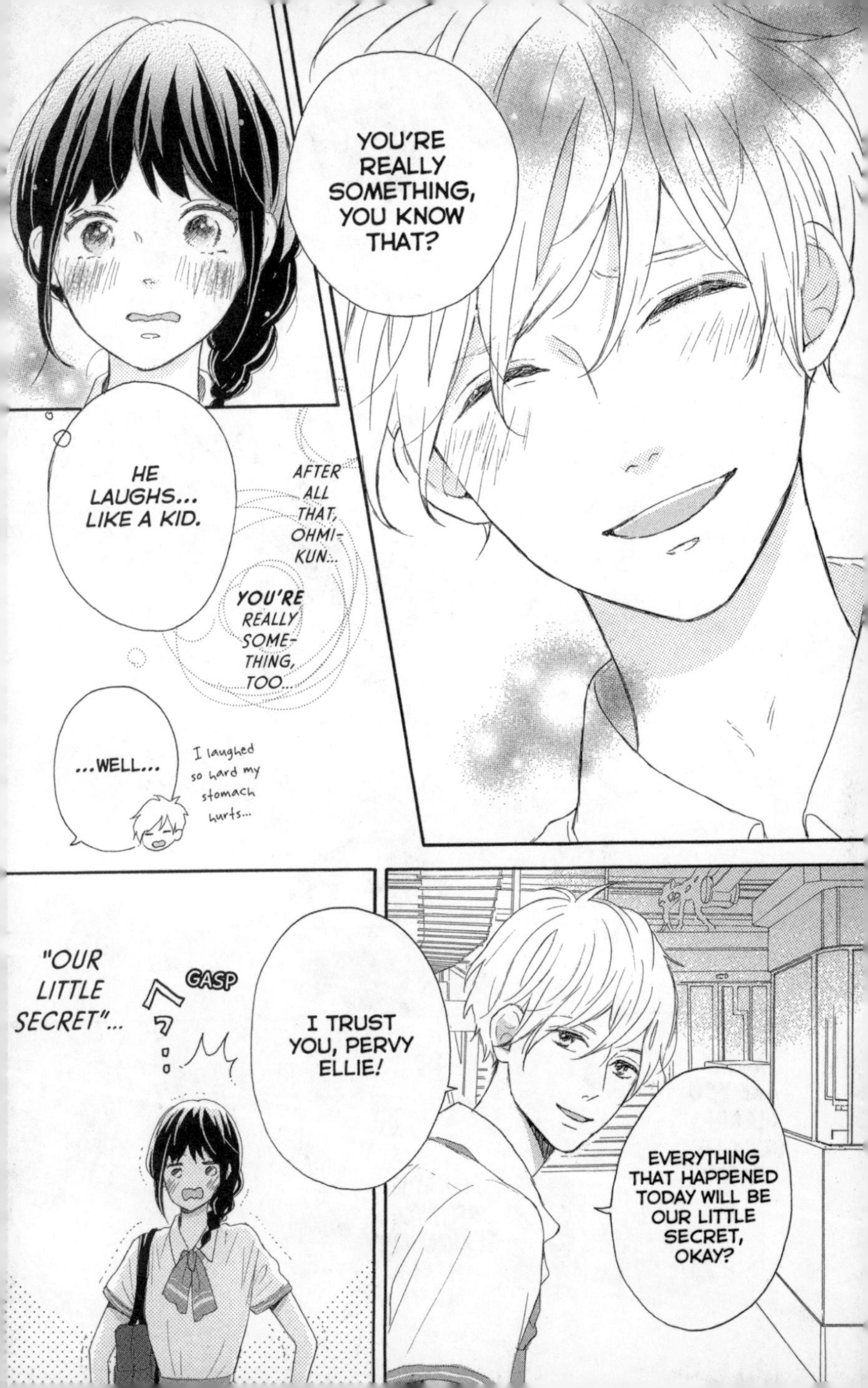
YOU'RE REALLY SOMETHING, YOU KNOW THAT?
HE LAUGHS... LIKE A KID.
AFTER ALL THAT, OHMI-KUN...
YOU'RE REALLY SOMETHING, TOO...
...WELL...
I laughed so hard my stomach hurts...
EVERYTHING THAT HAPPENED TODAY WILL BE OUR LITTLE SECRET, OKAY?
I TRUST YOU, PERVY ELLIE!
GASP
"OUR LITTLE SECRET"...

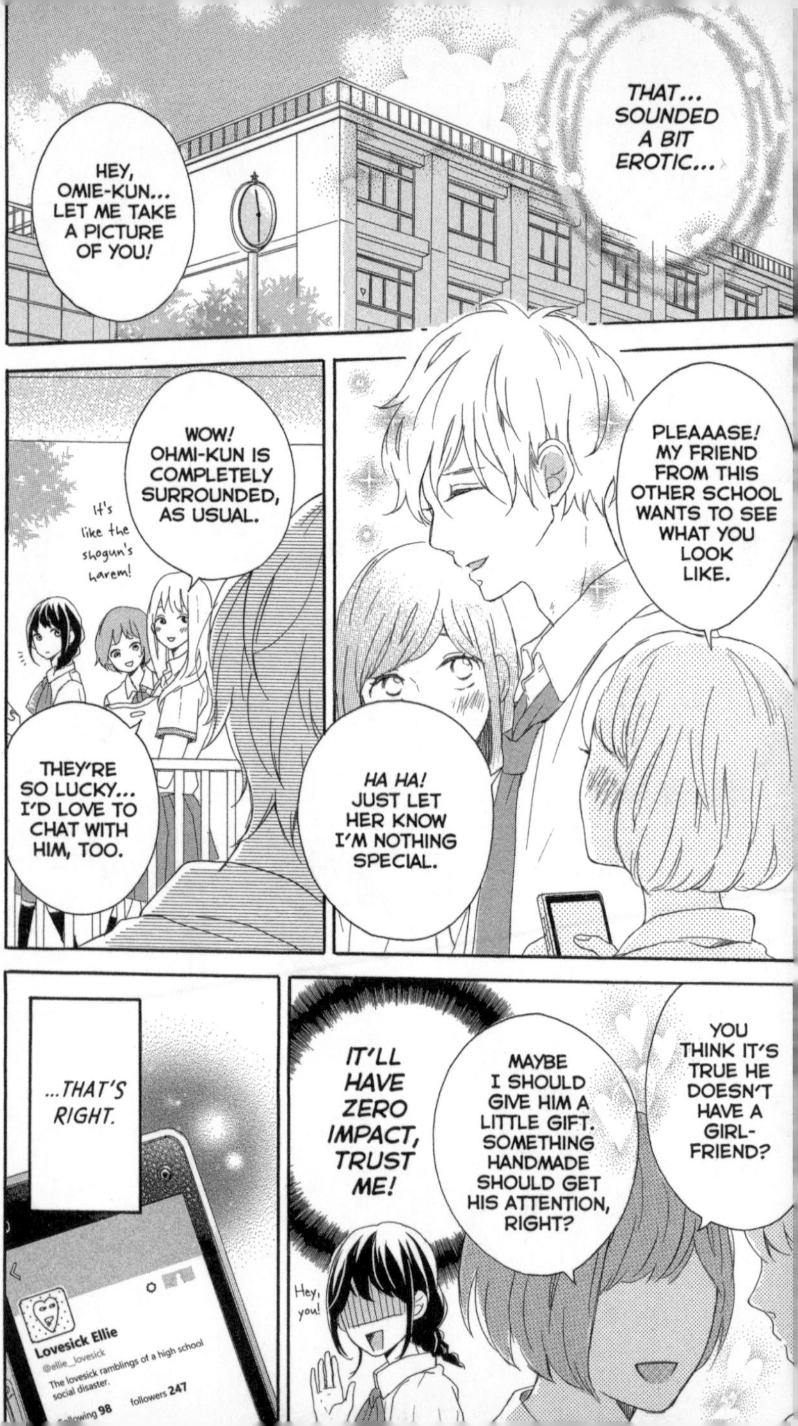
THAT... SOUNDED A BIT EROTIC...
HEY, OMIE-KUN... LET ME TAKE A PICTURE OF YOU!
PLEAAASE! MY FRIEND FROM THIS OTHER SCHOOL WANTS TO SEE WHAT YOU LOOK LIKE.
HA HA! JUST LET HER KNOW I'M NOTHING SPECIAL.
WOW! OHMI-KUN IS COMPLETELY SURROUNDED, AS USUAL.
It's like the shogun's harem!
THEY'RE SO LUCKY... I'D LOVE TO CHAT WITH HIM, TOO.
YOU THINK IT'S TRUE HE DOESN'T HAVE A GIRL-FRIEND?
MAYBE I SHOULD GIVE HIM A LITTLE GIFT. SOMETHING HANDMADE SHOULD GET HIS ATTENTION, RIGHT?
IT'LL HAVE ZERO IMPACT, TRUST ME!
Hey, you!
...THAT'S RIGHT.
Lovesick Ellie
@ellie_lovesick
The lovesick ramblings of a high school social disaster.
Following 98
followers 247

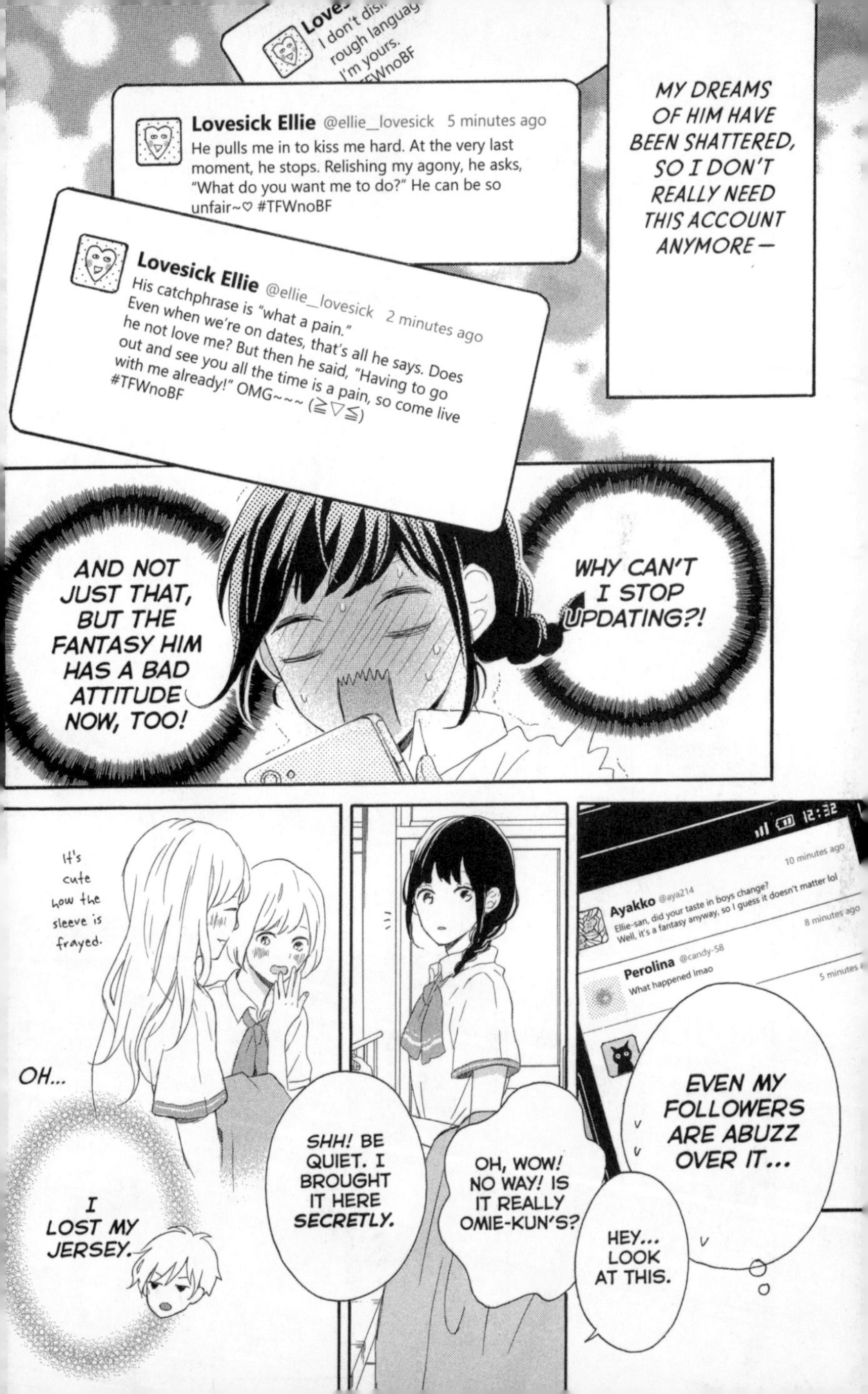
MY DREAMS OF HIM HAVE BEEN SHATTERED, SO I DON'T REALLY NEED THIS ACCOUNT ANYMORE—
Lovesick Ellie @ellie__lovesick 5 minutes ago
He pulls me in to kiss me hard. At the very last moment, he stops. Relishing my agony, he asks, "What do you want me to do?" He can be so unfair~♡ #TFWnoBF
Lovesick Ellie @ellie__lovesick 2 minutes ago
His catchphrase is "what a pain." Even when we're on dates, that's all he says. Does he not love me? But then he said, "Having to go out and see you all the time is a pain, so come live with me already!" OMG~~~ (≧▽≦) #TFWnoBF
WHY CAN'T I STOP UPDATING?!
AND NOT JUST THAT, BUT THE FANTASY HIM HAS A BAD ATTITUDE NOW, TOO!
12:32
Ayakko @aya214 10 minutes ago
Ellie-san, did your taste in boys change? Well, it's a fantasy anyway, so I guess it doesn't matter lol
Perolina @candy-58 8 minutes ago
What happened lmao
5 minutes
EVEN MY FOLLOWERS ARE ABUZZ OVER IT...
HEY... LOOK AT THIS.
OH, WOW! NO WAY! IS IT REALLY OMIE-KUN'S?
SHH! BE QUIET. I BROUGHT IT HERE SECRETLY.
It's cute how the sleeve is frayed.
OH...
I LOST MY JERSEY.

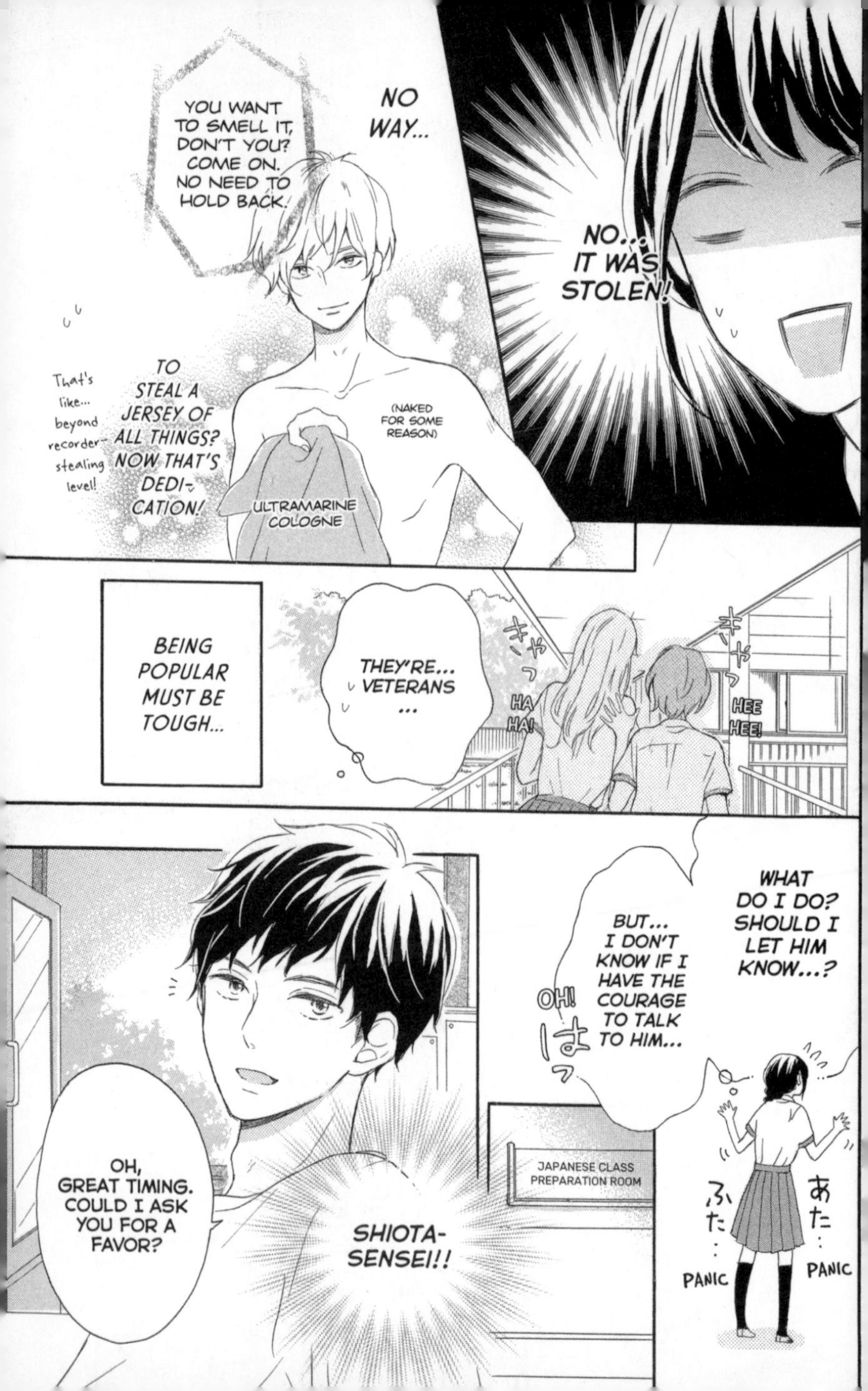
NO... IT WAS STOLEN!
NO WAY...
YOU WANT TO SMELL IT, DON'T YOU? COME ON. NO NEED TO HOLD BACK.
(NAKED FOR SOME REASON)
TO STEAL A JERSEY OF ALL THINGS? NOW THAT'S DEDI-CATION!
That's like... beyond recorder-stealing level!
ULTRAMARINE COLOGNE
きゃっ
HEE HEE!
きゃっ
HA HA!
THEY'RE... VETERANS ...
BEING POPULAR MUST BE TOUGH...
WHAT DO I DO? SHOULD I LET HIM KNOW...?
BUT... I DON'T KNOW IF I HAVE THE COURAGE TO TALK TO HIM...
はっ
OH!
あた…
PANIC
ふた…
PANIC
JAPANESE CLASS PREPARATION ROOM
SHIOTA-SENSEI!!
OH, GREAT TIMING. COULD I ASK YOU FOR A FAVOR?

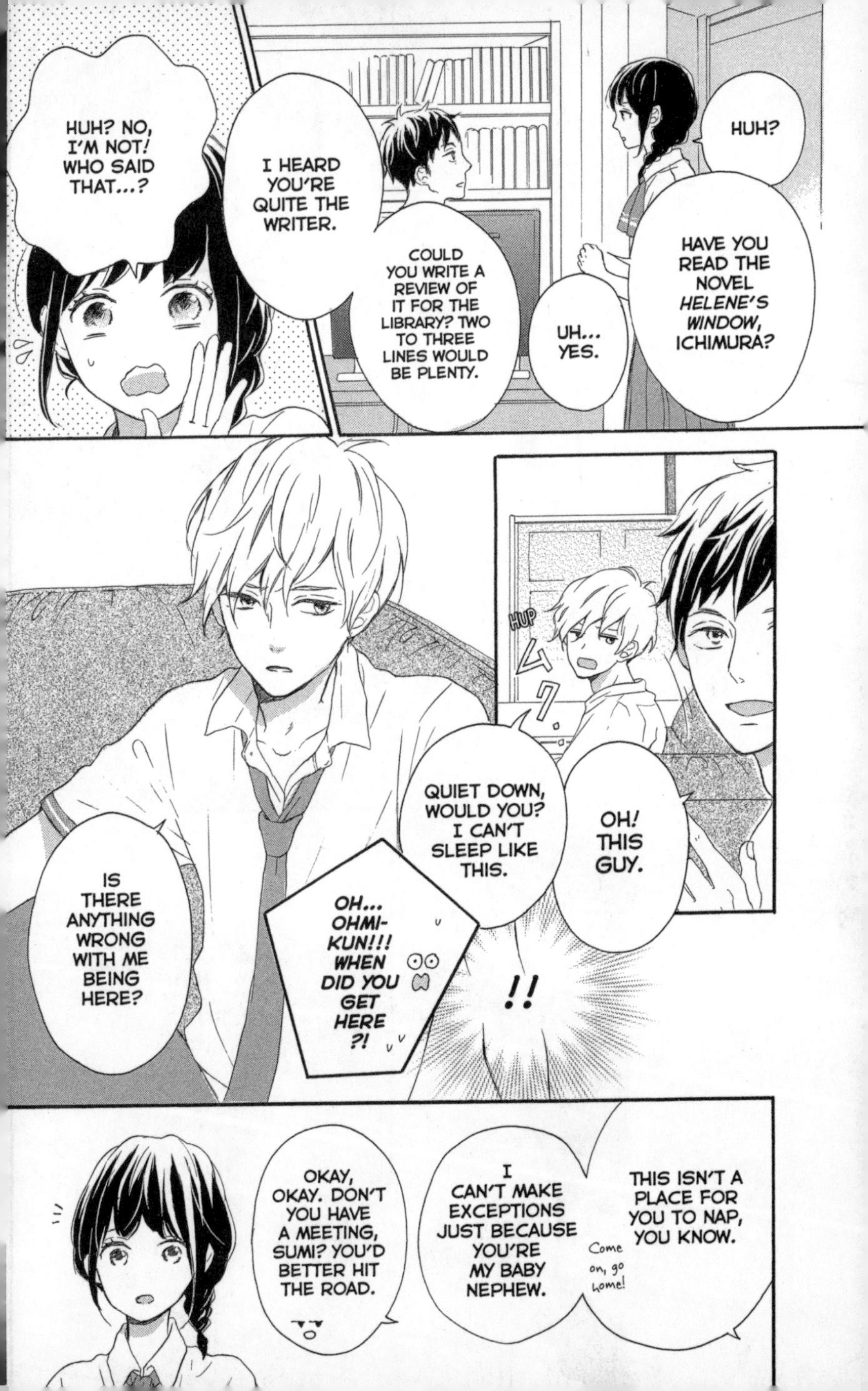
HUH?
HAVE YOU READ THE NOVEL *HELENE'S WINDOW*, ICHIMURA?
UH... YES.
COULD YOU WRITE A REVIEW OF IT FOR THE LIBRARY? TWO TO THREE LINES WOULD BE PLENTY.
I HEARD YOU'RE QUITE THE WRITER.
HUH? NO, I'M NOT! WHO SAID THAT...?
HUP
QUIET DOWN, WOULD YOU? I CAN'T SLEEP LIKE THIS.
OH! THIS GUY.
!!
OH... OHMI-KUN!!! WHEN DID YOU GET HERE ?!
IS THERE ANYTHING WRONG WITH ME BEING HERE?
THIS ISN'T A PLACE FOR YOU TO NAP, YOU KNOW.
Come on, go home!
I CAN'T MAKE EXCEPTIONS JUST BECAUSE YOU'RE MY BABY NEPHEW.
OKAY, OKAY. DON'T YOU HAVE A MEETING, SUMI? YOU'D BETTER HIT THE ROAD.

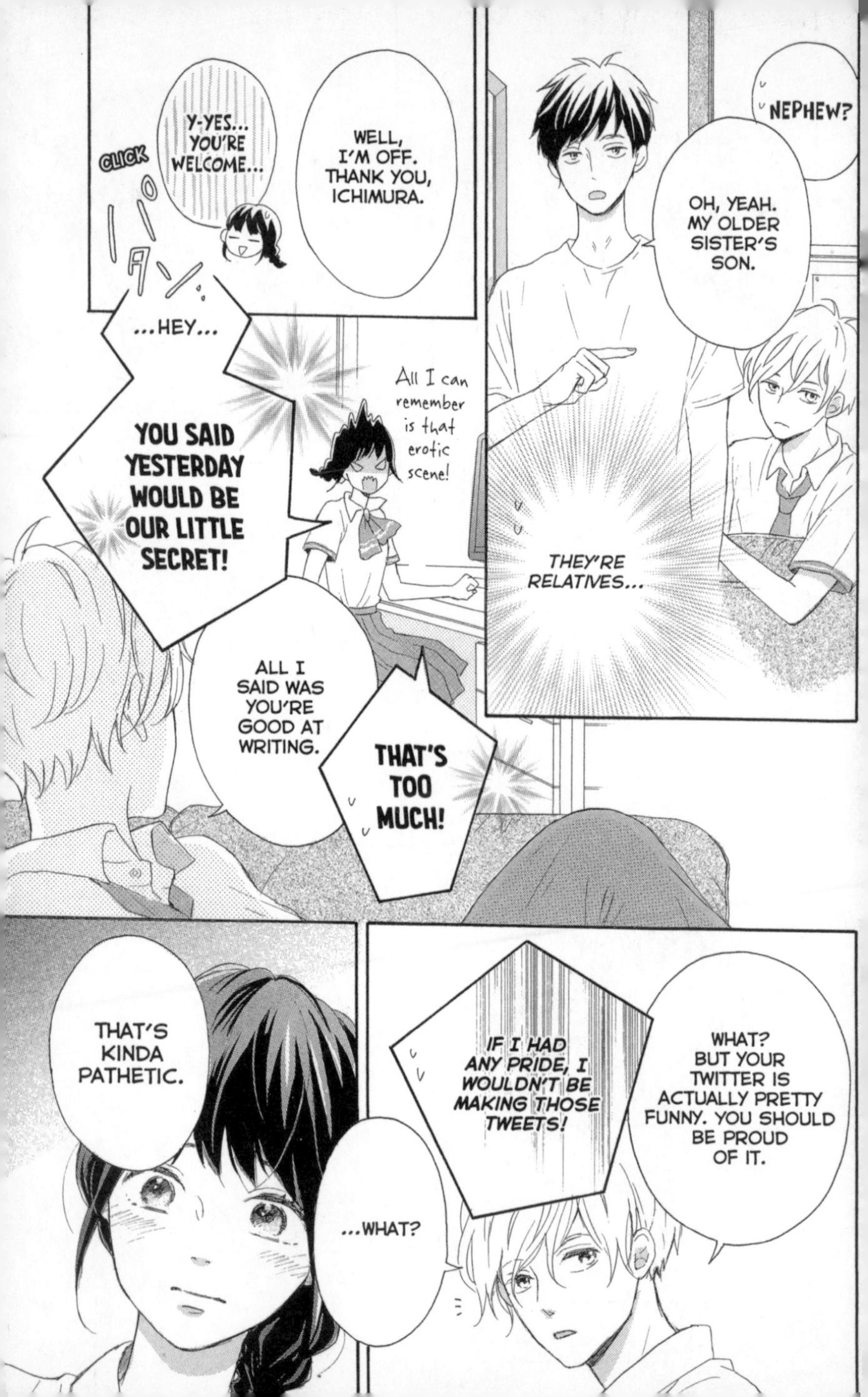
NEPHEW?
OH, YEAH. MY OLDER SISTER'S SON.
THEY'RE RELATIVES...
WELL, I'M OFF. THANK YOU, ICHIMURA.
Y-YES... YOU'RE WELCOME...
CLICK
...HEY...
YOU SAID YESTERDAY WOULD BE OUR LITTLE SECRET!
All I can remember is that erotic scene!
ALL I SAID WAS YOU'RE GOOD AT WRITING.
THAT'S TOO MUCH!
WHAT? BUT YOUR TWITTER IS ACTUALLY PRETTY FUNNY. YOU SHOULD BE PROUD OF IT.
IF I HAD ANY PRIDE, I WOULDN'T BE MAKING THOSE TWEETS!
THAT'S KINDA PATHETIC.
...WHAT?

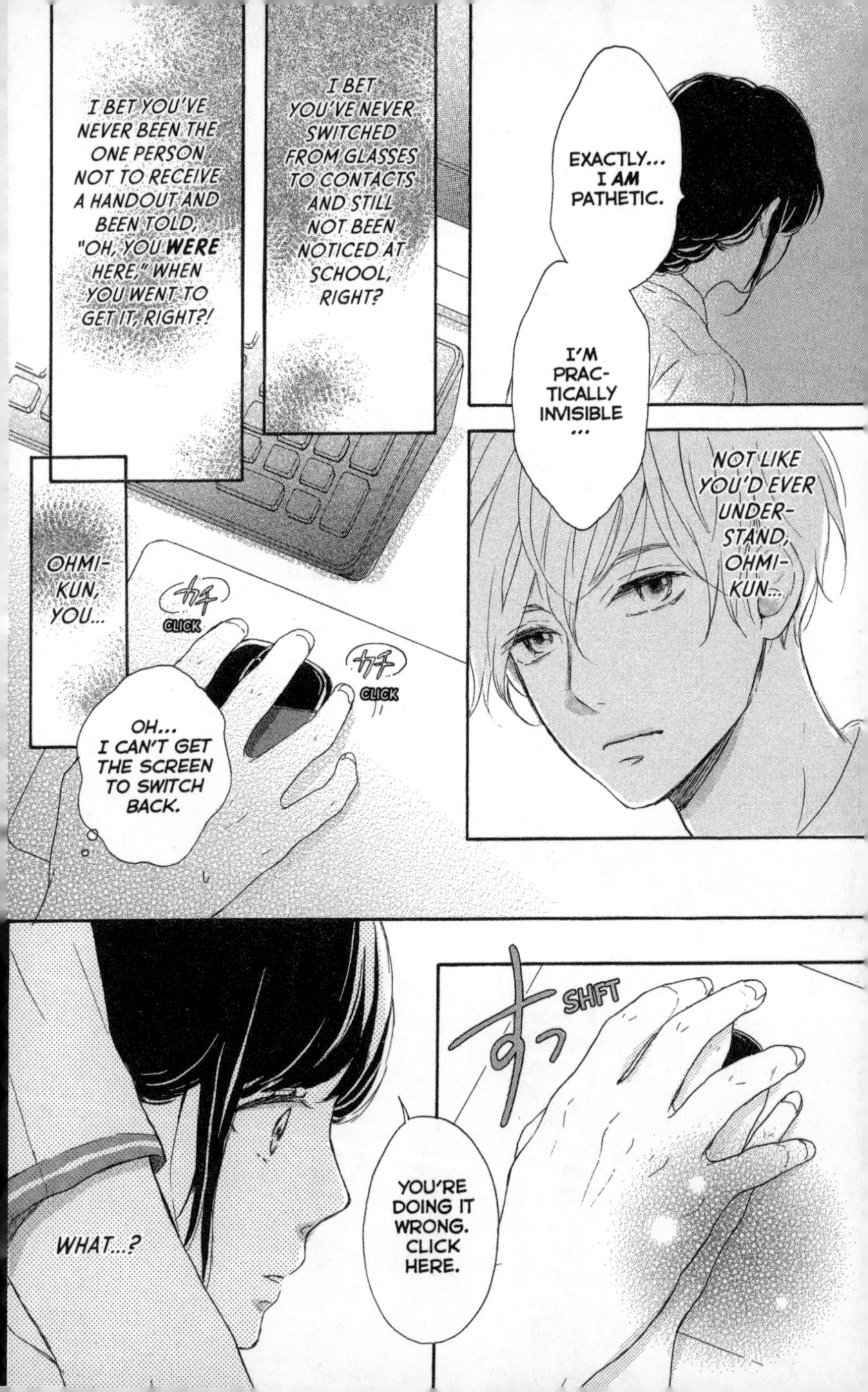
EXACTLY... I AM PATHETIC.
I'M PRACTICALLY INVISIBLE...
I BET YOU'VE NEVER SWITCHED FROM GLASSES TO CONTACTS AND STILL NOT BEEN NOTICED AT SCHOOL, RIGHT?
I BET YOU'VE NEVER BEEN THE ONE PERSON NOT TO RECEIVE A HANDOUT AND BEEN TOLD, "OH, YOU WERE HERE," WHEN YOU WENT TO GET IT, RIGHT?!
NOT LIKE YOU'D EVER UNDERSTAND, OHMI-KUN...
OHMI-KUN, YOU...
カチ
CLICK
カチ
CLICK
OH... I CAN'T GET THE SCREEN TO SWITCH BACK.
すっ
SHFT
YOU'RE DOING IT WRONG. CLICK HERE.
WHAT...?

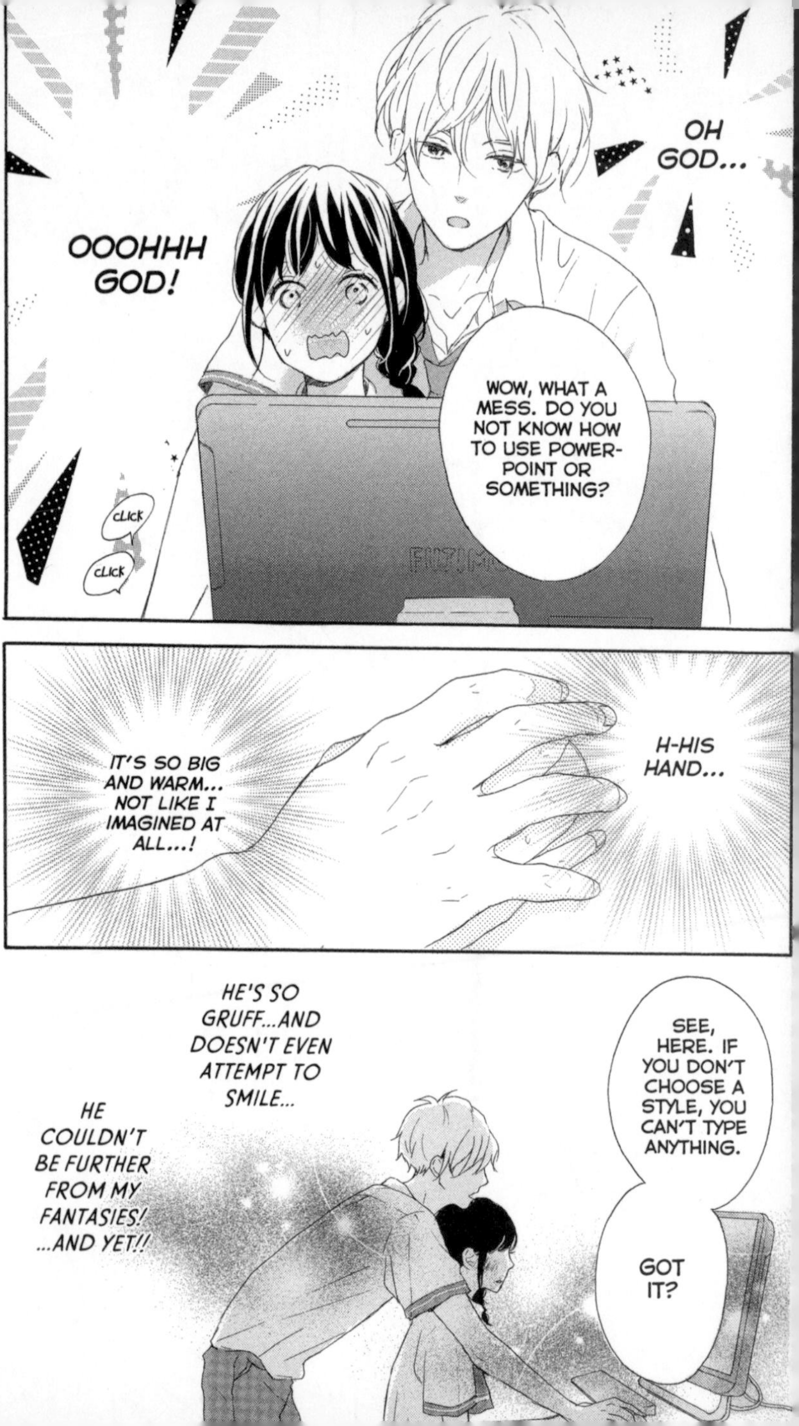
OH GOD...
WOW, WHAT A MESS. DO YOU NOT KNOW HOW TO USE POWER-POINT OR SOMETHING?
OOOHHH GOD!
CLICK
CLICK
H-HIS HAND...
IT'S SO BIG AND WARM... NOT LIKE I IMAGINED AT ALL...!
SEE, HERE. IF YOU DON'T CHOOSE A STYLE, YOU CAN'T TYPE ANYTHING.
GOT IT?
HE'S SO GRUFF...AND DOESN'T EVEN ATTEMPT TO SMILE...
HE COULDN'T BE FURTHER FROM MY FANTASIES! ...AND YET!!

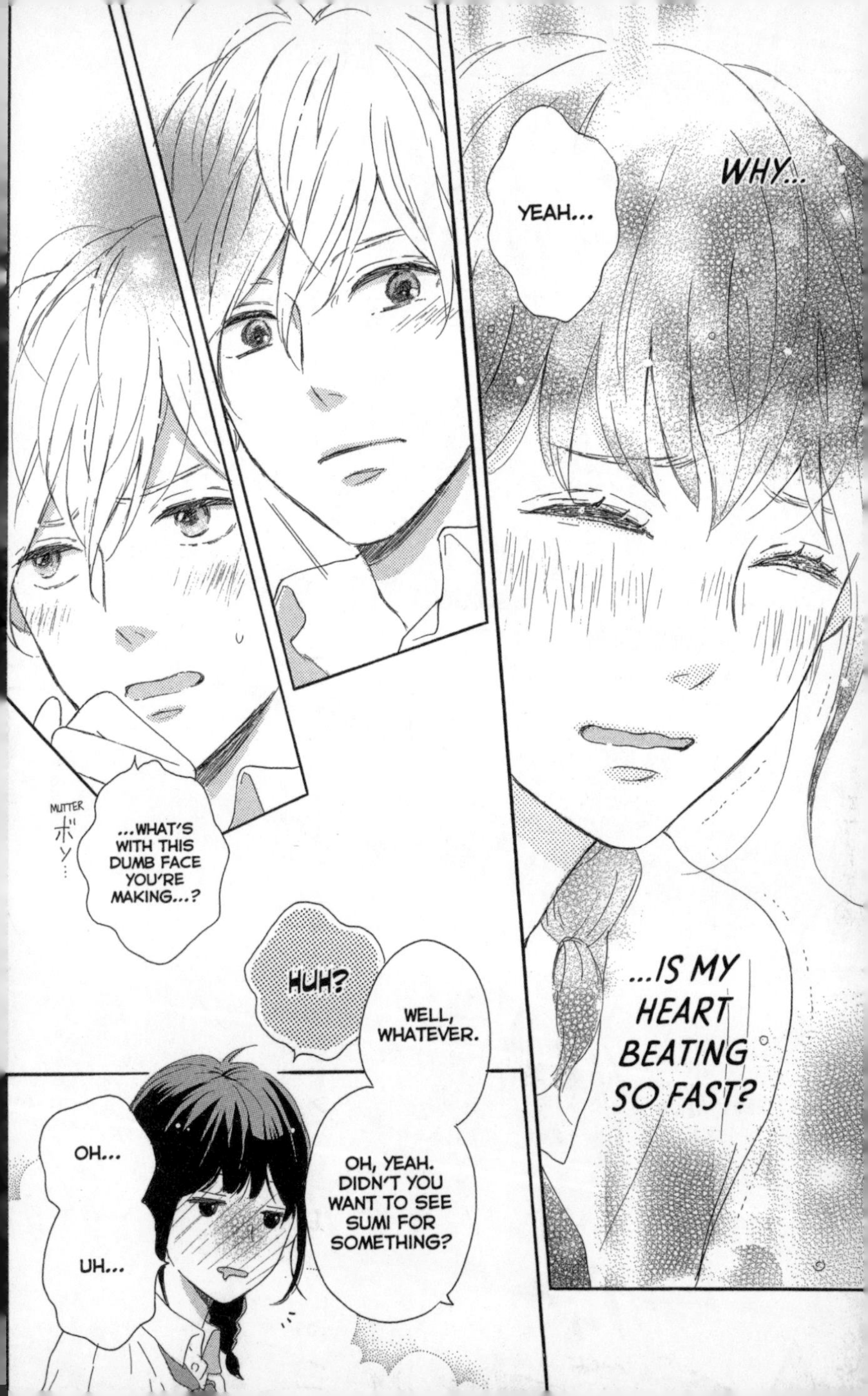

YEAH...
WHY...
...IS MY HEART BEATING SO FAST?
MUTTER ボソ…
...WHAT'S WITH THIS DUMB FACE YOU'RE MAKING...?
HUH?
WELL, WHATEVER.
OH, YEAH. DIDN'T YOU WANT TO SEE SUMI FOR SOMETHING?
OH...
UH...

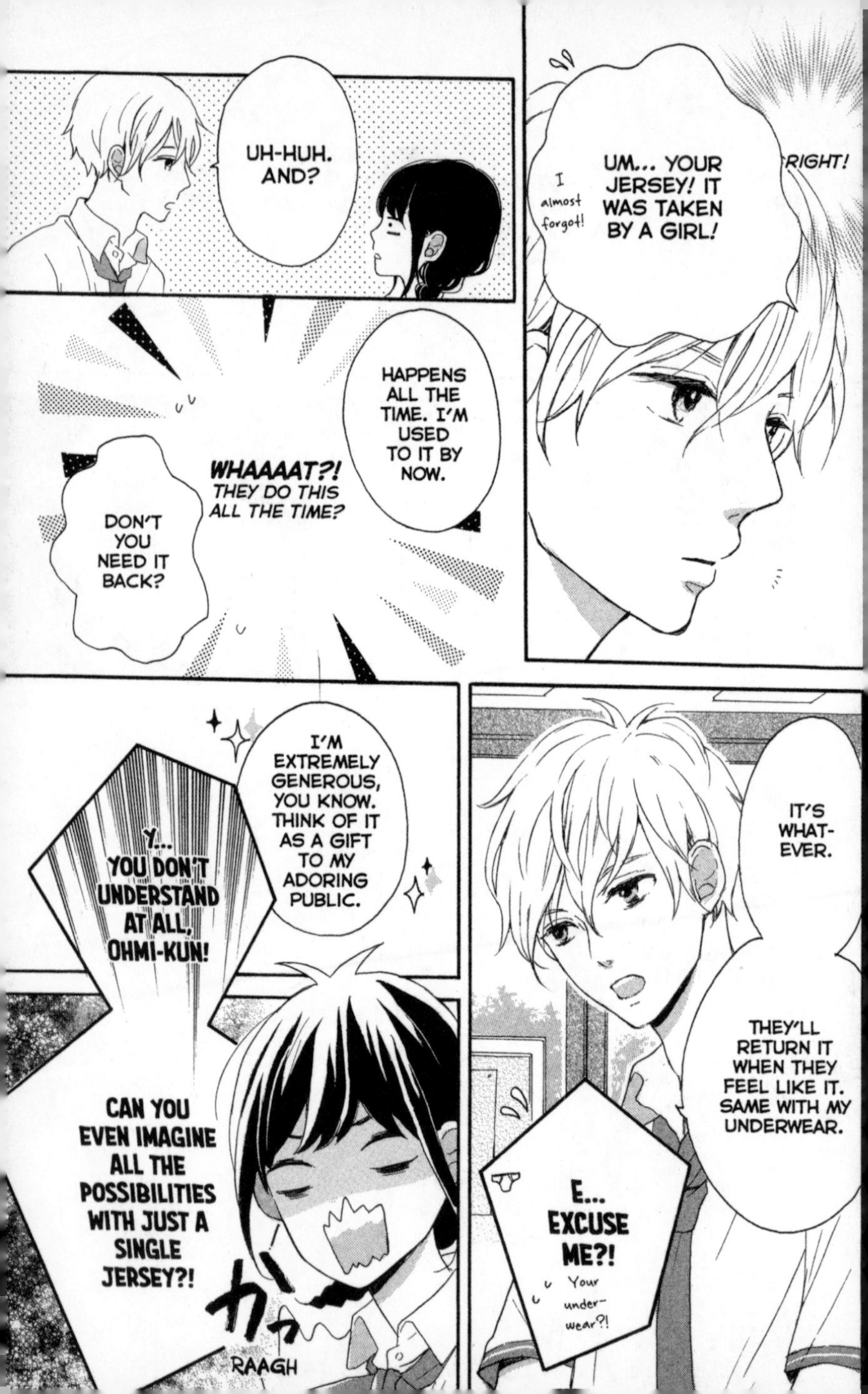
RIGHT!
I almost forgot!
UM... YOUR JERSEY! IT WAS TAKEN BY A GIRL!
UH-HUH. AND?
HAPPENS ALL THE TIME. I'M USED TO IT BY NOW.
WHAAAAT?! THEY DO THIS ALL THE TIME?
DON'T YOU NEED IT BACK?
IT'S WHAT-EVER.
THEY'LL RETURN IT WHEN THEY FEEL LIKE IT. SAME WITH MY UNDERWEAR.
E... EXCUSE ME?!
Your under-wear?!
I'M EXTREMELY GENEROUS, YOU KNOW. THINK OF IT AS A GIFT TO MY ADORING PUBLIC.
Y... YOU DON'T UNDERSTAND AT ALL, OHMI-KUN!
CAN YOU EVEN IMAGINE ALL THE POSSIBILITIES WITH JUST A SINGLE JERSEY?!
RAAGH

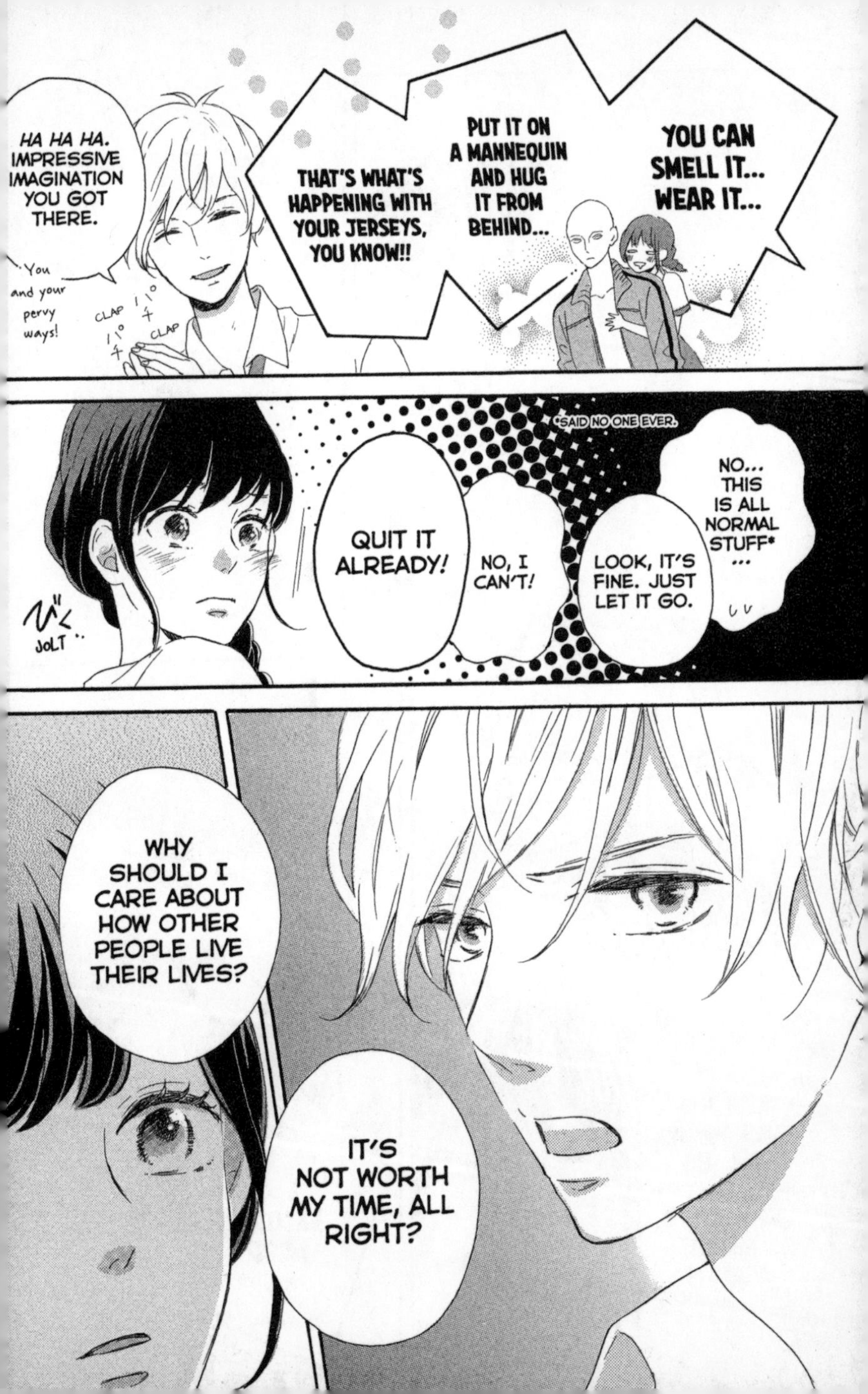
YOU CAN SMELL IT... WEAR IT...
PUT IT ON A MANNEQUIN AND HUG IT FROM BEHIND...
THAT'S WHAT'S HAPPENING WITH YOUR JERSEYS, YOU KNOW!!
HA HA HA. IMPRESSIVE IMAGINATION YOU GOT THERE.
CLAP CLAP
...You and your pervy ways!
*SAID NO ONE EVER.
NO... THIS IS ALL NORMAL STUFF*...
LOOK, IT'S FINE. JUST LET IT GO.
NO, I CAN'T!
QUIT IT ALREADY!
JOLT
WHY SHOULD I CARE ABOUT HOW OTHER PEOPLE LIVE THEIR LIVES?
IT'S NOT WORTH MY TIME, ALL RIGHT?

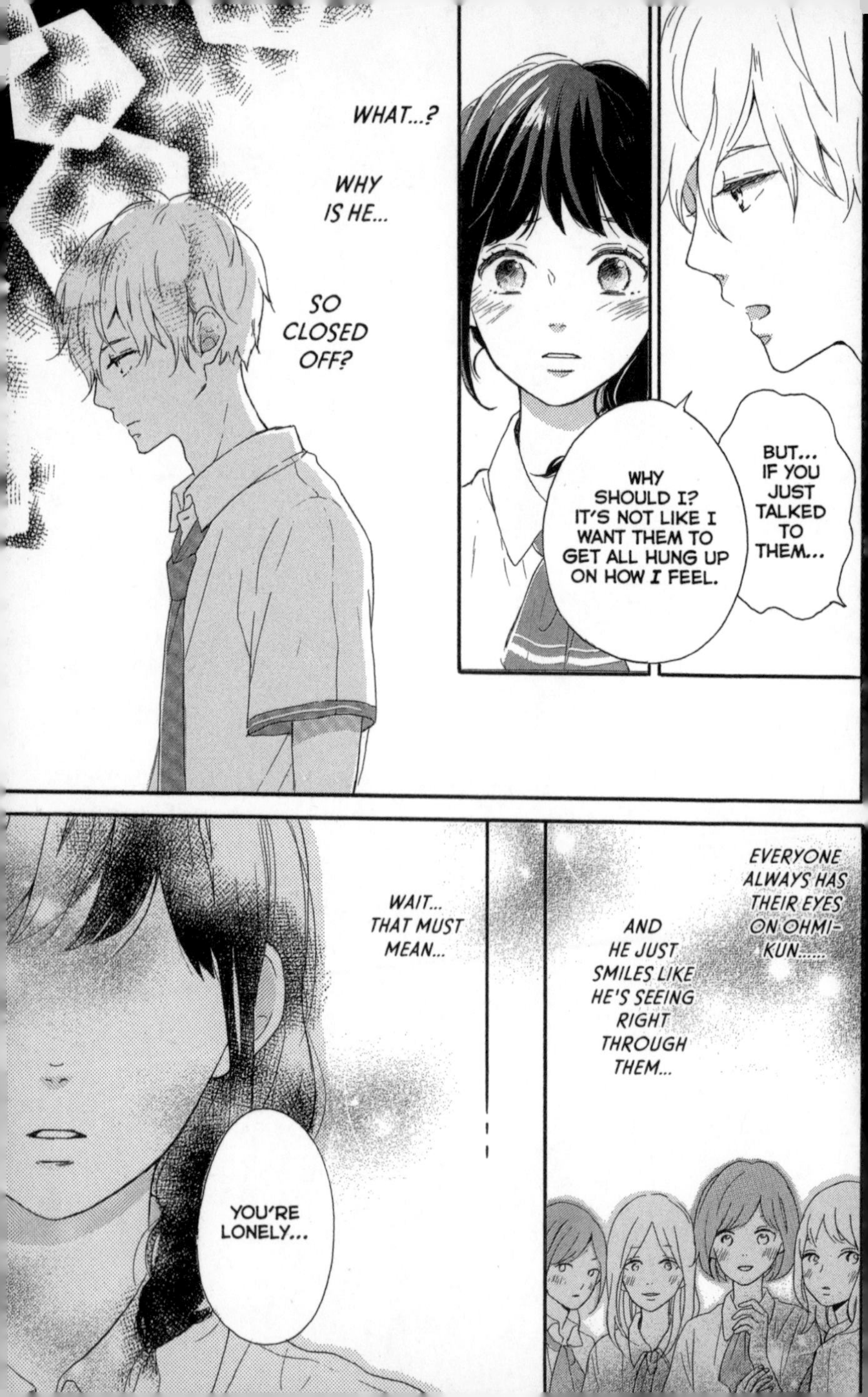
BUT... IF YOU JUST TALKED TO THEM...
WHY SHOULD I? IT'S NOT LIKE I WANT THEM TO GET ALL HUNG UP ON HOW *I* FEEL.
WHAT...?
WHY IS HE...
SO CLOSED OFF?
EVERYONE ALWAYS HAS THEIR EYES ON OHMI-KUN.....
AND HE JUST SMILES LIKE HE'S SEEING RIGHT THROUGH THEM...
WAIT... THAT MUST MEAN...
YOU'RE LONELY...

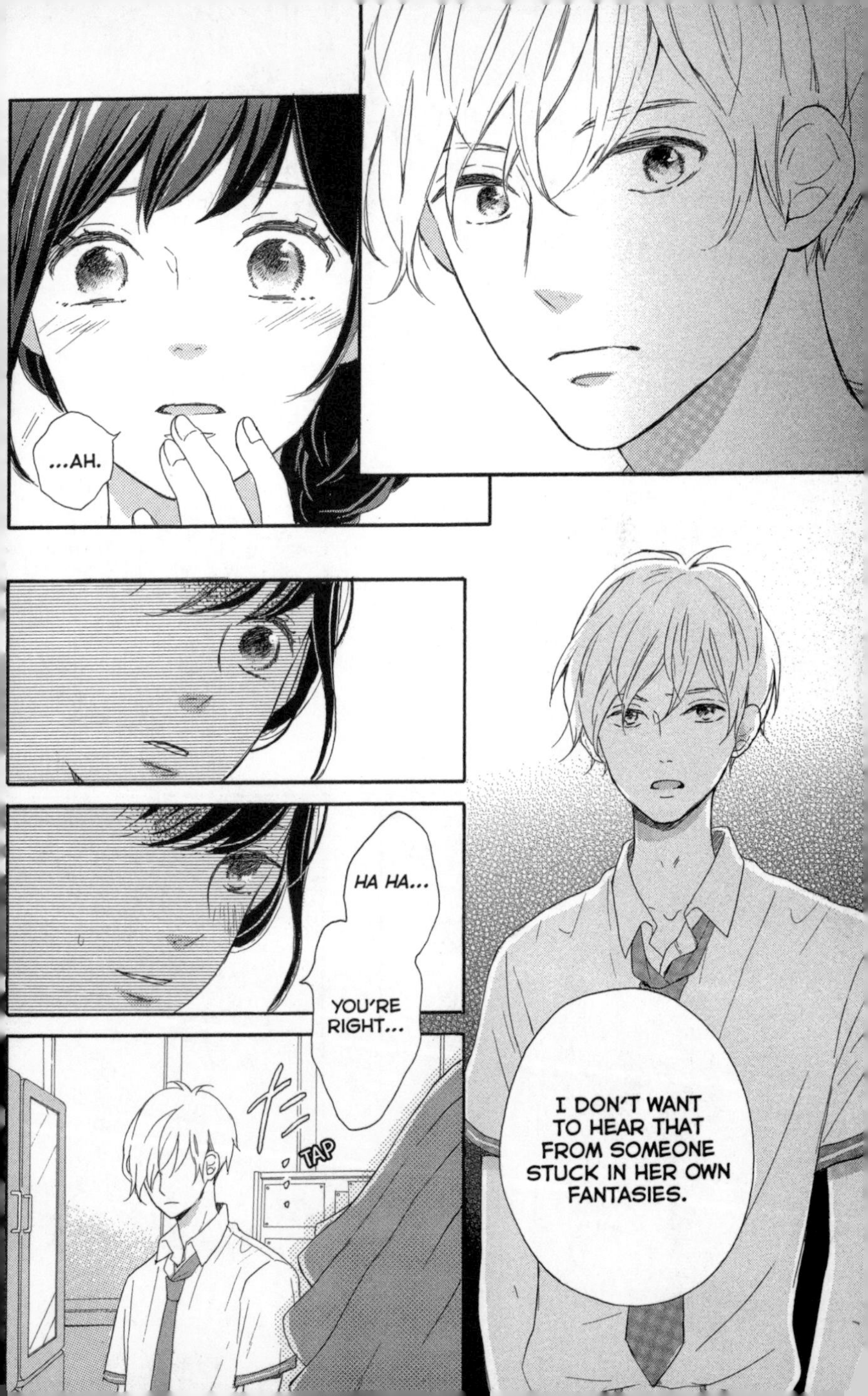
...AH.
I DON'T WANT TO HEAR THAT FROM SOMEONE STUCK IN HER OWN FANTASIES.
HA HA...
YOU'RE RIGHT...
TAP

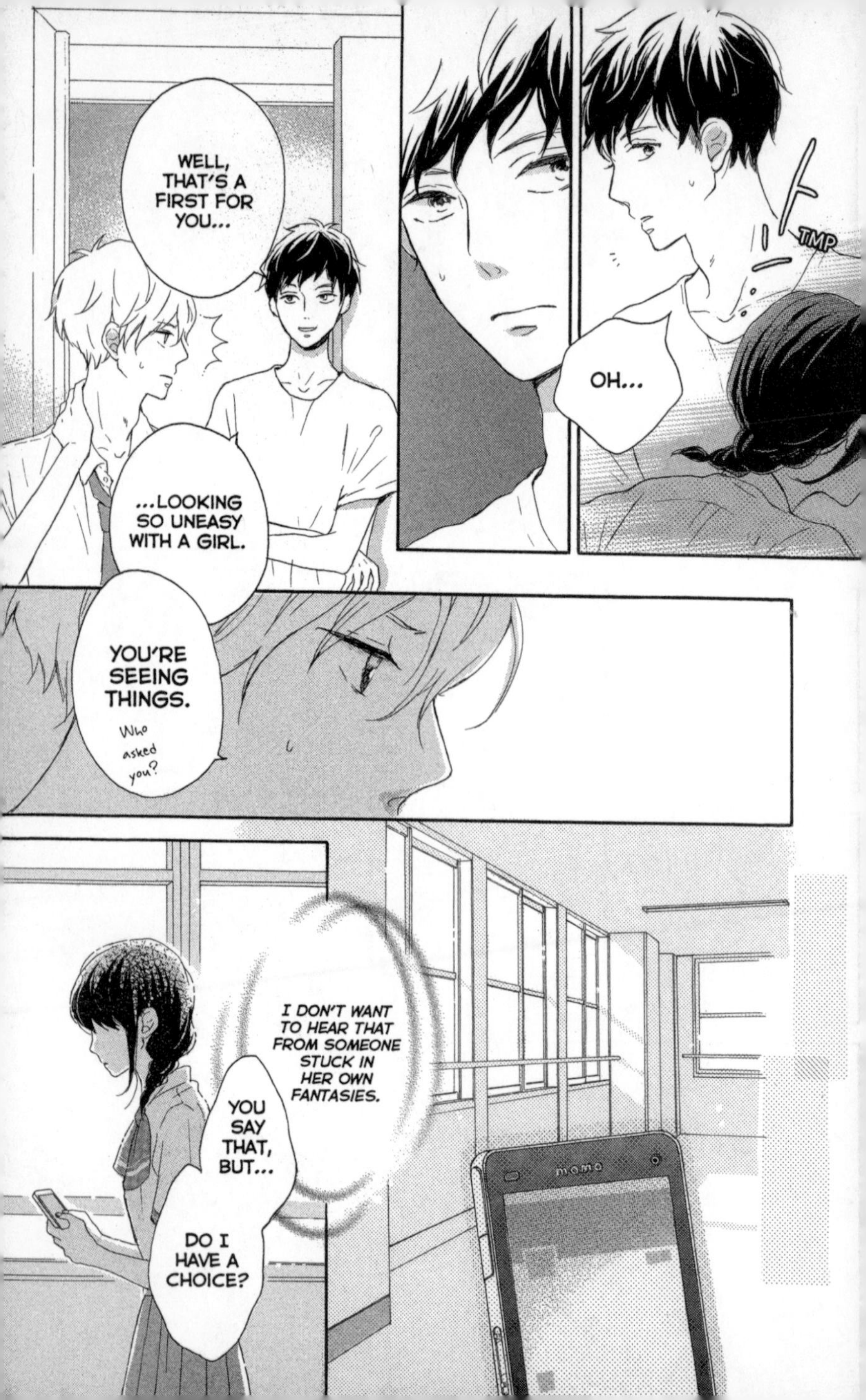
TMP
OH...
WELL, THAT'S A FIRST FOR YOU...
...LOOKING SO UNEASY WITH A GIRL.
YOU'RE SEEING THINGS.
Who asked you?
momo
I DON'T WANT TO HEAR THAT FROM SOMEONE STUCK IN HER OWN FANTASIES.
YOU SAY THAT, BUT...
DO I HAVE A CHOICE?

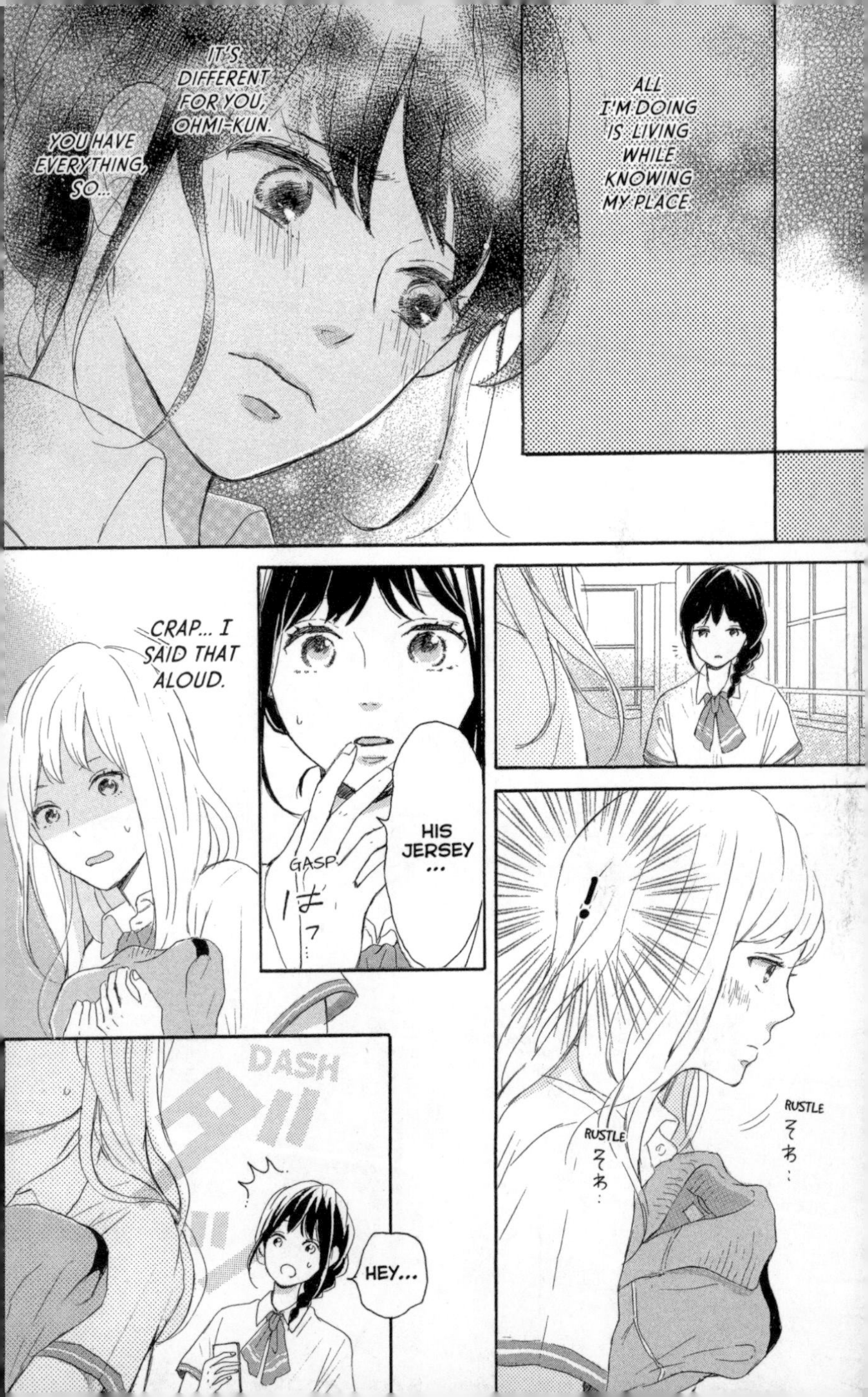
ALL I'M DOING IS LIVING WHILE KNOWING MY PLACE.
IT'S DIFFERENT FOR YOU, OHMI-KUN.
YOU HAVE EVERYTHING, SO...
HIS JERSEY...
GASP
ぱっ
CRAP... I SAID THAT ALOUD.
!
RUSTLE
そわ…
RUSTLE
そわ…
DASH
HEY...

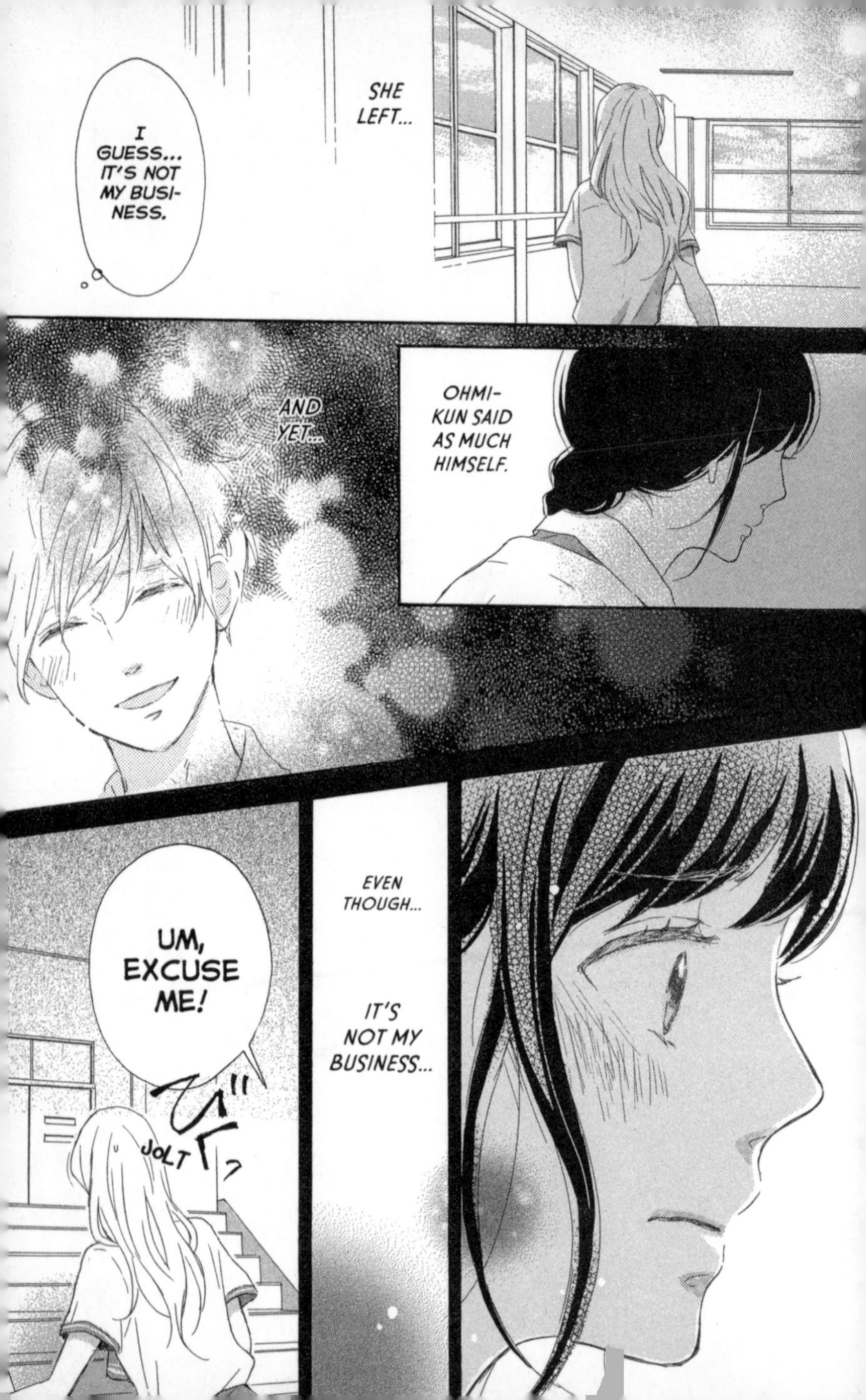
SHE LEFT...
I GUESS... IT'S NOT MY BUSINESS.
OHMI-KUN SAID AS MUCH HIMSELF.
AND YET...
EVEN THOUGH...
IT'S NOT MY BUSINESS...
UM, EXCUSE ME!
JOLT

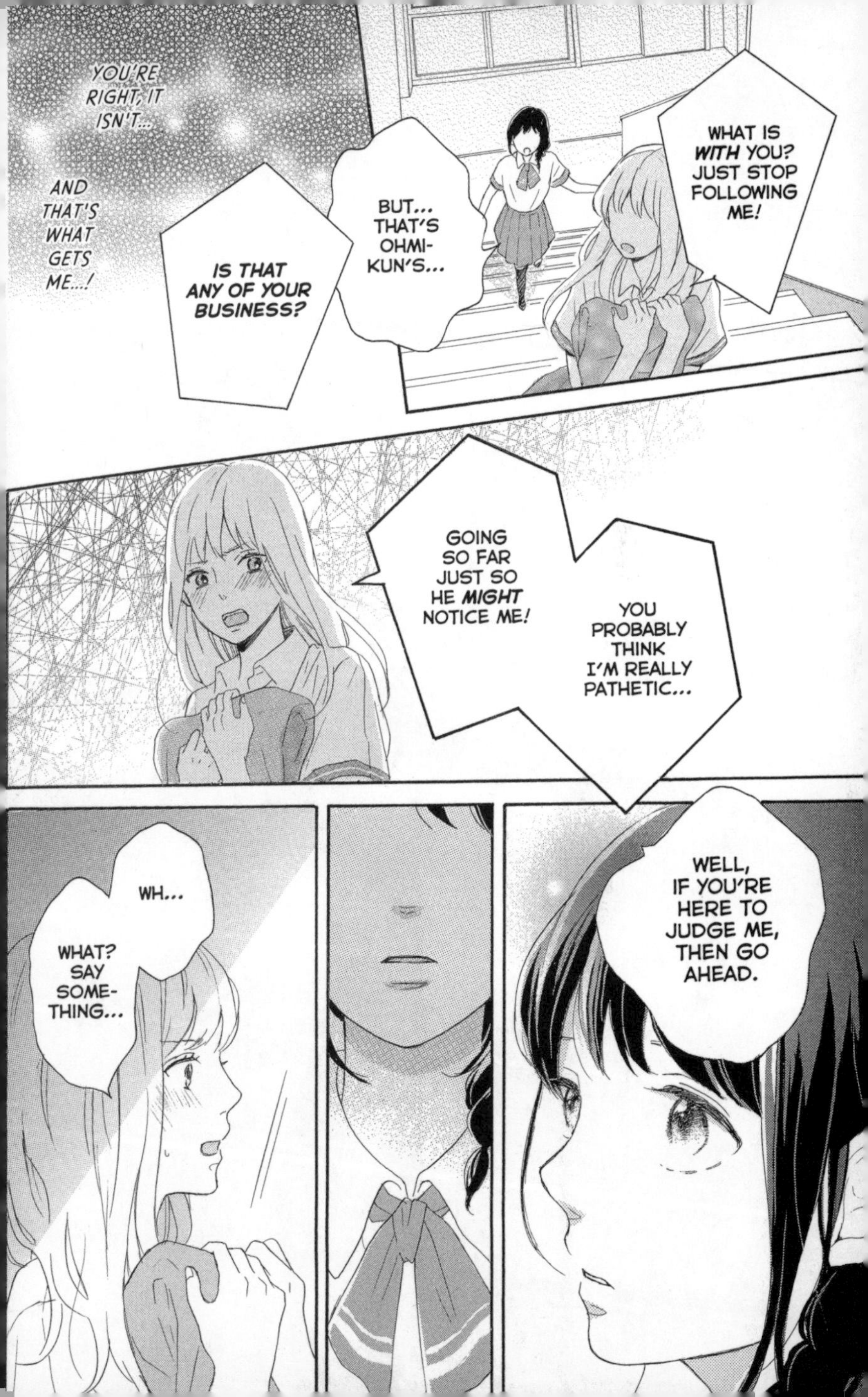
WHAT IS WITH YOU? JUST STOP FOLLOWING ME!
BUT... THAT'S OHMI-KUN'S...
IS THAT ANY OF YOUR BUSINESS?
YOU'RE RIGHT, IT ISN'T...
AND THAT'S WHAT GETS ME...!
GOING SO FAR JUST SO HE MIGHT NOTICE ME!
YOU PROBABLY THINK I'M REALLY PATHETIC...
WELL, IF YOU'RE HERE TO JUDGE ME, THEN GO AHEAD.
WH...
WHAT? SAY SOME-THING...

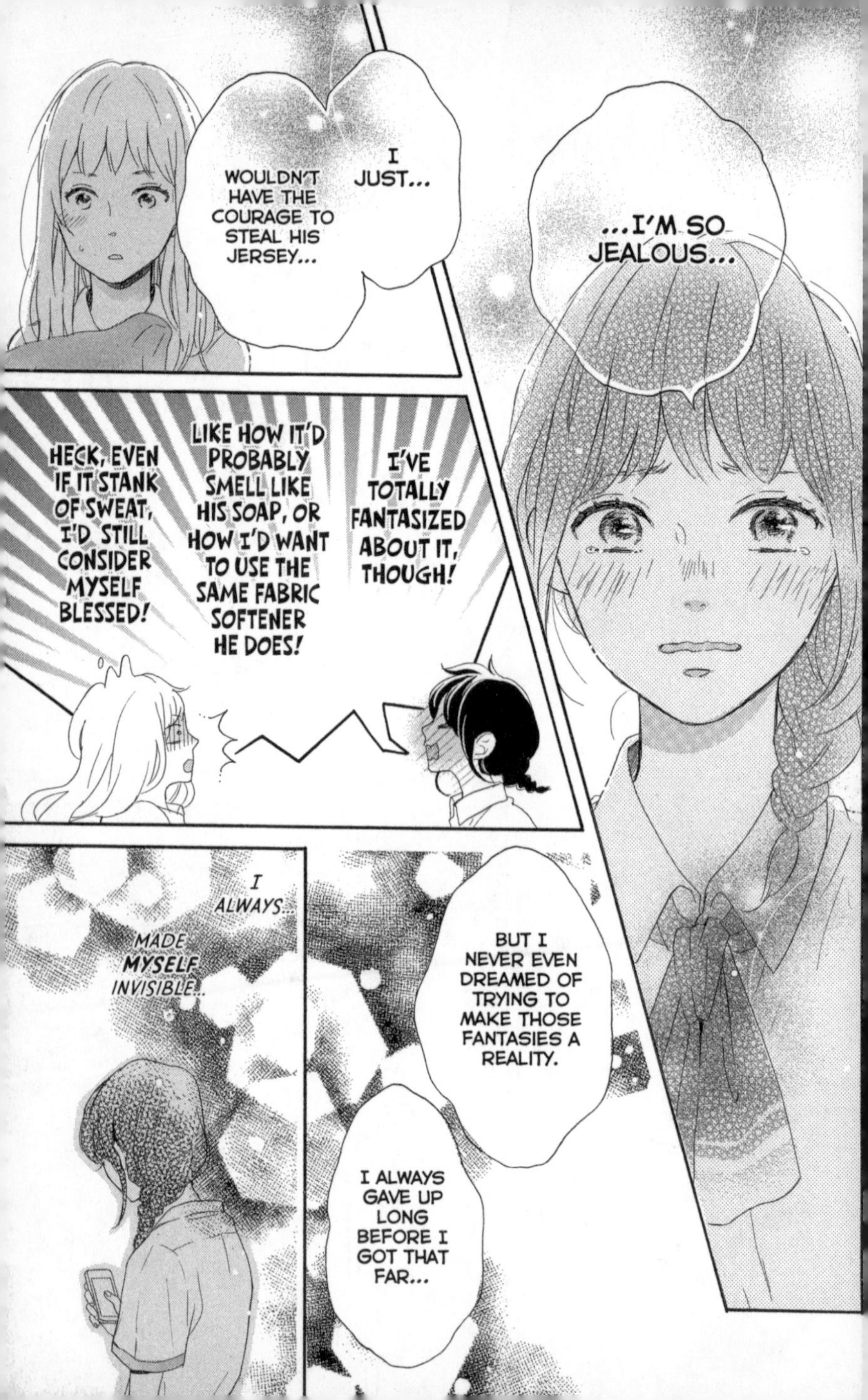

...I'M SO JEALOUS...
I JUST...
WOULDN'T HAVE THE COURAGE TO STEAL HIS JERSEY...
I'VE TOTALLY FANTASIZED ABOUT IT, THOUGH!
LIKE HOW IT'D PROBABLY SMELL LIKE HIS SOAP, OR HOW I'D WANT TO USE THE SAME FABRIC SOFTENER HE DOES!
HECK, EVEN IF IT STANK OF SWEAT, I'D STILL CONSIDER MYSELF BLESSED!
BUT I NEVER EVEN DREAMED OF TRYING TO MAKE THOSE FANTASIES A REALITY.
I ALWAYS GAVE UP LONG BEFORE I GOT THAT FAR...
I ALWAYS...
MADE MYSELF INVISIBLE...

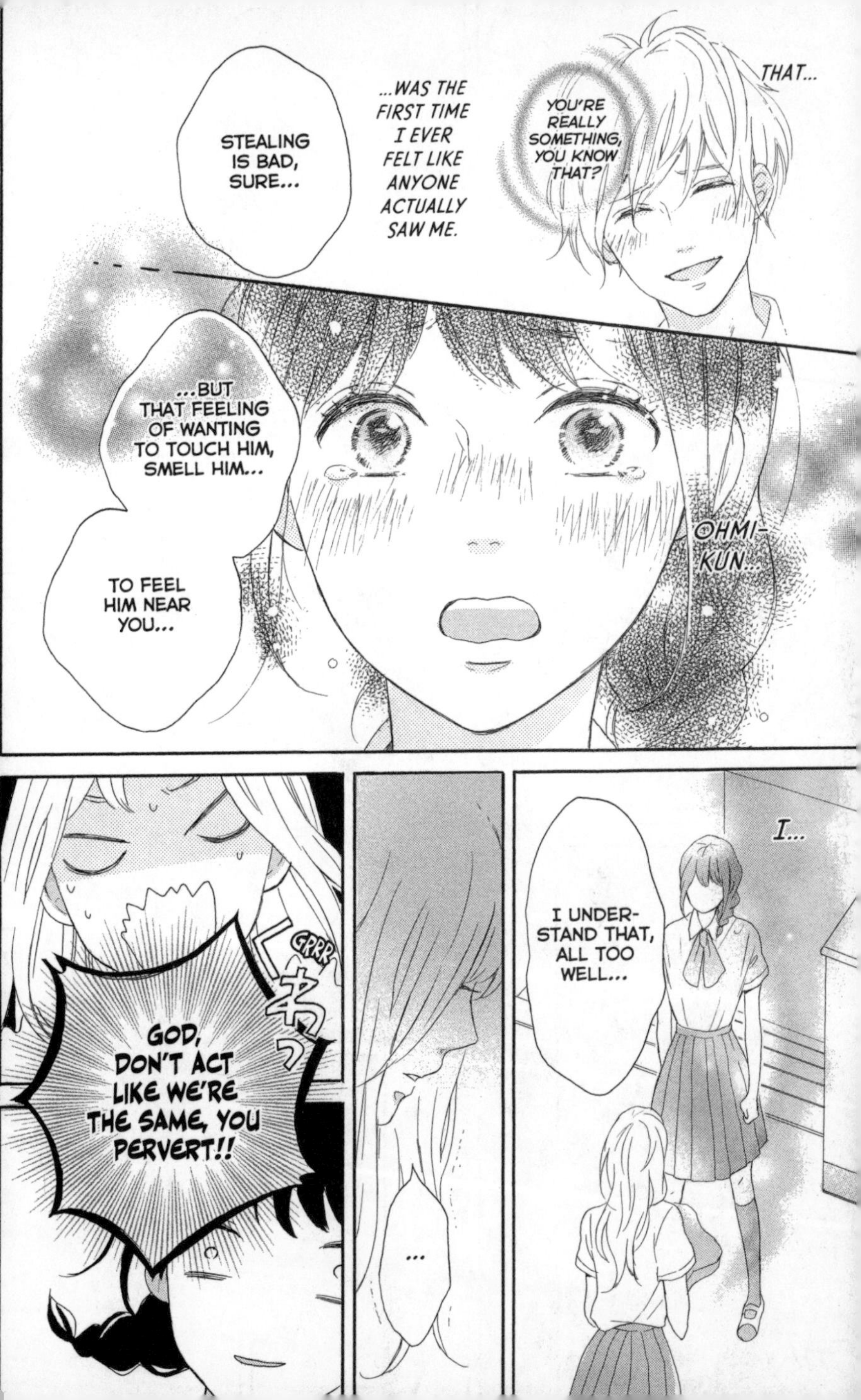
THAT...
YOU'RE REALLY SOMETHING, YOU KNOW THAT?
...WAS THE FIRST TIME I EVER FELT LIKE ANYONE ACTUALLY SAW ME.
STEALING IS BAD, SURE...
OHMI-KUN...
...BUT THAT FEELING OF WANTING TO TOUCH HIM, SMELL HIM...
TO FEEL HIM NEAR YOU...
I...
I UNDER-STAND THAT, ALL TOO WELL...
...
GRRR
GOD, DON'T ACT LIKE WE'RE THE SAME, YOU PERVERT!!

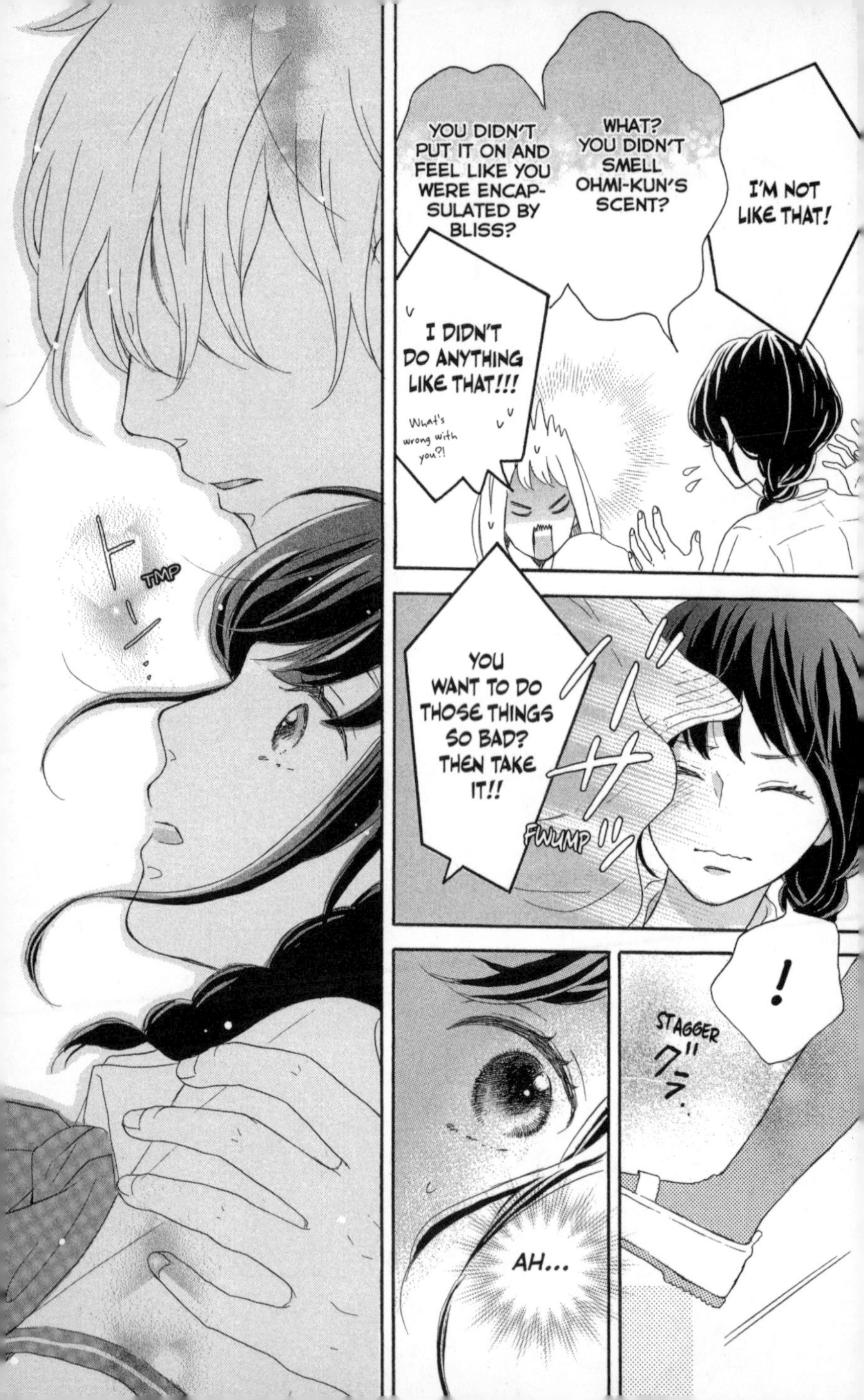
WHAT? YOU DIDN'T SMELL OHMI-KUN'S SCENT?
YOU DIDN'T PUT IT ON AND FEEL LIKE YOU WERE ENCAP-SULATED BY BLISS?
I'M NOT LIKE THAT!
I DIDN'T DO ANYTHING LIKE THAT!!!
What's wrong with you?!
YOU WANT TO DO THOSE THINGS SO BAD? THEN TAKE IT!!
FWUMP
!
STAGGER
AH...
TMP

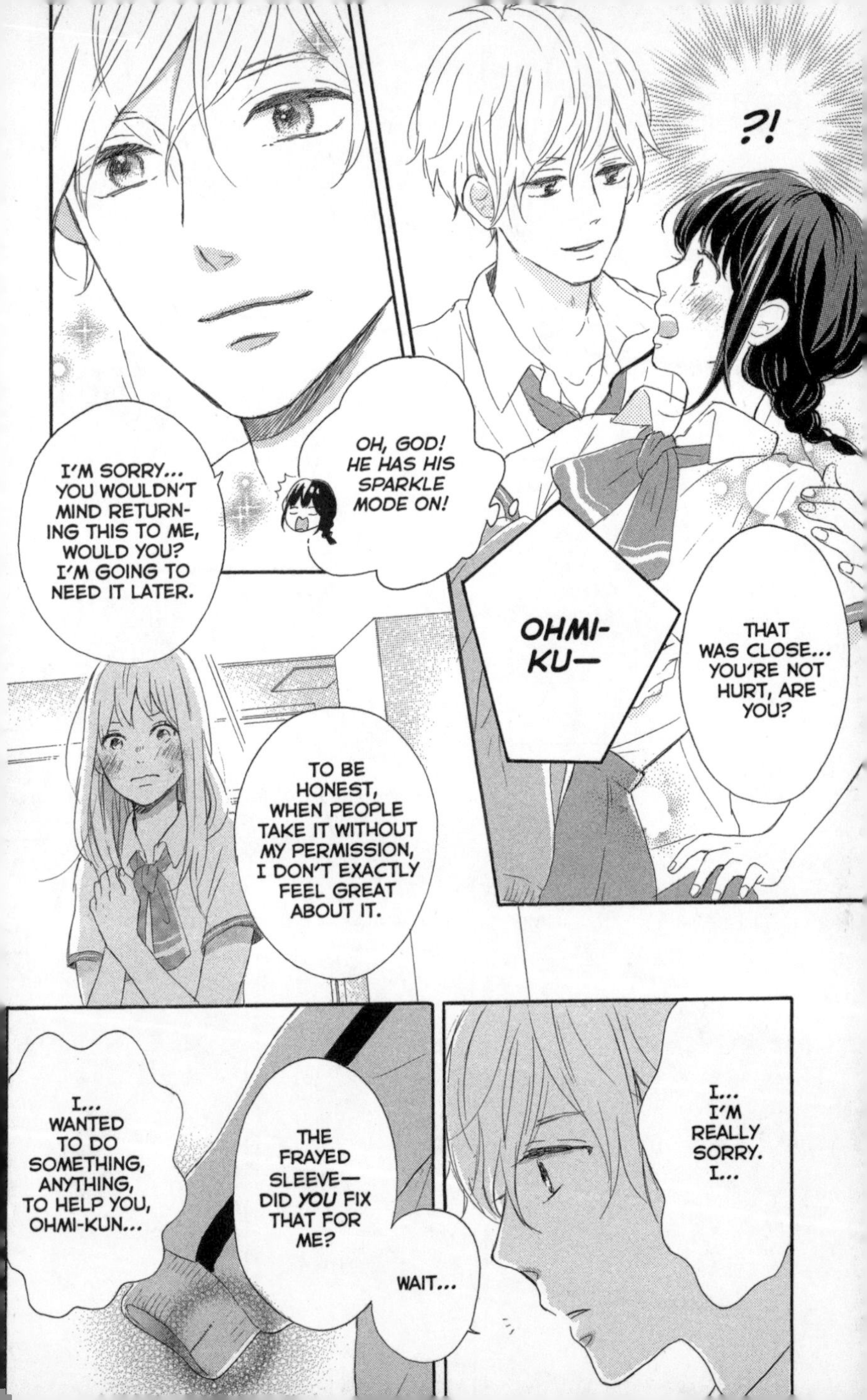
?!
THAT WAS CLOSE... YOU'RE NOT HURT, ARE YOU?
OHMI-KU—
OH, GOD! HE HAS HIS SPARKLE MODE ON!
I'M SORRY... YOU WOULDN'T MIND RETURNING THIS TO ME, WOULD YOU? I'M GOING TO NEED IT LATER.
TO BE HONEST, WHEN PEOPLE TAKE IT WITHOUT MY PERMISSION, I DON'T EXACTLY FEEL GREAT ABOUT IT.
I... I'M REALLY SORRY. I...
WAIT...
THE FRAYED SLEEVE— DID *YOU* FIX THAT FOR ME?
I... WANTED TO DO SOMETHING, ANYTHING, TO HELP YOU, OHMI-KUN...

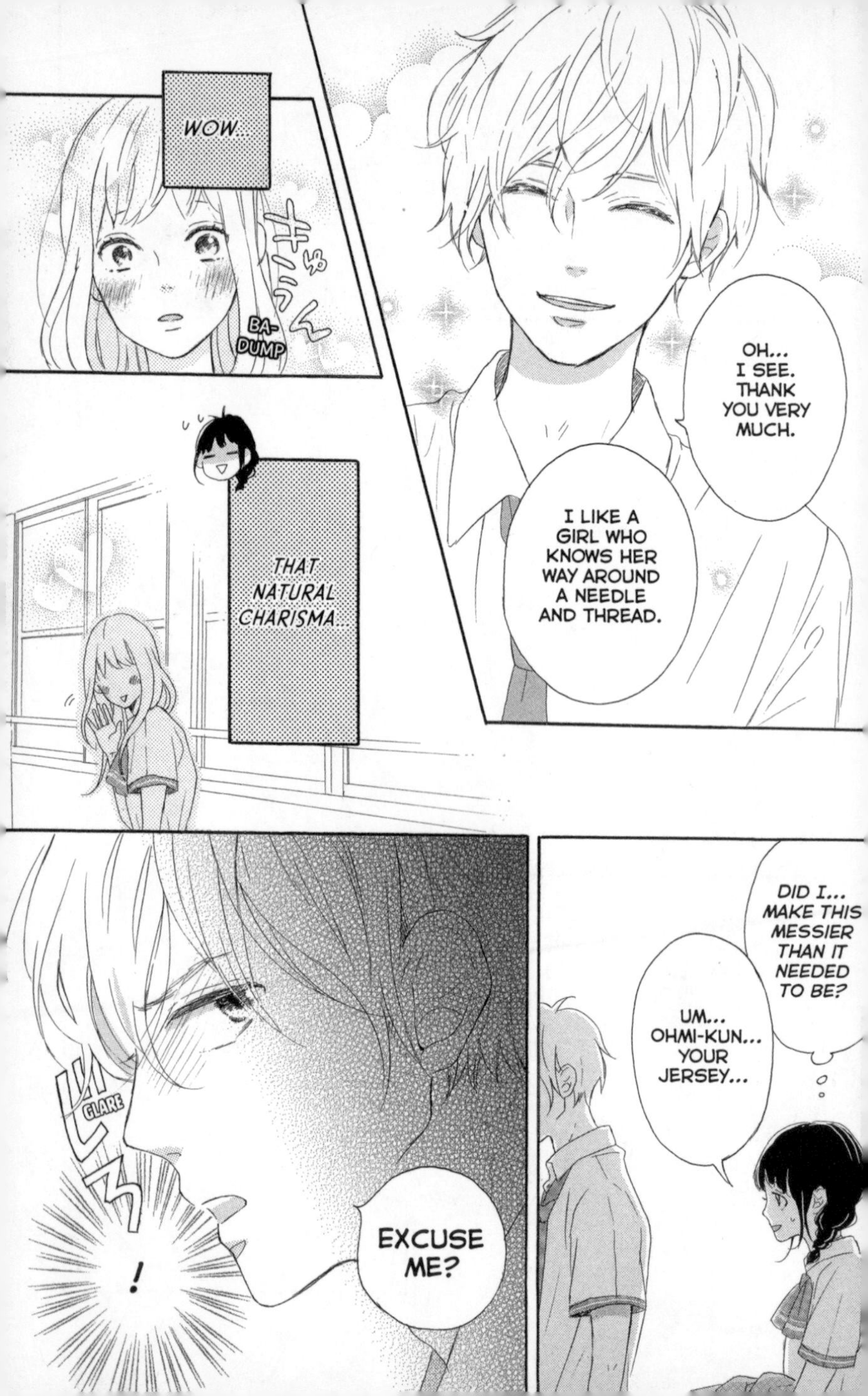
OH... I SEE. THANK YOU VERY MUCH.
I LIKE A GIRL WHO KNOWS HER WAY AROUND A NEEDLE AND THREAD.
WOW...
BA-DUMP
THAT NATURAL CHARISMA...
DID I... MAKE THIS MESSIER THAN IT NEEDED TO BE?
UM... OHMI-KUN... YOUR JERSEY...
GLARE
EXCUSE ME?
!

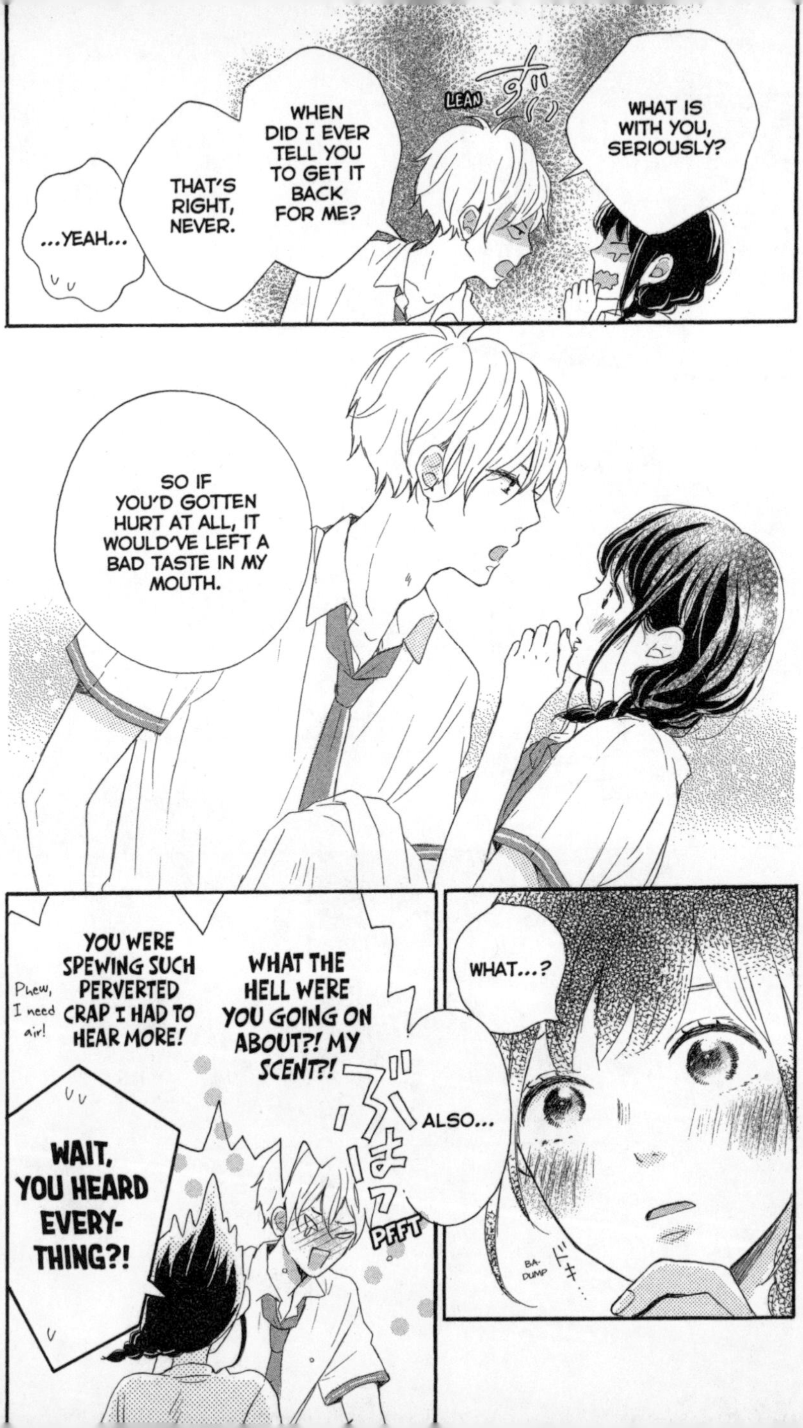
WHAT IS WITH YOU, SERIOUSLY?
LEAN
WHEN DID I EVER TELL YOU TO GET IT BACK FOR ME?
THAT'S RIGHT, NEVER.
...YEAH...
SO IF YOU'D GOTTEN HURT AT ALL, IT WOULD'VE LEFT A BAD TASTE IN MY MOUTH.
ALSO...
WHAT...?
BA-DUMP
PFFT
WHAT THE HELL WERE YOU GOING ON ABOUT?! MY SCENT?!
YOU WERE SPEWING SUCH PERVERTED CRAP I HAD TO HEAR MORE!
Phew, I need air!
WAIT, YOU HEARD EVERYTHING?!

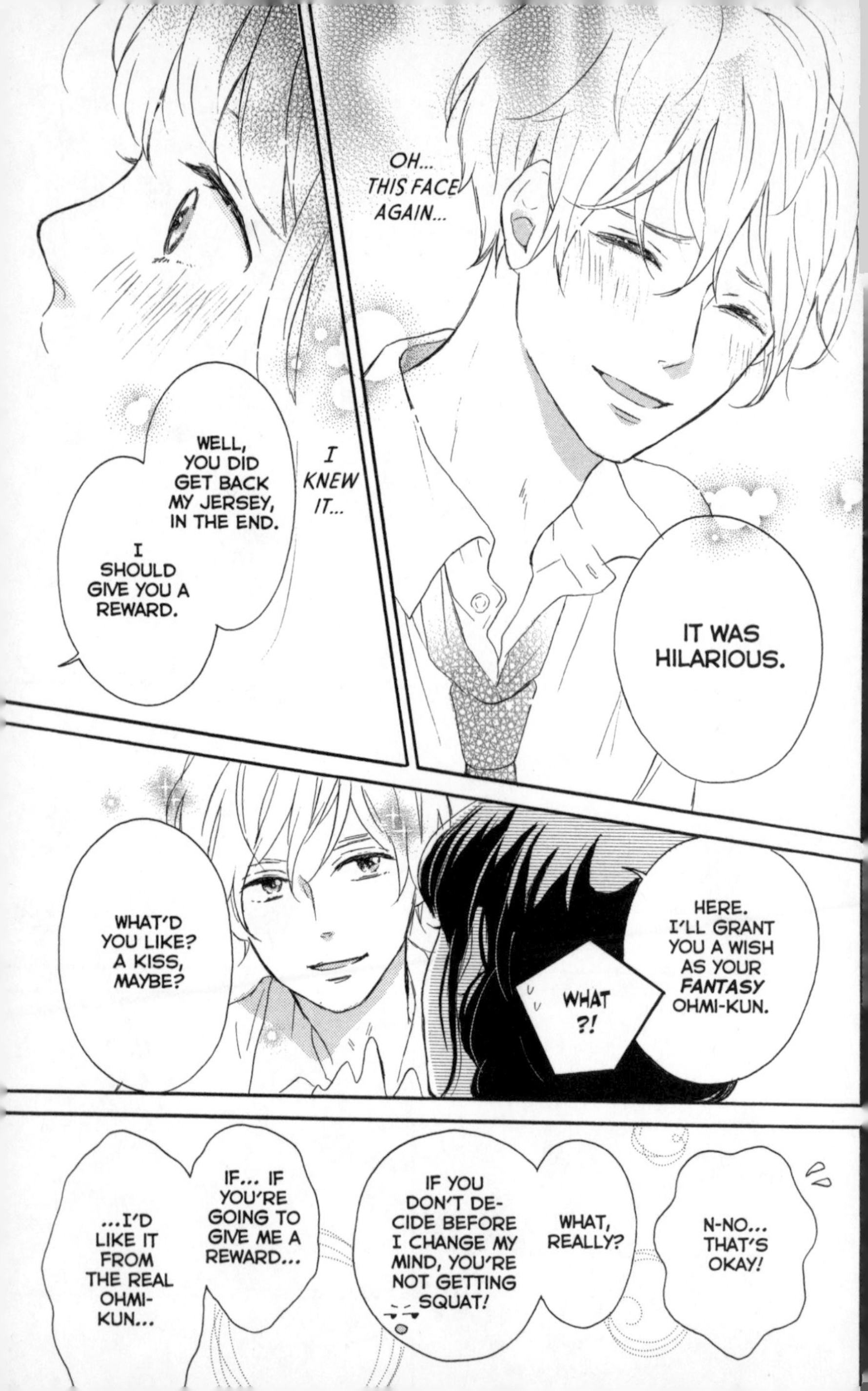
IT WAS HILARIOUS.
OH... THIS FACE AGAIN...
I KNEW IT...
WELL, YOU DID GET BACK MY JERSEY, IN THE END.
I SHOULD GIVE YOU A REWARD.
HERE. I'LL GRANT YOU A WISH AS YOUR *FANTASY* OHMI-KUN.
WHAT ?!
WHAT'D YOU LIKE? A KISS, MAYBE?
N-NO... THAT'S OKAY!
WHAT, REALLY?
IF YOU DON'T DE-CIDE BEFORE I CHANGE MY MIND, YOU'RE NOT GETTING SQUAT!
IF... IF YOU'RE GOING TO GIVE ME A REWARD...
...I'D LIKE IT FROM THE REAL OHMI-KUN...

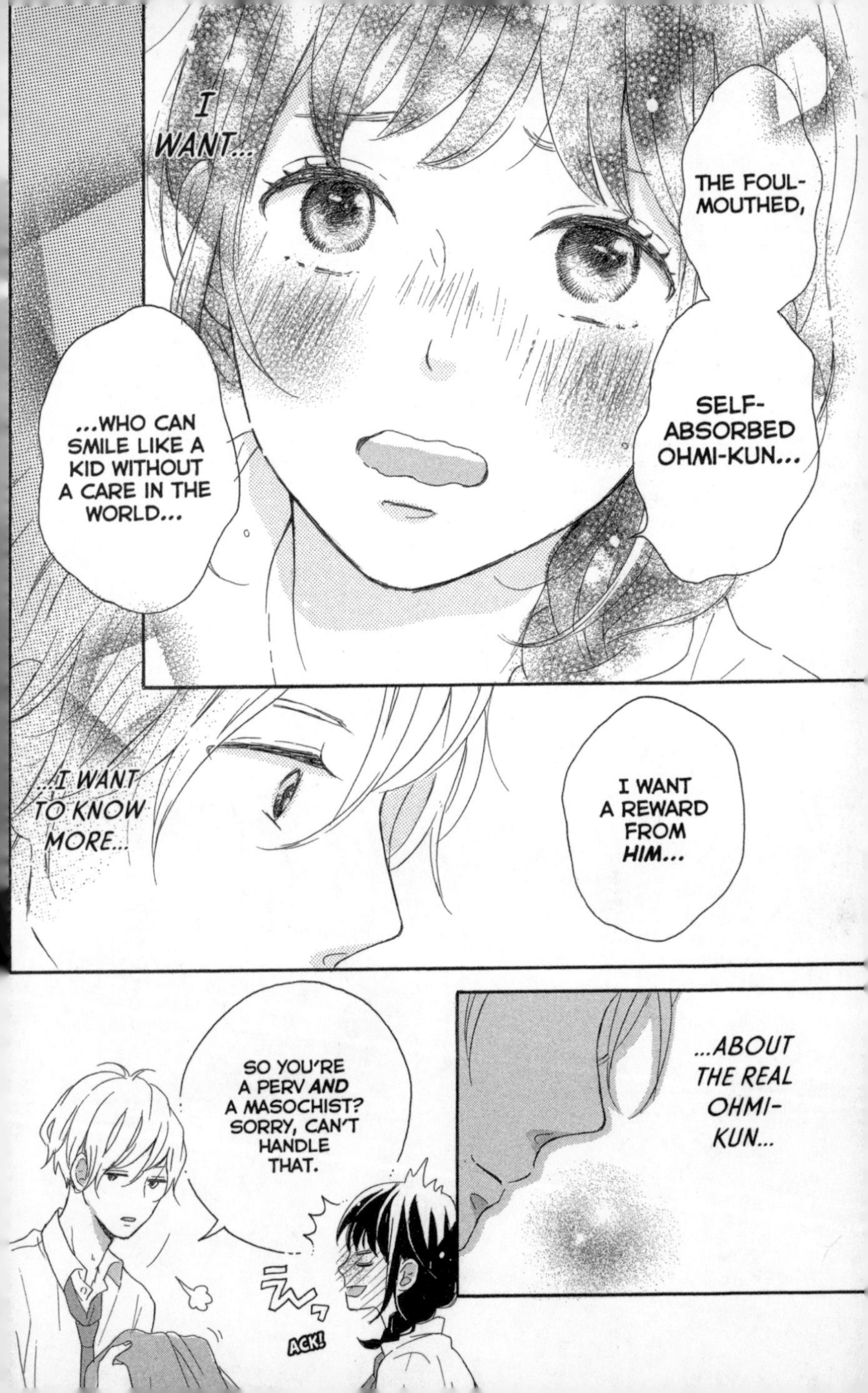
I WANT...
THE FOUL-MOUTHED,
SELF-ABSORBED OHMI-KUN...
...WHO CAN SMILE LIKE A KID WITHOUT A CARE IN THE WORLD...
I WANT A REWARD FROM *HIM*...
...I WANT TO KNOW MORE...
...ABOUT THE REAL OHMI-KUN...
SO YOU'RE A PERV *AND* A MASOCHIST? SORRY, CAN'T HANDLE THAT.
ACK!

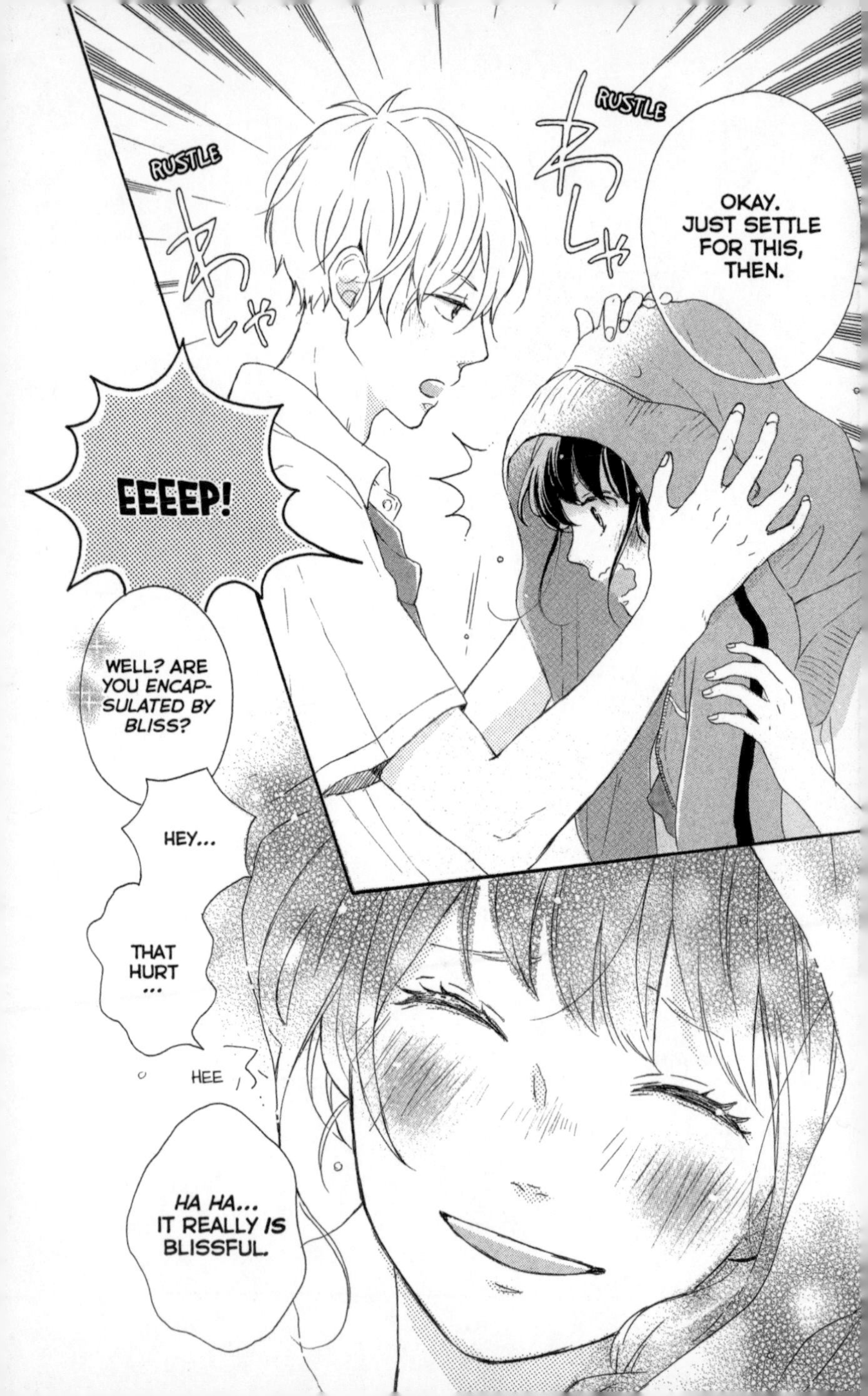
RUSTLE
わしゃ
OKAY. JUST SETTLE FOR THIS, THEN.
RUSTLE
わしゃ
EEEEP!
WELL? ARE YOU ENCAP-SULATED BY BLISS?
HEY...
THAT HURT...
HEE
HA HA... IT REALLY *IS* BLISSFUL.

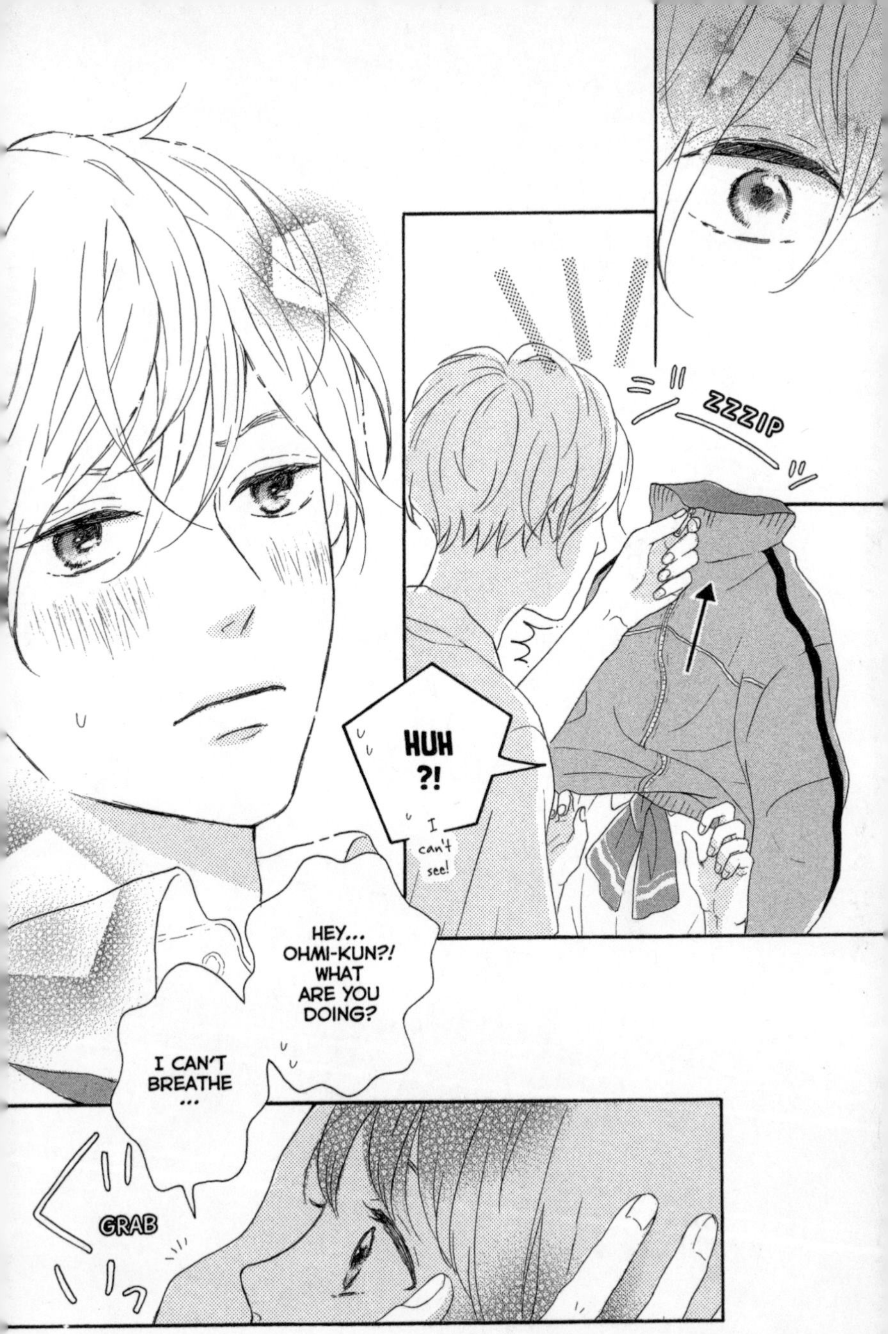
ZZZIP
HUH ?!
I can't see!
HEY... OHMI-KUN?! WHAT ARE YOU DOING?
I CAN'T BREATHE ...
GRAB

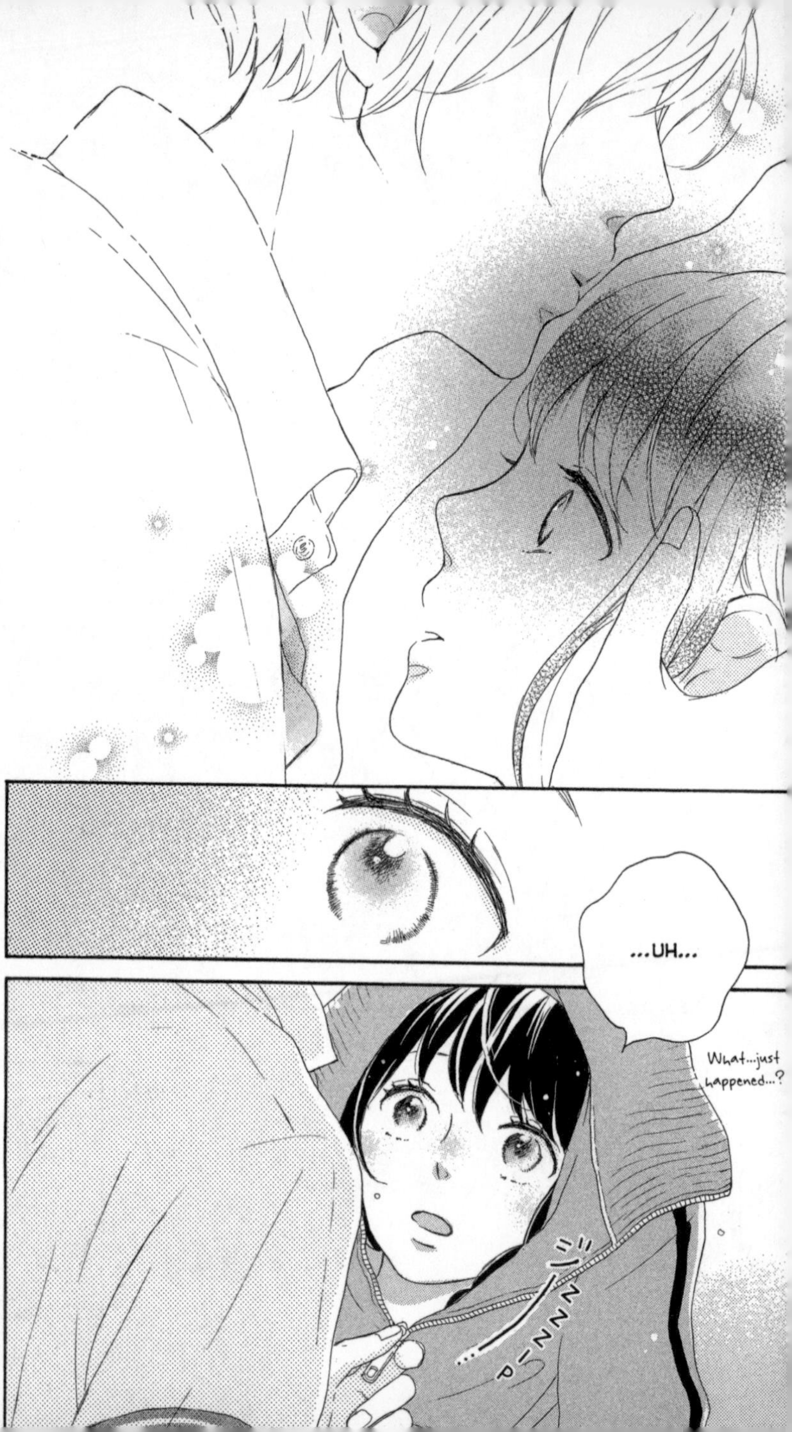
...UH...
What...just happened...?
ZZZZZ-P

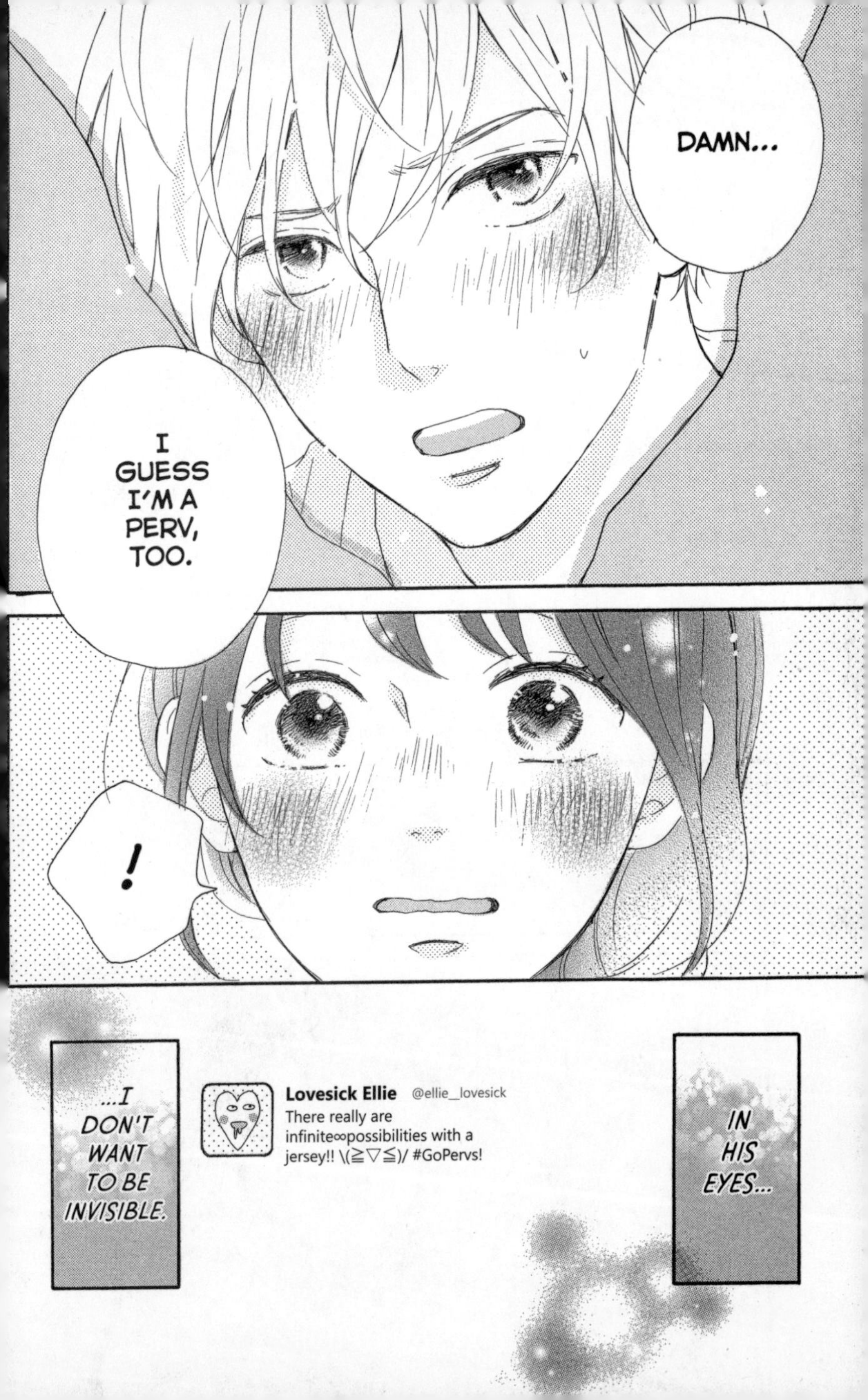
DAMN...
I GUESS I'M A PERV, TOO.
!
IN HIS EYES...
...I DON'T WANT TO BE INVISIBLE.
Lovesick Ellie @ellie_lovesick
There really are infinite∞possibilities with a jersey!! \(≧▽≦)/ #GoPervs!

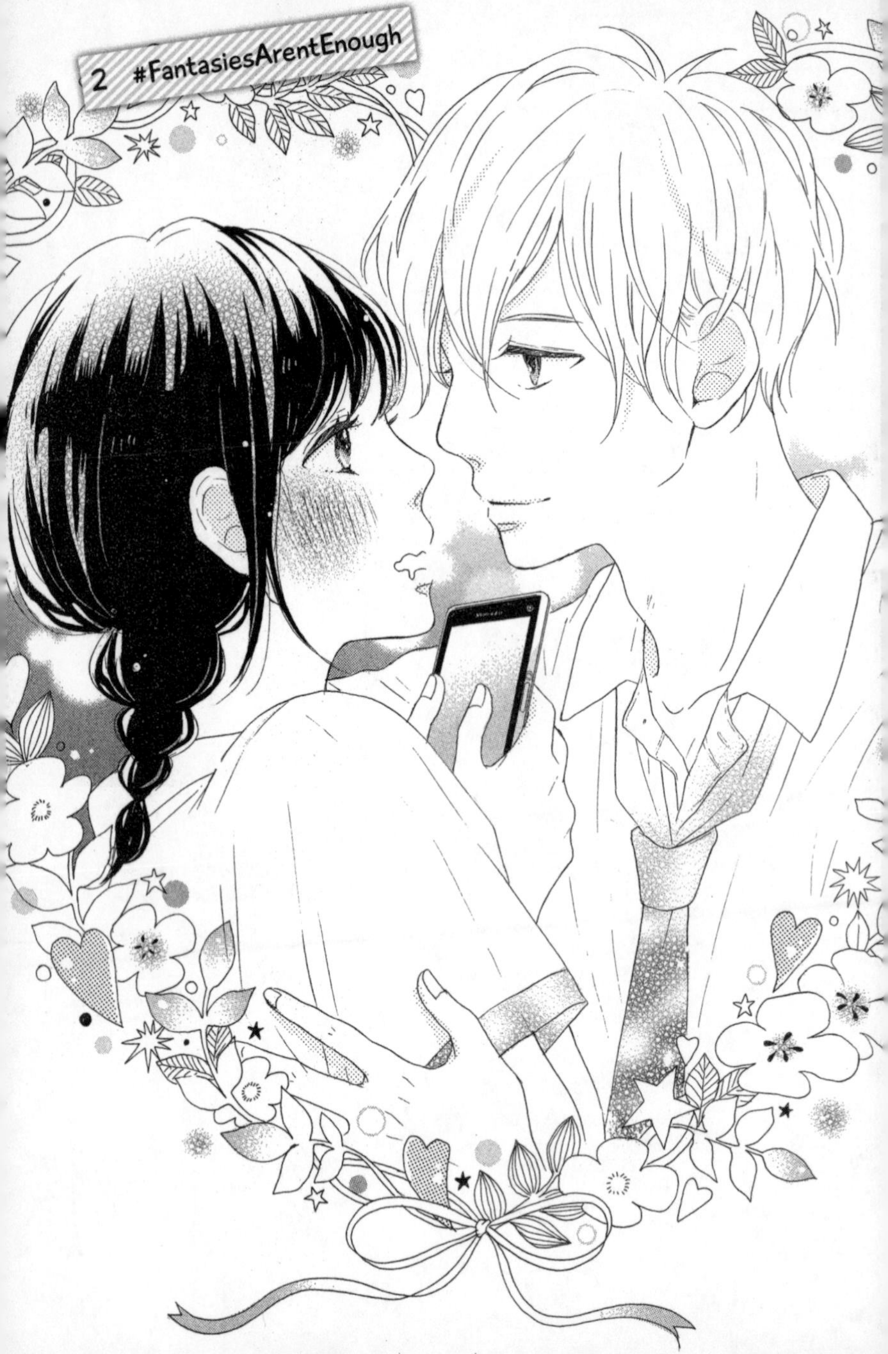
2 #FantasiesArentEnough

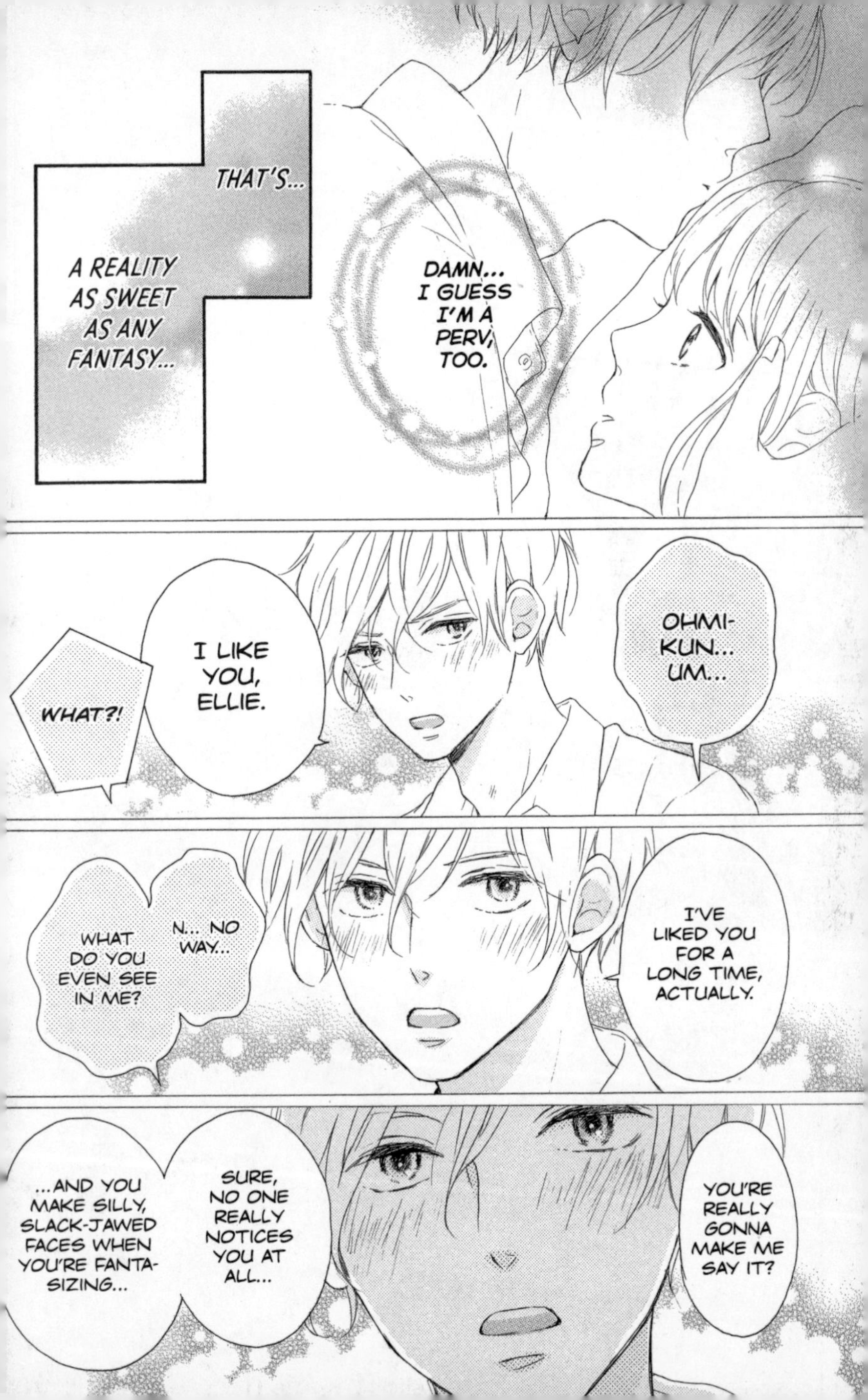
DAMN... I GUESS I'M A PERV, TOO.
THAT'S...
A REALITY AS SWEET AS ANY FANTASY...
OHMI-KUN... UM...
I LIKE YOU, ELLIE.
WHAT?!
I'VE LIKED YOU FOR A LONG TIME, ACTUALLY.
N... NO WAY...
WHAT DO YOU EVEN SEE IN ME?
YOU'RE REALLY GONNA MAKE ME SAY IT?
SURE, NO ONE REALLY NOTICES YOU AT ALL...
...AND YOU MAKE SILLY, SLACK-JAWED FACES WHEN YOU'RE FANTA-SIZING...

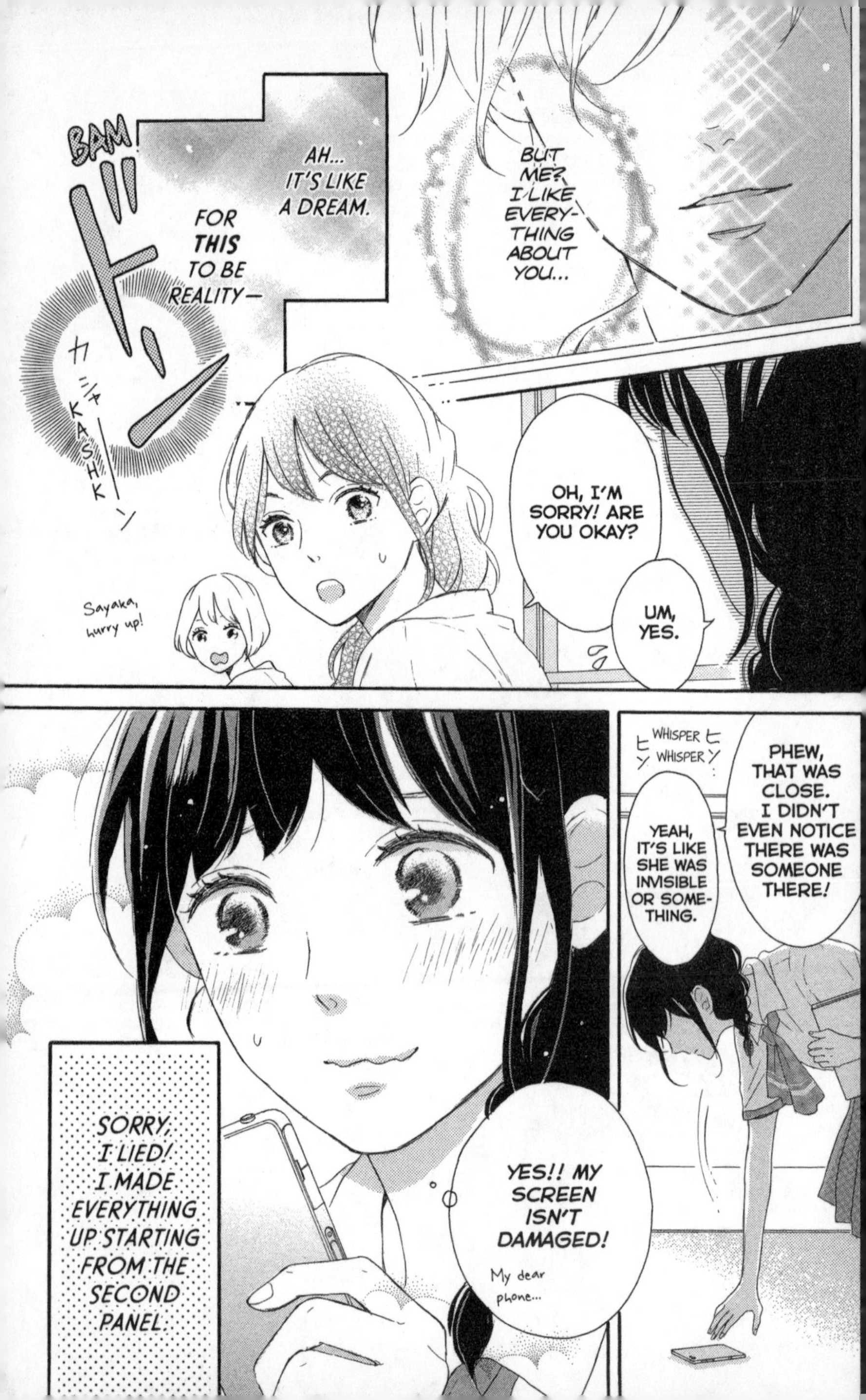
BUT ME? I LIKE EVERYTHING ABOUT YOU...
AH... IT'S LIKE A DREAM.
FOR **THIS** TO BE REALITY—
BAM
KASHK
OH, I'M SORRY! ARE YOU OKAY?
UM, YES.
Sayaka, hurry up!
WHISPER WHISPER
PHEW, THAT WAS CLOSE. I DIDN'T EVEN NOTICE THERE WAS SOMEONE THERE!
YEAH, IT'S LIKE SHE WAS INVISIBLE OR SOMETHING.
YES!! MY SCREEN ISN'T DAMAGED!
My dear phone...
SORRY, I LIED! I MADE EVERYTHING UP STARTING FROM THE SECOND PANEL.

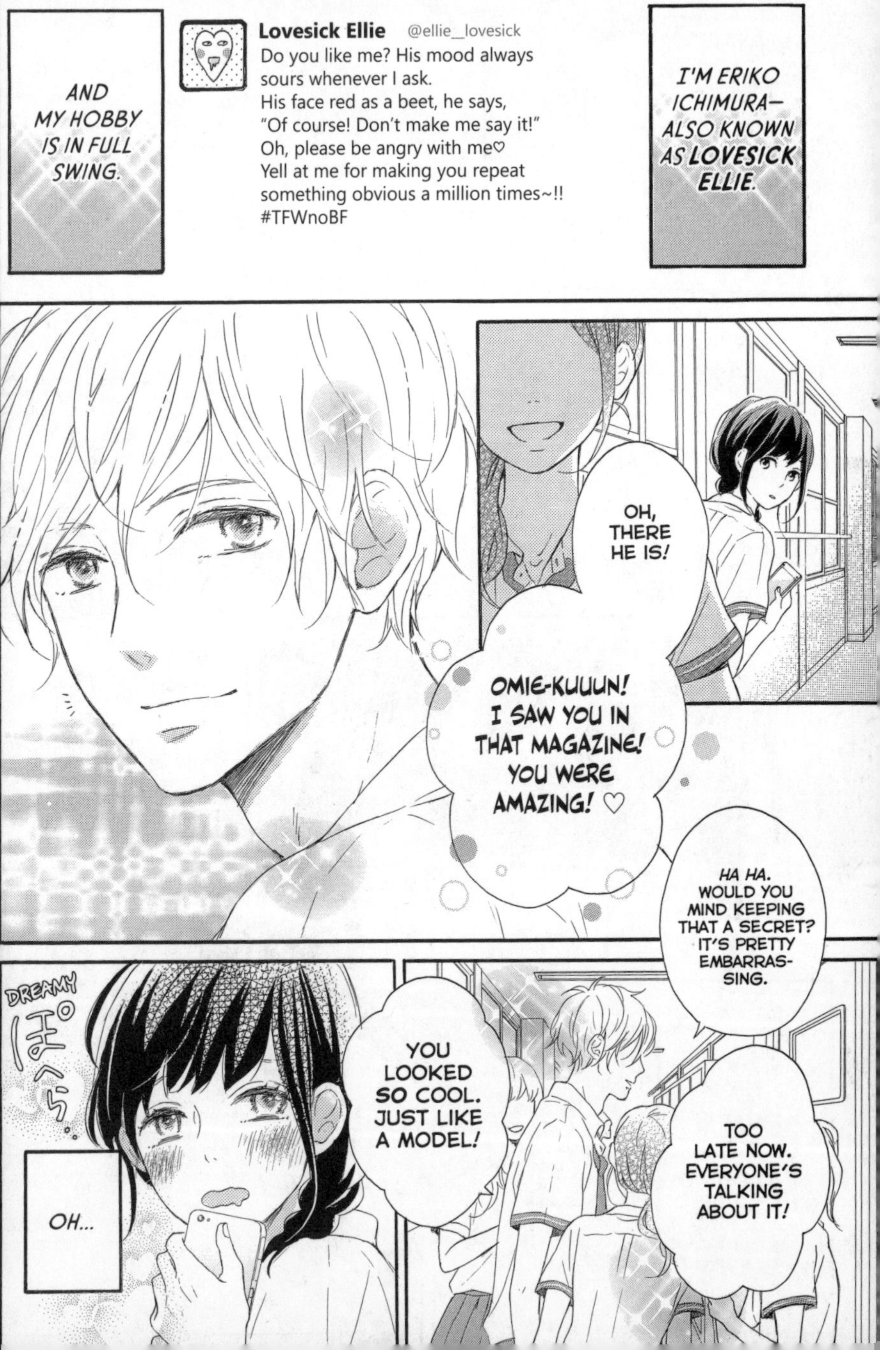
I'M ERIKO ICHIMURA—ALSO KNOWN AS LOVESICK ELLIE.
Lovesick Ellie @ellie__lovesick
Do you like me? His mood always sours whenever I ask.
His face red as a beet, he says, "Of course! Don't make me say it!"
Oh, please be angry with me♡
Yell at me for making you repeat something obvious a million times~!!
#TFWnoBF
AND MY HOBBY IS IN FULL SWING.
OH, THERE HE IS!
OMIE-KUUUN! I SAW YOU IN THAT MAGAZINE! YOU WERE AMAZING! ♡
HA HA. WOULD YOU MIND KEEPING THAT A SECRET? IT'S PRETTY EMBARRAS-SING.
TOO LATE NOW. EVERYONE'S TALKING ABOUT IT!
YOU LOOKED SO COOL. JUST LIKE A MODEL!
DREAMY
ぽへら
OH...

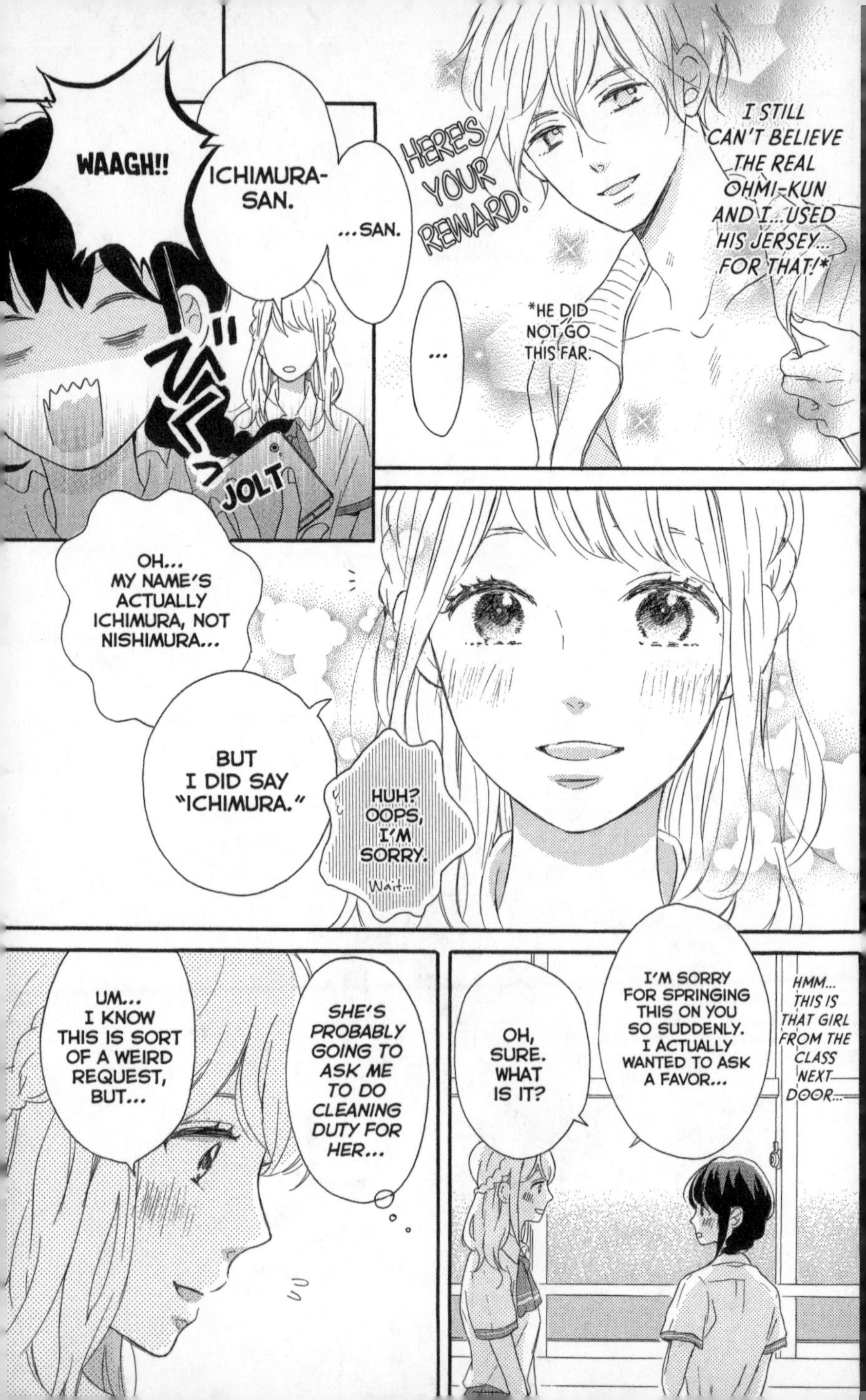
I STILL CAN'T BELIEVE THE REAL OHMI-KUN AND I...USED HIS JERSEY... FOR THAT!*
HERE'S YOUR REWARD.
*HE DID NOT GO THIS FAR.
...
...SAN.
ICHIMURA-SAN.
WAAGH!!
JOLT
OH... MY NAME'S ACTUALLY ICHIMURA, NOT NISHIMURA...
BUT I DID SAY "ICHIMURA."
HUH? OOPS, I'M SORRY.
Wait...
HMM... THIS IS THAT GIRL FROM THE CLASS NEXT DOOR...
I'M SORRY FOR SPRINGING THIS ON YOU SO SUDDENLY. I ACTUALLY WANTED TO ASK A FAVOR...
OH, SURE. WHAT IS IT?
SHE'S PROBABLY GOING TO ASK ME TO DO CLEANING DUTY FOR HER...
UM... I KNOW THIS IS SORT OF A WEIRD REQUEST, BUT...

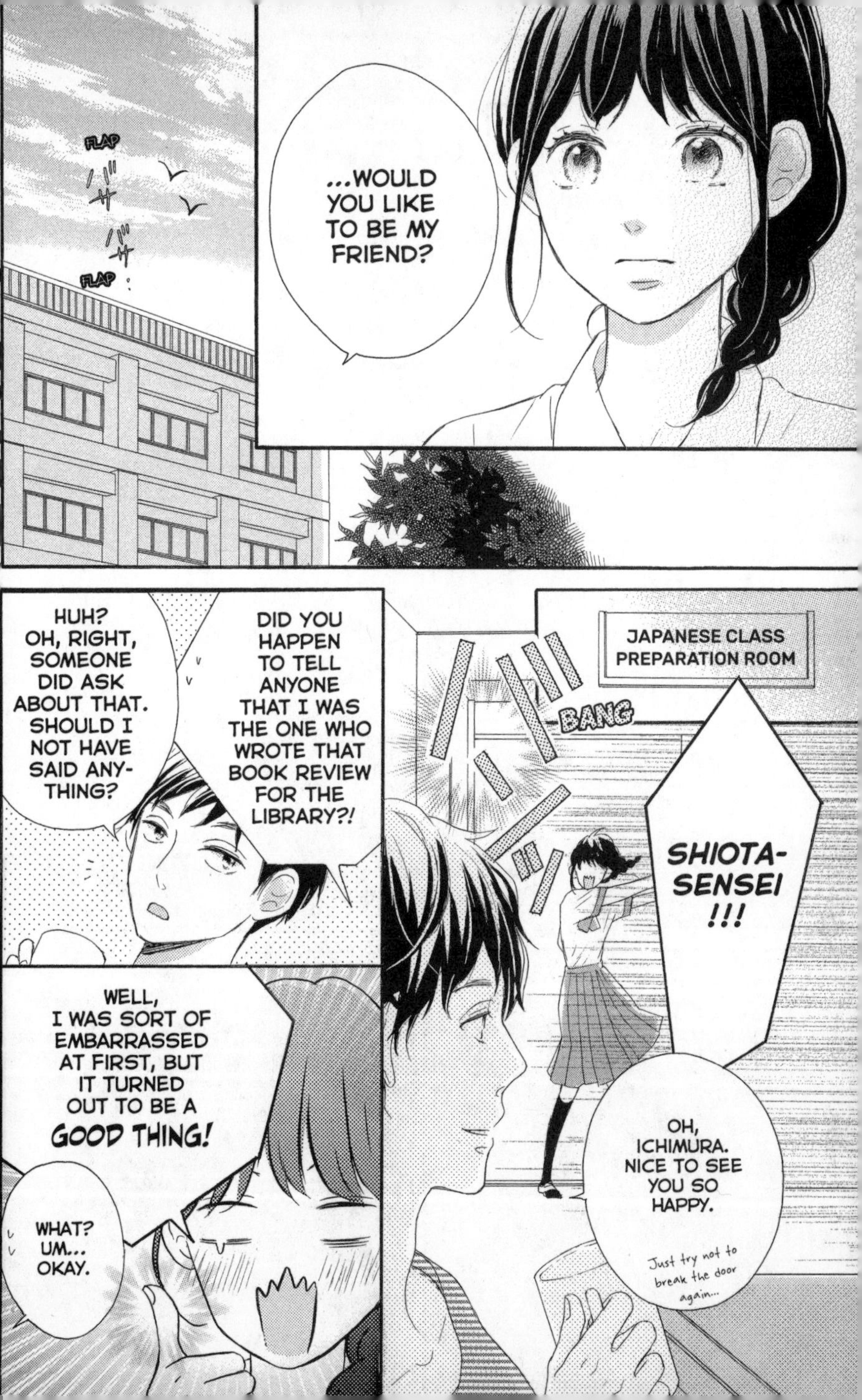
...WOULD YOU LIKE TO BE MY FRIEND?
FLAP
FLAP
JAPANESE CLASS PREPARATION ROOM
BANG
SHIOTA-SENSEI!!!
OH, ICHIMURA. NICE TO SEE YOU SO HAPPY.
Just try not to break the door again...
DID YOU HAPPEN TO TELL ANYONE THAT I WAS THE ONE WHO WROTE THAT BOOK REVIEW FOR THE LIBRARY?!
HUH? OH, RIGHT, SOMEONE DID ASK ABOUT THAT. SHOULD I NOT HAVE SAID ANY-THING?
WELL, I WAS SORT OF EMBARRASSED AT FIRST, BUT IT TURNED OUT TO BE A GOOD THING!
WHAT? UM... OKAY.

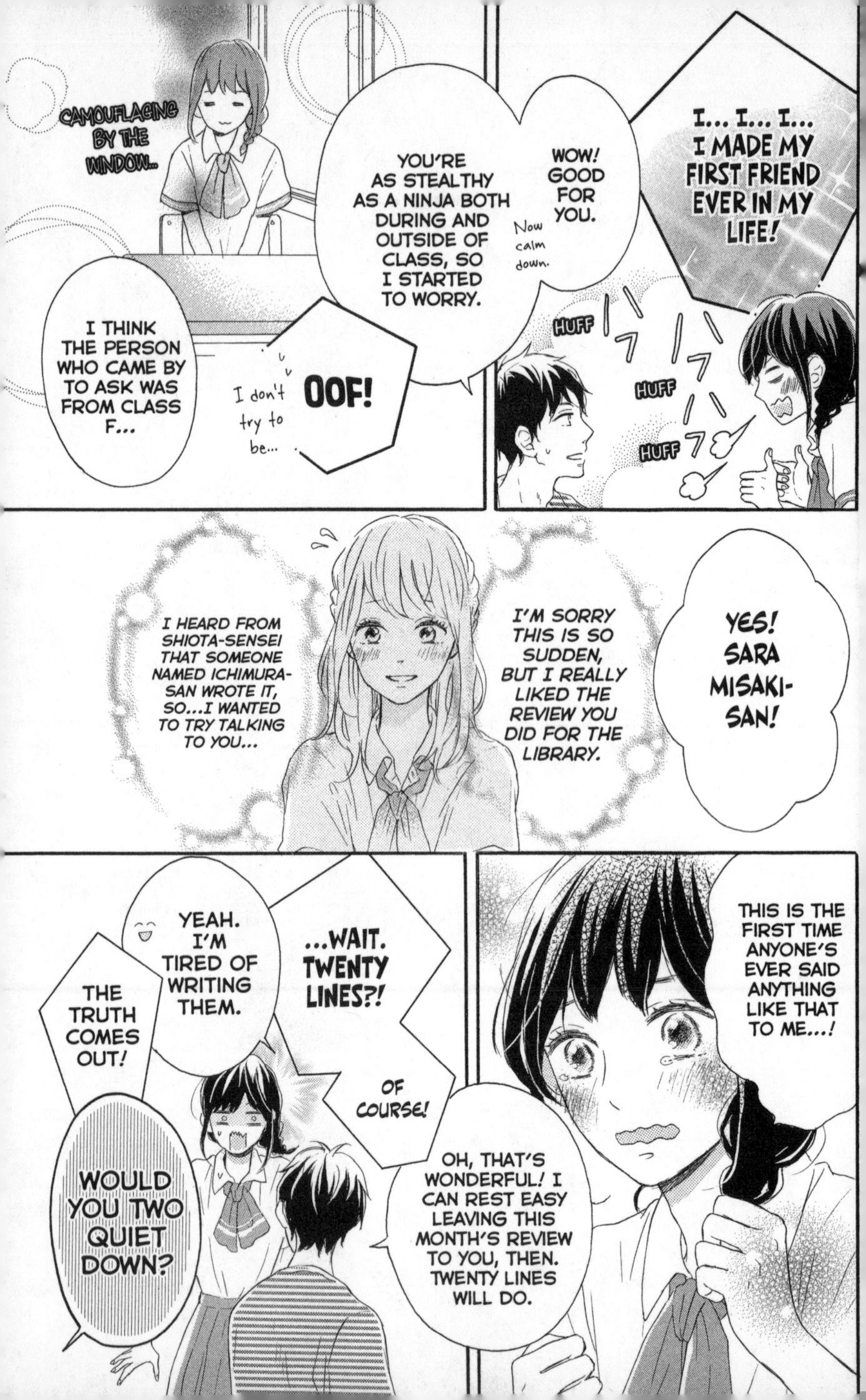
I... I... I... I MADE MY FIRST FRIEND EVER IN MY LIFE!
HUFF
HUFF
HUFF
WOW! GOOD FOR YOU.
Now calm down.
YOU'RE AS STEALTHY AS A NINJA BOTH DURING AND OUTSIDE OF CLASS, SO I STARTED TO WORRY.
OOF!
I don't try to be...
CAMOUFLAGING BY THE WINDOW...
I THINK THE PERSON WHO CAME BY TO ASK WAS FROM CLASS F...
YES! SARA MISAKI-SAN!
I'M SORRY THIS IS SO SUDDEN, BUT I REALLY LIKED THE REVIEW YOU DID FOR THE LIBRARY.
I HEARD FROM SHIOTA-SENSEI THAT SOMEONE NAMED ICHIMURA-SAN WROTE IT, SO...I WANTED TO TRY TALKING TO YOU...
THIS IS THE FIRST TIME ANYONE'S EVER SAID ANYTHING LIKE THAT TO ME...!
OH, THAT'S WONDERFUL! I CAN REST EASY LEAVING THIS MONTH'S REVIEW TO YOU, THEN. TWENTY LINES WILL DO.
...WAIT. TWENTY LINES?!
OF COURSE!
YEAH. I'M TIRED OF WRITING THEM.
THE TRUTH COMES OUT!
WOULD YOU TWO QUIET DOWN?

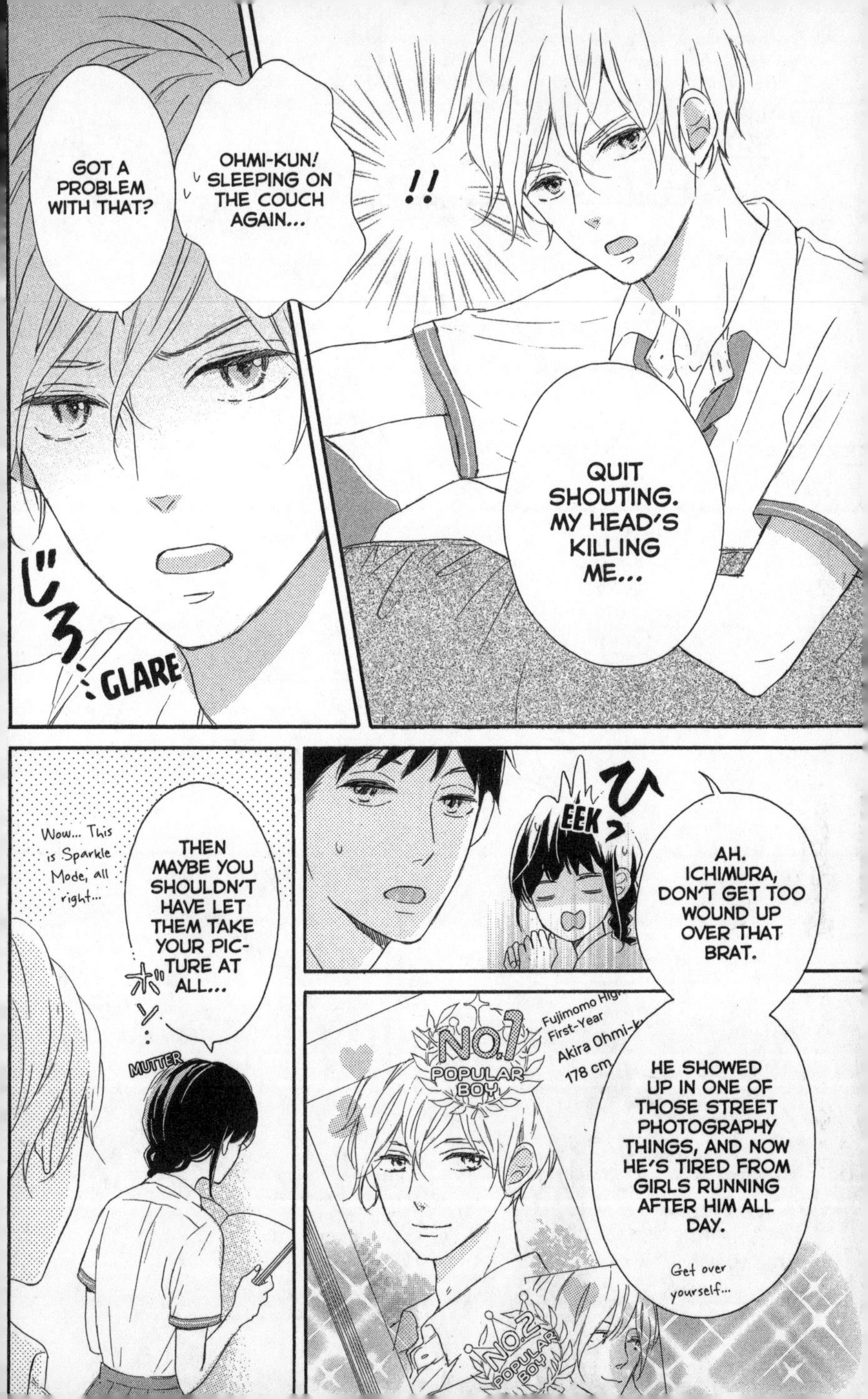
OHMI-KUN! SLEEPING ON THE COUCH AGAIN...
!!
QUIT SHOUTING. MY HEAD'S KILLING ME...
GOT A PROBLEM WITH THAT?
じろ
GLARE
ひっ
EEK
AH. ICHIMURA, DON'T GET TOO WOUND UP OVER THAT BRAT.
HE SHOWED UP IN ONE OF THOSE STREET PHOTOGRAPHY THINGS, AND NOW HE'S TIRED FROM GIRLS RUNNING AFTER HIM ALL DAY.
Get over yourself...
NO.1 POPULAR BOY
Fujimomo High
First-Year
Akira Ohmi-k
178 cm
NO.2 POPULAR BOY
THEN MAYBE YOU SHOULDN'T HAVE LET THEM TAKE YOUR PICTURE AT ALL...
ボソ
MUTTER
Wow... This is Sparkle Mode, all right...

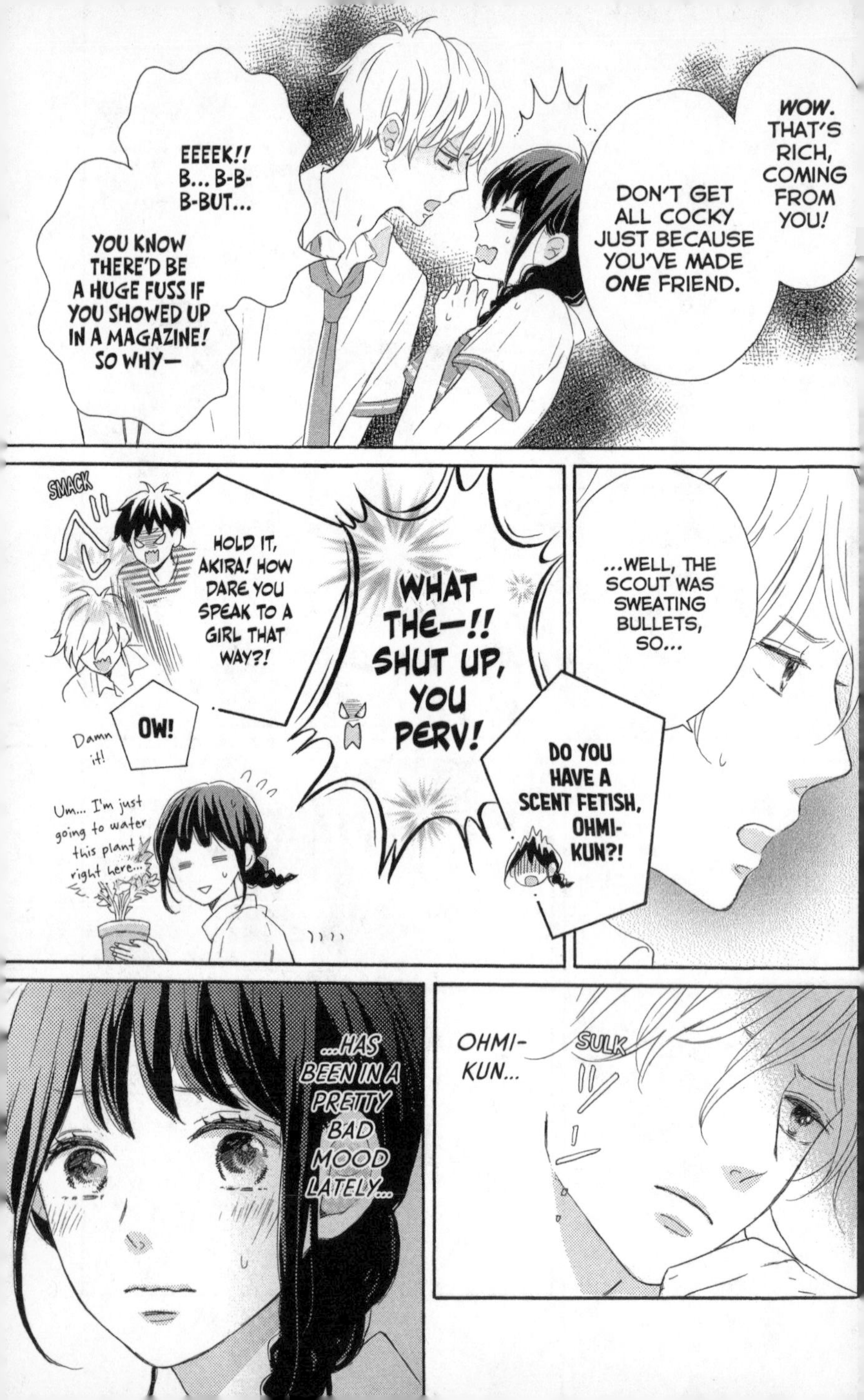
WOW. THAT'S RICH, COMING FROM YOU!
DON'T GET ALL COCKY JUST BECAUSE YOU'VE MADE ONE FRIEND.
EEEEK!! B... B-B-B-BUT...
YOU KNOW THERE'D BE A HUGE FUSS IF YOU SHOWED UP IN A MAGAZINE! SO WHY—
...WELL, THE SCOUT WAS SWEATING BULLETS, SO...
DO YOU HAVE A SCENT FETISH, OHMI-KUN?!
WHAT THE—!! SHUT UP, YOU PERV!
HOLD IT, AKIRA! HOW DARE YOU SPEAK TO A GIRL THAT WAY?!
SMACK
OW!
Damn it!
Um... I'm just going to water this plant right here...
OHMI-KUN...
SULK
...HAS BEEN IN A PRETTY BAD MOOD LATELY...

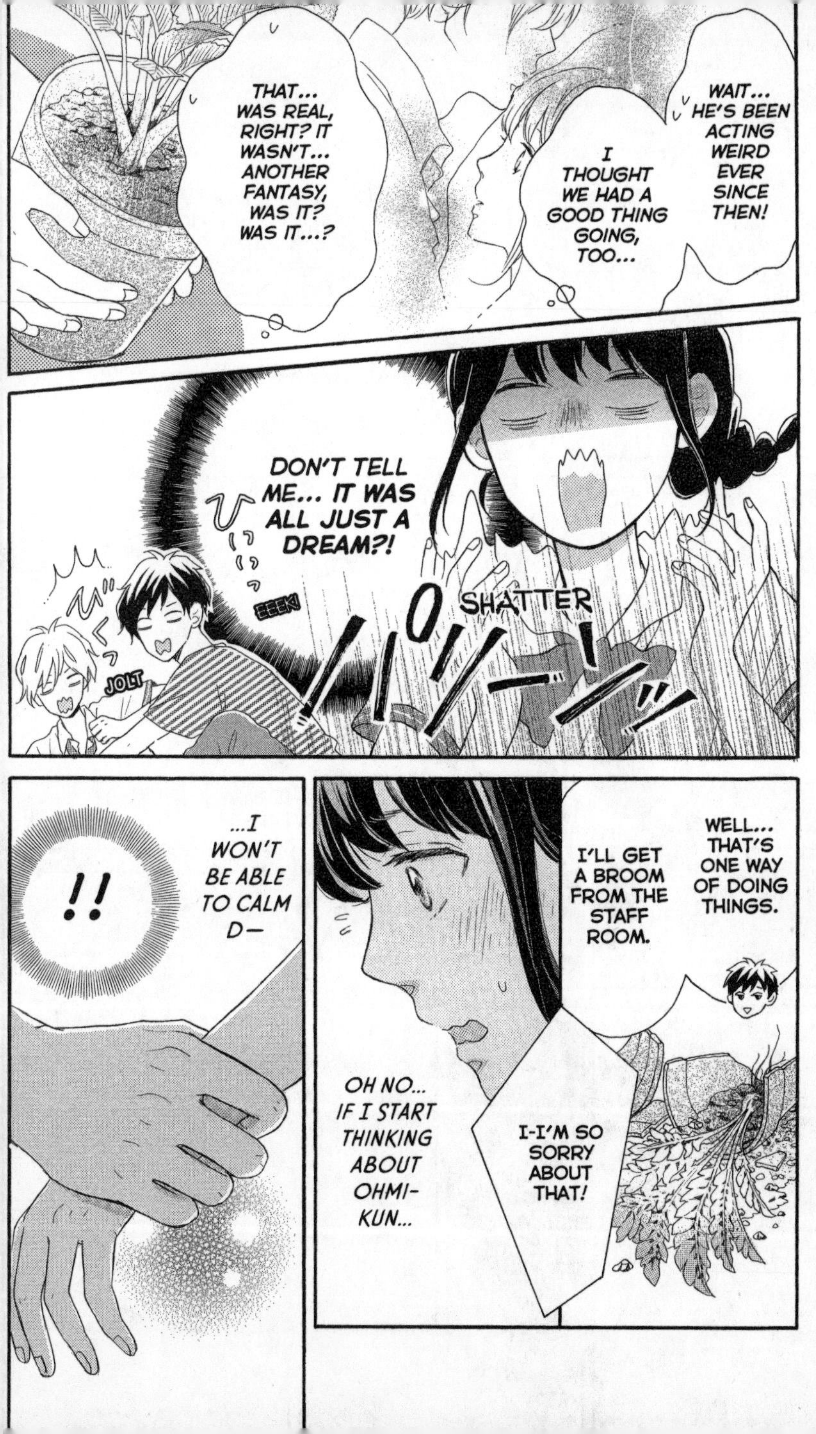
WAIT... HE'S BEEN ACTING WEIRD EVER SINCE THEN!
I THOUGHT WE HAD A GOOD THING GOING, TOO...
THAT... WAS REAL, RIGHT? IT WASN'T... ANOTHER FANTASY, WAS IT? WAS IT...?
DON'T TELL ME... IT WAS ALL JUST A DREAM?!
SHATTER
EEEK!
JOLT
WELL... THAT'S ONE WAY OF DOING THINGS.
I'LL GET A BROOM FROM THE STAFF ROOM.
I-I'M SO SORRY ABOUT THAT!
OH NO... IF I START THINKING ABOUT OHMI-KUN...
!!
...I WON'T BE ABLE TO CALM D—

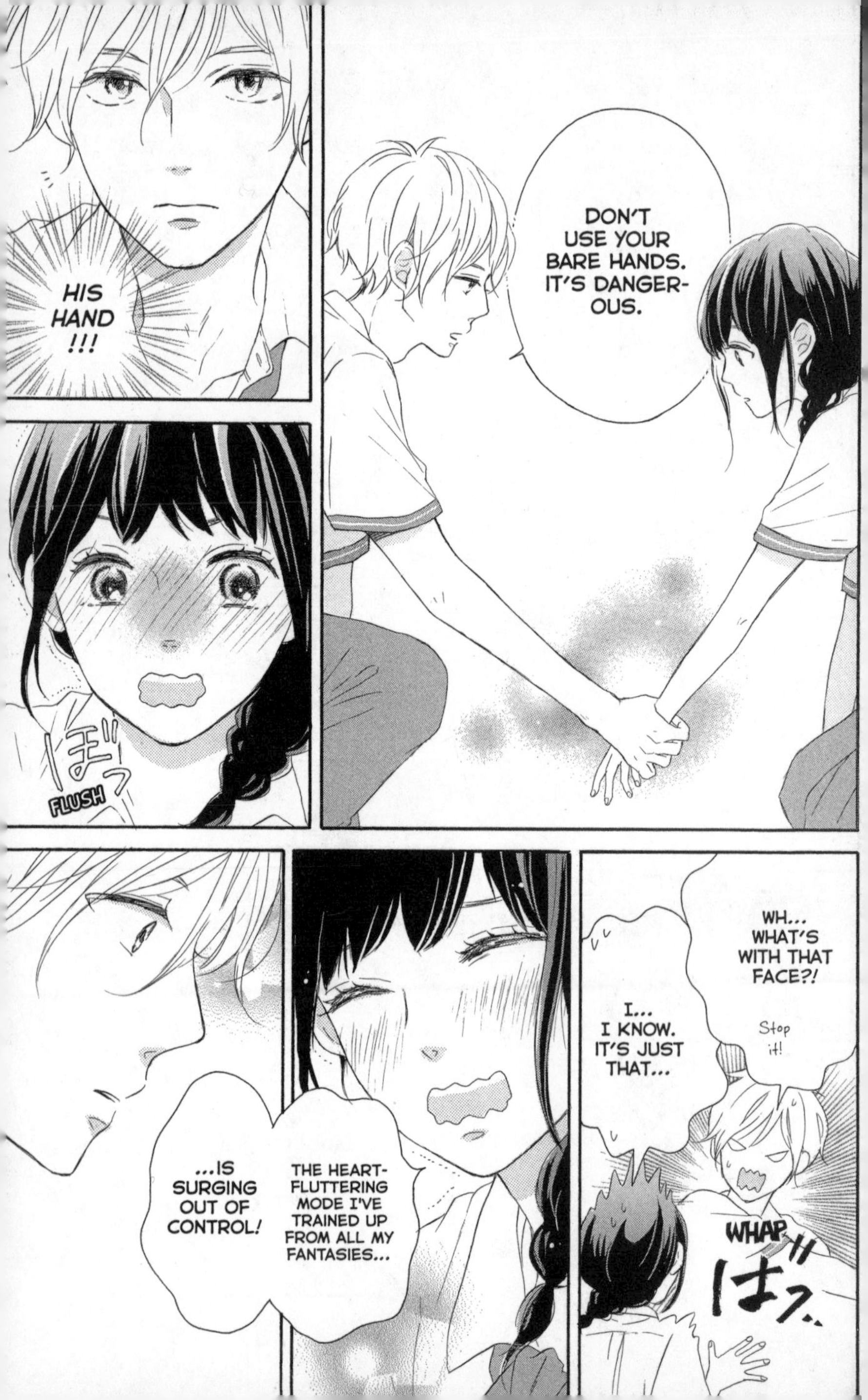
DON'T USE YOUR BARE HANDS. IT'S DANGER-OUS.
HIS HAND!!!
FLUSH
WH... WHAT'S WITH THAT FACE?!
Stop it!
I... I KNOW. IT'S JUST THAT...
WHAP
THE HEART-FLUTTERING MODE I'VE TRAINED UP FROM ALL MY FANTASIES...
...IS SURGING OUT OF CONTROL!

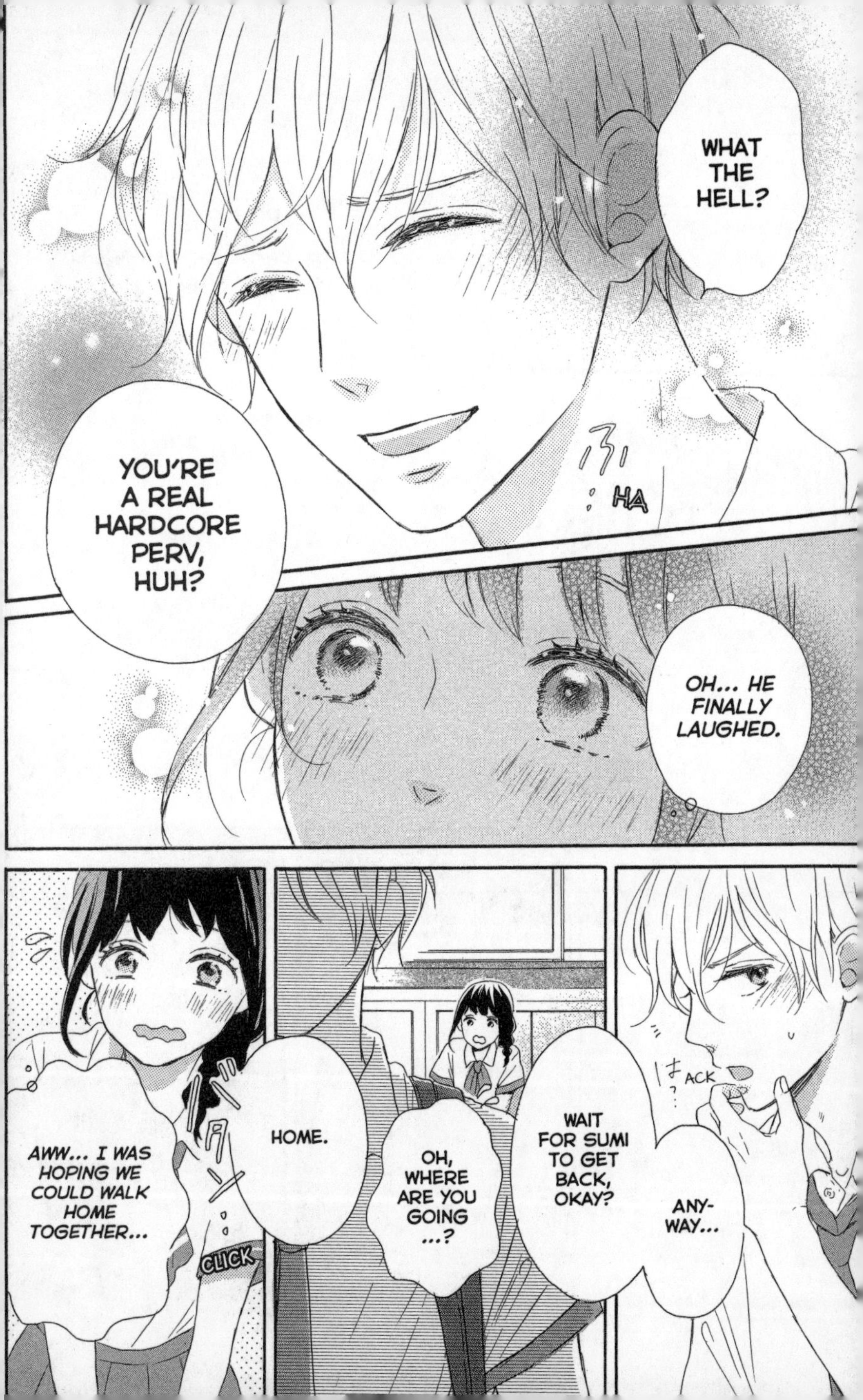
WHAT THE HELL?
HA
YOU'RE A REAL HARDCORE PERV, HUH?
OH... HE FINALLY LAUGHED.
ACK
ANY-WAY...
WAIT FOR SUMI TO GET BACK, OKAY?
OH, WHERE ARE YOU GOING ...?
HOME.
CLICK
AWW... I WAS HOPING WE COULD WALK HOME TOGETHER...

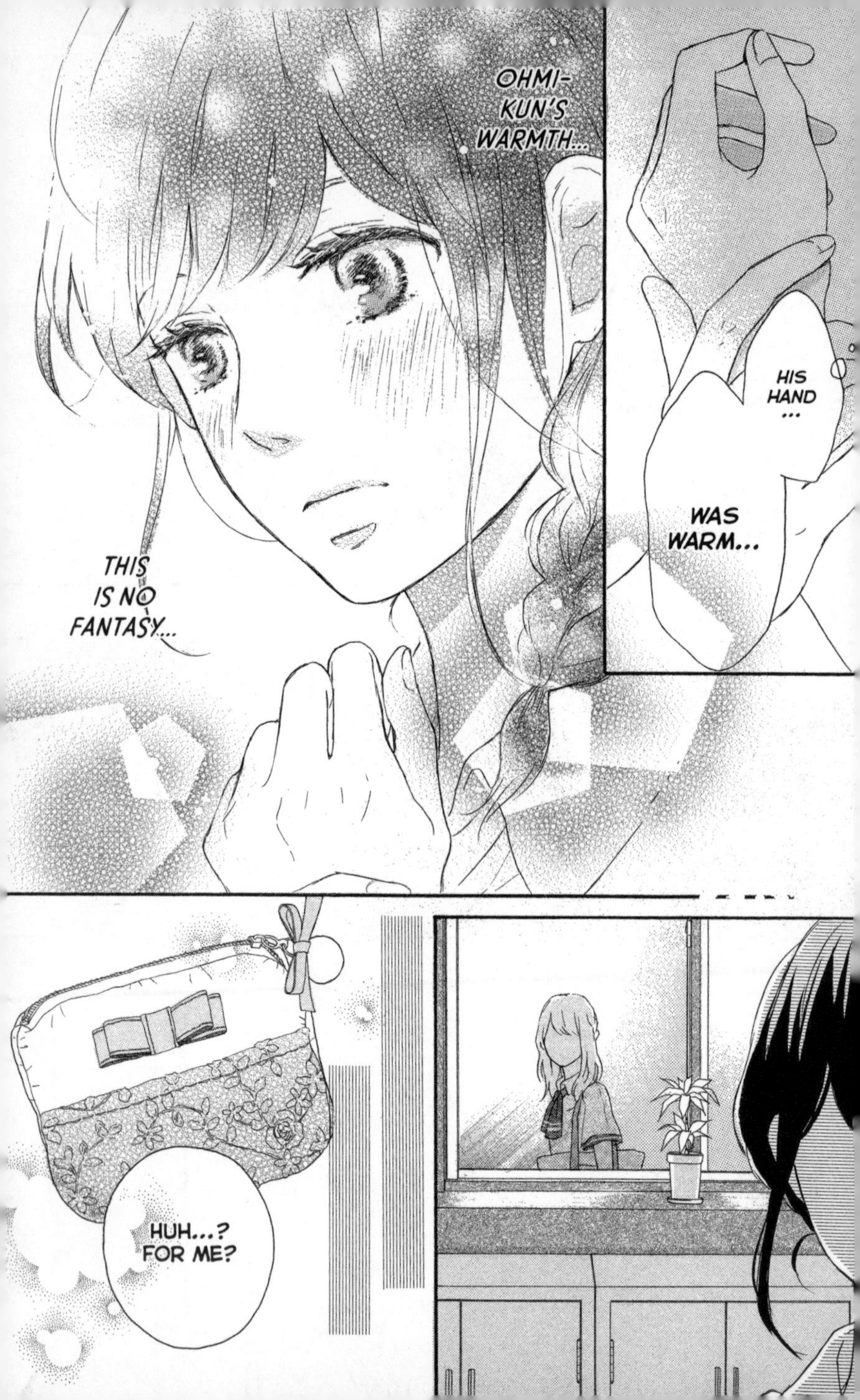
HIS HAND ...
WAS WARM...
OHMI-KUN'S WARMTH...
THIS IS NO FANTASY...
HUH...? FOR ME?

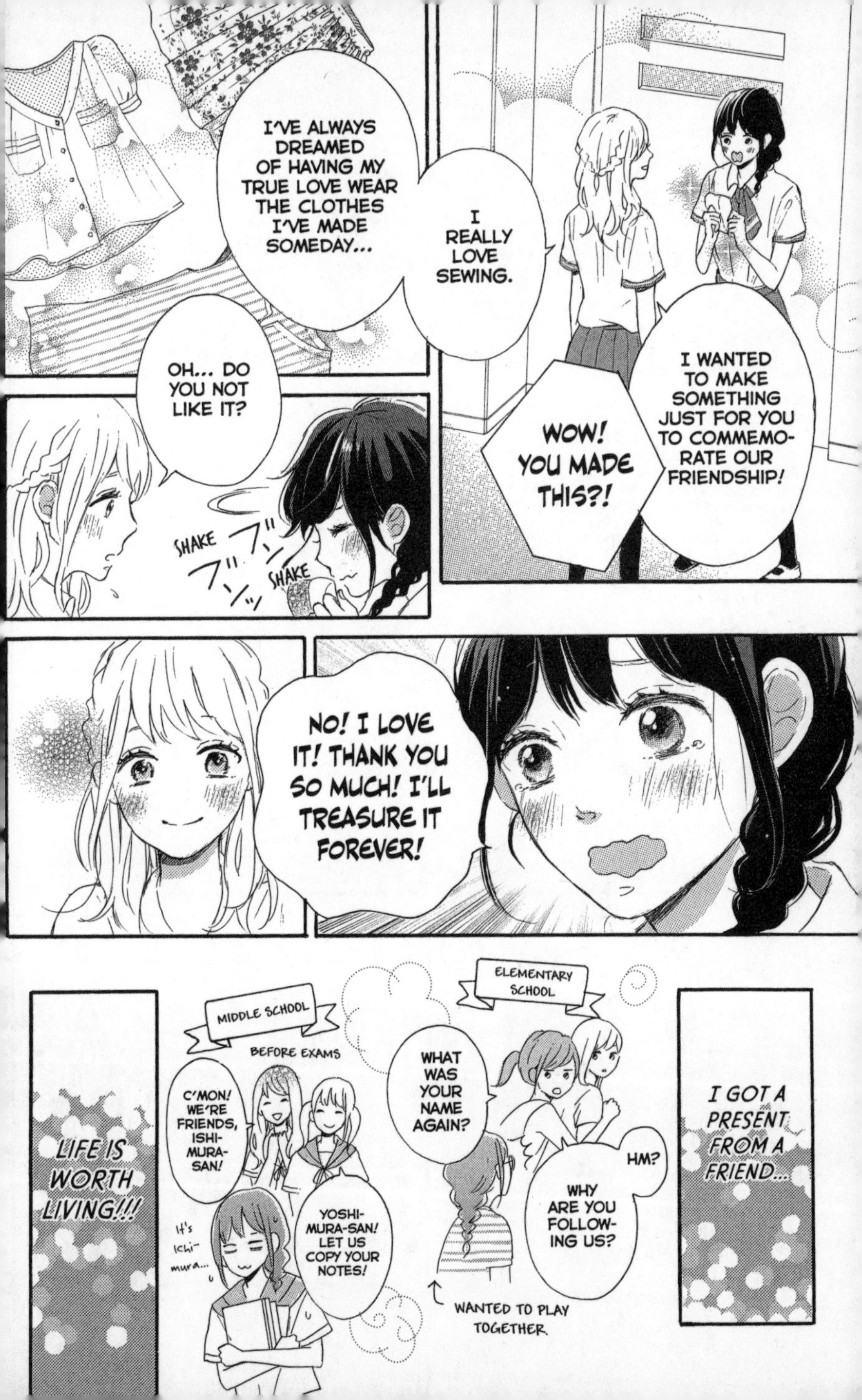
I WANTED TO MAKE SOMETHING JUST FOR YOU TO COMMEMORATE OUR FRIENDSHIP!
WOW! YOU MADE THIS?!
I REALLY LOVE SEWING.
I'VE ALWAYS DREAMED OF HAVING MY TRUE LOVE WEAR THE CLOTHES I'VE MADE SOMEDAY...
OH... DO YOU NOT LIKE IT?
SHAKE
ブン
ブンッ
SHAKE
NO! I LOVE IT! THANK YOU SO MUCH! I'LL TREASURE IT FOREVER!
I GOT A PRESENT FROM A FRIEND...
ELEMENTARY SCHOOL
WHAT WAS YOUR NAME AGAIN?
HM?
WHY ARE YOU FOLLOWING US?
WANTED TO PLAY TOGETHER.
MIDDLE SCHOOL
BEFORE EXAMS
C'MON! WE'RE FRIENDS, ISHIMURA-SAN!
YOSHIMURA-SAN! LET US COPY YOUR NOTES!
It's Ichimura...
LIFE IS WORTH LIVING!!!

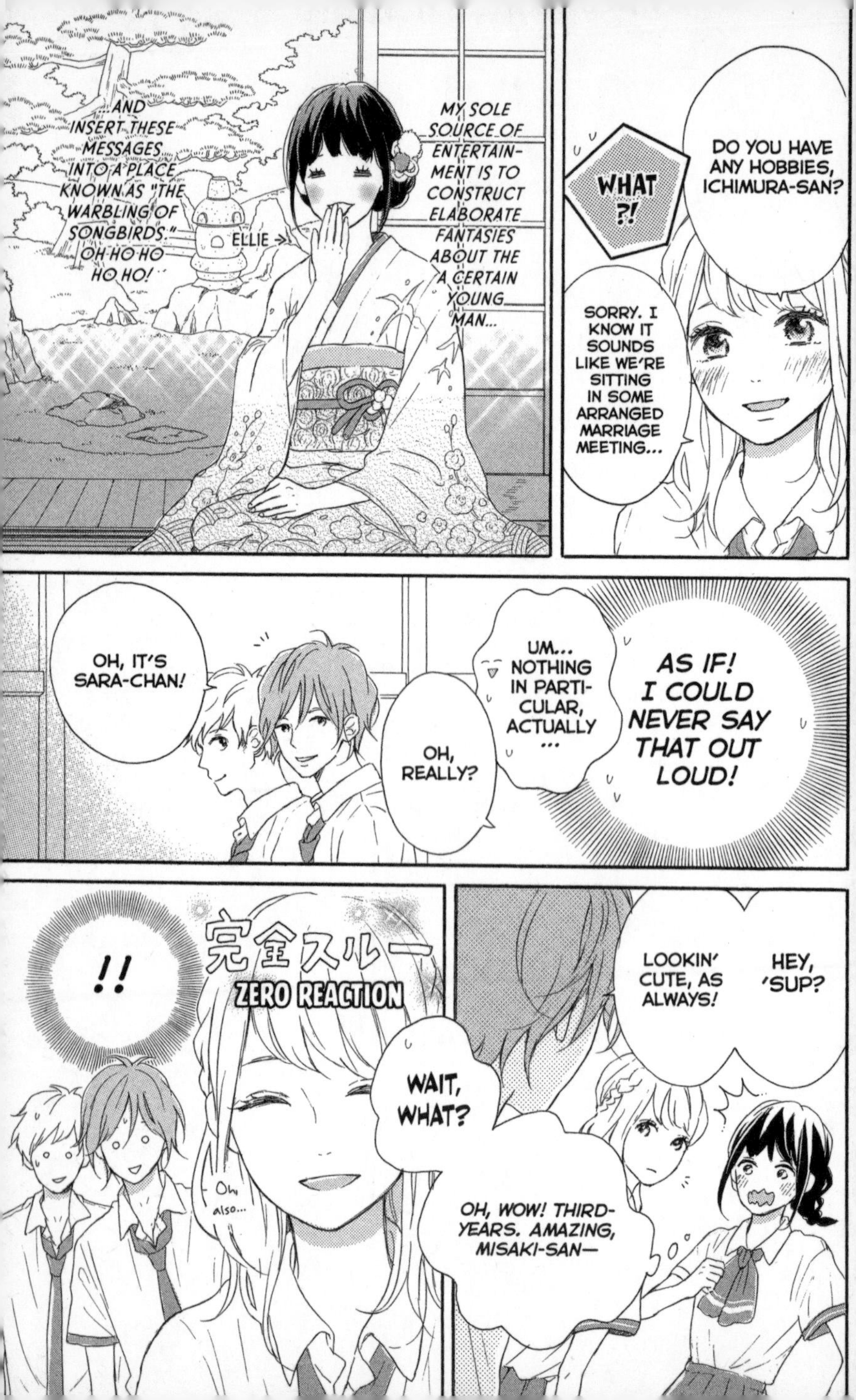

DO YOU HAVE ANY HOBBIES, ICHIMURA-SAN?
WHAT ?!
SORRY. I KNOW IT SOUNDS LIKE WE'RE SITTING IN SOME ARRANGED MARRIAGE MEETING...
MY SOLE SOURCE OF ENTERTAINMENT IS TO CONSTRUCT ELABORATE FANTASIES ABOUT THE A CERTAIN YOUNG MAN...
...AND INSERT THESE MESSAGES INTO A PLACE KNOWN AS "THE WARBLING OF SONGBIRDS." OH HO HO HO HO!
ELLIE →
AS IF! I COULD NEVER SAY THAT OUT LOUD!
UM... NOTHING IN PARTICULAR, ACTUALLY ...
OH, REALLY?
OH, IT'S SARA-CHAN!
HEY, 'SUP?
LOOKIN' CUTE, AS ALWAYS!
WAIT, WHAT?
OH, WOW! THIRD-YEARS. AMAZING, MISAKI-SAN—
完全スルー
ZERO REACTION
!!
Oh also...

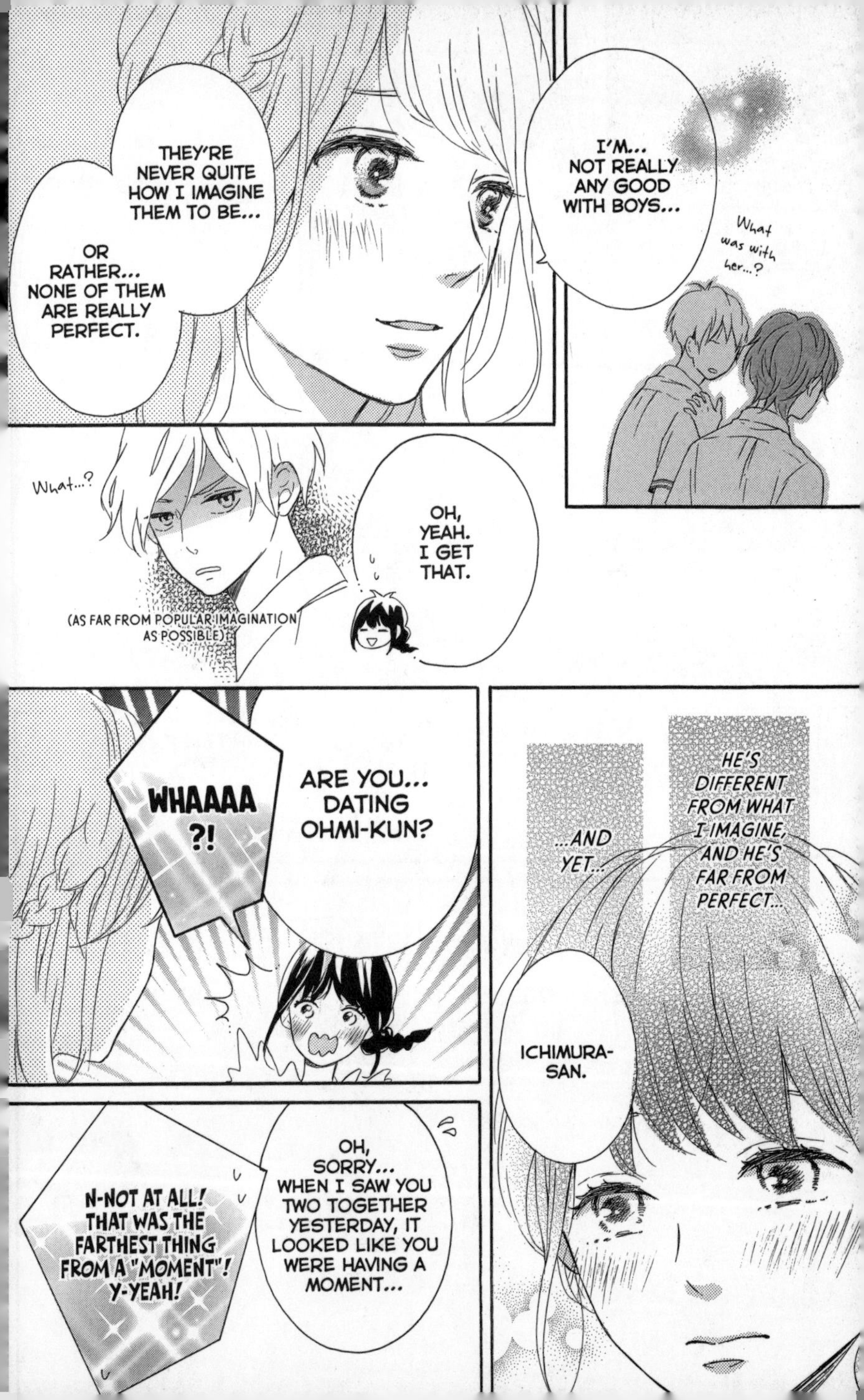
I'M... NOT REALLY ANY GOOD WITH BOYS...
What was with her...?
THEY'RE NEVER QUITE HOW I IMAGINE THEM TO BE...
OR RATHER... NONE OF THEM ARE REALLY PERFECT.
OH, YEAH. I GET THAT.
What...?
(AS FAR FROM POPULAR IMAGINATION AS POSSIBLE)
HE'S DIFFERENT FROM WHAT I IMAGINE, AND HE'S FAR FROM PERFECT...
...AND YET...
ICHIMURA-SAN.
ARE YOU... DATING OHMI-KUN?
WHAAAA?!
OH, SORRY... WHEN I SAW YOU TWO TOGETHER YESTERDAY, IT LOOKED LIKE YOU WERE HAVING A MOMENT...
N-NOT AT ALL! THAT WAS THE FARTHEST THING FROM A "MOMENT"! Y-YEAH!

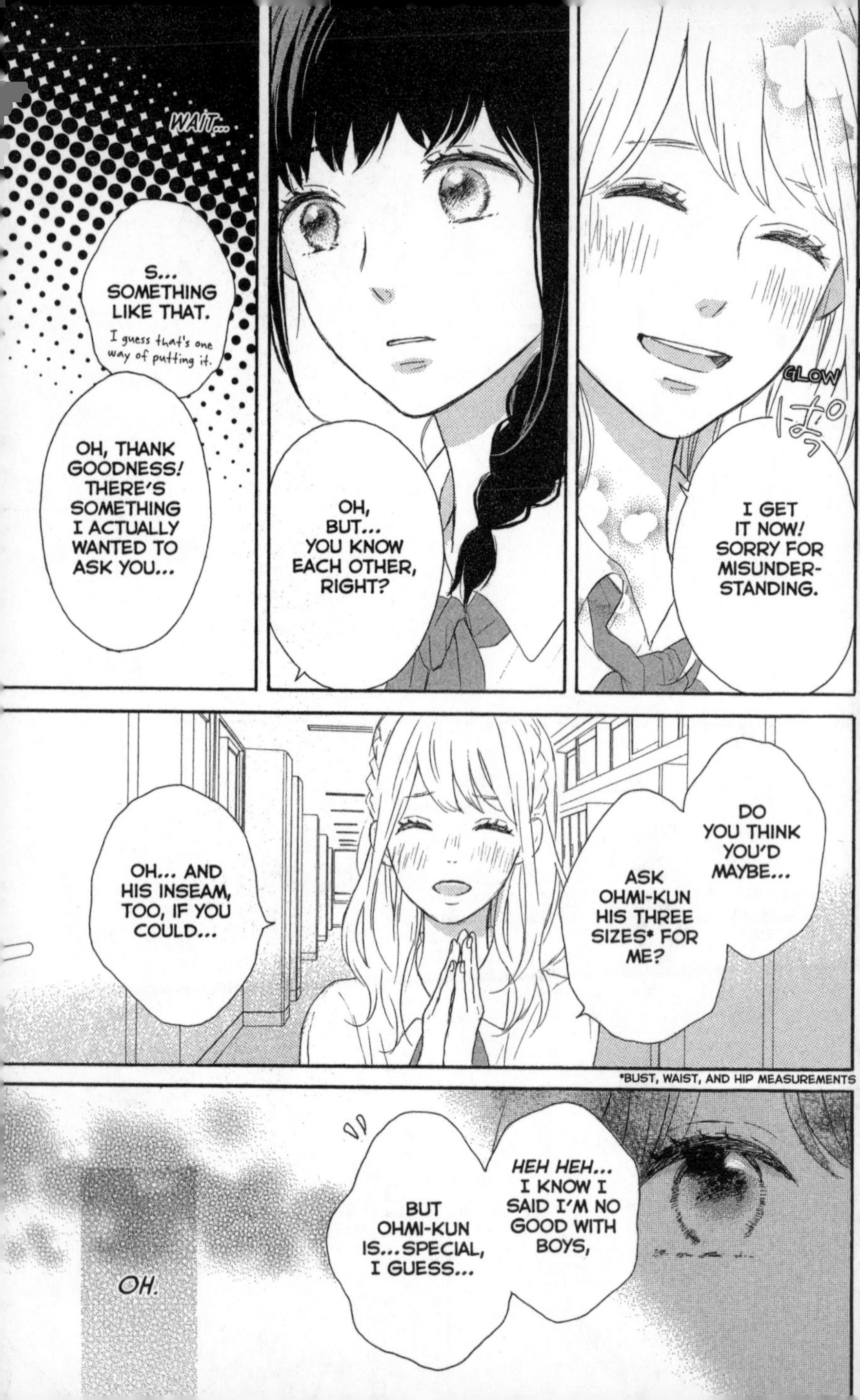
GLOW
I GET IT NOW! SORRY FOR MISUNDER-STANDING.
OH, BUT... YOU KNOW EACH OTHER, RIGHT?
WAIT...
S... SOMETHING LIKE THAT.
I guess that's one way of putting it.
OH, THANK GOODNESS! THERE'S SOMETHING I ACTUALLY WANTED TO ASK YOU...
DO YOU THINK YOU'D MAYBE...
ASK OHMI-KUN HIS THREE SIZES* FOR ME?
OH... AND HIS INSEAM, TOO, IF YOU COULD...
HEH HEH... I KNOW I SAID I'M NO GOOD WITH BOYS,
BUT OHMI-KUN IS...SPECIAL, I GUESS...
OH.

*BUST, WAIST, AND HIP MEASUREMENTS

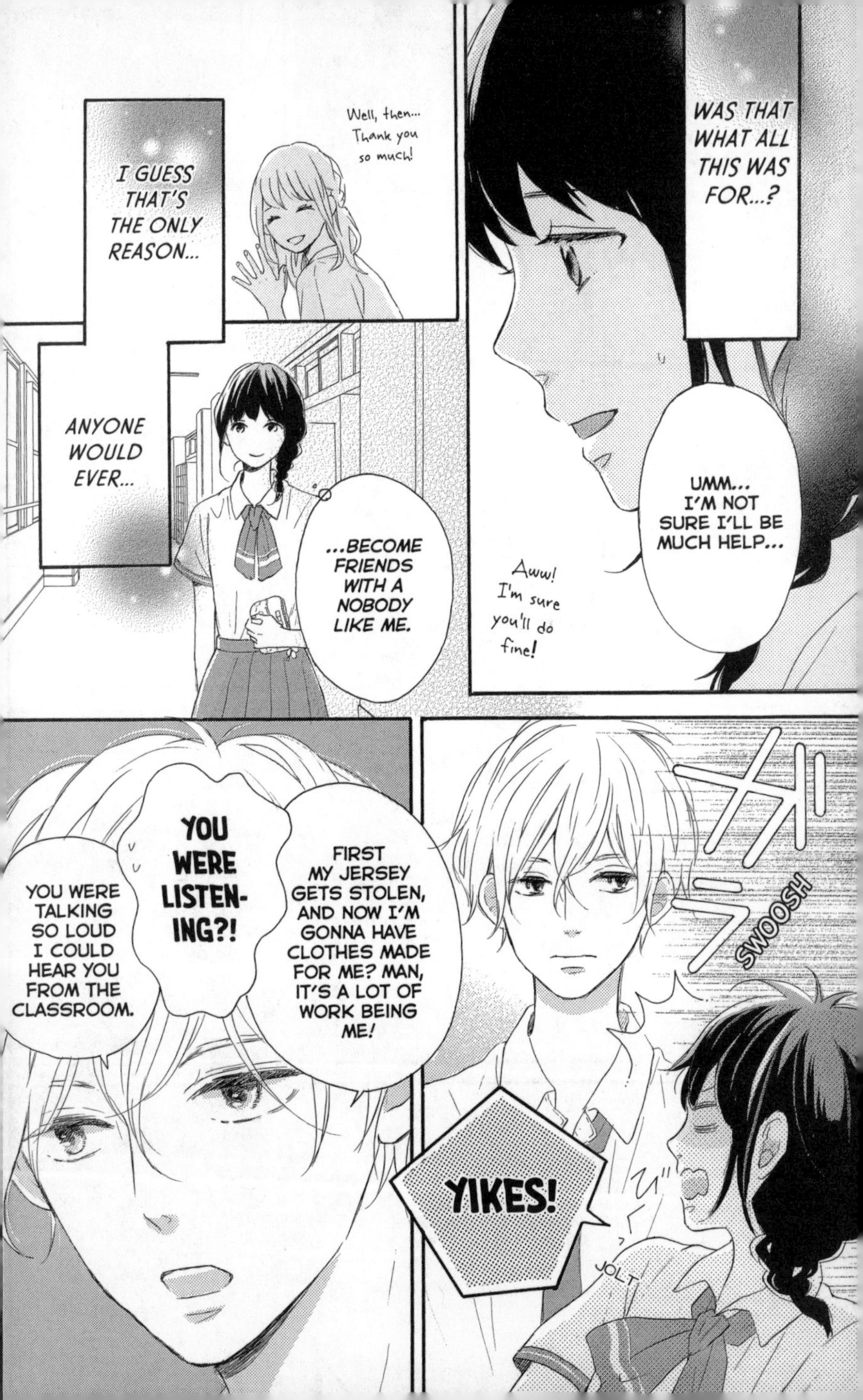
WAS THAT WHAT ALL THIS WAS FOR...?
UMM... I'M NOT SURE I'LL BE MUCH HELP...
Aww! I'm sure you'll do fine!
Well, then... Thank you so much!
I GUESS THAT'S THE ONLY REASON...
ANYONE WOULD EVER...
...BECOME FRIENDS WITH A NOBODY LIKE ME.
SWOOSH
YIKES!
JOLT
FIRST MY JERSEY GETS STOLEN, AND NOW I'M GONNA HAVE CLOTHES MADE FOR ME? MAN, IT'S A LOT OF WORK BEING ME!
YOU WERE LISTENING?!
YOU WERE TALKING SO LOUD I COULD HEAR YOU FROM THE CLASSROOM.

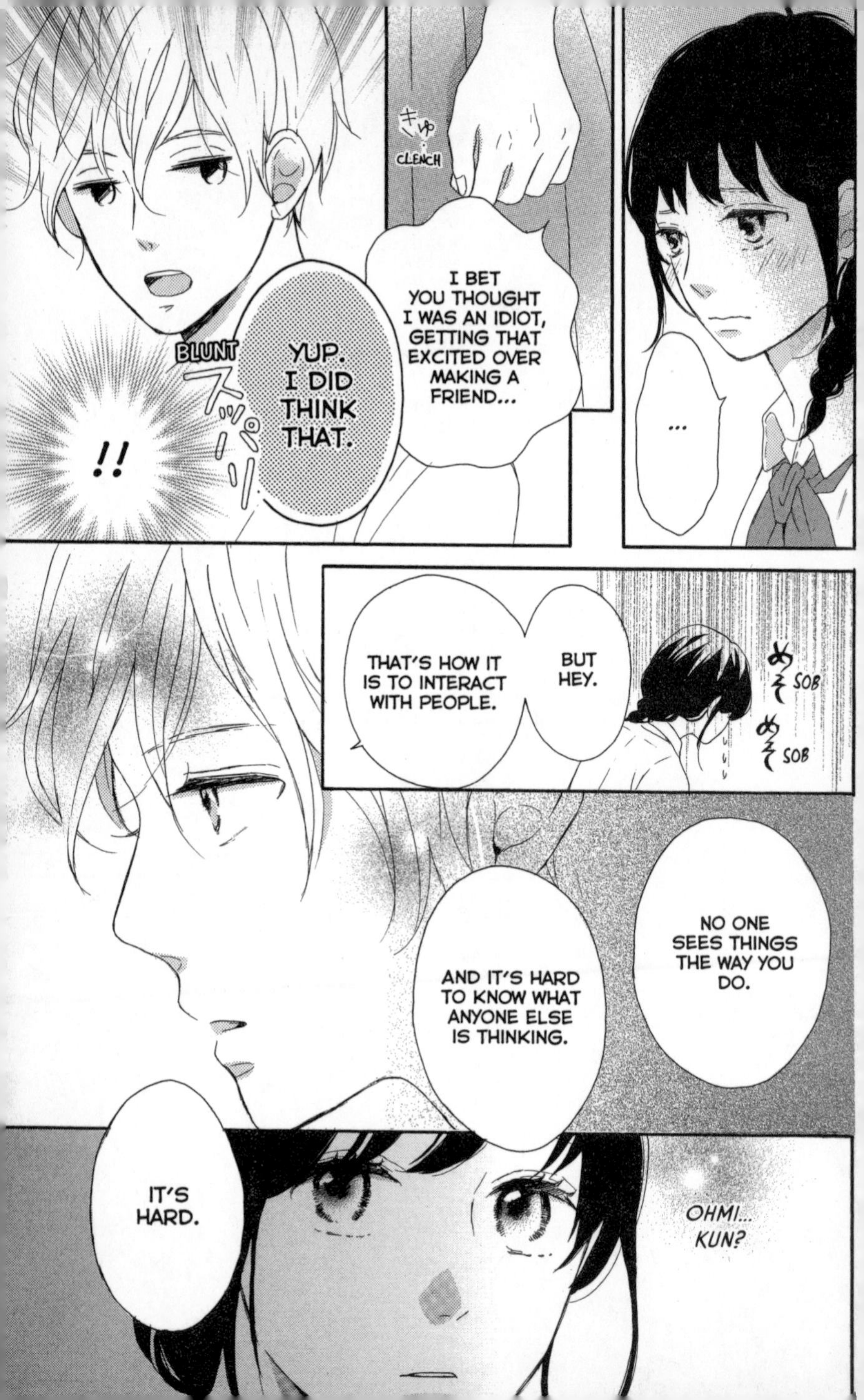
...
キュ
CLENCH
I BET YOU THOUGHT I WAS AN IDIOT, GETTING THAT EXCITED OVER MAKING A FRIEND...
YUP. I DID THINK THAT.
BLUNT
スッパリ
!!
めそ SOB
めそ SOB
BUT HEY.
THAT'S HOW IT IS TO INTERACT WITH PEOPLE.
NO ONE SEES THINGS THE WAY YOU DO.
AND IT'S HARD TO KNOW WHAT ANYONE ELSE IS THINKING.
IT'S HARD.
OHMI... KUN?

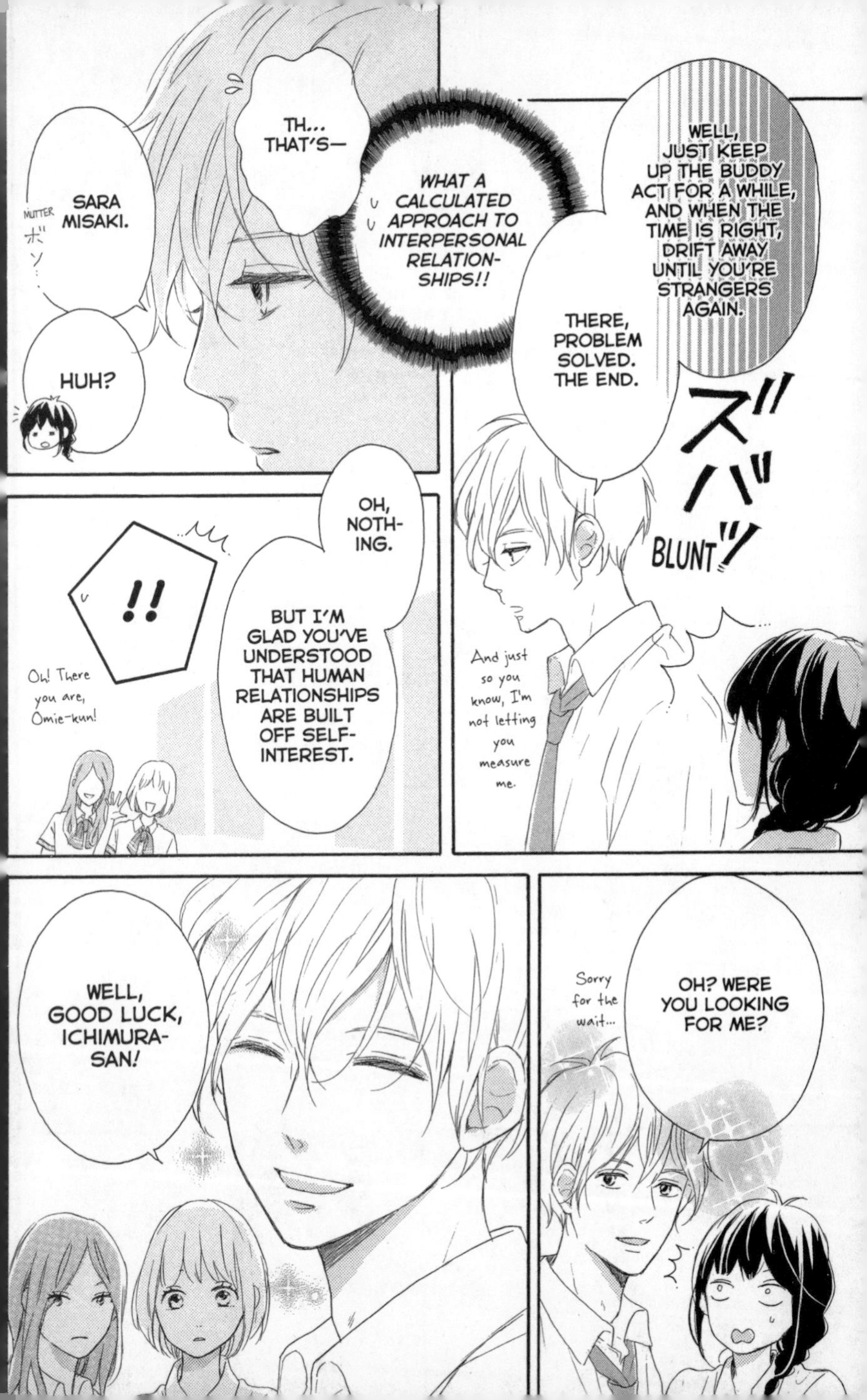
WELL, JUST KEEP UP THE BUDDY ACT FOR A WHILE, AND WHEN THE TIME IS RIGHT, DRIFT AWAY UNTIL YOU'RE STRANGERS AGAIN.
THERE, PROBLEM SOLVED. THE END.
ズバッ
BLUNT
And just so you know, I'm not letting you measure me.
WHAT A CALCULATED APPROACH TO INTERPERSONAL RELATIONSHIPS!!
TH... THAT'S—
MUTTER
ボソ
SARA MISAKI.
HUH?
OH, NOTHING.
BUT I'M GLAD YOU'VE UNDERSTOOD THAT HUMAN RELATIONSHIPS ARE BUILT OFF SELF-INTEREST.
!!
Oh! There you are, Omie-kun!
OH? WERE YOU LOOKING FOR ME?
Sorry for the wait...
WELL, GOOD LUCK, ICHIMURA-SAN!

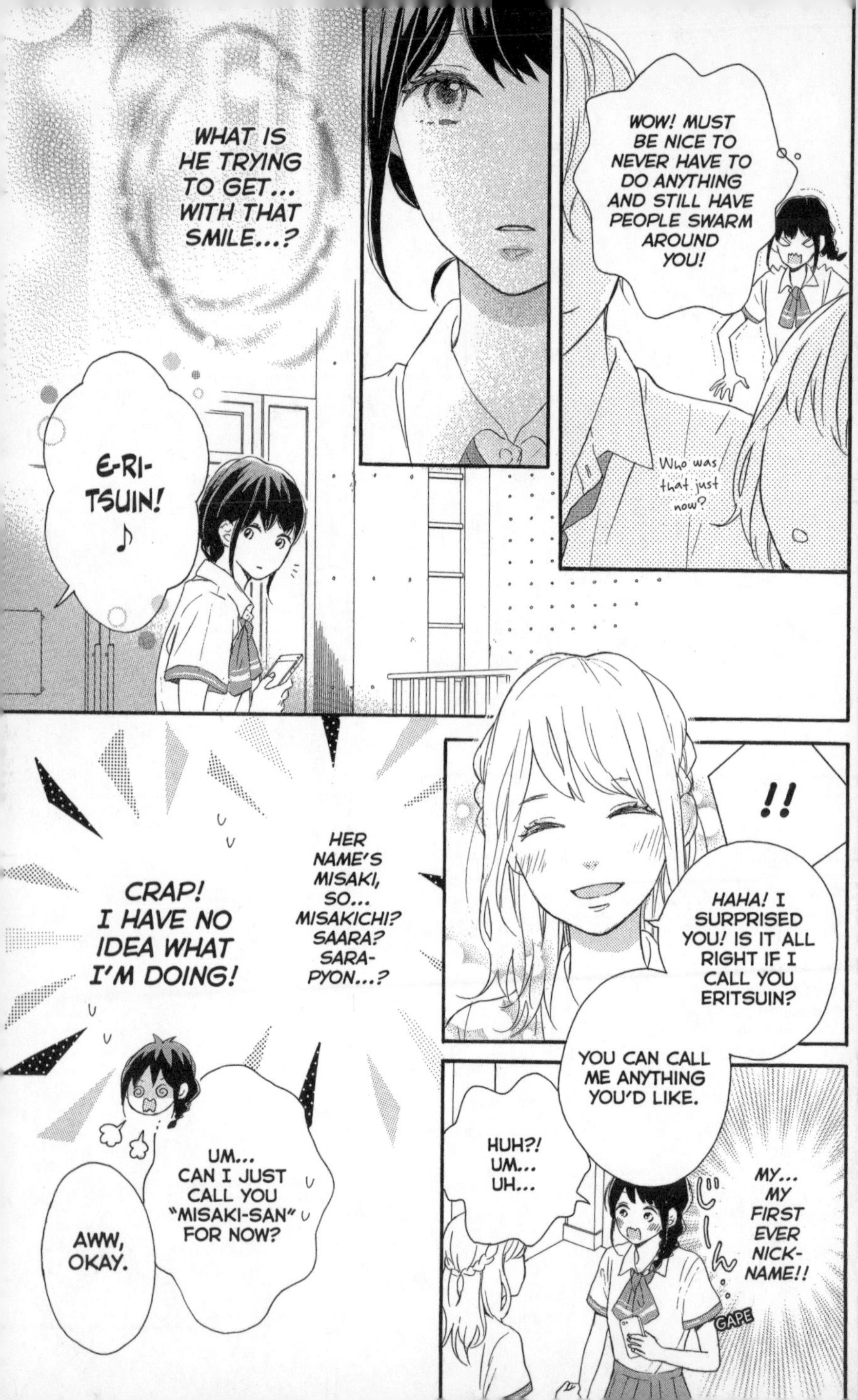
WOW! MUST BE NICE TO NEVER HAVE TO DO ANYTHING AND STILL HAVE PEOPLE SWARM AROUND YOU!
Who was that just now?
WHAT IS HE TRYING TO GET... WITH THAT SMILE...?
E-RI-TSUIN! ♪
!!
HAHA! I SURPRISED YOU! IS IT ALL RIGHT IF I CALL YOU ERITSUIN?
YOU CAN CALL ME ANYTHING YOU'D LIKE.
MY... MY FIRST EVER NICK-NAME!!
じーん
HUH?! UM... UH...
GAPE
HER NAME'S MISAKI, SO... MISAKICHI? SAARA? SARA-PYON...?
CRAP! I HAVE NO IDEA WHAT I'M DOING!
UM... CAN I JUST CALL YOU "MISAKI-SAN" FOR NOW?
AWW, OKAY.

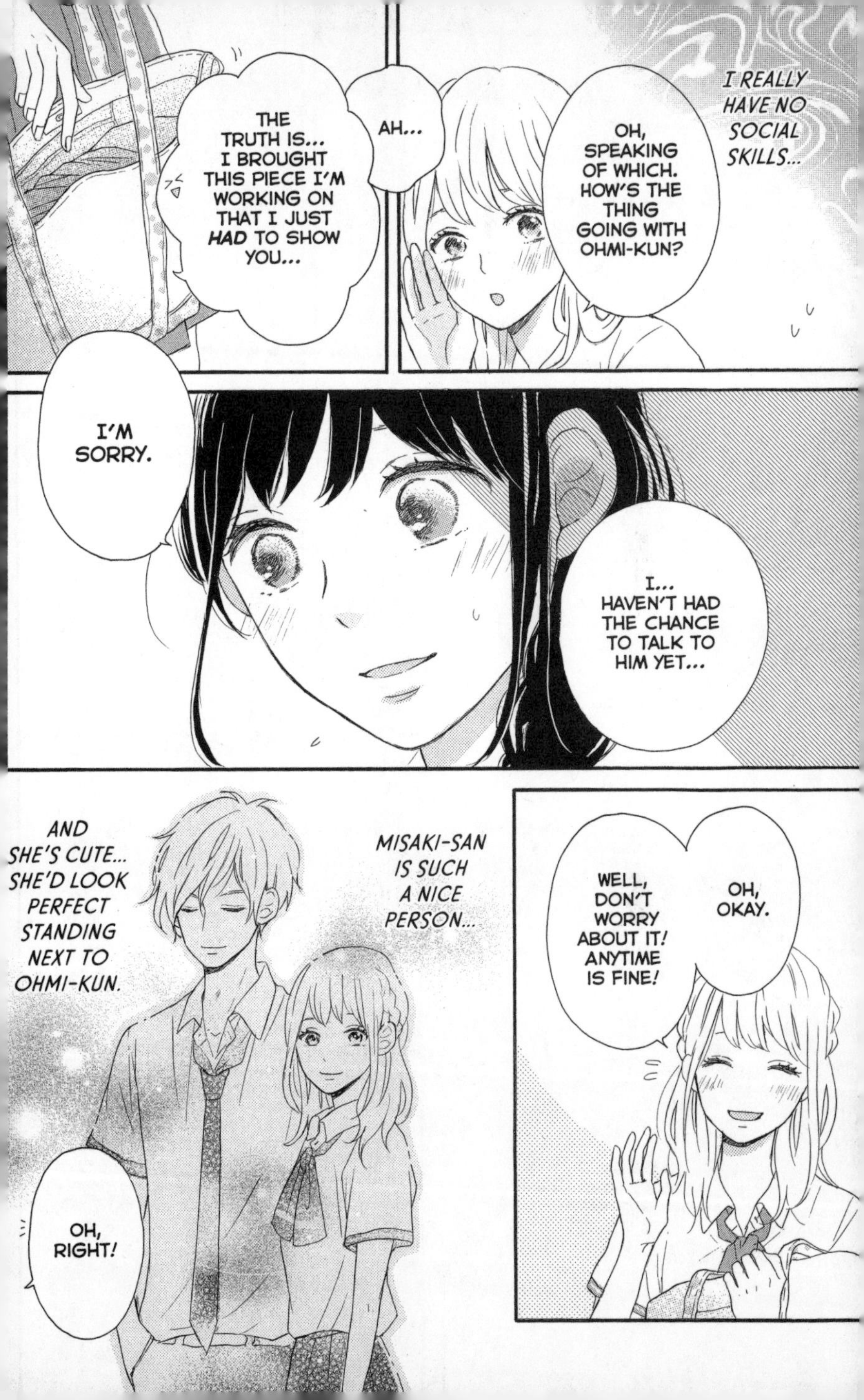
I REALLY HAVE NO SOCIAL SKILLS...
OH, SPEAKING OF WHICH. HOW'S THE THING GOING WITH OHMI-KUN?
AH...
THE TRUTH IS... I BROUGHT THIS PIECE I'M WORKING ON THAT I JUST *HAD* TO SHOW YOU...
I... HAVEN'T HAD THE CHANCE TO TALK TO HIM YET...
I'M SORRY.
OH, OKAY.
WELL, DON'T WORRY ABOUT IT! ANYTIME IS FINE!
MISAKI-SAN IS SUCH A NICE PERSON...
AND SHE'S CUTE... SHE'D LOOK PERFECT STANDING NEXT TO OHMI-KUN.
OH, RIGHT!

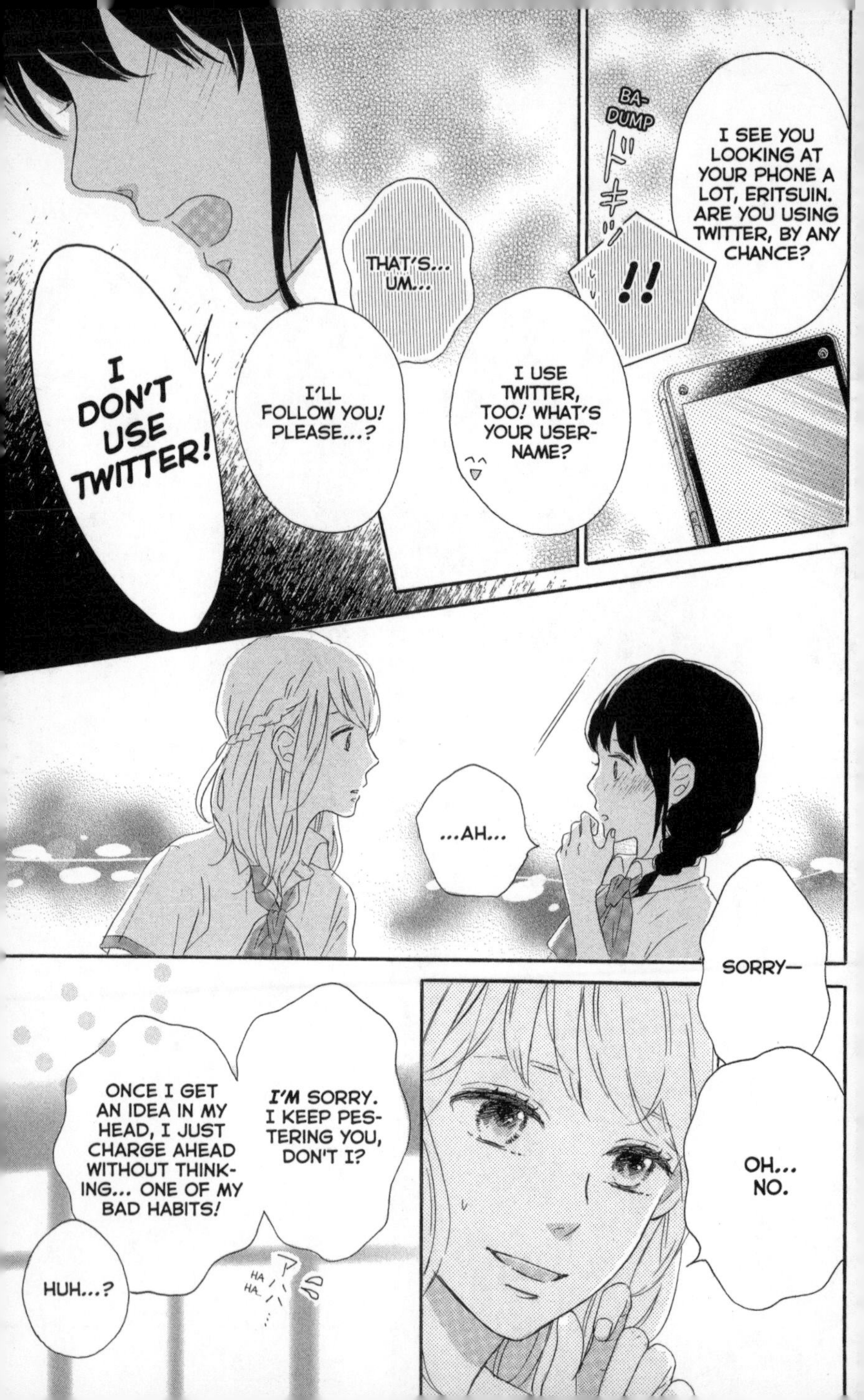
I SEE YOU LOOKING AT YOUR PHONE A LOT, ERITSUIN. ARE YOU USING TWITTER, BY ANY CHANCE?
BA-DUMP
!!
I USE TWITTER, TOO! WHAT'S YOUR USER-NAME?
I'LL FOLLOW YOU! PLEASE...?
THAT'S... UM...
I DON'T USE TWITTER!
...AH...
SORRY—
OH... NO.
I'M SORRY. I KEEP PES-TERING YOU, DON'T I?
ONCE I GET AN IDEA IN MY HEAD, I JUST CHARGE AHEAD WITHOUT THINK-ING... ONE OF MY BAD HABITS!
HA HA
HUH...?

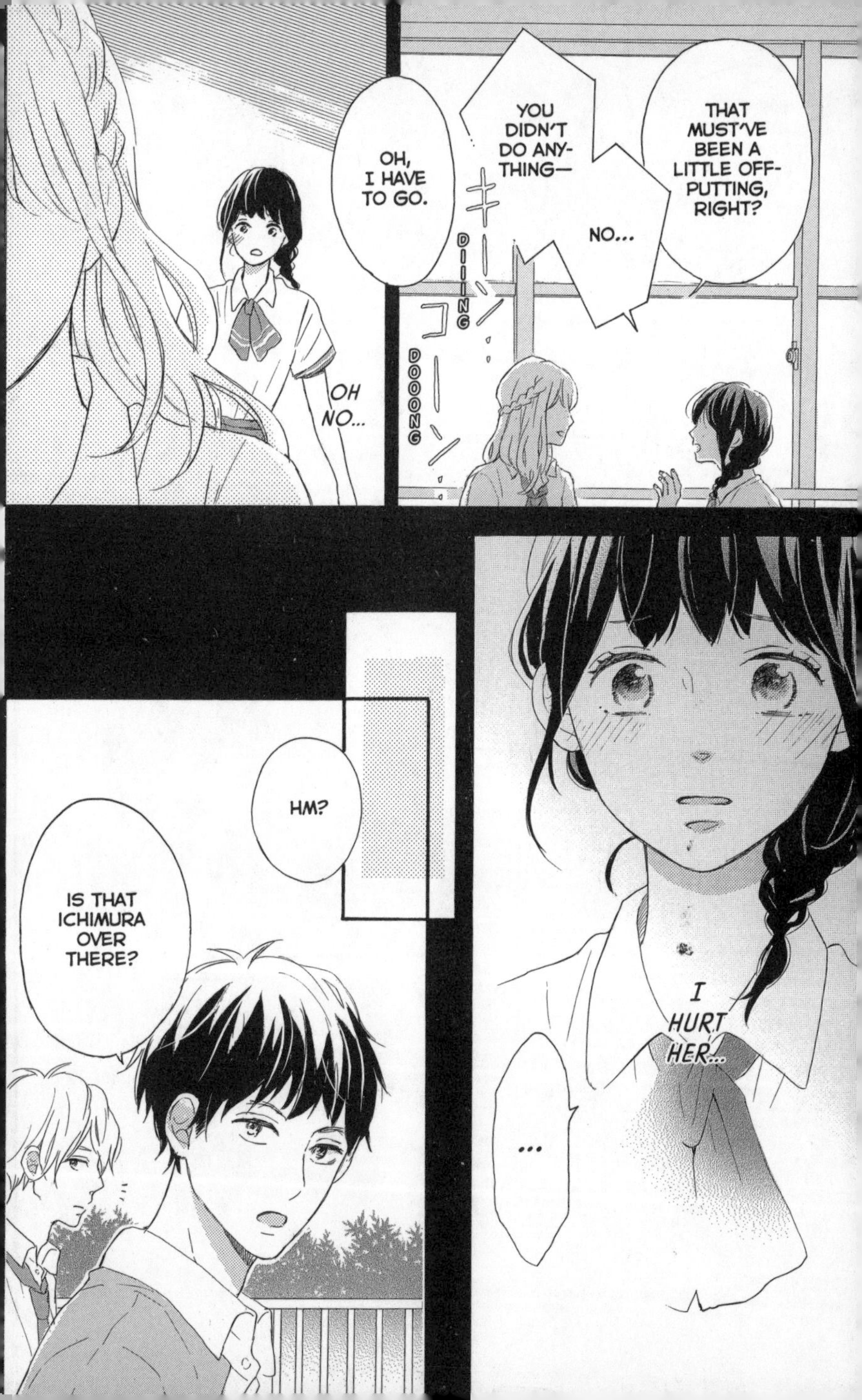
THAT MUST'VE BEEN A LITTLE OFF-PUTTING, RIGHT?
NO...
YOU DIDN'T DO ANY-THING—
OH, I HAVE TO GO.
DIIIING
DOOOONG
OH NO...
I HURT HER...
...
HM?
IS THAT ICHIMURA OVER THERE?

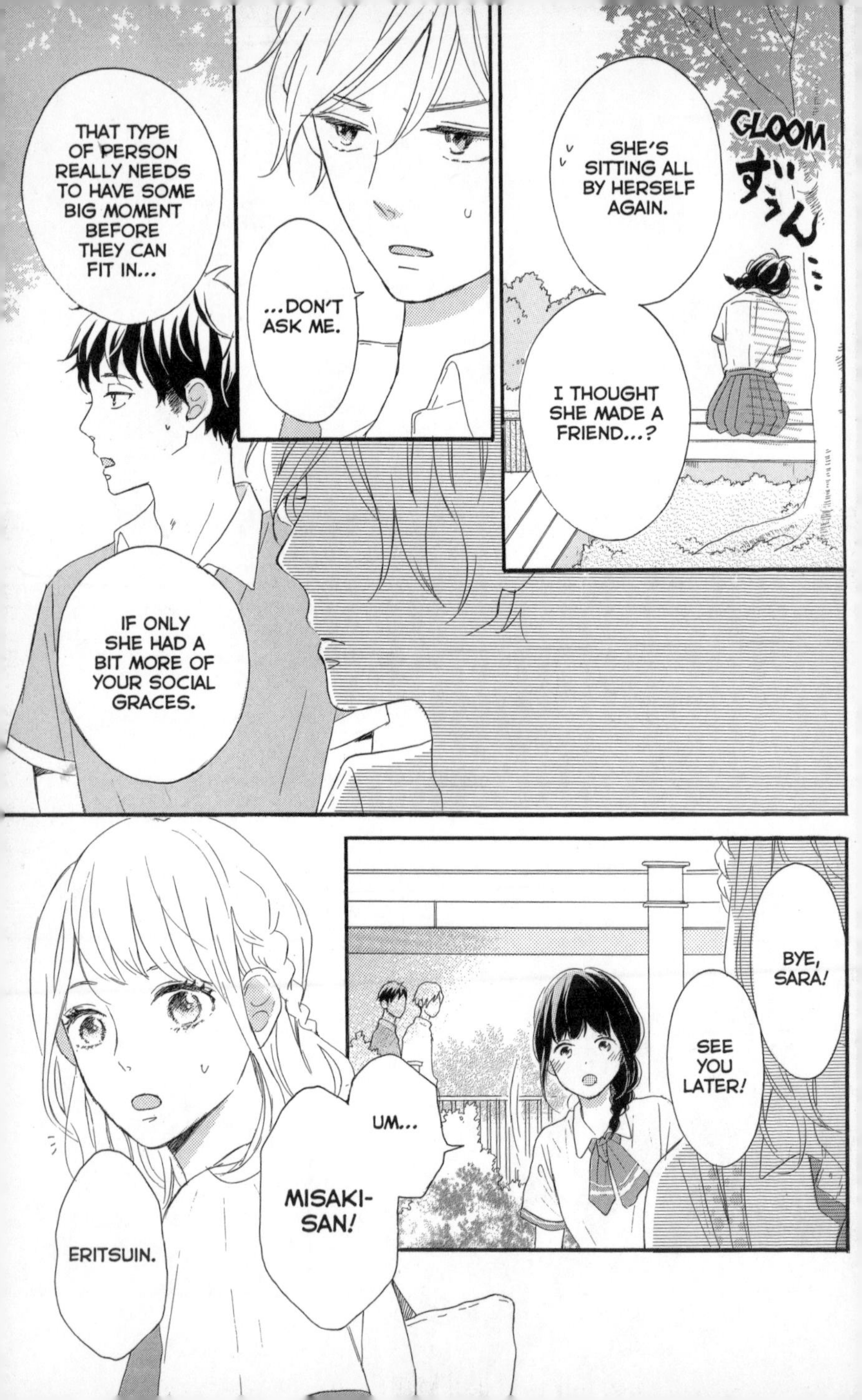
GLOOM
ずぅん
SHE'S SITTING ALL BY HERSELF AGAIN.
I THOUGHT SHE MADE A FRIEND...?
...DON'T ASK ME.
THAT TYPE OF PERSON REALLY NEEDS TO HAVE SOME BIG MOMENT BEFORE THEY CAN FIT IN...
IF ONLY SHE HAD A BIT MORE OF YOUR SOCIAL GRACES.
BYE, SARA!
SEE YOU LATER!
UM...
MISAKI-SAN!
ERITSUIN.

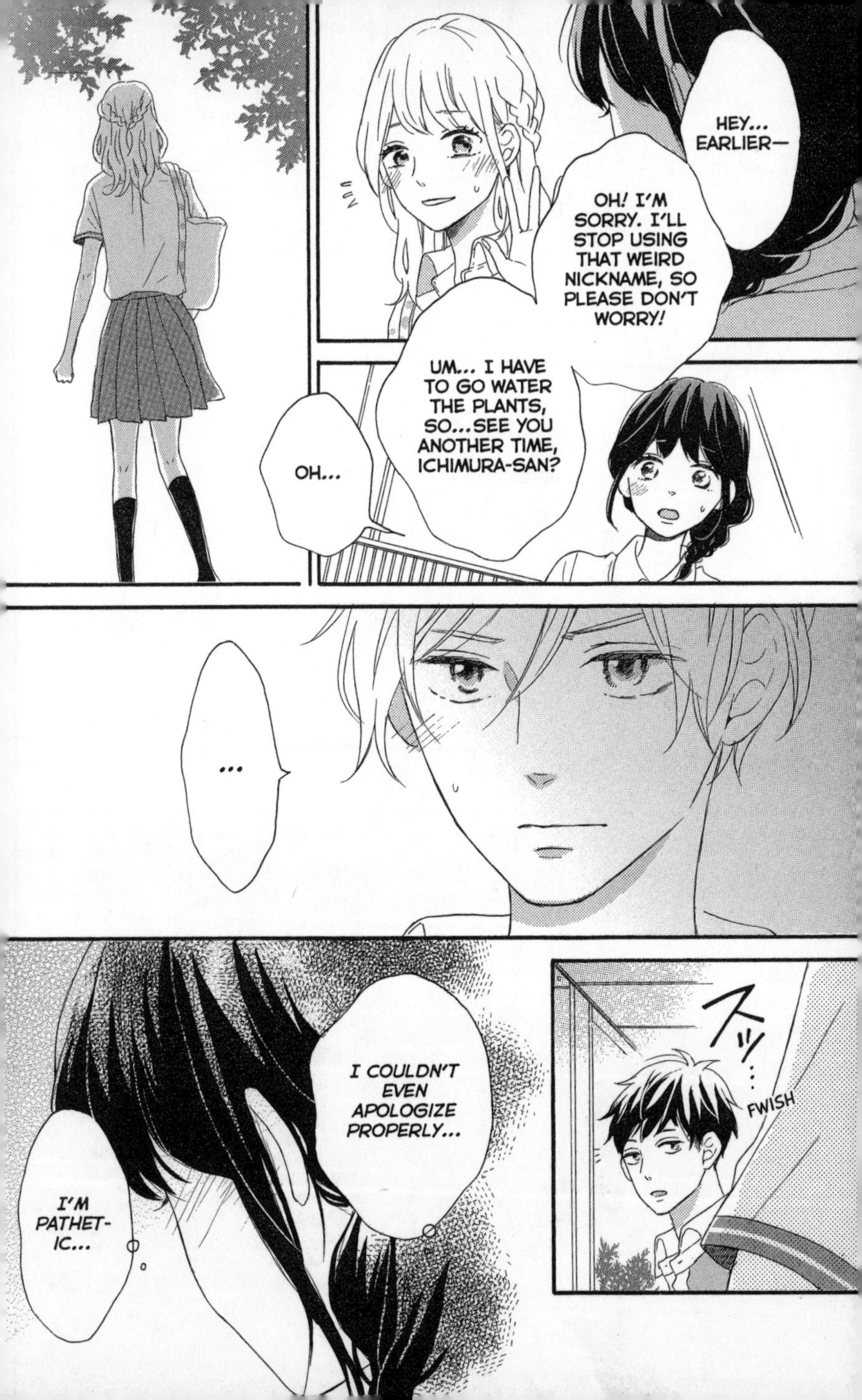
HEY... EARLIER—
OH! I'M SORRY. I'LL STOP USING THAT WEIRD NICKNAME, SO PLEASE DON'T WORRY!
UM... I HAVE TO GO WATER THE PLANTS, SO...SEE YOU ANOTHER TIME, ICHIMURA-SAN?
OH...
...
スッ...
FWISH
I COULDN'T EVEN APOLOGIZE PROPERLY...
I'M PATHET-IC...

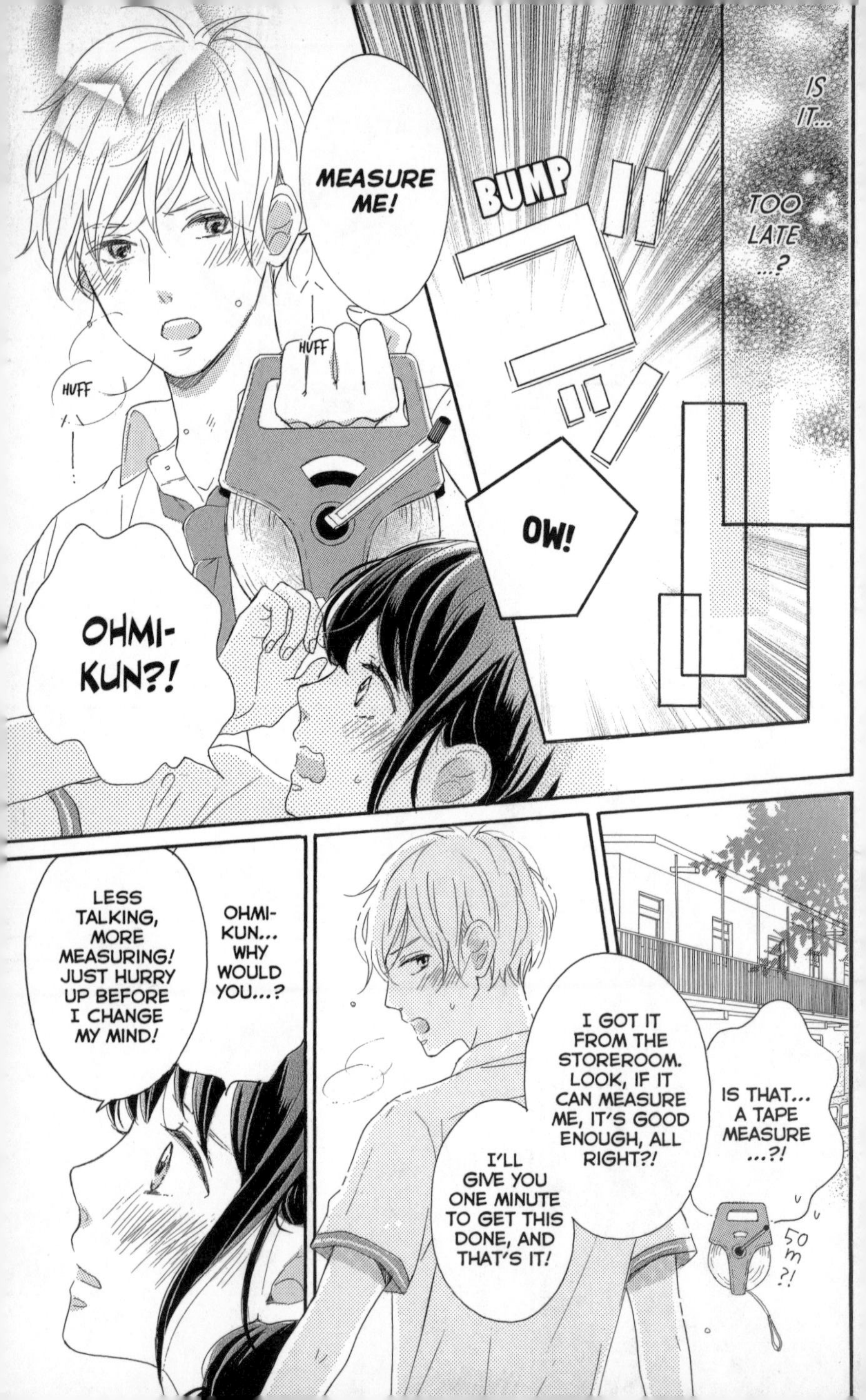
IS IT... TOO LATE ...?
BUMP
OW!
MEASURE ME!
HUFF
HUFF
OHMI-KUN?!
IS THAT... A TAPE MEASURE ...?!
50 m ?!
I GOT IT FROM THE STOREROOM. LOOK, IF IT CAN MEASURE ME, IT'S GOOD ENOUGH, ALL RIGHT?!
I'LL GIVE YOU ONE MINUTE TO GET THIS DONE, AND THAT'S IT!
OHMI-KUN... WHY WOULD YOU...?
LESS TALKING, MORE MEASURING! JUST HURRY UP BEFORE I CHANGE MY MIND!

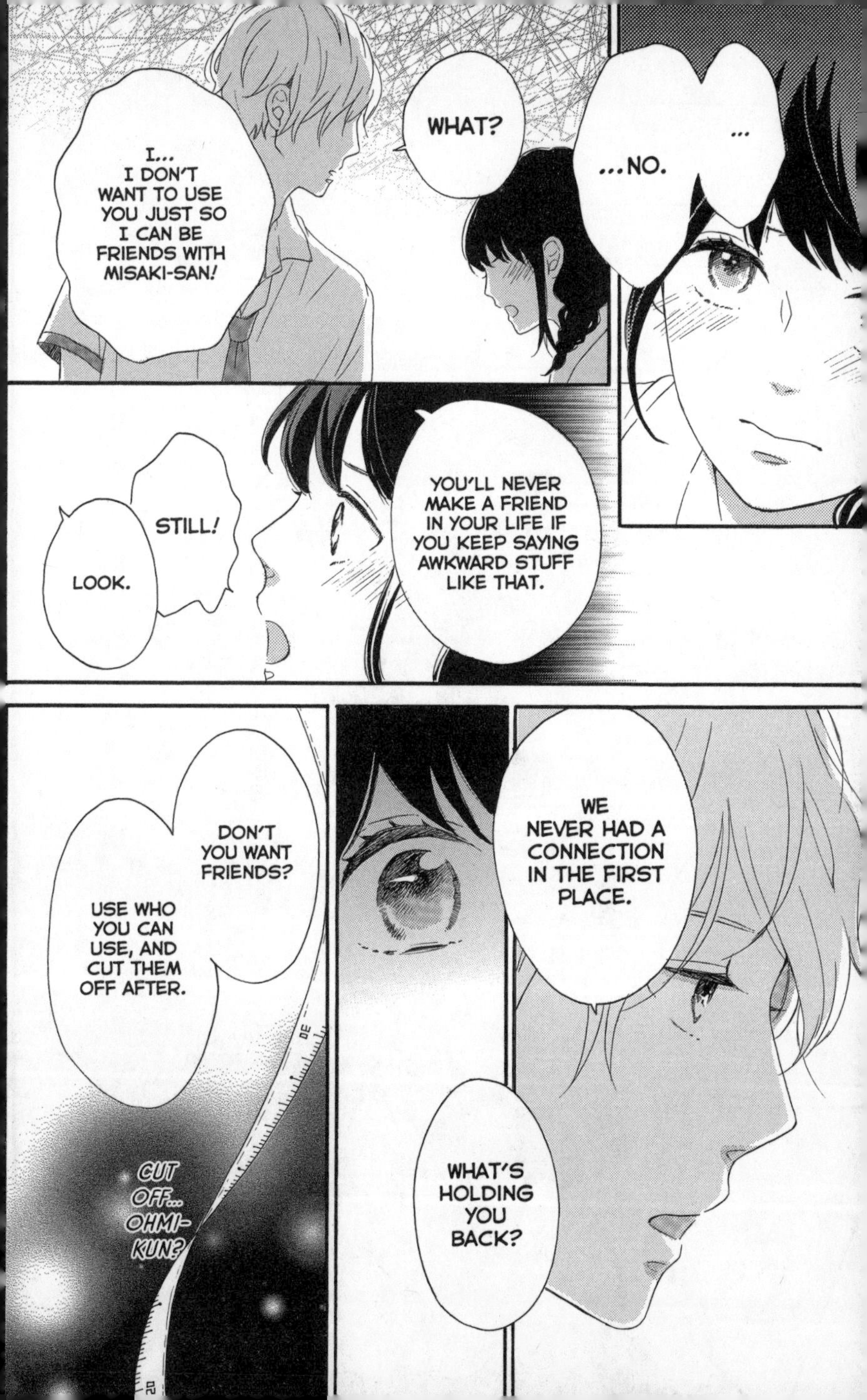
...
...NO.
WHAT?
I... I DON'T WANT TO USE YOU JUST SO I CAN BE FRIENDS WITH MISAKI-SAN!
YOU'LL NEVER MAKE A FRIEND IN YOUR LIFE IF YOU KEEP SAYING AWKWARD STUFF LIKE THAT.
STILL!
LOOK.
WE NEVER HAD A CONNECTION IN THE FIRST PLACE.
WHAT'S HOLDING YOU BACK?
DON'T YOU WANT FRIENDS?
USE WHO YOU CAN USE, AND CUT THEM OFF AFTER.
CUT OFF... OHMI-KUN?

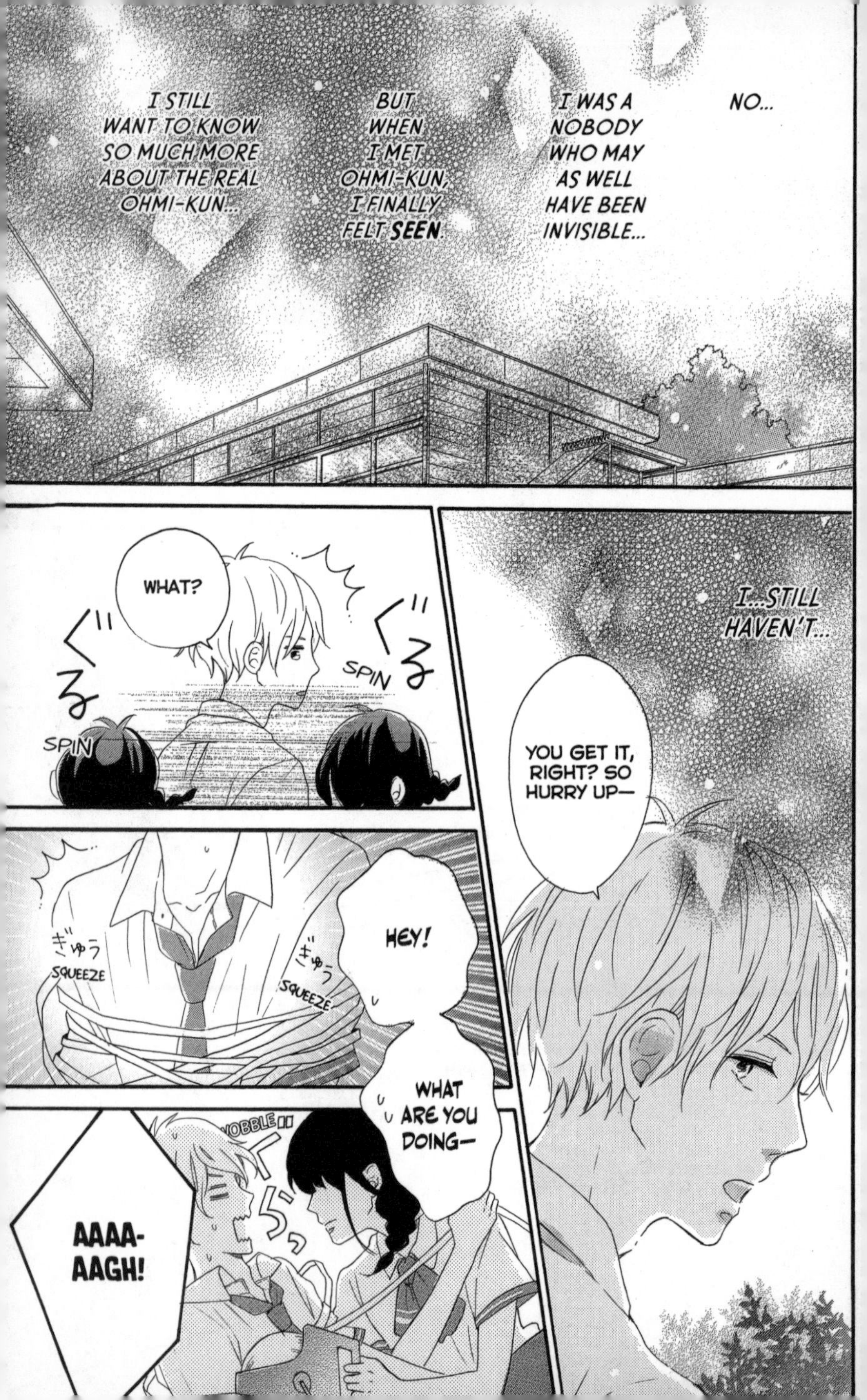
NO...
I WAS A NOBODY WHO MAY AS WELL HAVE BEEN INVISIBLE...
BUT WHEN I MET OHMI-KUN, I FINALLY FELT **SEEN**.
I STILL WANT TO KNOW SO MUCH MORE ABOUT THE REAL OHMI-KUN...
I...STILL HAVEN'T...
YOU GET IT, RIGHT? SO HURRY UP—
ぐる SPIN
WHAT?
ぐる SPIN
HEY!
ぎゅう SQUEEZE
ぎゅう SQUEEZE
WHAT ARE YOU DOING—
ぐらっ WOBBLE!!
AAAA-AAGH!

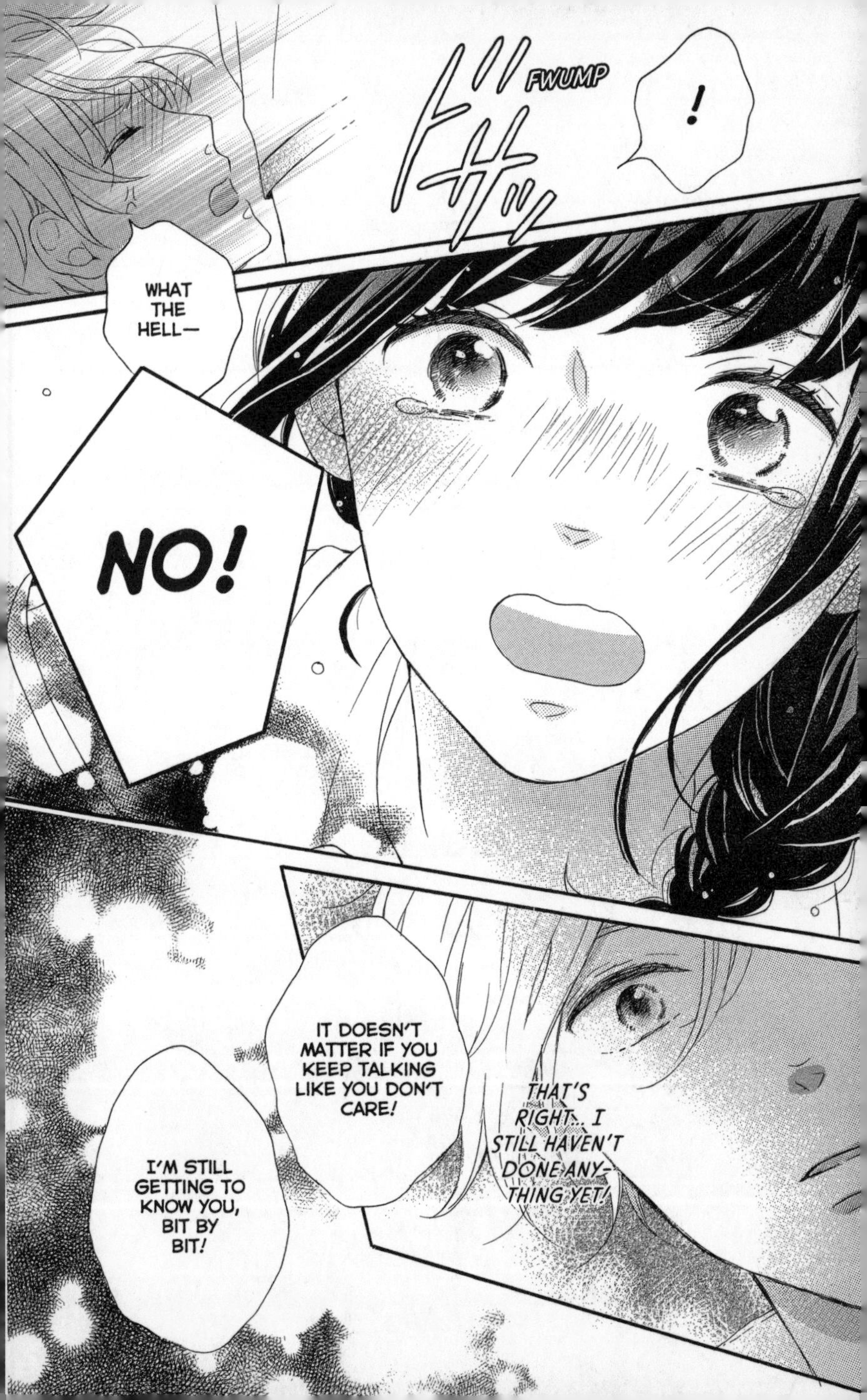
!
ドサッ
FWUMP
WHAT THE HELL—
NO!
THAT'S RIGHT... I STILL HAVEN'T DONE ANYTHING YET!
IT DOESN'T MATTER IF YOU KEEP TALKING LIKE YOU DON'T CARE!
I'M STILL GETTING TO KNOW YOU, BIT BY BIT!

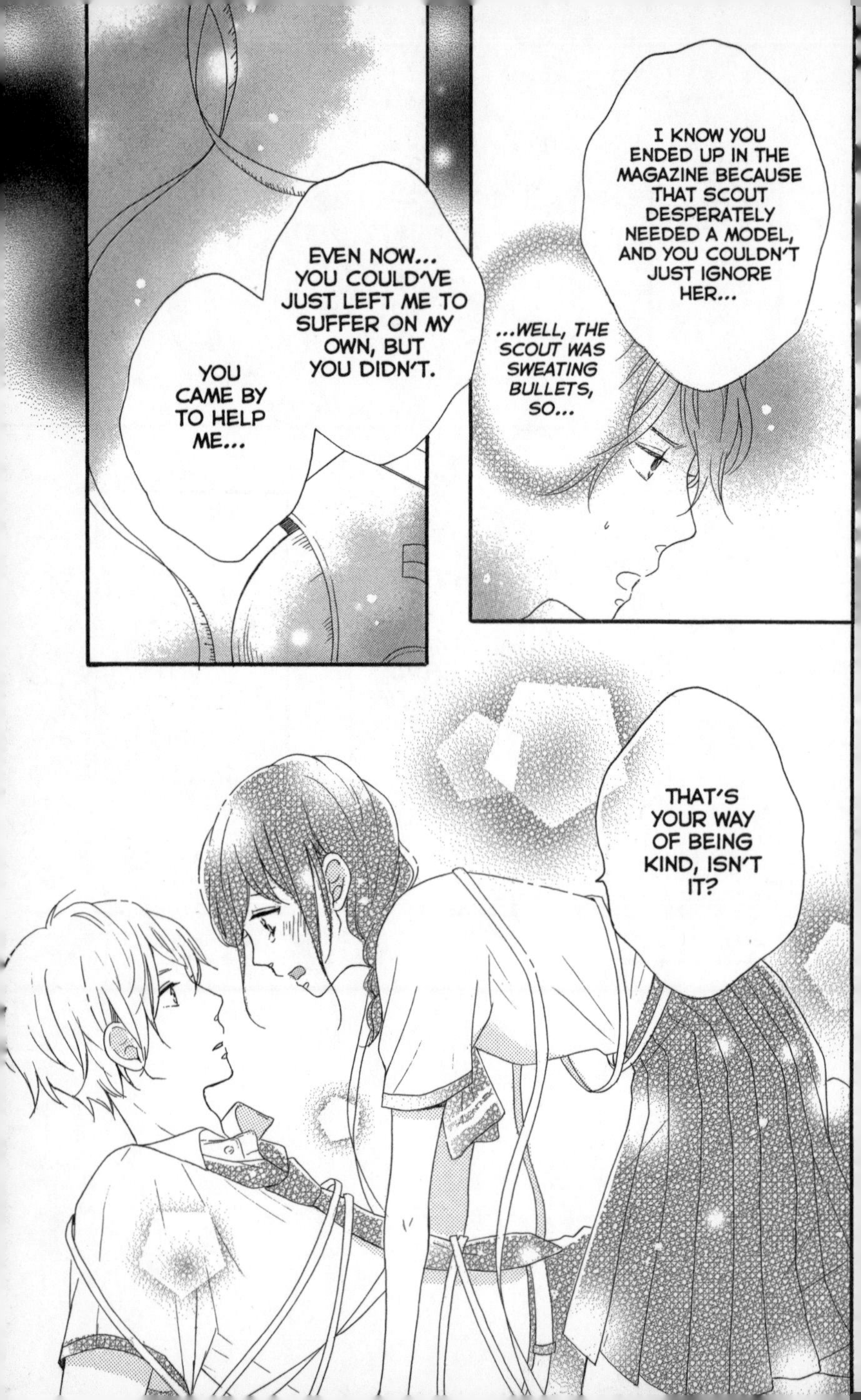
I KNOW YOU ENDED UP IN THE MAGAZINE BECAUSE THAT SCOUT DESPERATELY NEEDED A MODEL, AND YOU COULDN'T JUST IGNORE HER...
...WELL, THE SCOUT WAS SWEATING BULLETS, SO...
EVEN NOW... YOU COULD'VE JUST LEFT ME TO SUFFER ON MY OWN, BUT YOU DIDN'T.
YOU CAME BY TO HELP ME...
THAT'S YOUR WAY OF BEING KIND, ISN'T IT?

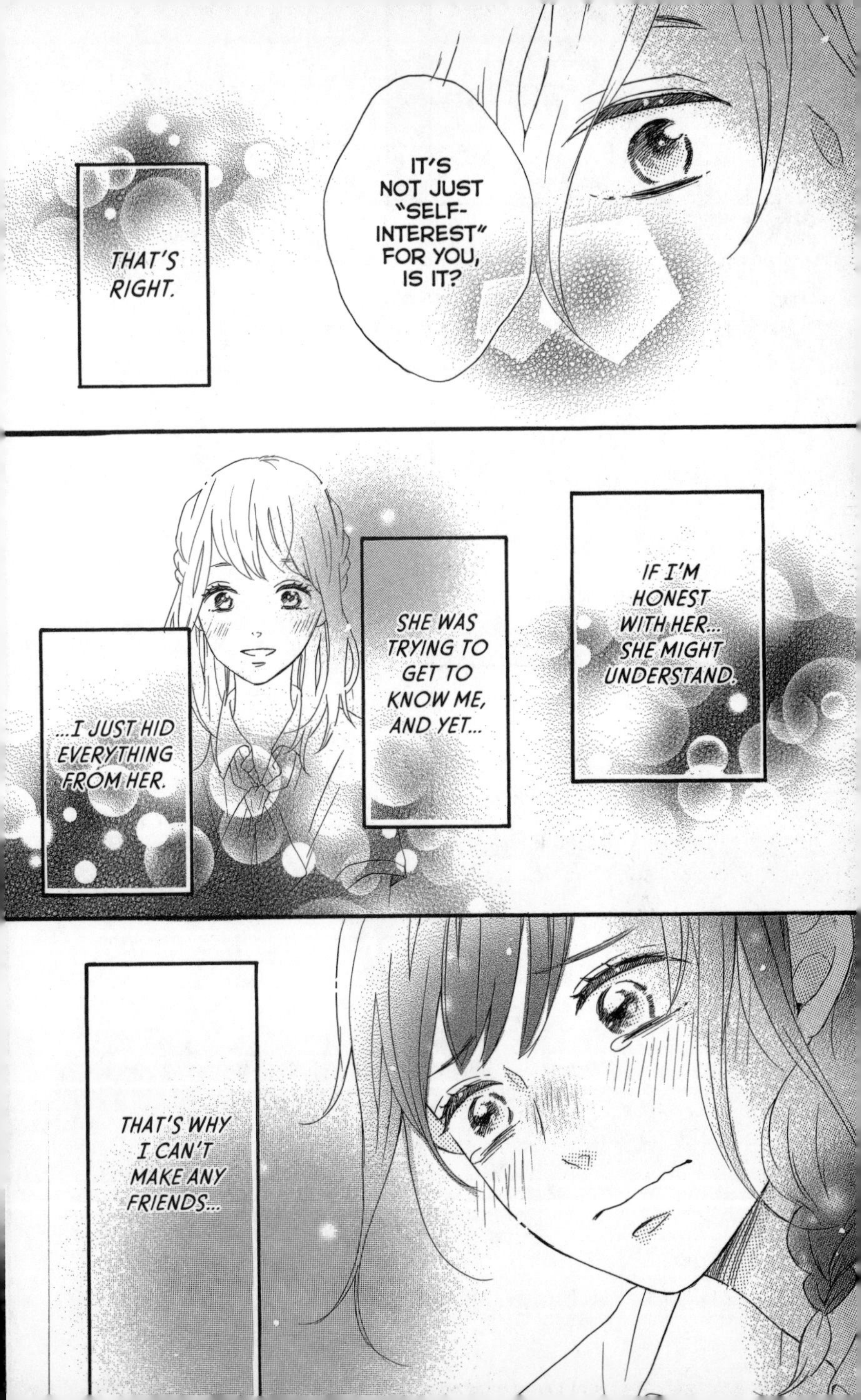
IT'S NOT JUST "SELF-INTEREST" FOR YOU, IS IT?
THAT'S RIGHT.
IF I'M HONEST WITH HER... SHE MIGHT UNDERSTAND.
SHE WAS TRYING TO GET TO KNOW ME, AND YET...
...I JUST HID EVERYTHING FROM HER.
THAT'S WHY I CAN'T MAKE ANY FRIENDS...

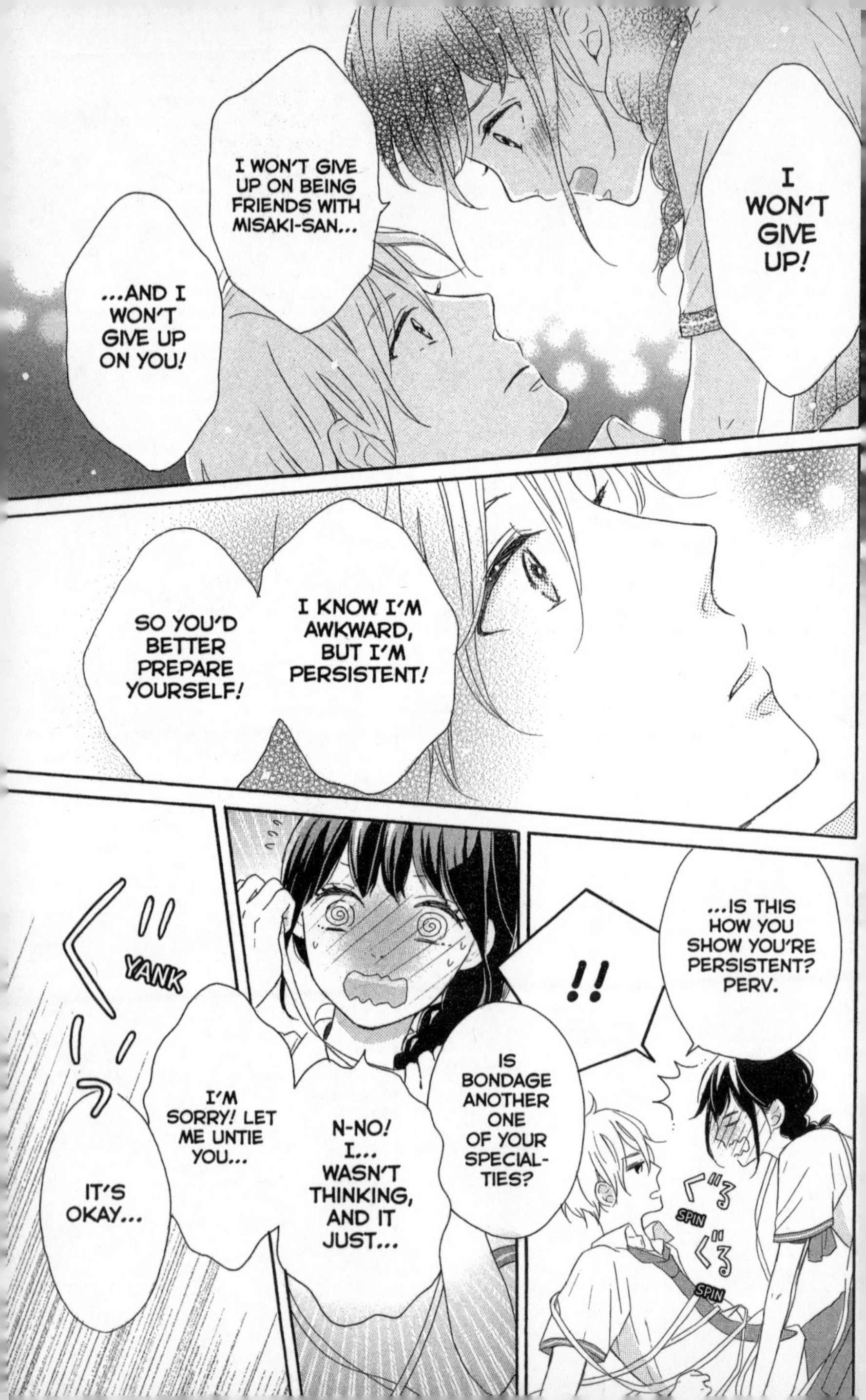

I WON'T GIVE UP!
I WON'T GIVE UP ON BEING FRIENDS WITH MISAKI-SAN...
...AND I WON'T GIVE UP ON YOU!
I KNOW I'M AWKWARD, BUT I'M PERSISTENT!
SO YOU'D BETTER PREPARE YOURSELF!
...IS THIS HOW YOU SHOW YOU'RE PERSISTENT? PERV.
!!
ぐる
SPIN
ぐる
SPIN
IS BONDAGE ANOTHER ONE OF YOUR SPECIAL-TIES?
N-NO! I... WASN'T THINKING, AND IT JUST...
YANK
I'M SORRY! LET ME UNTIE YOU...
IT'S OKAY...

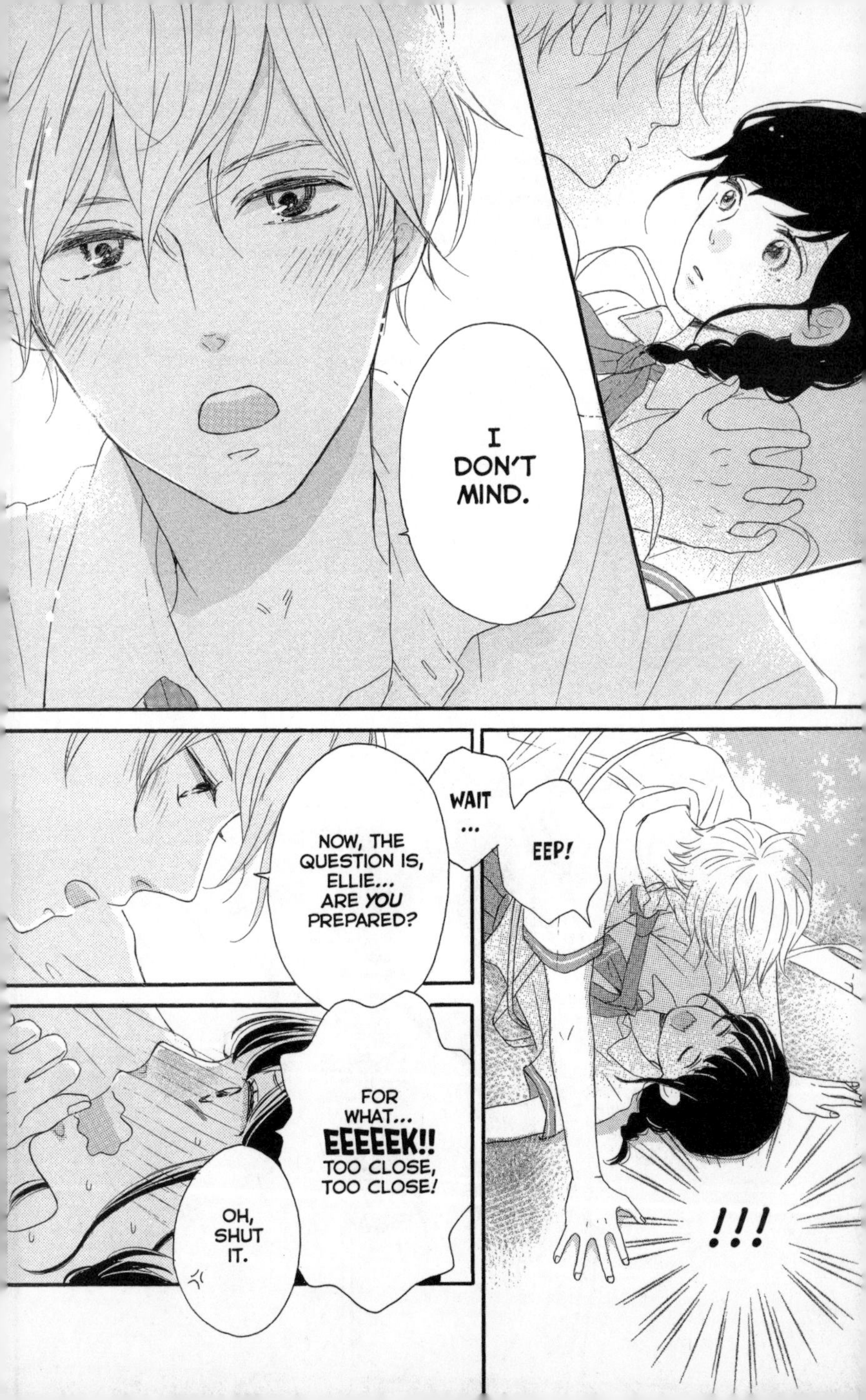
I DON'T MIND.
WAIT ...
EEP!
!!!
NOW, THE QUESTION IS, ELLIE... ARE *YOU* PREPARED?
FOR WHAT... **EEEEEK!!** TOO CLOSE, TOO CLOSE!
OH, SHUT IT.

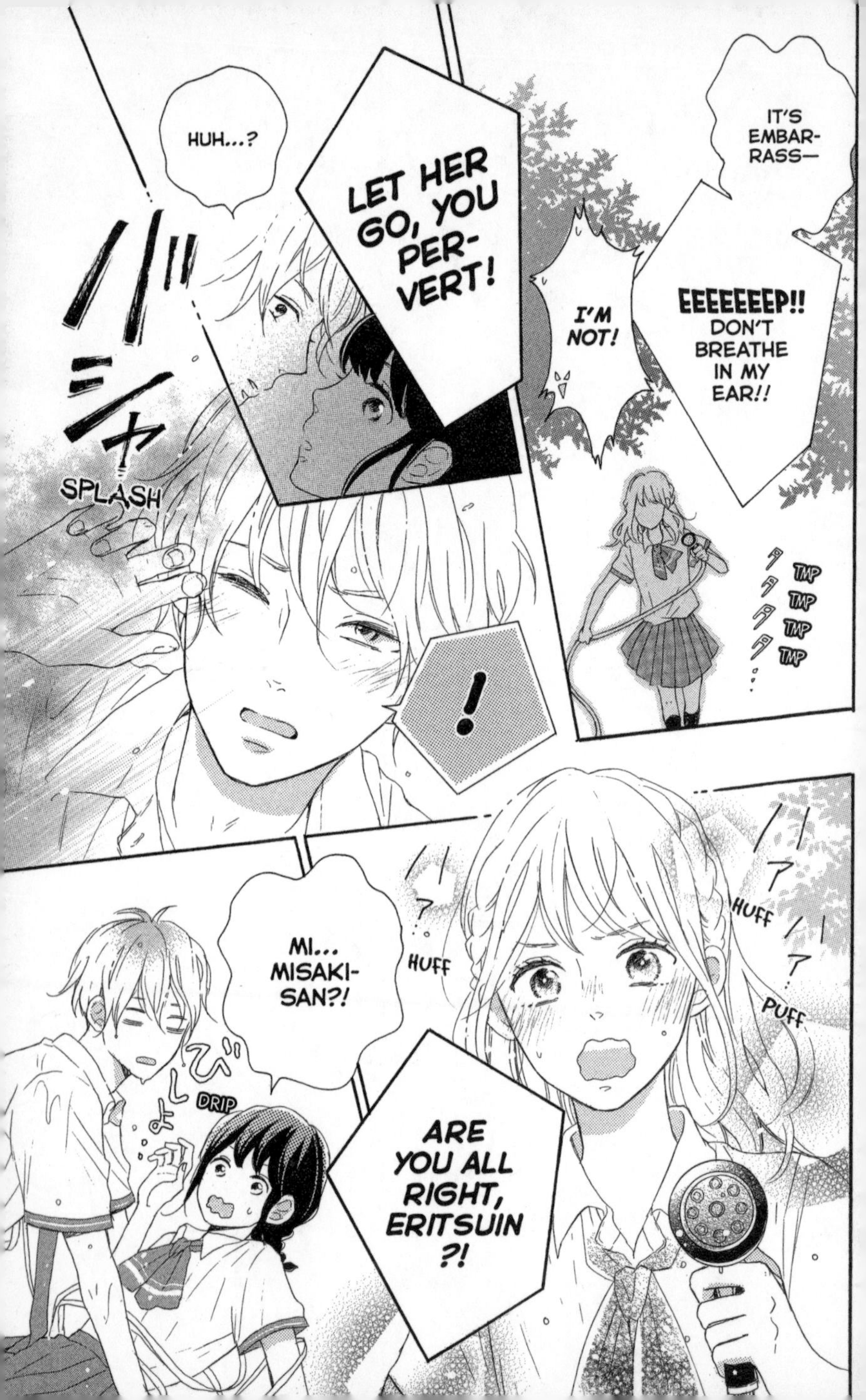
IT'S EMBARRASS—
EEEEEEEP!! DON'T BREATHE IN MY EAR!!
I'M NOT!
TMP TMP TMP TMP
LET HER GO, YOU PERVERT!
HUH...?
SPLASH
!
HUFF
PUFF
HUFF
ARE YOU ALL RIGHT, ERITSUIN?!
MI... MISAKI-SAN?!
DRIP

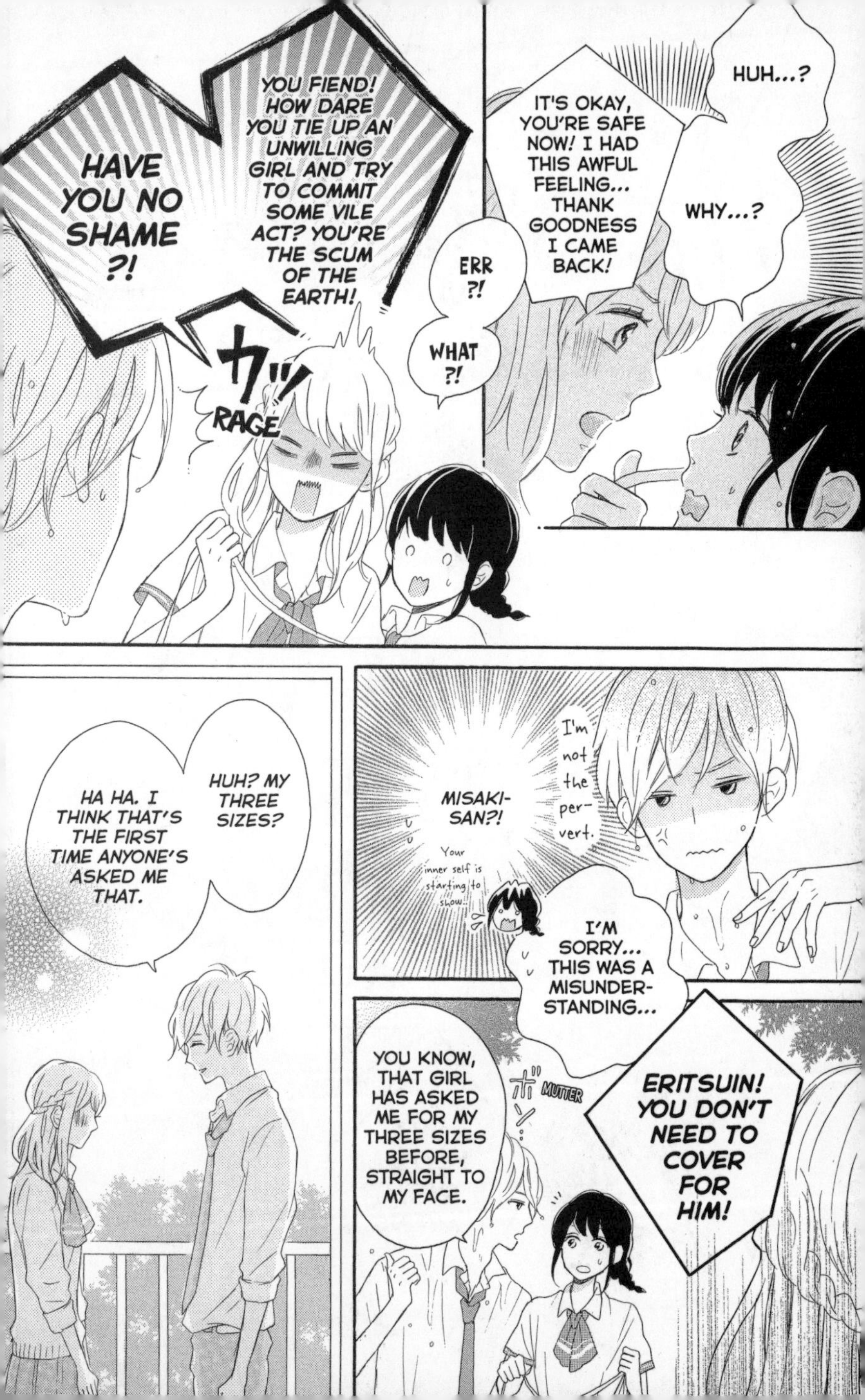
HUH...?
IT'S OKAY, YOU'RE SAFE NOW! I HAD THIS AWFUL FEELING... THANK GOODNESS I CAME BACK!
WHY...?
ERR ?!
WHAT ?!
YOU FIEND! HOW DARE YOU TIE UP AN UNWILLING GIRL AND TRY TO COMMIT SOME VILE ACT? YOU'RE THE SCUM OF THE EARTH!
HAVE YOU NO SHAME ?!
カッ
RAGE
I'm not the per-vert.
MISAKI-SAN?!
Your inner self is starting to show...
I'M SORRY... THIS WAS A MISUNDER-STANDING...
ERITSUIN! YOU DON'T NEED TO COVER FOR HIM!
ボソ
MUTTER
YOU KNOW, THAT GIRL HAS ASKED ME FOR MY THREE SIZES BEFORE, STRAIGHT TO MY FACE.
HUH? MY THREE SIZES?
HA HA. I THINK THAT'S THE FIRST TIME ANYONE'S ASKED ME THAT.

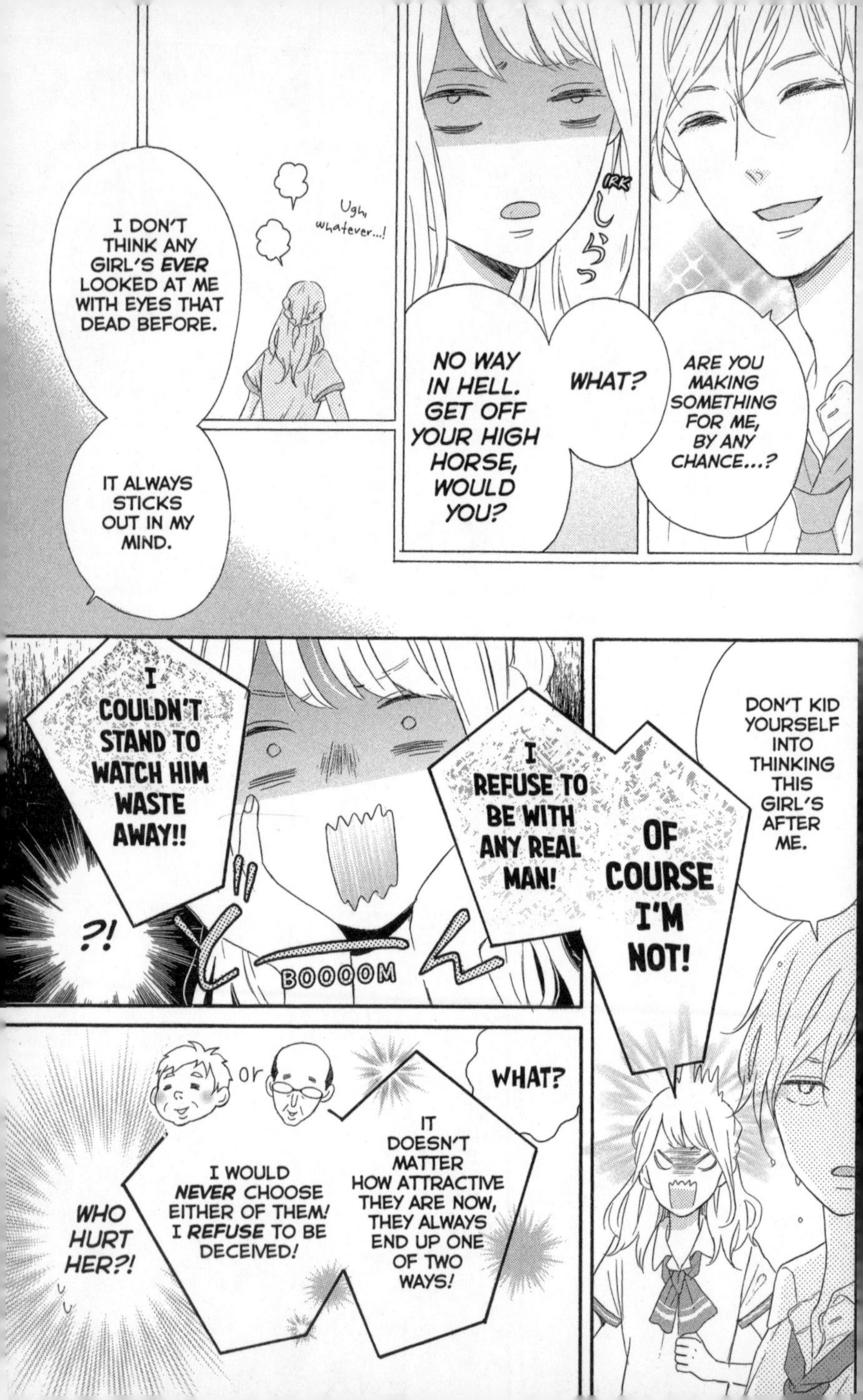
ARE YOU MAKING SOMETHING FOR ME, BY ANY CHANCE...?
IRK
WHAT?
NO WAY IN HELL. GET OFF YOUR HIGH HORSE, WOULD YOU?
Ugh, whatever...!
I DON'T THINK ANY GIRL'S *EVER* LOOKED AT ME WITH EYES THAT DEAD BEFORE.
IT ALWAYS STICKS OUT IN MY MIND.
DON'T KID YOURSELF INTO THINKING THIS GIRL'S AFTER ME.
OF COURSE I'M NOT!
I REFUSE TO BE WITH ANY REAL MAN!
I COULDN'T STAND TO WATCH HIM WASTE AWAY!!
BOOOOM
?!
WHAT?
IT DOESN'T MATTER HOW ATTRACTIVE THEY ARE NOW, THEY ALWAYS END UP ONE OF TWO WAYS!
or
I WOULD *NEVER* CHOOSE EITHER OF THEM! I *REFUSE* TO BE DECEIVED!
WHO HURT HER?!

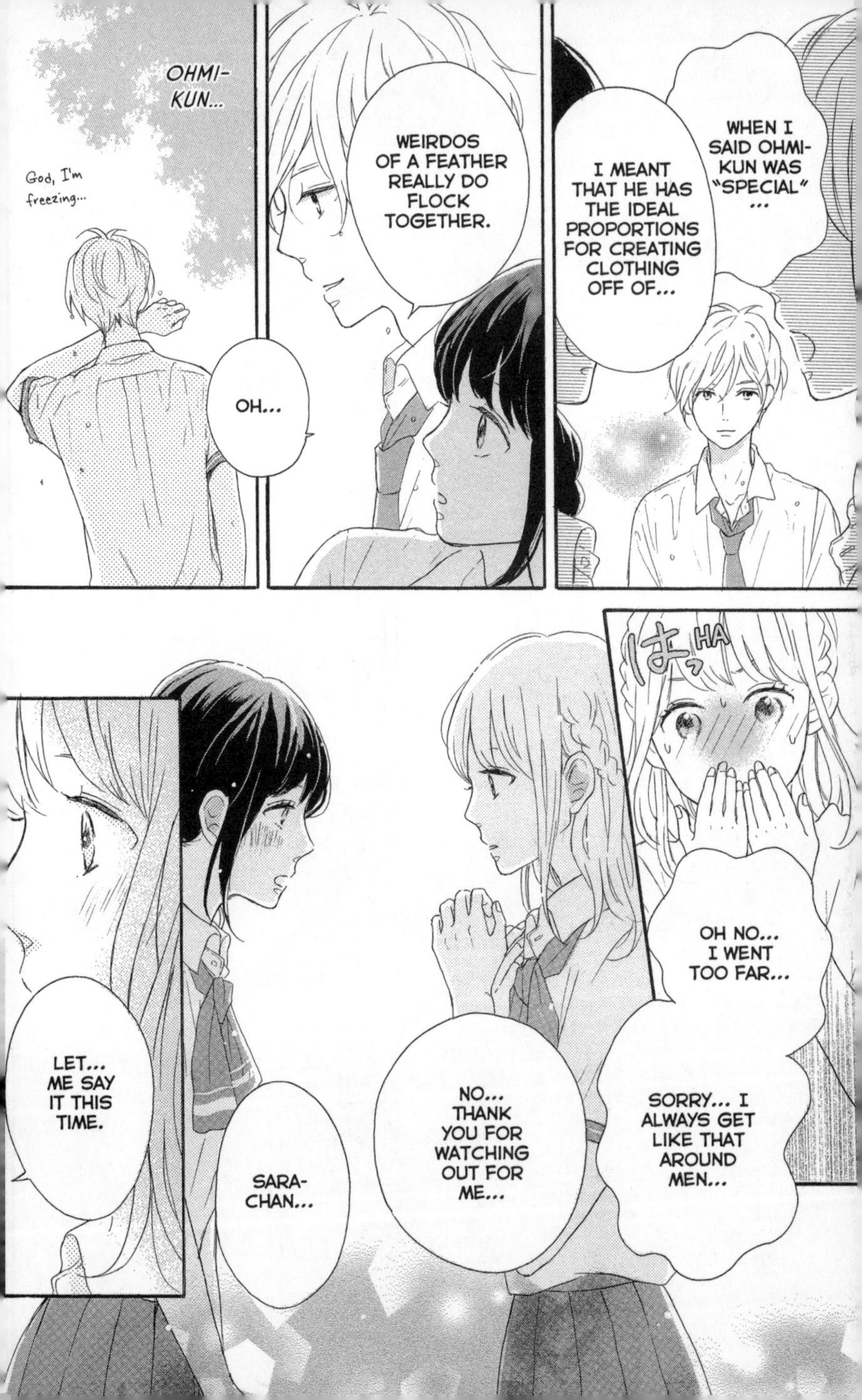
WHEN I SAID OHMI-KUN WAS "SPECIAL"...
I MEANT THAT HE HAS THE IDEAL PROPORTIONS FOR CREATING CLOTHING OFF OF...
WEIRDOS OF A FEATHER REALLY DO FLOCK TOGETHER.
OH...
OHMI-KUN...
God, I'm freezing...
HA
OH NO... I WENT TOO FAR...
SORRY... I ALWAYS GET LIKE THAT AROUND MEN...
NO... THANK YOU FOR WATCHING OUT FOR ME...
SARA-CHAN...
LET... ME SAY IT THIS TIME.

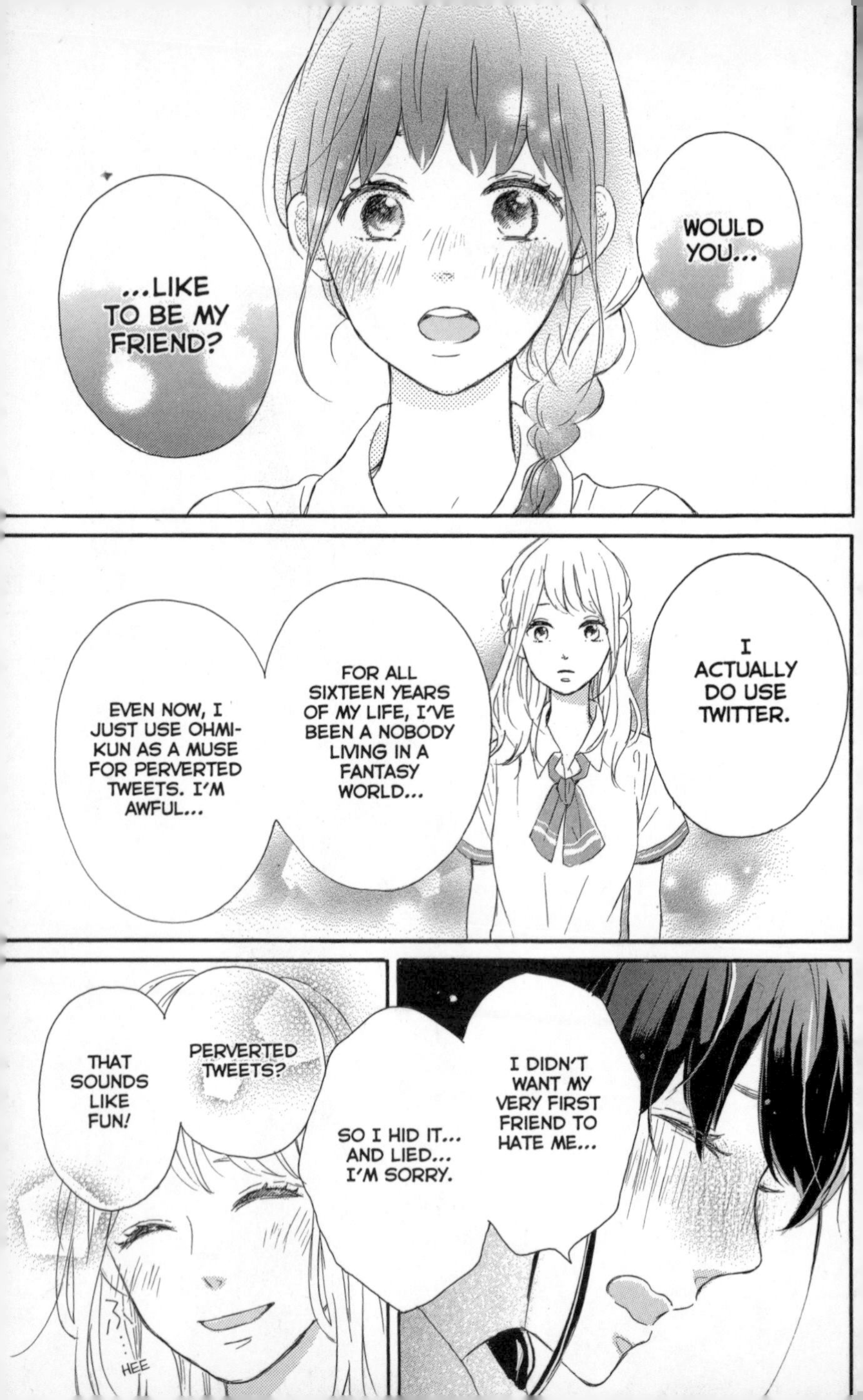
WOULD YOU...
...LIKE TO BE MY FRIEND?
I ACTUALLY DO USE TWITTER.
FOR ALL SIXTEEN YEARS OF MY LIFE, I'VE BEEN A NOBODY LIVING IN A FANTASY WORLD...
EVEN NOW, I JUST USE OHMI-KUN AS A MUSE FOR PERVERTED TWEETS. I'M AWFUL...
I DIDN'T WANT MY VERY FIRST FRIEND TO HATE ME...
SO I HID IT... AND LIED... I'M SORRY.
PERVERTED TWEETS?
THAT SOUNDS LIKE FUN!
HEE

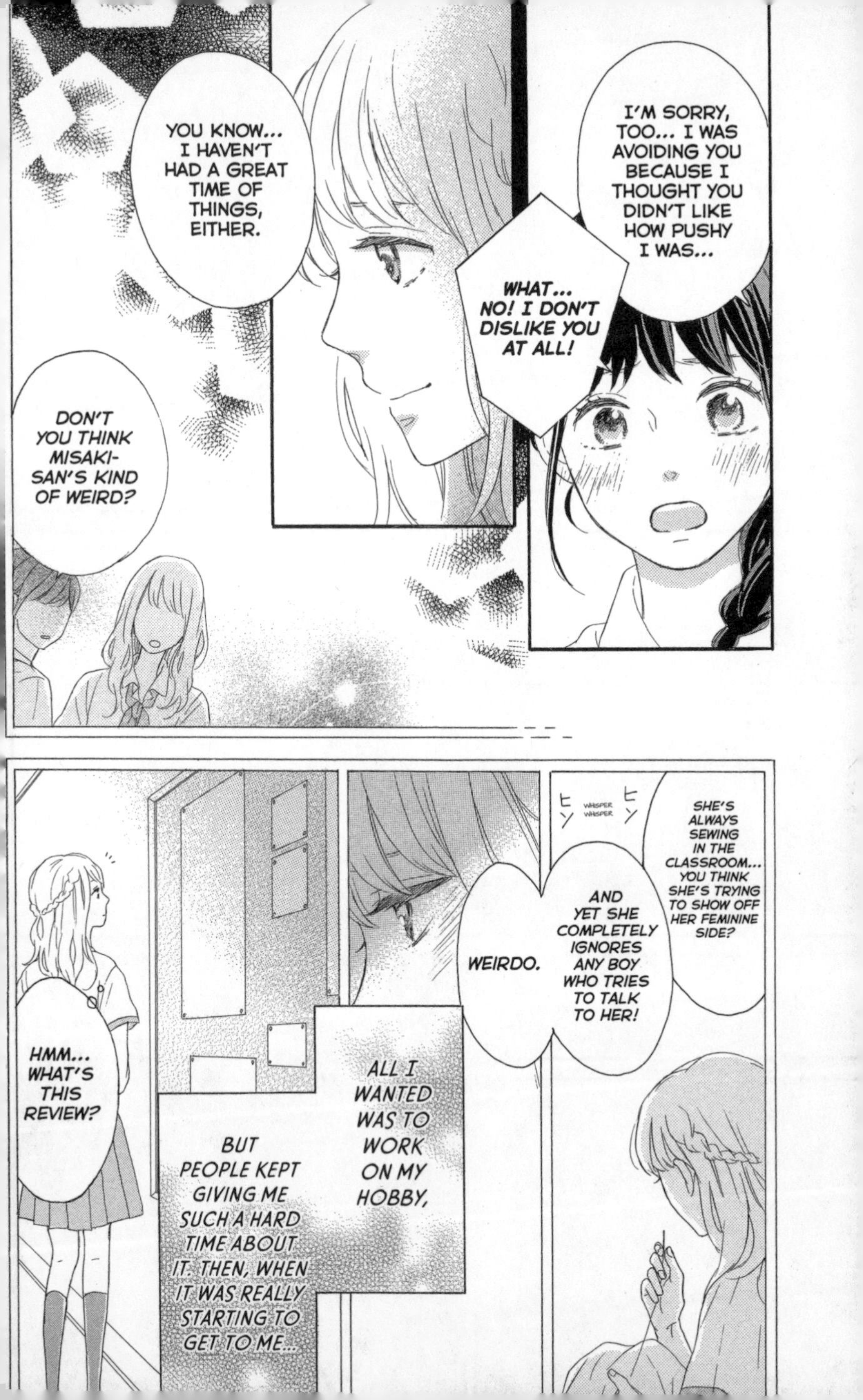
I'M SORRY, TOO... I WAS AVOIDING YOU BECAUSE I THOUGHT YOU DIDN'T LIKE HOW PUSHY I WAS...
WHAT... NO! I DON'T DISLIKE YOU AT ALL!
YOU KNOW... I HAVEN'T HAD A GREAT TIME OF THINGS, EITHER.
DON'T YOU THINK MISAKI-SAN'S KIND OF WEIRD?
ヒソ WHISPER WHISPER ヒソ
SHE'S ALWAYS SEWING IN THE CLASSROOM... YOU THINK SHE'S TRYING TO SHOW OFF HER FEMININE SIDE?
AND YET SHE COMPLETELY IGNORES ANY BOY WHO TRIES TO TALK TO HER!
WEIRDO.
ALL I WANTED WAS TO WORK ON MY HOBBY,
BUT PEOPLE KEPT GIVING ME SUCH A HARD TIME ABOUT IT. THEN, WHEN IT WAS REALLY STARTING TO GET TO ME...
HMM... WHAT'S THIS REVIEW?

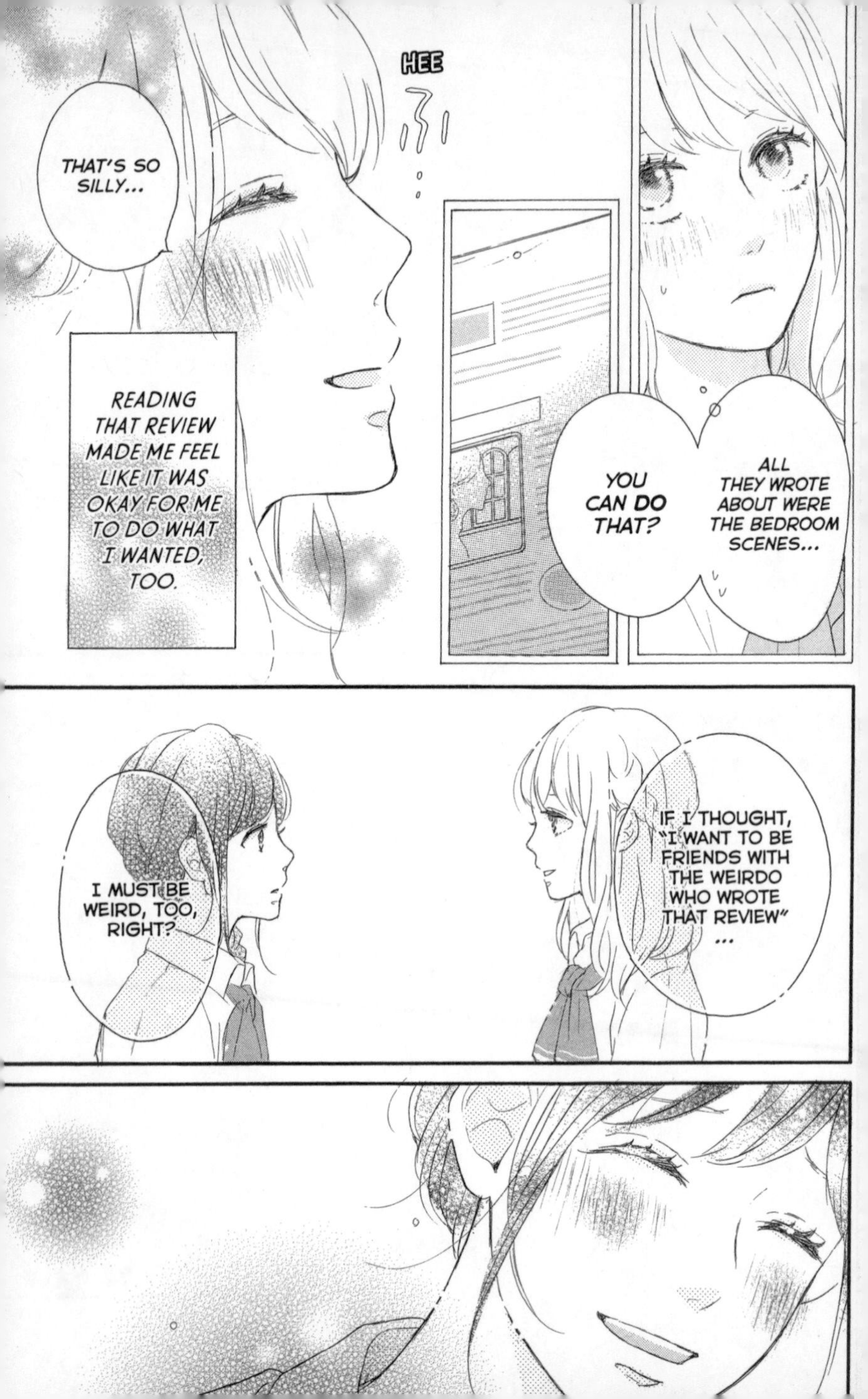
ALL THEY WROTE ABOUT WERE THE BEDROOM SCENES...
YOU CAN DO THAT?
HEE
THAT'S SO SILLY...
READING THAT REVIEW MADE ME FEEL LIKE IT WAS OKAY FOR ME TO DO WHAT I WANTED, TOO.
IF I THOUGHT, "I WANT TO BE FRIENDS WITH THE WEIRDO WHO WROTE THAT REVIEW"...
I MUST BE WEIRD, TOO, RIGHT?

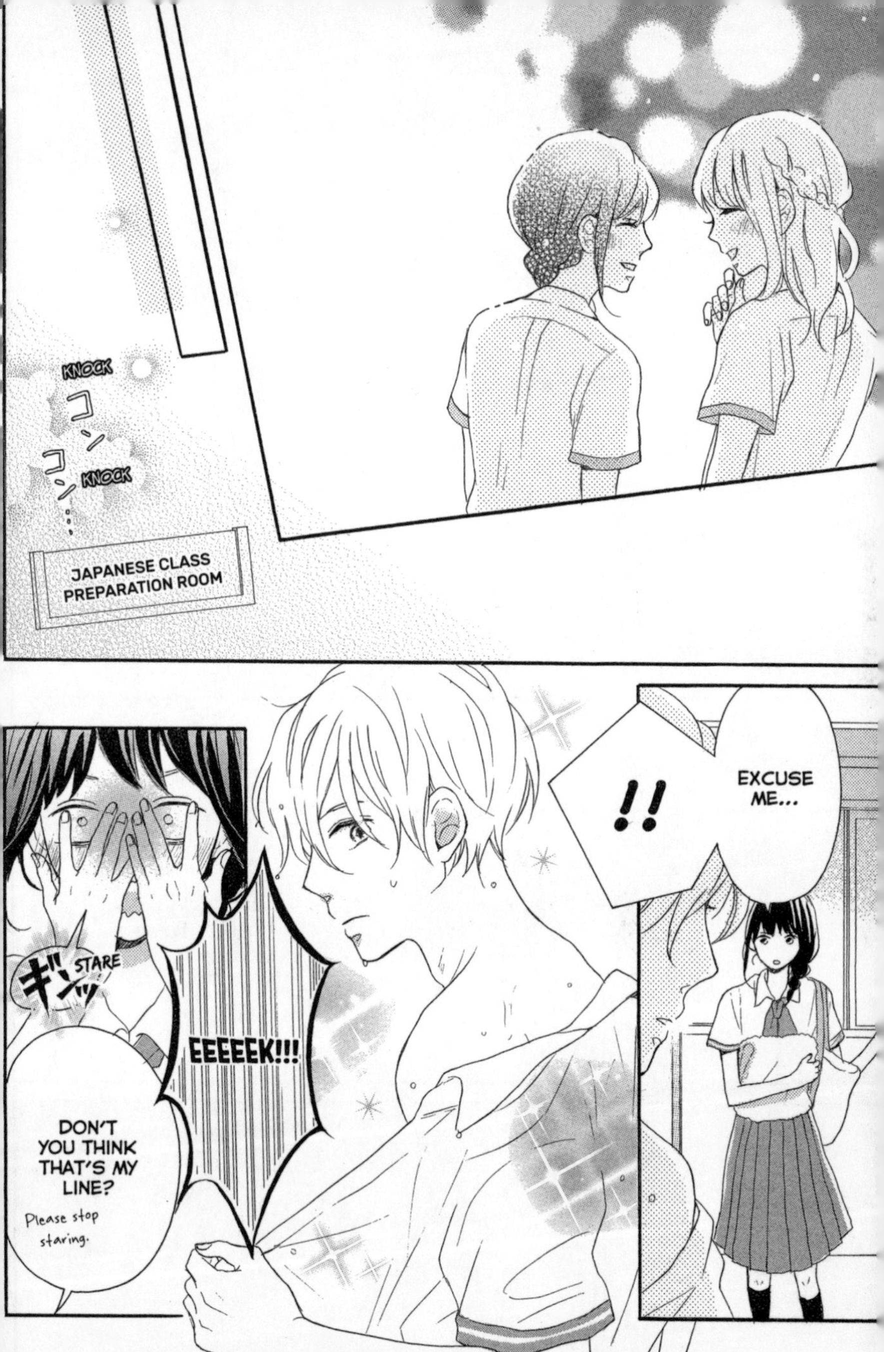
KNOCK
コン
コン…
KNOCK
JAPANESE CLASS PREPARATION ROOM
EXCUSE ME...
!!
EEEEEK!!!
ギンッ
STARE
DON'T YOU THINK THAT'S MY LINE?
Please stop staring.

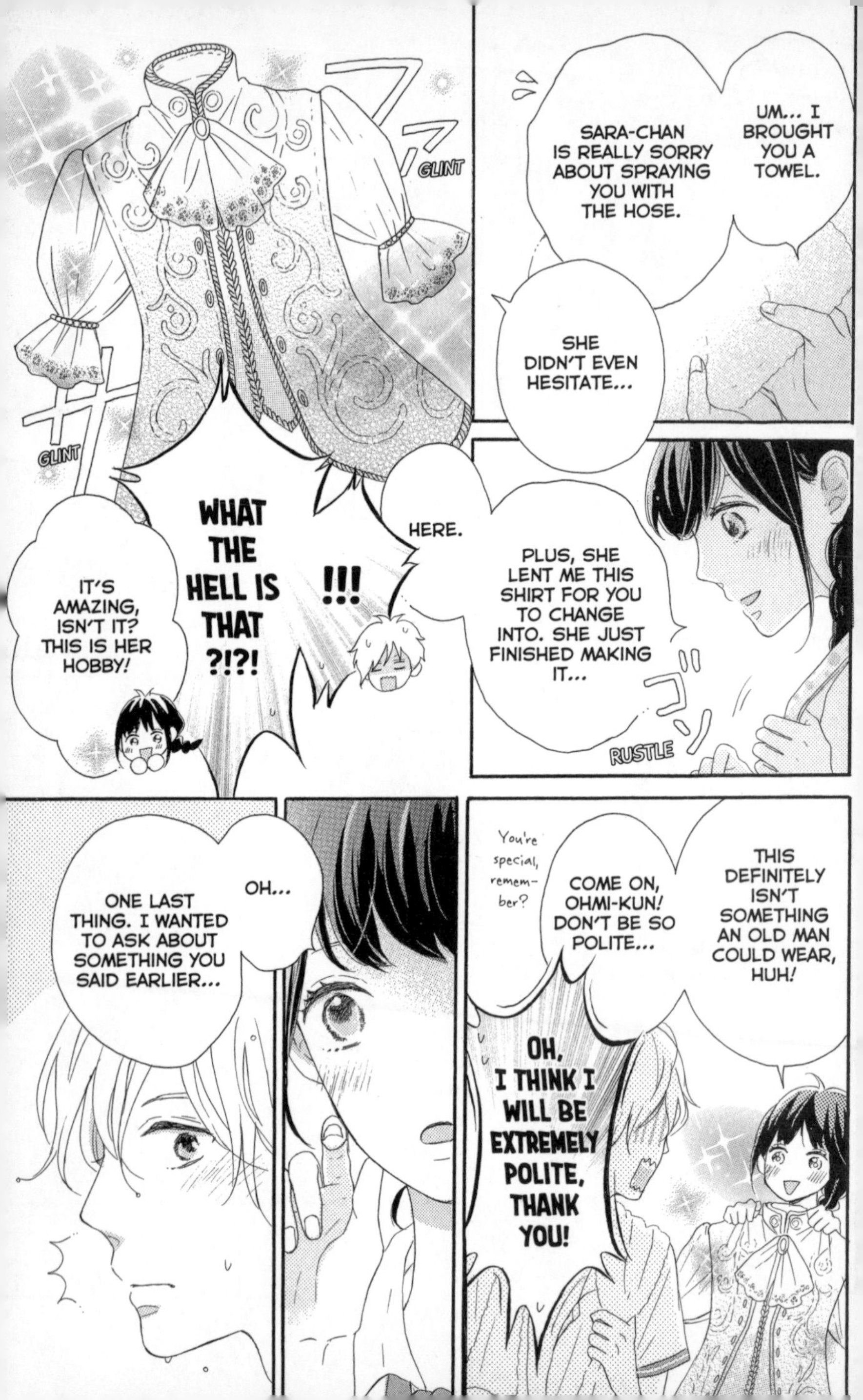
UM... I BROUGHT YOU A TOWEL.
SARA-CHAN IS REALLY SORRY ABOUT SPRAYING YOU WITH THE HOSE.
SHE DIDN'T EVEN HESITATE...
PLUS, SHE LENT ME THIS SHIRT FOR YOU TO CHANGE INTO. SHE JUST FINISHED MAKING IT...
RUSTLE
HERE.
GLINT
GLINT
WHAT THE HELL IS THAT ?!?!
!!!
IT'S AMAZING, ISN'T IT? THIS IS HER HOBBY!
THIS DEFINITELY ISN'T SOMETHING AN OLD MAN COULD WEAR, HUH!
COME ON, OHMI-KUN! DON'T BE SO POLITE...
You're special, remember?
OH, I THINK I WILL BE EXTREMELY POLITE, THANK YOU!
OH...
ONE LAST THING. I WANTED TO ASK ABOUT SOMETHING YOU SAID EARLIER...

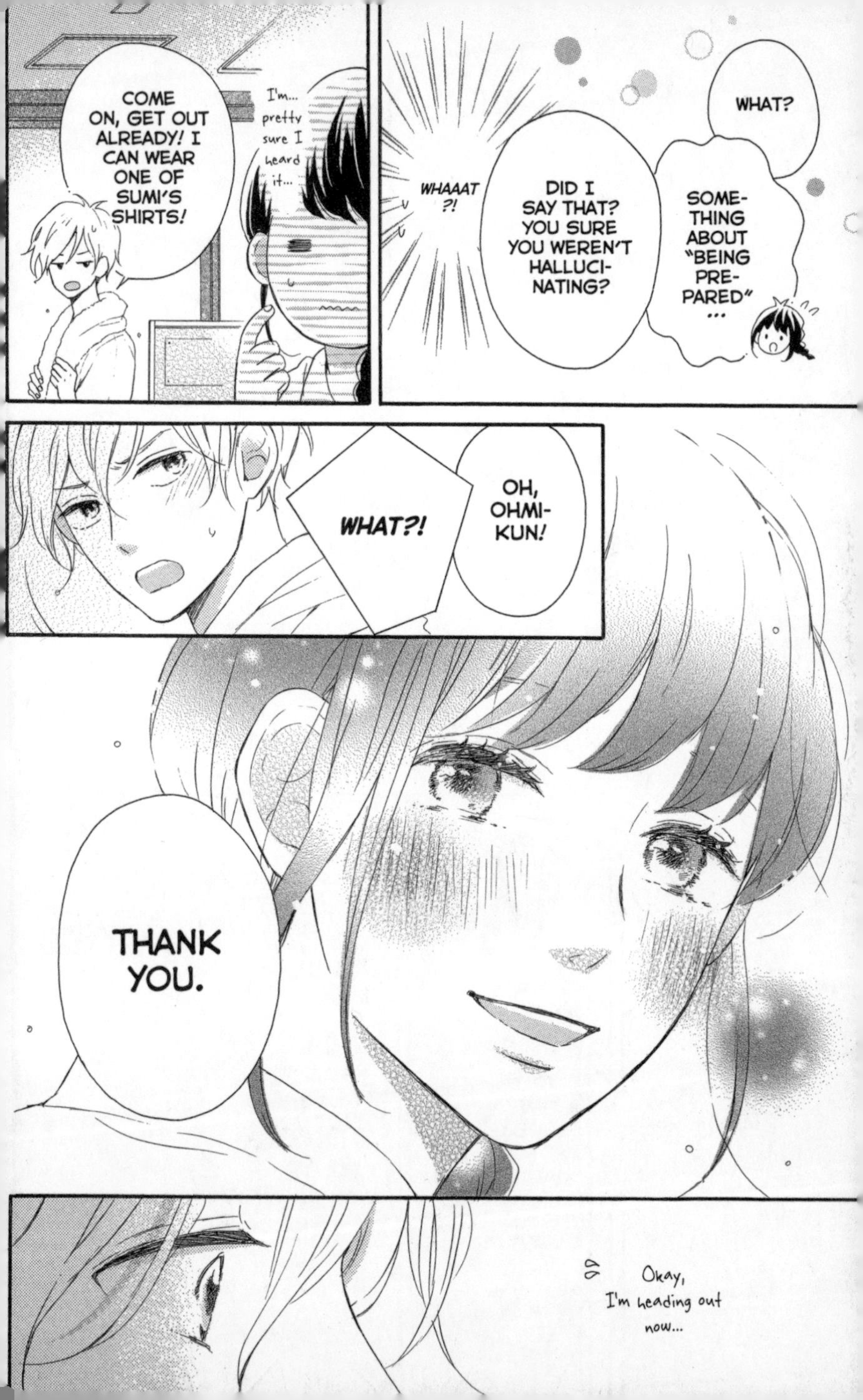
WHAT?
SOMETHING ABOUT "BEING PREPARED"...
DID I SAY THAT? YOU SURE YOU WEREN'T HALLUCINATING?
WHAAAT?!
I'm... pretty sure I heard it...
COME ON, GET OUT ALREADY! I CAN WEAR ONE OF SUMI'S SHIRTS!
OH, OHMI-KUN!
WHAT?!
THANK YOU.
Okay, I'm heading out now...

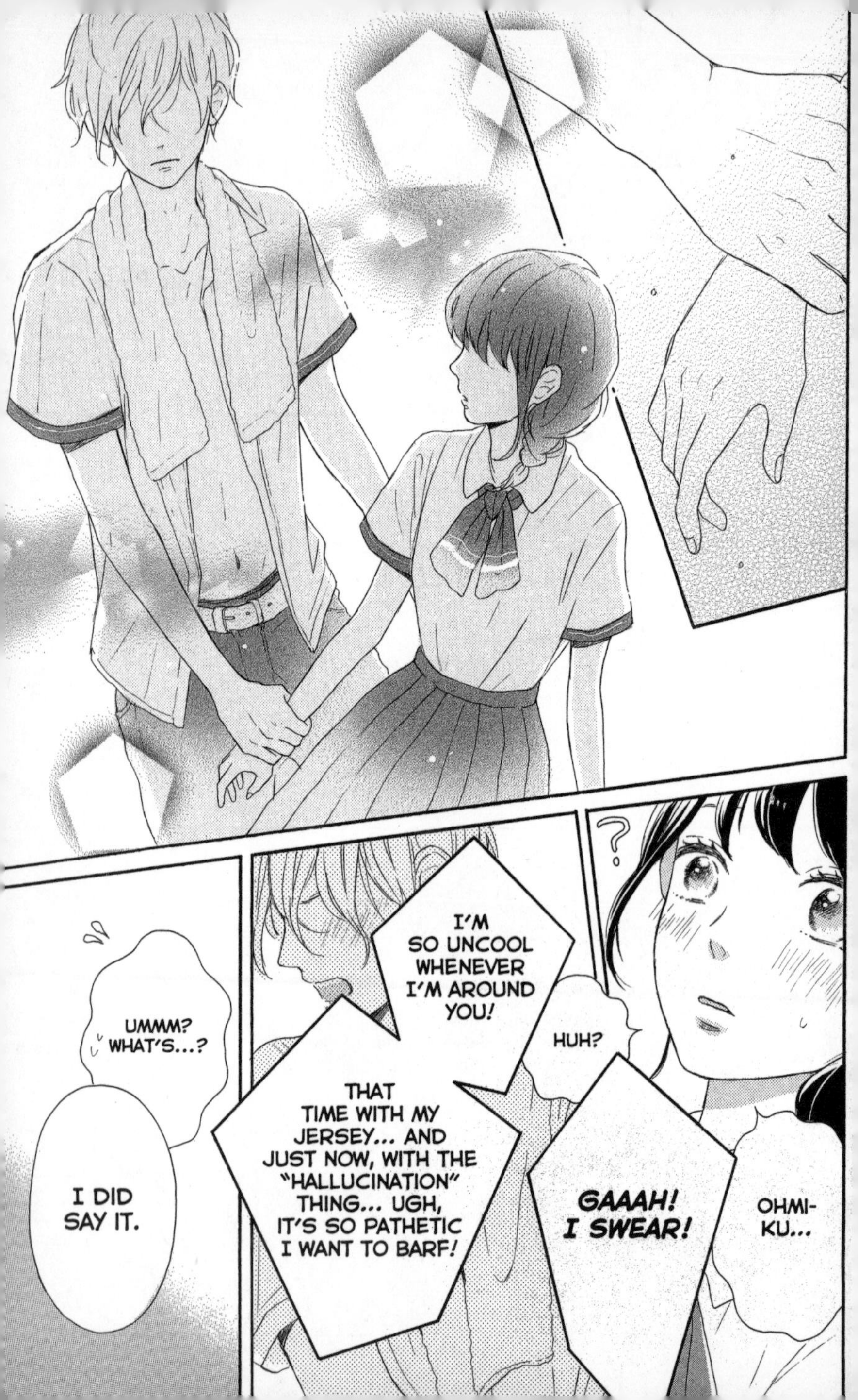
?
HUH?
OHMI-KU...
GAAAH! I SWEAR!
I'M SO UNCOOL WHENEVER I'M AROUND YOU!
THAT TIME WITH MY JERSEY... AND JUST NOW, WITH THE "HALLUCINATION" THING... UGH, IT'S SO PATHETIC I WANT TO BARF!
UMMM? WHAT'S...?
I DID SAY IT.

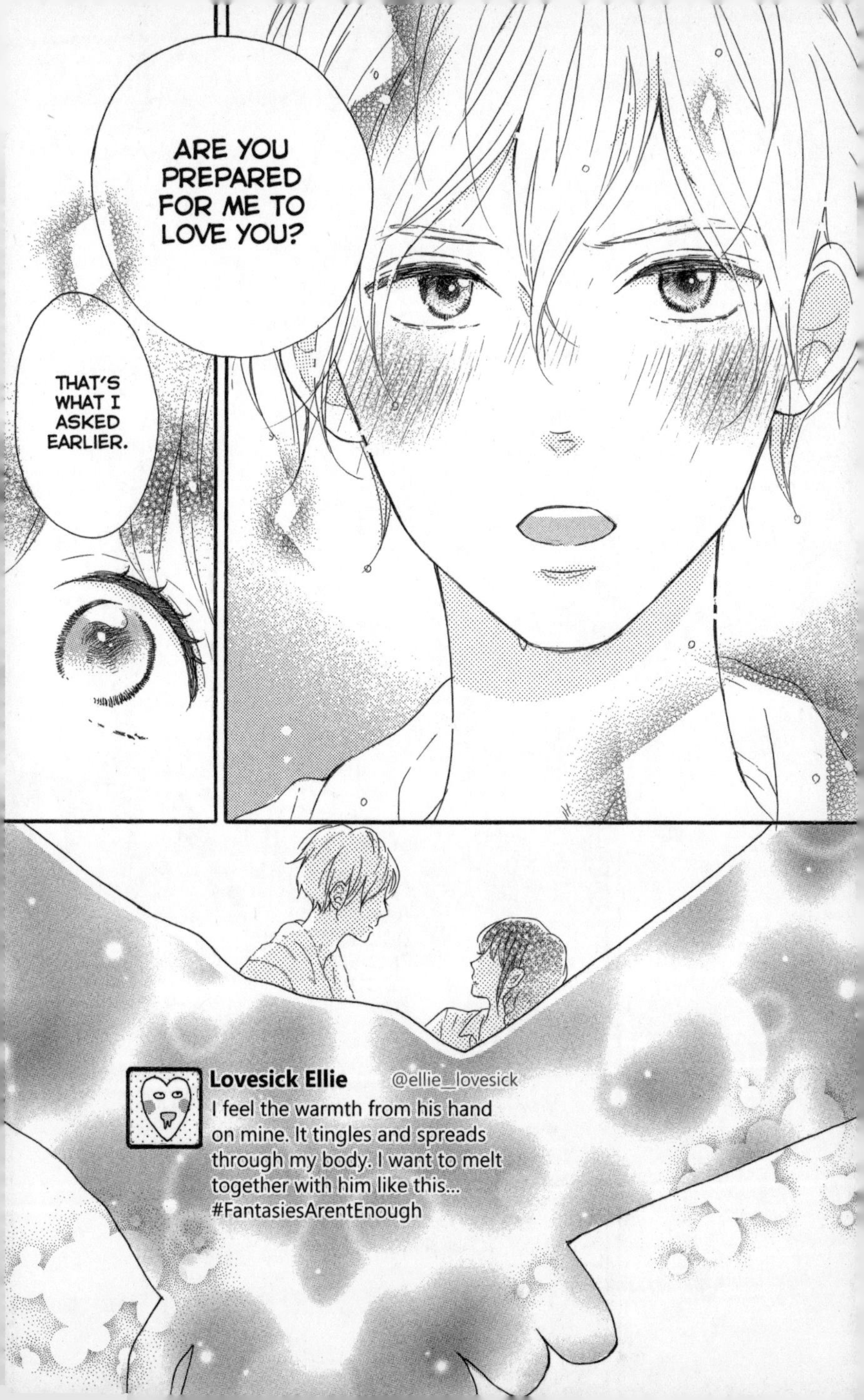
ARE YOU PREPARED FOR ME TO LOVE YOU?
THAT'S WHAT I ASKED EARLIER.
Lovesick Ellie @ellie_lovesick
I feel the warmth from his hand on mine. It tingles and spreads through my body. I want to melt together with him like this... #FantasiesArentEnough

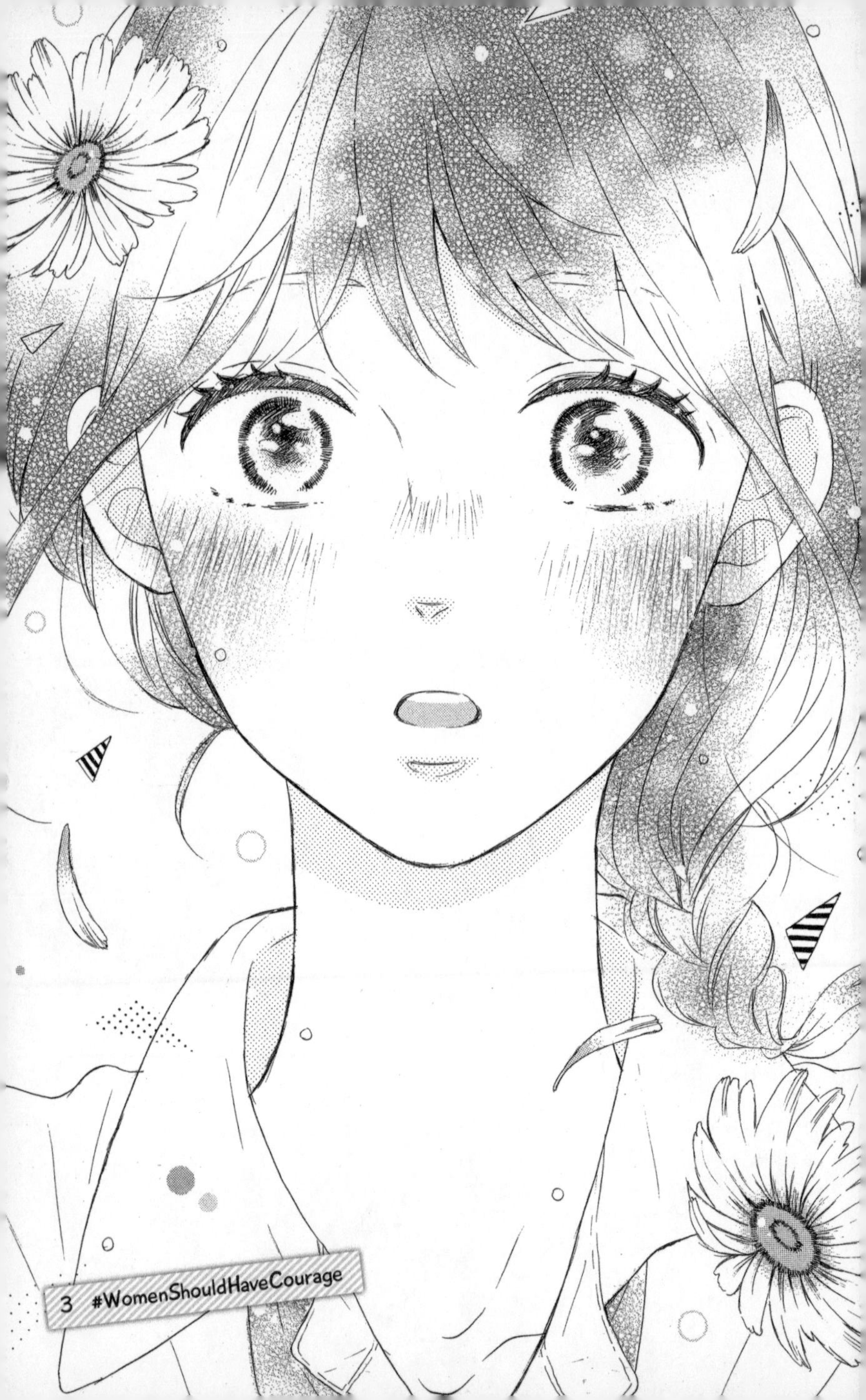
3 #WomenShouldHaveCourage

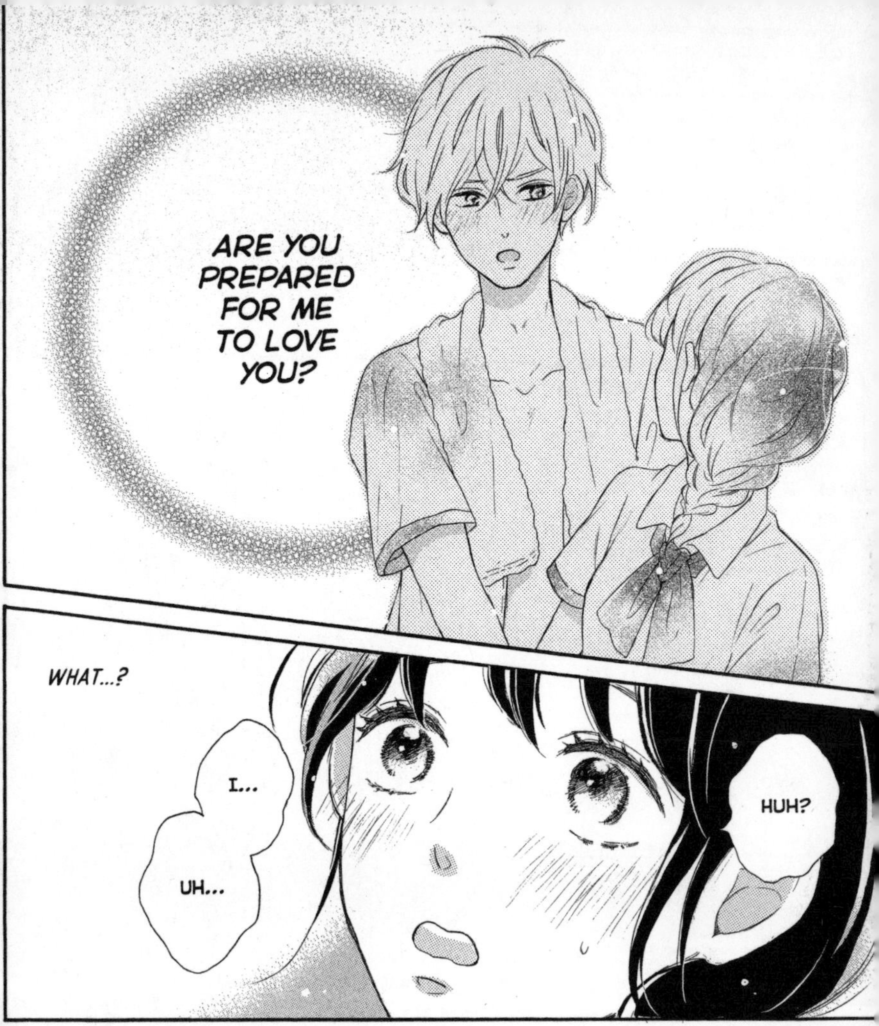
ARE YOU PREPARED FOR ME TO LOVE YOU?
HUH?
I...
UH...
WHAT...?

Lovesick Ellie 1

Thank you for picking up this volume! I'm drawing this shojo manga in hopes it can give all the fantasizing, pervy girls out there (like me!) some hopes and dreams!

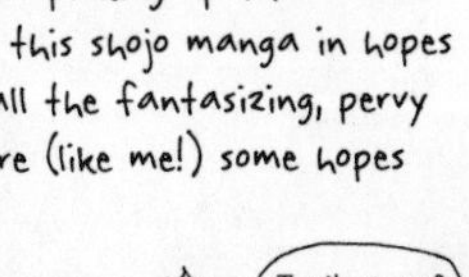
That's kind of a tall order!
My editor

Ellie's Twitter exists (in Japanese)!

@ellie__lovesick
(that's two underscores)

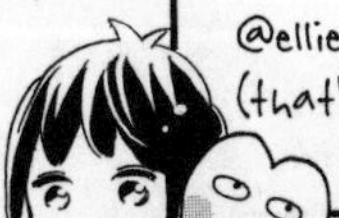

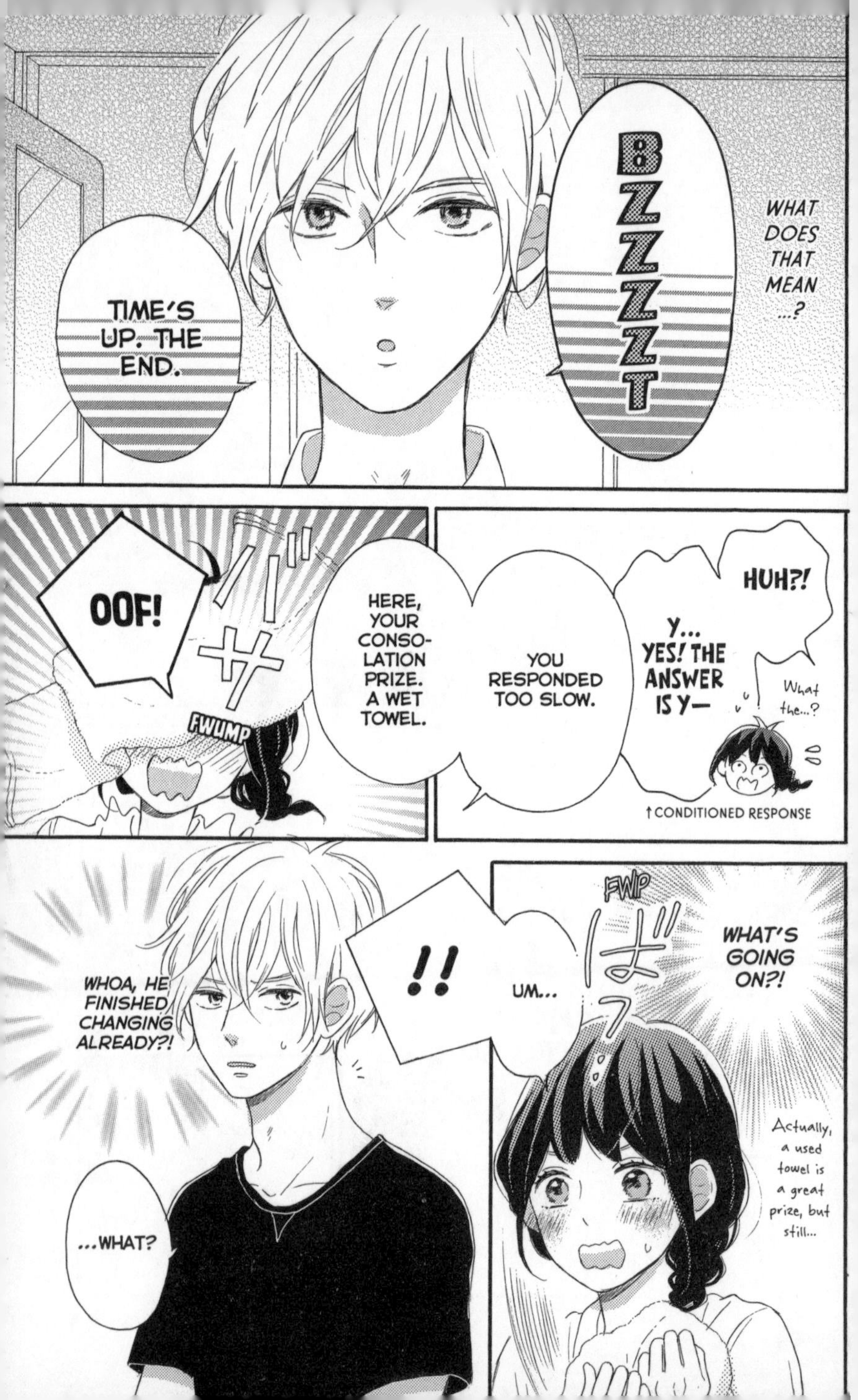
WHAT DOES THAT MEAN ...?
BZZZZT
TIME'S UP. THE END.
HUH?!
What the...?
Y... YES! THE ANSWER IS Y—
↑CONDITIONED RESPONSE
YOU RESPONDED TOO SLOW.
HERE, YOUR CONSOLATION PRIZE. A WET TOWEL.
FWUMP
OOF!
FWIP
WHAT'S GOING ON?!
UM...
Actually, a used towel is a great prize, but still...
!!
WHOA, HE FINISHED CHANGING ALREADY?!
...WHAT?

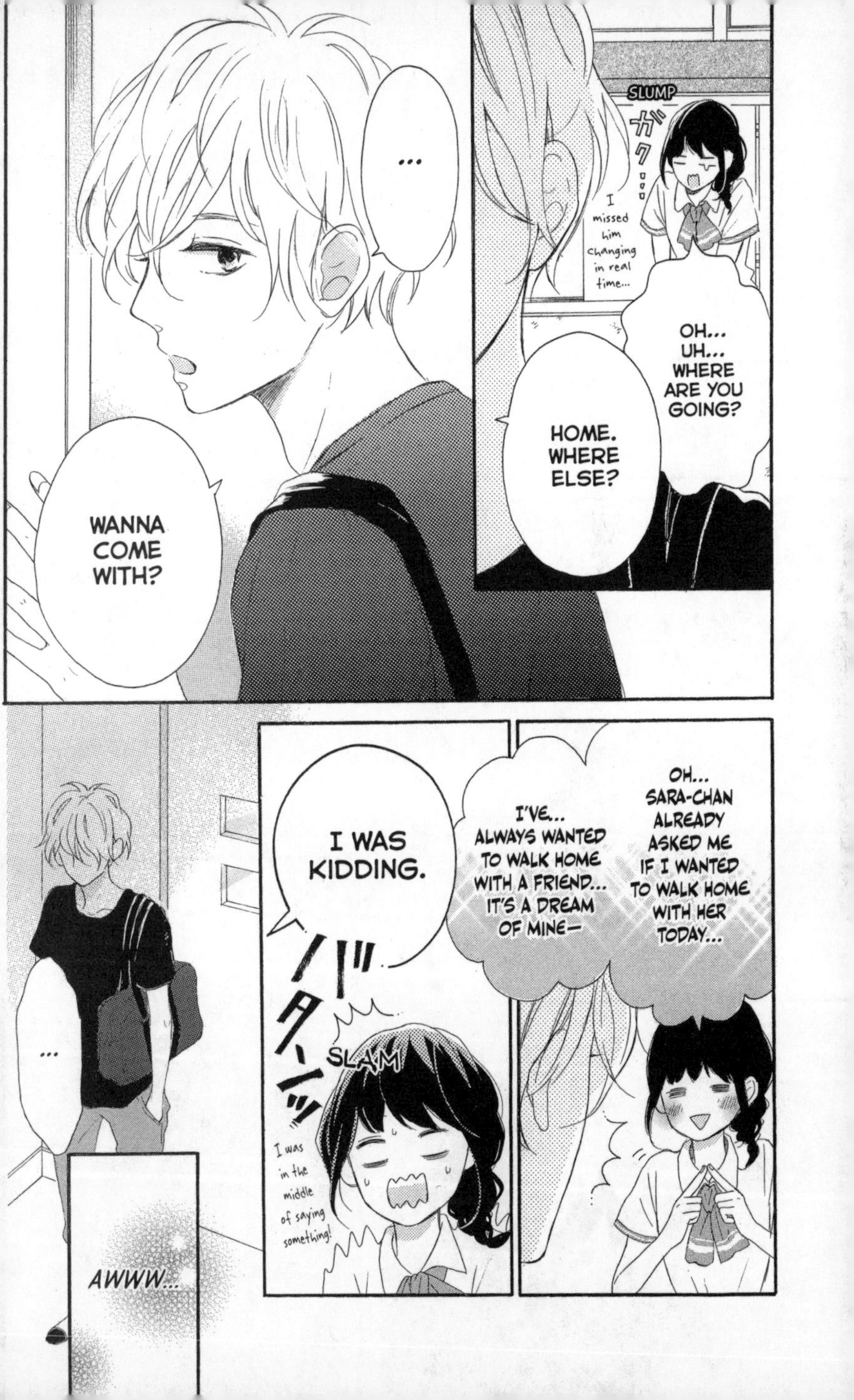
SLUMP
ガク
I missed him changing in real time...
OH... UH... WHERE ARE YOU GOING?
HOME. WHERE ELSE?
...
WANNA COME WITH?
OH... SARA-CHAN ALREADY ASKED ME IF I WANTED TO WALK HOME WITH HER TODAY...
I'VE... ALWAYS WANTED TO WALK HOME WITH A FRIEND... IT'S A DREAM OF MINE—
I WAS KIDDING.
SLAM
I was in the middle of saying something!
...
AWWW...

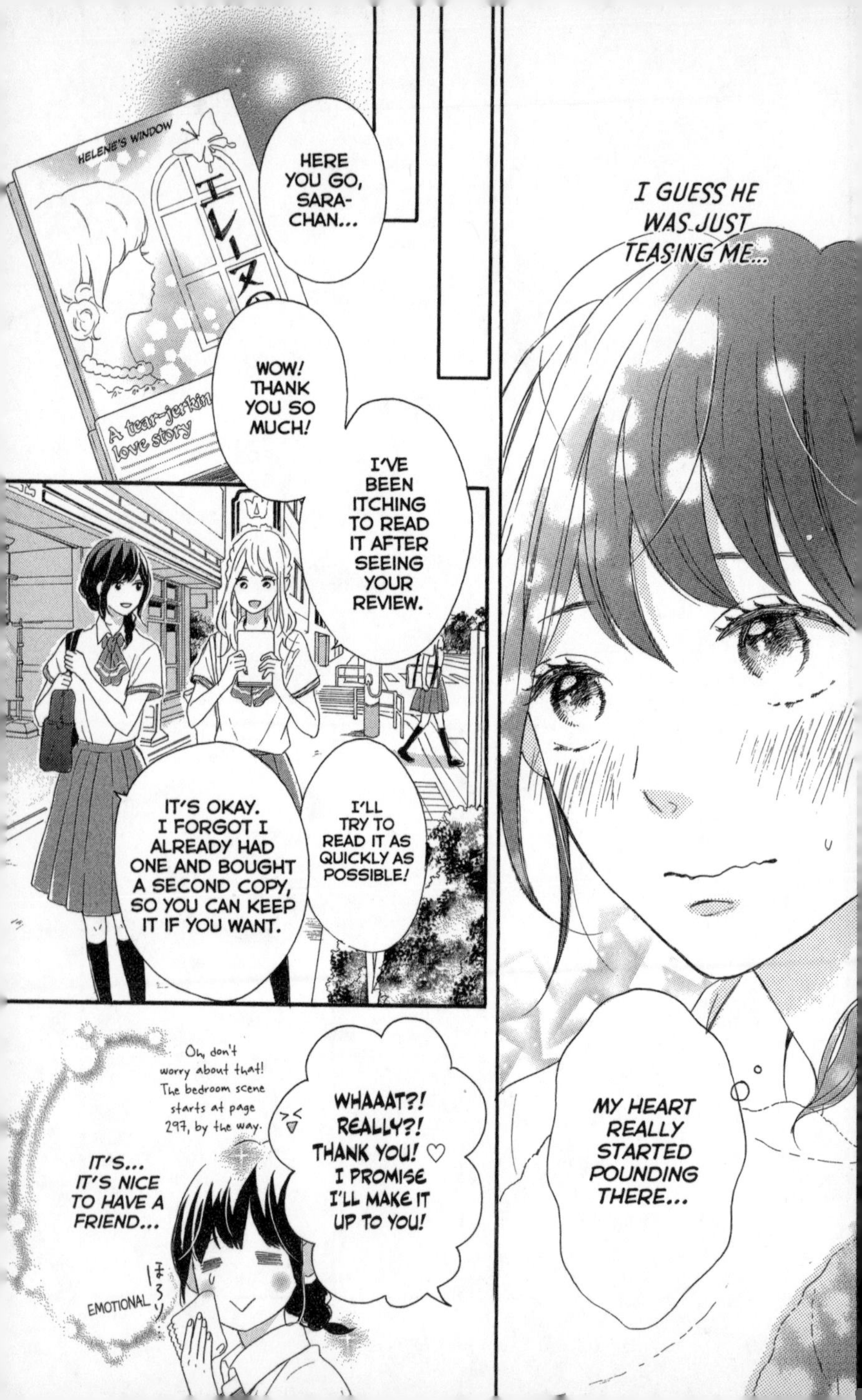
I GUESS HE WAS JUST TEASING ME...
MY HEART REALLY STARTED POUNDING THERE...
HELENE'S WINDOW
A tear-jerkin love story
HERE YOU GO, SARA-CHAN...
WOW! THANK YOU SO MUCH!
I'VE BEEN ITCHING TO READ IT AFTER SEEING YOUR REVIEW.
I'LL TRY TO READ IT AS QUICKLY AS POSSIBLE!
IT'S OKAY. I FORGOT I ALREADY HAD ONE AND BOUGHT A SECOND COPY, SO YOU CAN KEEP IT IF YOU WANT.
Oh, don't worry about that! The bedroom scene starts at page 297, by the way.
WHAAAT?! REALLY?! THANK YOU! ♡ I PROMISE I'LL MAKE IT UP TO YOU!
IT'S... IT'S NICE TO HAVE A FRIEND...
ほろり
EMOTIONAL

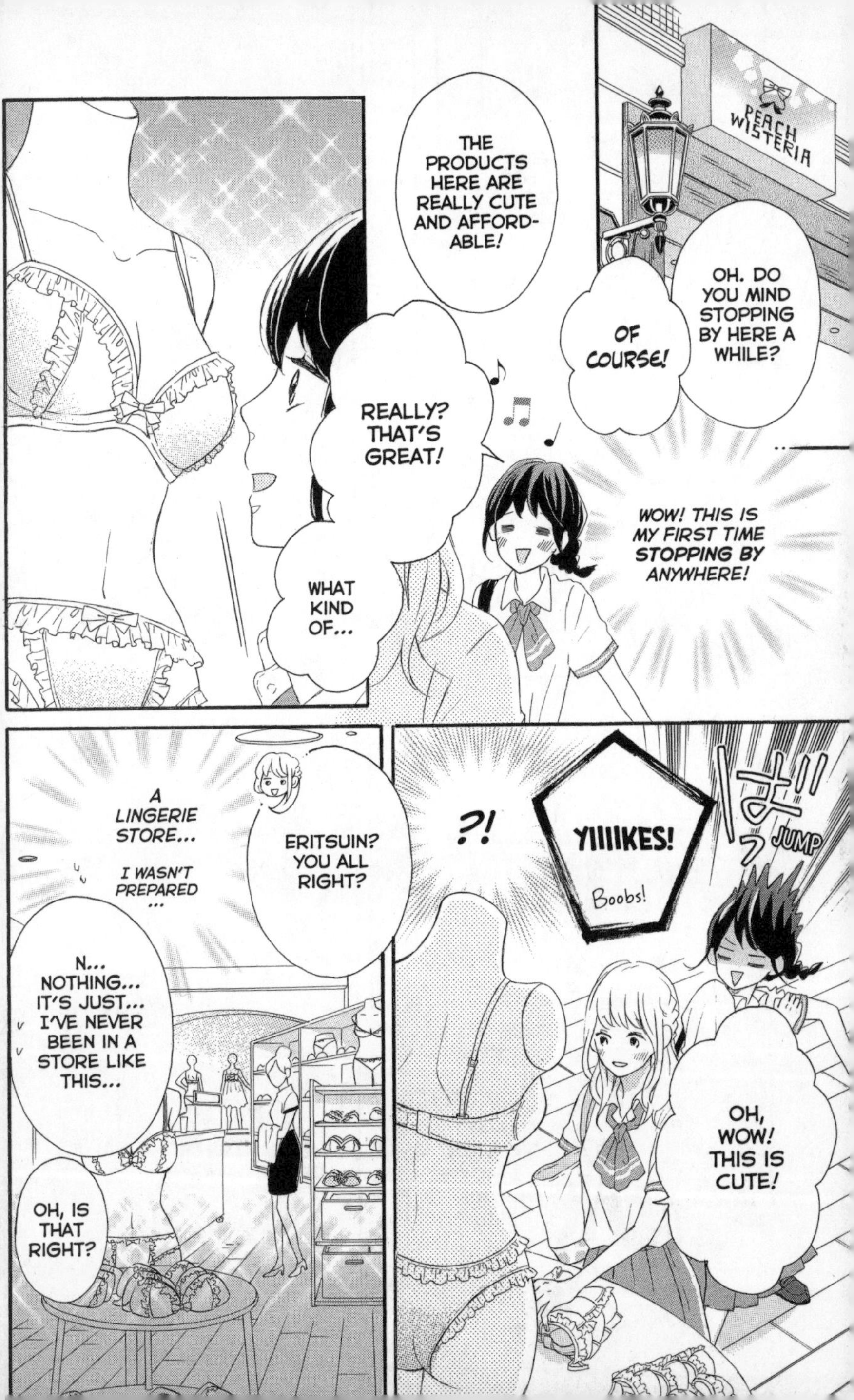
PEACH WISTERIA
OH. DO YOU MIND STOPPING BY HERE A WHILE?
OF COURSE!
...
WOW! THIS IS MY FIRST TIME STOPPING BY ANYWHERE!
THE PRODUCTS HERE ARE REALLY CUTE AND AFFORD-ABLE!
REALLY? THAT'S GREAT!
WHAT KIND OF...
はっ!!
JUMP
YIIIIKES!
Boobs!
?!
OH, WOW! THIS IS CUTE!
ERITSUIN? YOU ALL RIGHT?
A LINGERIE STORE...
I WASN'T PREPARED...
N... NOTHING... IT'S JUST... I'VE NEVER BEEN IN A STORE LIKE THIS...
OH, IS THAT RIGHT?

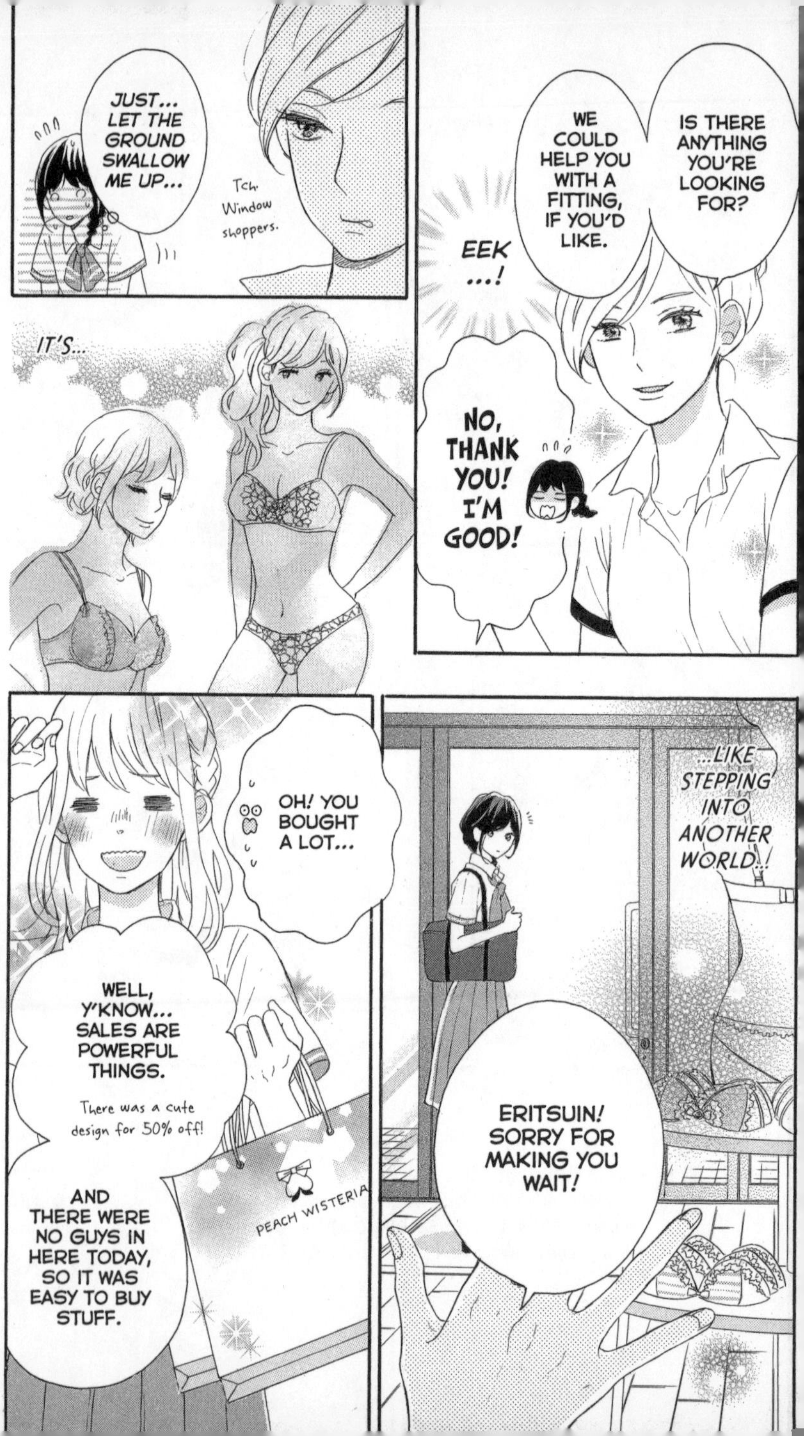
IS THERE ANYTHING YOU'RE LOOKING FOR?
WE COULD HELP YOU WITH A FITTING, IF YOU'D LIKE.
EEK ...!
NO, THANK YOU! I'M GOOD!
JUST... LET THE GROUND SWALLOW ME UP...
Tch. Window shoppers.
IT'S...
...LIKE STEPPING INTO ANOTHER WORLD..!
ERITSUIN! SORRY FOR MAKING YOU WAIT!
OH! YOU BOUGHT A LOT...
WELL, Y'KNOW... SALES ARE POWERFUL THINGS.
There was a cute design for 50% off!
AND THERE WERE NO GUYS IN HERE TODAY, SO IT WAS EASY TO BUY STUFF.
PEACH WISTERIA

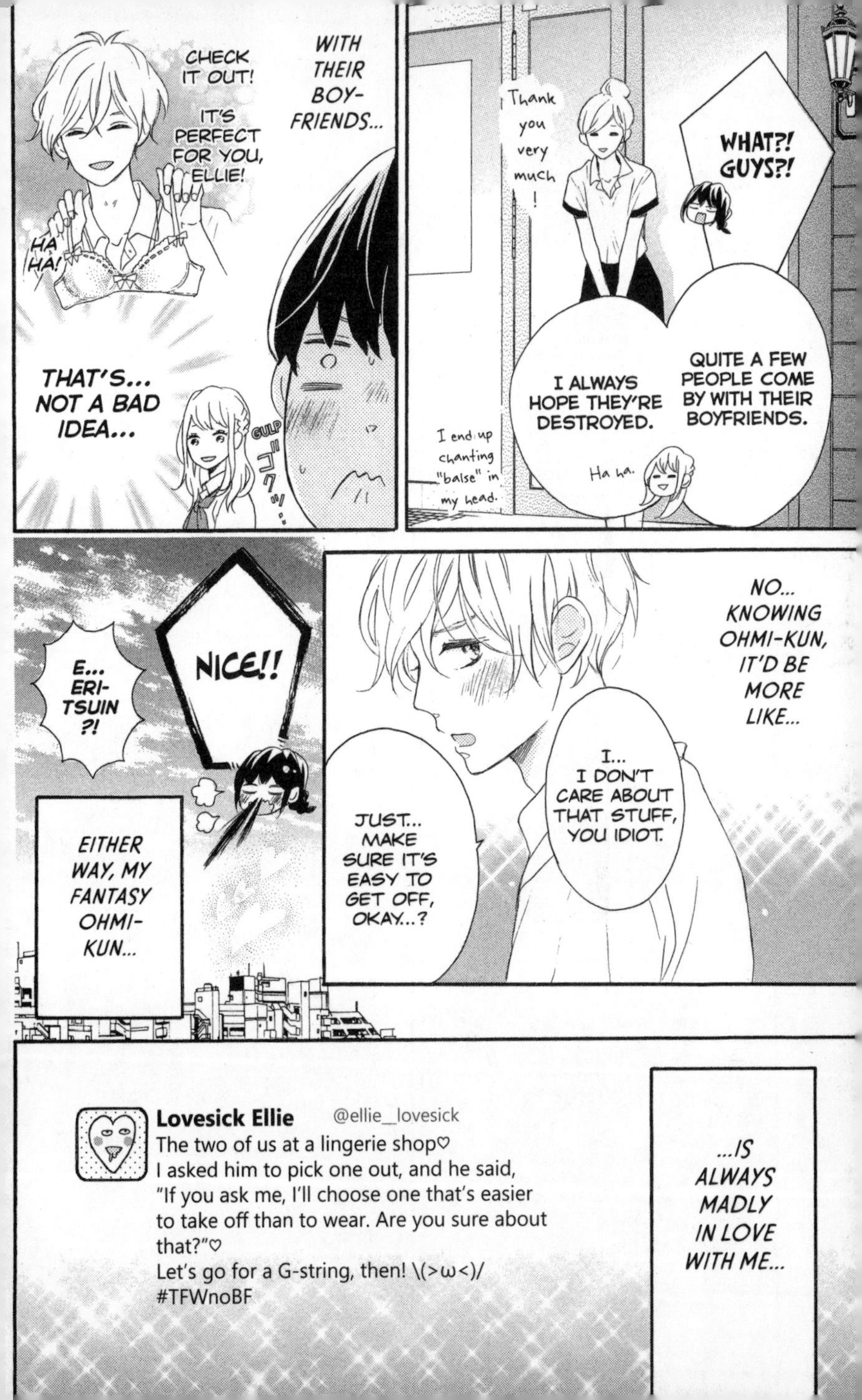
Thank you very much!
WHAT?! GUYS?!
QUITE A FEW PEOPLE COME BY WITH THEIR BOYFRIENDS.
I ALWAYS HOPE THEY'RE DESTROYED.
Ha ha.
I end up chanting "balse" in my head.
WITH THEIR BOYFRIENDS...
CHECK IT OUT!
IT'S PERFECT FOR YOU, ELLIE!
HA HA!
GULP
THAT'S... NOT A BAD IDEA...
NO... KNOWING OHMI-KUN, IT'D BE MORE LIKE...
I... I DON'T CARE ABOUT THAT STUFF, YOU IDIOT.
JUST... MAKE SURE IT'S EASY TO GET OFF, OKAY...?
NICE!!
E... ERI-TSUIN ?!
EITHER WAY, MY FANTASY OHMI-KUN...
...IS ALWAYS MADLY IN LOVE WITH ME...
Lovesick Ellie @ellie__lovesick
The two of us at a lingerie shop♡
I asked him to pick one out, and he said,
"If you ask me, I'll choose one that's easier to take off than to wear. Are you sure about that?"♡
Let's go for a G-string, then! \(>ω<)/
#TFWnoBF

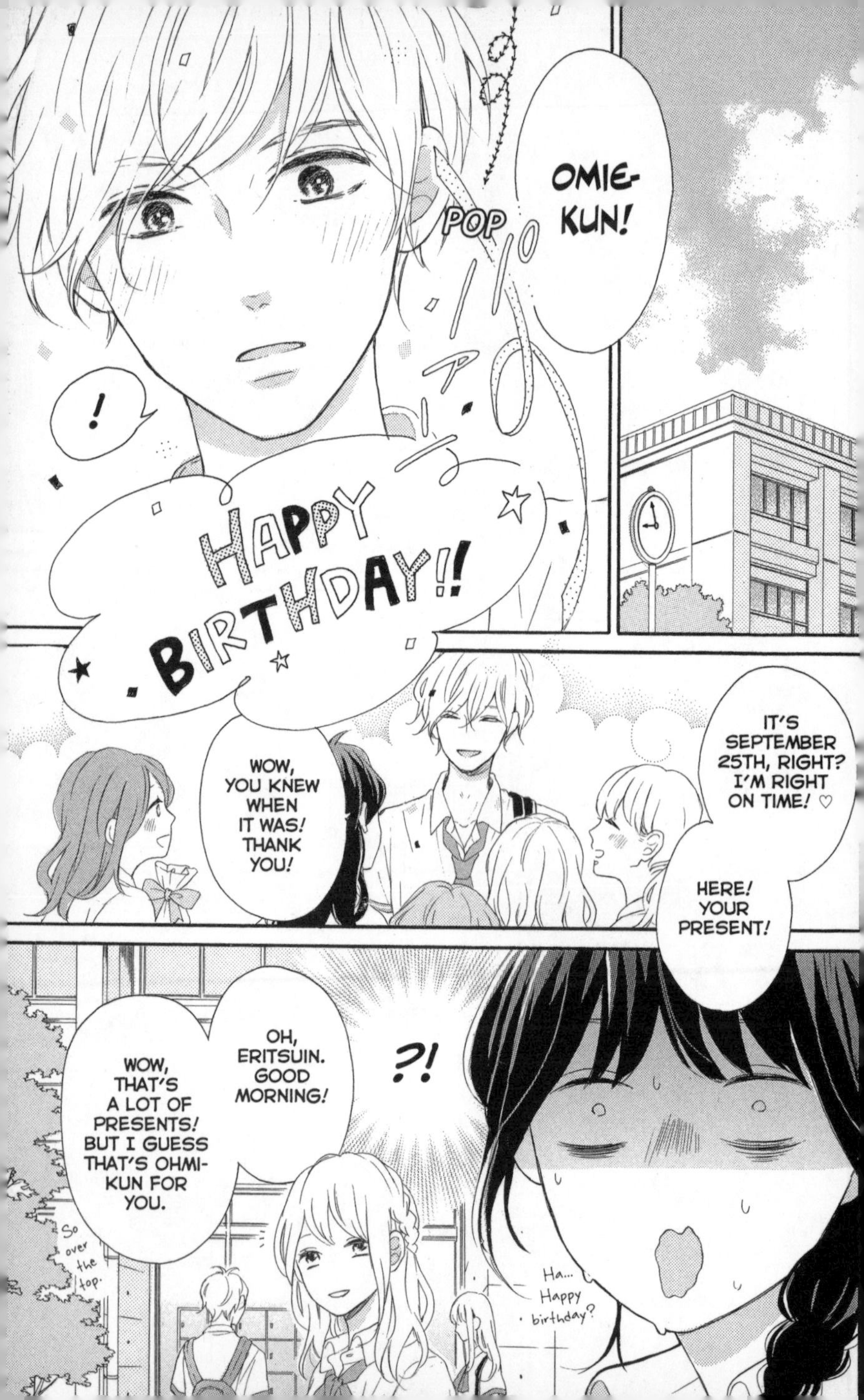
OMIE-KUN!
POP
!
HAPPY BIRTHDAY!!
IT'S SEPTEMBER 25TH, RIGHT? I'M RIGHT ON TIME! ♡
WOW, YOU KNEW WHEN IT WAS! THANK YOU!
HERE! YOUR PRESENT!
?!
Ha... Happy birthday?
OH, ERITSUIN. GOOD MORNING!
WOW, THAT'S A LOT OF PRESENTS! BUT I GUESS THAT'S OHMI-KUN FOR YOU.
So over the top.

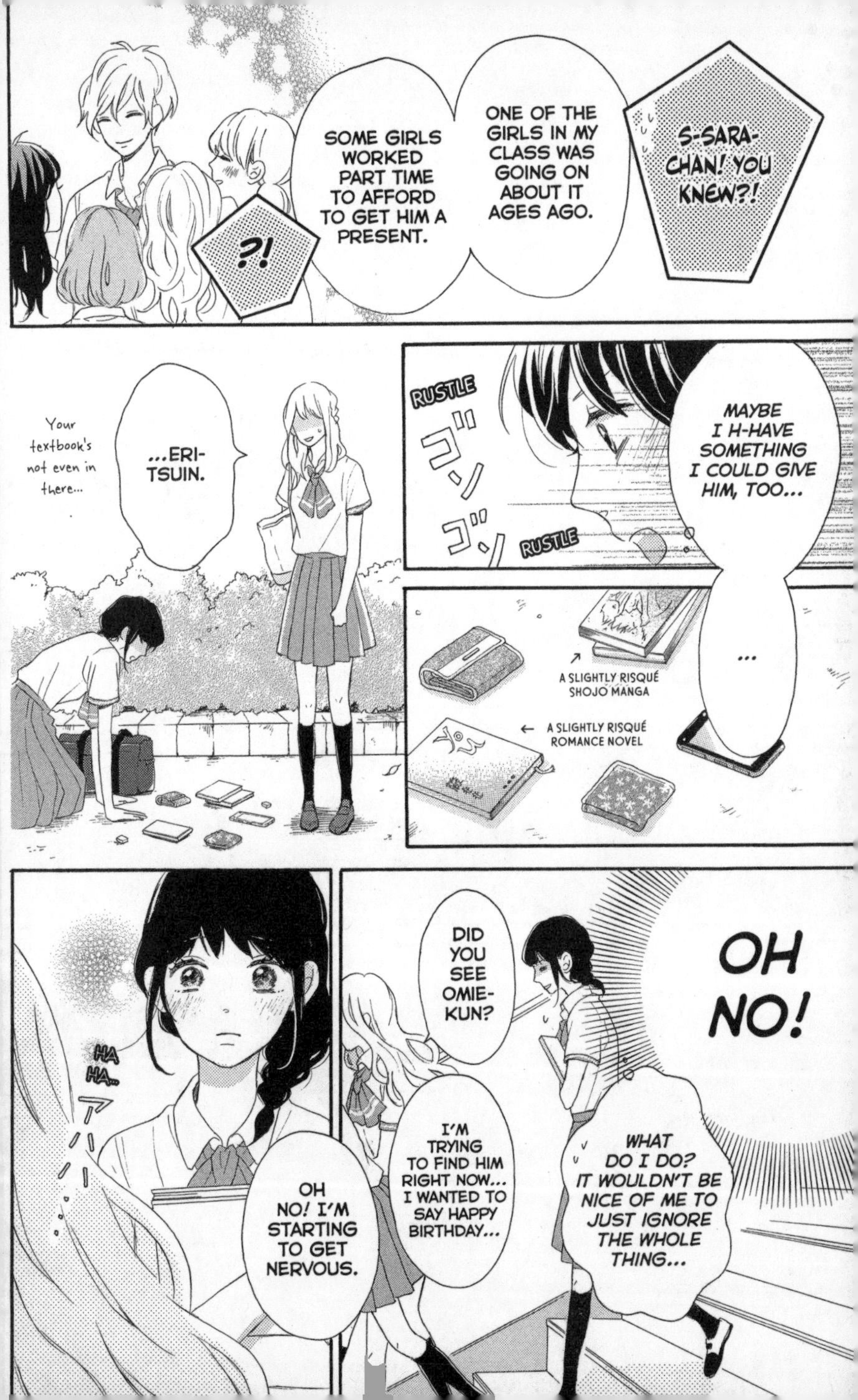
S-SARA-CHAN! YOU KNEW?!
ONE OF THE GIRLS IN MY CLASS WAS GOING ON ABOUT IT AGES AGO.
SOME GIRLS WORKED PART TIME TO AFFORD TO GET HIM A PRESENT.
?!
MAYBE I H-HAVE SOMETHING I COULD GIVE HIM, TOO...
RUSTLE
ゴソゴソ
RUSTLE
...
A SLIGHTLY RISQUÉ SHOJO MANGA
A SLIGHTLY RISQUÉ ROMANCE NOVEL
...ERI-TSUIN.
Your textbook's not even in there...
OH NO!
DID YOU SEE OMIE-KUN?
WHAT DO I DO? IT WOULDN'T BE NICE OF ME TO JUST IGNORE THE WHOLE THING...
I'M TRYING TO FIND HIM RIGHT NOW... I WANTED TO SAY HAPPY BIRTHDAY...
OH NO! I'M STARTING TO GET NERVOUS.
HA HA...

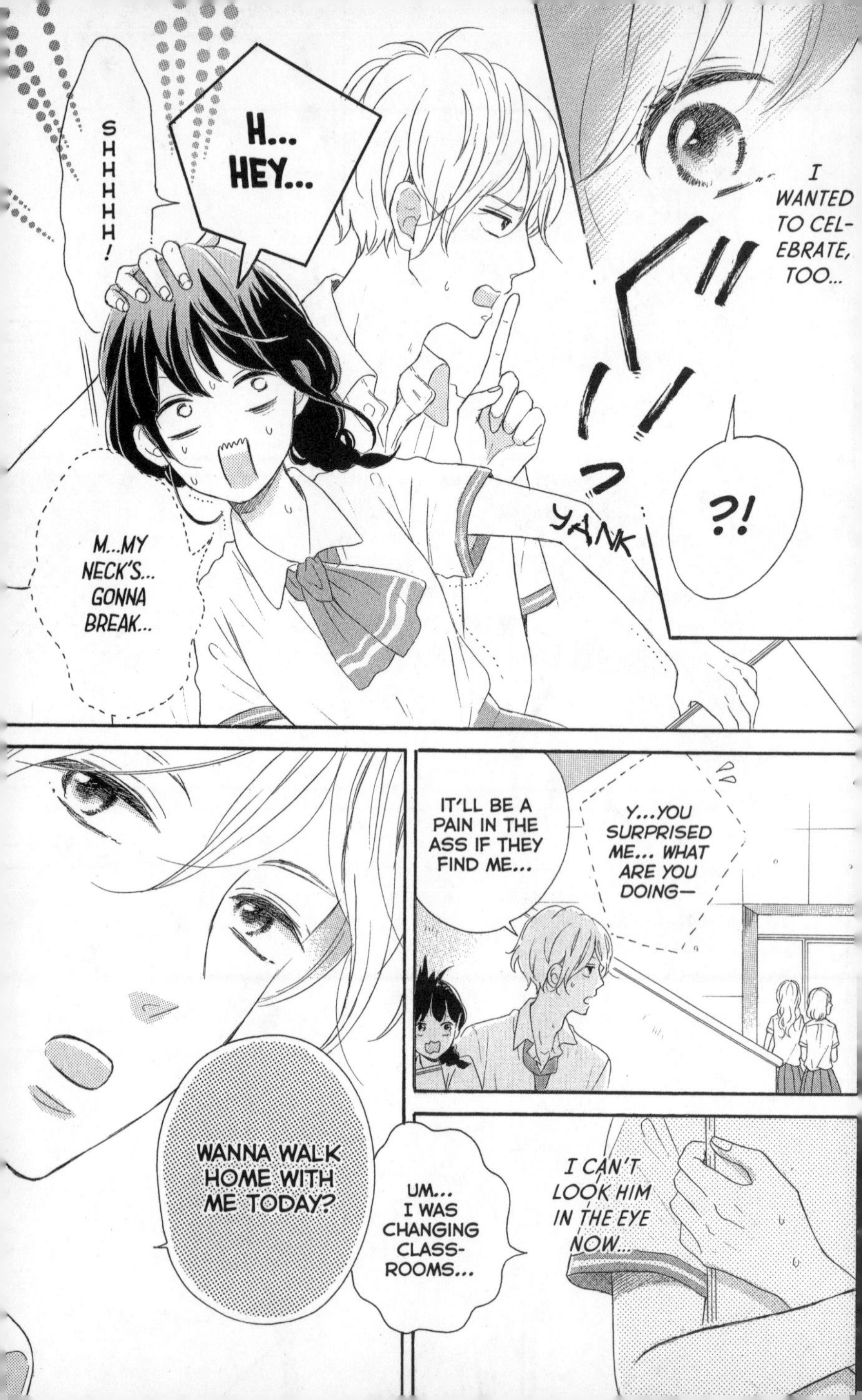
I WANTED TO CELEBRATE, TOO...
?!
YANK
H... HEY...
SHHHHHH!
M...MY NECK'S... GONNA BREAK...
Y...YOU SURPRISED ME... WHAT ARE YOU DOING—
IT'LL BE A PAIN IN THE ASS IF THEY FIND ME...
I CAN'T LOOK HIM IN THE EYE NOW...
UM... I WAS CHANGING CLASS-ROOMS...
WANNA WALK HOME WITH ME TODAY?

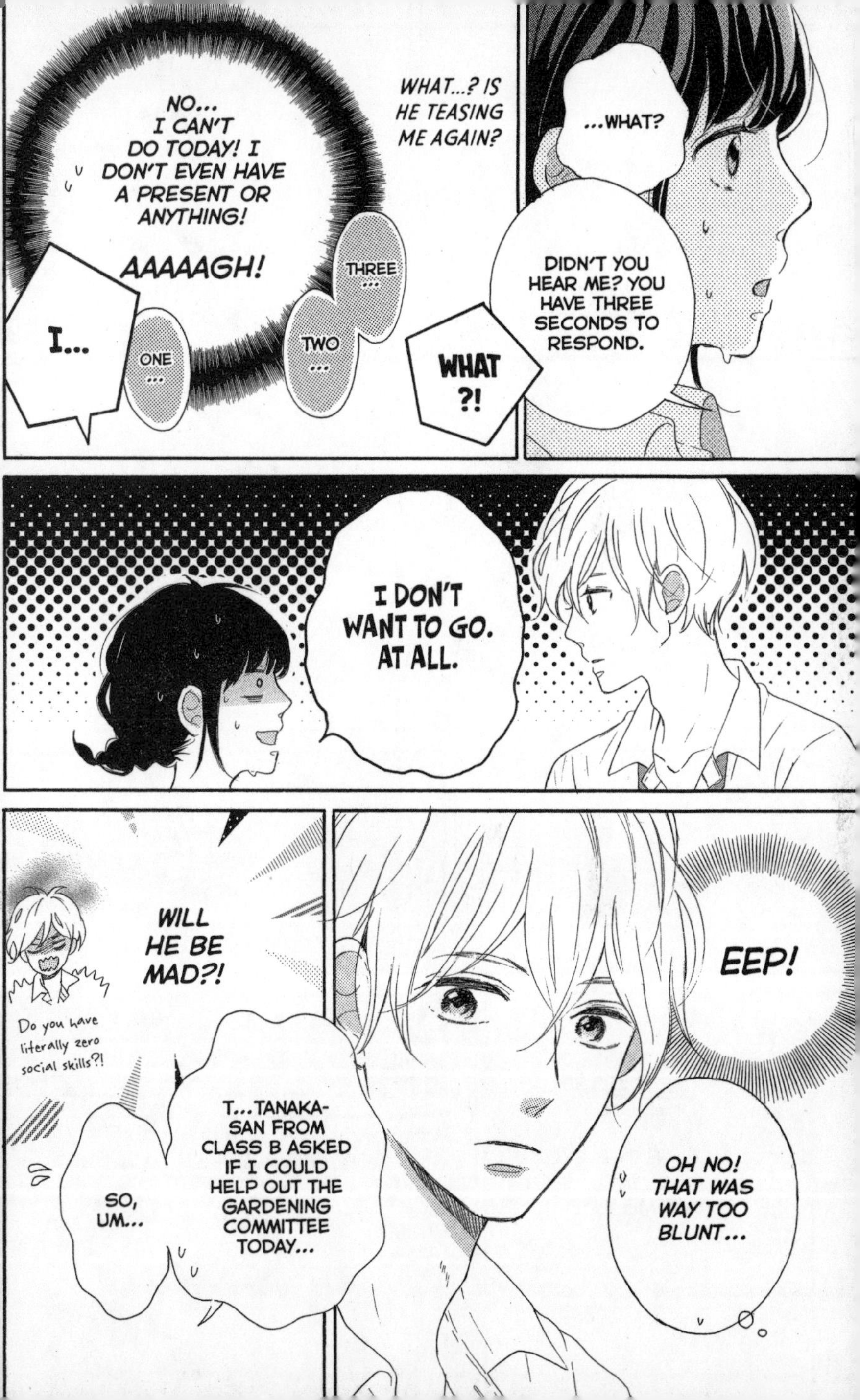
...WHAT?
DIDN'T YOU HEAR ME? YOU HAVE THREE SECONDS TO RESPOND.
WHAT...? IS HE TEASING ME AGAIN?
WHAT ?!
NO... I CAN'T DO TODAY! I DON'T EVEN HAVE A PRESENT OR ANYTHING!
AAAAAGH!
THREE...
TWO...
ONE...
I...
I DON'T WANT TO GO. AT ALL.
EEP!
OH NO! THAT WAS WAY TOO BLUNT...
WILL HE BE MAD?!
T...TANAKA-SAN FROM CLASS B ASKED IF I COULD HELP OUT THE GARDENING COMMITTEE TODAY...
SO, UM...
Do you have literally zero social skills?!

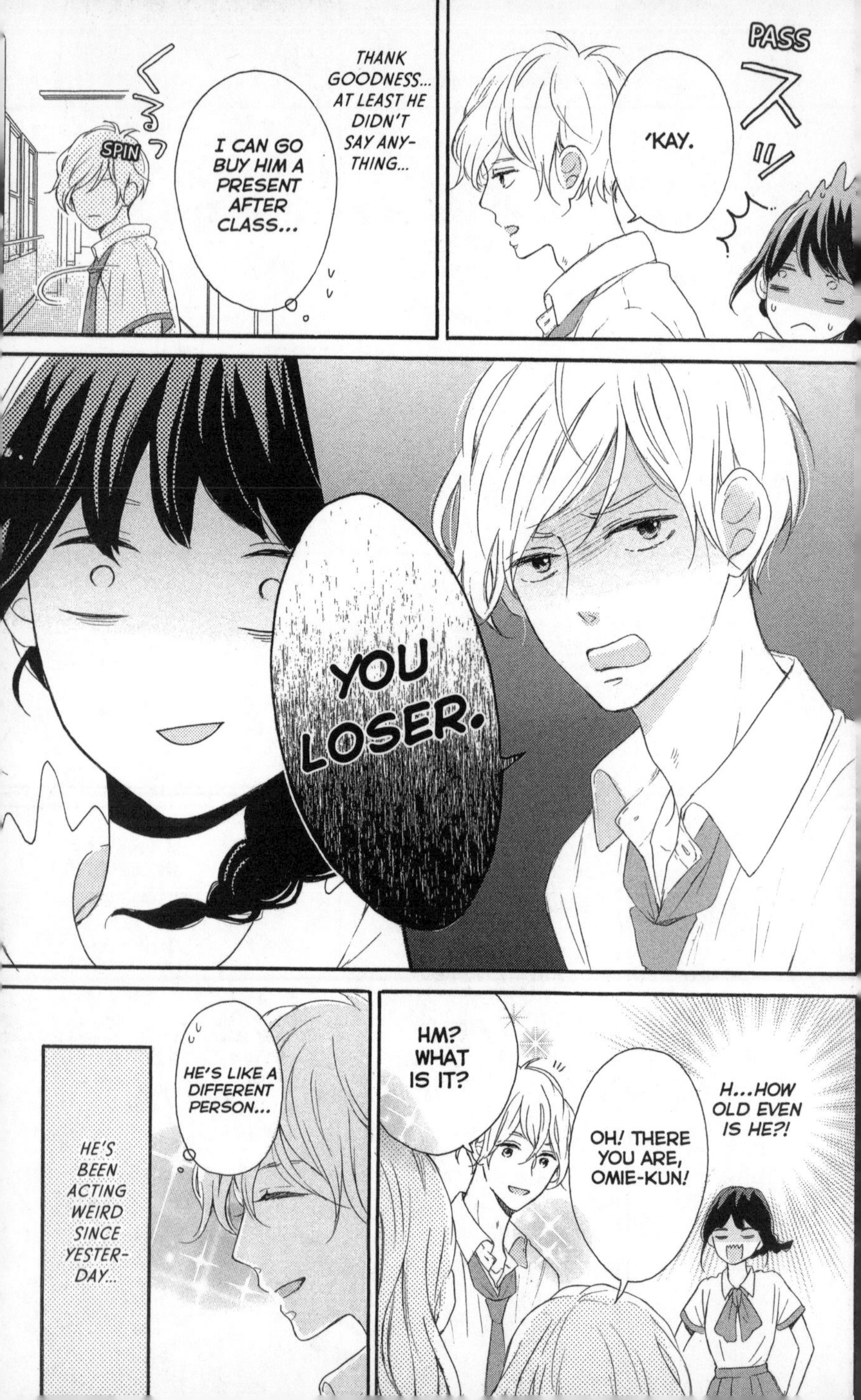
PASS
'KAY.
THANK GOODNESS... AT LEAST HE DIDN'T SAY ANYTHING...
I CAN GO BUY HIM A PRESENT AFTER CLASS...
SPIN
YOU LOSER.
H...HOW OLD EVEN IS HE?!
HM? WHAT IS IT?
OH! THERE YOU ARE, OMIE-KUN!
HE'S LIKE A DIFFERENT PERSON...
HE'S BEEN ACTING WEIRD SINCE YESTERDAY...

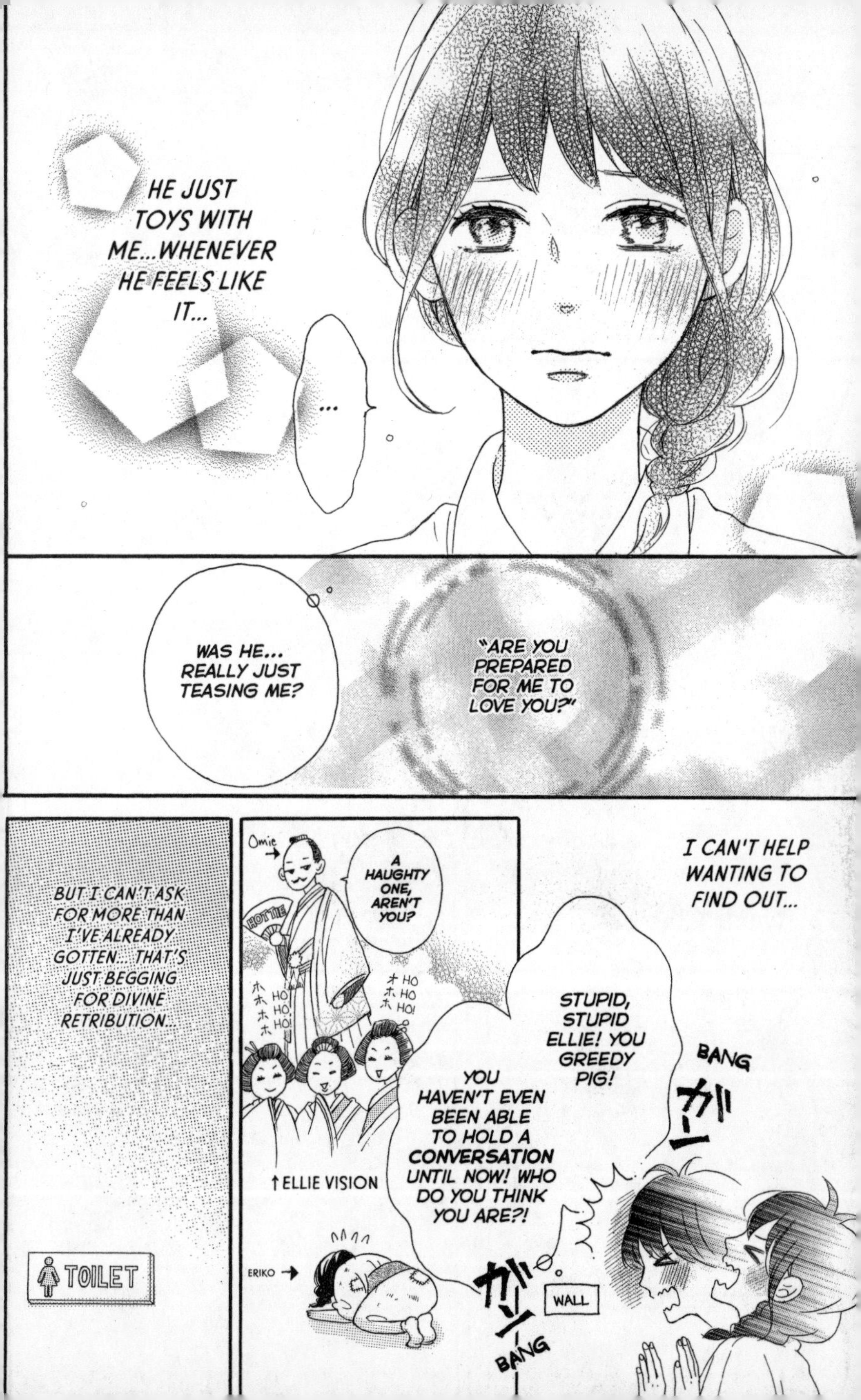

HE JUST TOYS WITH ME...WHENEVER HE FEELS LIKE IT...
...
"ARE YOU PREPARED FOR ME TO LOVE YOU?"
WAS HE... REALLY JUST TEASING ME?
I CAN'T HELP WANTING TO FIND OUT...
STUPID, STUPID ELLIE! YOU GREEDY PIG!
BANG
YOU HAVEN'T EVEN BEEN ABLE TO HOLD A CONVERSATION UNTIL NOW! WHO DO YOU THINK YOU ARE?!
WALL
BANG
Omie
A HAUGHTY ONE, AREN'T YOU?
HOTTIE
HO HO HO!
HO HO HO!
↑ELLIE VISION
ERIKO
BUT I CAN'T ASK FOR MORE THAN I'VE ALREADY GOTTEN... THAT'S JUST BEGGING FOR DIVINE RETRIBUTION...
TOILET

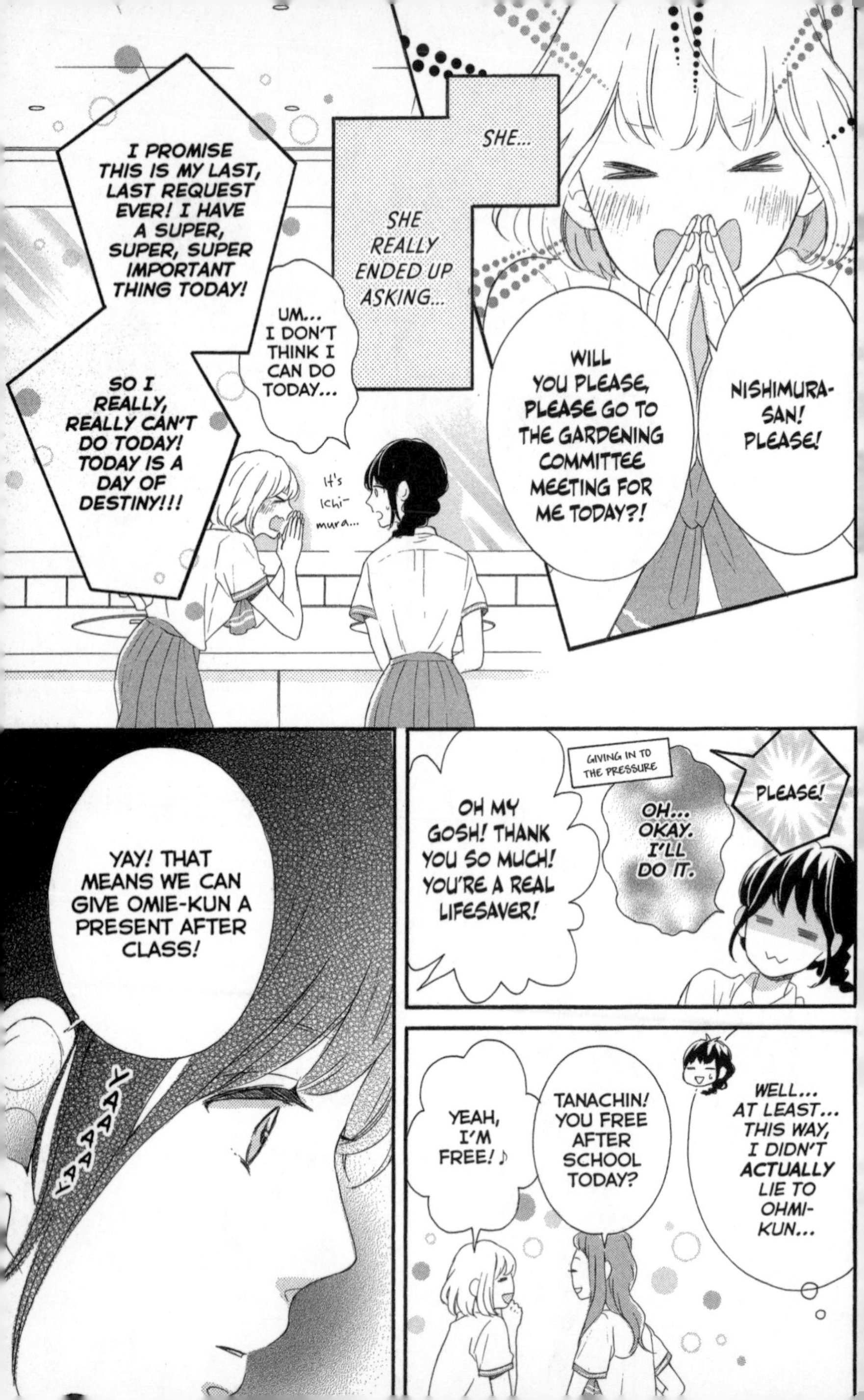
NISHIMURA-SAN! PLEASE!
WILL YOU PLEASE, PLEASE GO TO THE GARDENING COMMITTEE MEETING FOR ME TODAY?!
SHE...
SHE REALLY ENDED UP ASKING...
I PROMISE THIS IS MY LAST, LAST REQUEST EVER! I HAVE A SUPER, SUPER, SUPER IMPORTANT THING TODAY!
UM... I DON'T THINK I CAN DO TODAY...
It's Ichi-mura...
SO I REALLY, REALLY CAN'T DO TODAY! TODAY IS A DAY OF DESTINY!!!
PLEASE!
GIVING IN TO THE PRESSURE
OH... OKAY. I'LL DO IT.
OH MY GOSH! THANK YOU SO MUCH! YOU'RE A REAL LIFESAVER!
WELL... AT LEAST... THIS WAY, I DIDN'T ACTUALLY LIE TO OHMI-KUN...
TANACHIN! YOU FREE AFTER SCHOOL TODAY?
YEAH, I'M FREE! ♪
YAY! THAT MEANS WE CAN GIVE OMIE-KUN A PRESENT AFTER CLASS!
YAAAAAY

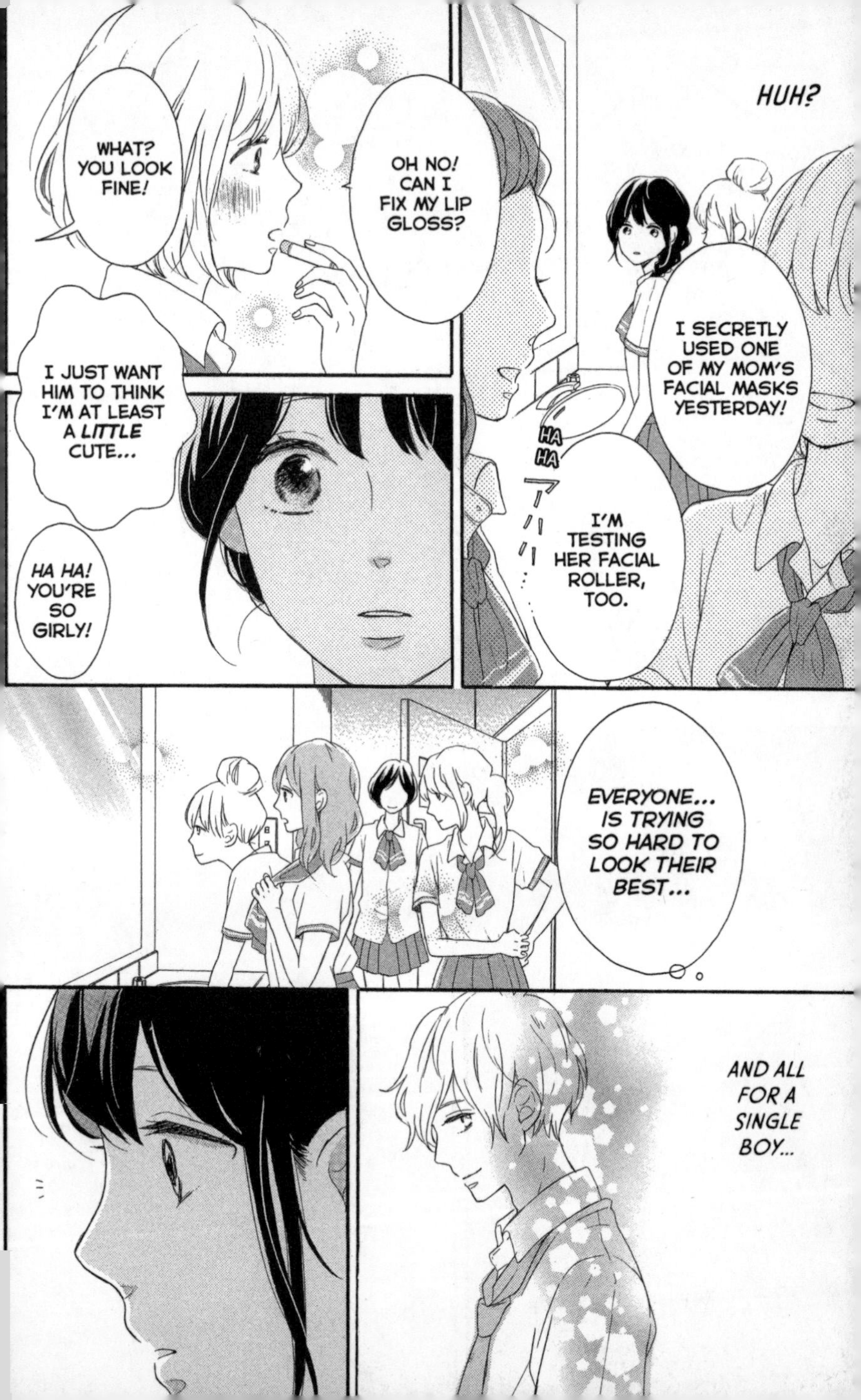

HUH?
I SECRETLY USED ONE OF MY MOM'S FACIAL MASKS YESTERDAY!
HA HA
I'M TESTING HER FACIAL ROLLER, TOO.
OH NO! CAN I FIX MY LIP GLOSS?
WHAT? YOU LOOK FINE!
I JUST WANT HIM TO THINK I'M AT LEAST A *LITTLE* CUTE...
HA HA! YOU'RE SO GIRLY!
EVERYONE... IS TRYING SO HARD TO LOOK THEIR BEST...
AND ALL FOR A SINGLE BOY...

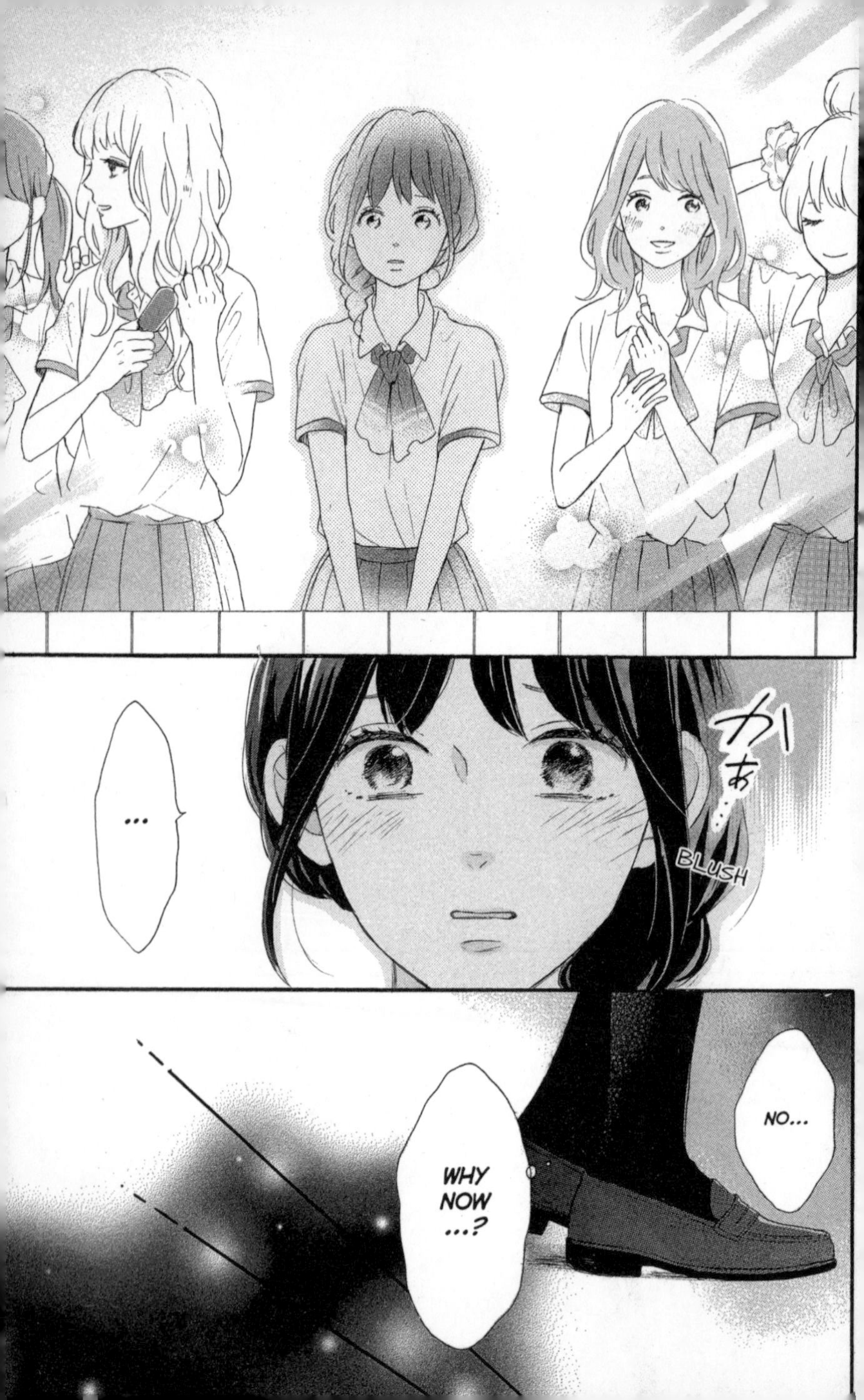
...
かぁ…
BLUSH
NO...
WHY NOW ...?

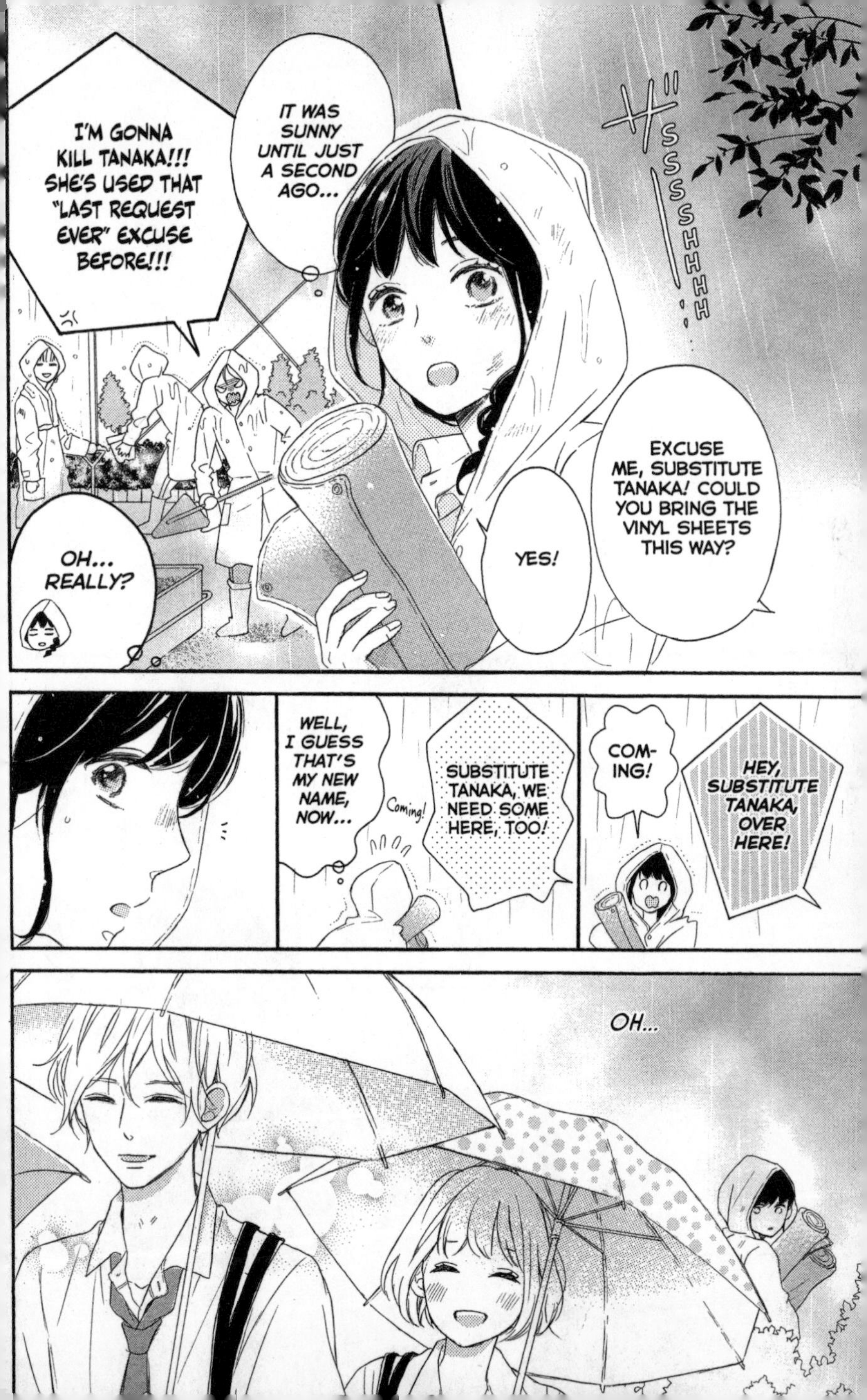
SSSSHHHHH
IT WAS SUNNY UNTIL JUST A SECOND AGO...
I'M GONNA KILL TANAKA!!! SHE'S USED THAT "LAST REQUEST EVER" EXCUSE BEFORE!!!
OH... REALLY?
EXCUSE ME, SUBSTITUTE TANAKA! COULD YOU BRING THE VINYL SHEETS THIS WAY?
YES!
HEY, SUBSTITUTE TANAKA, OVER HERE!
COM-ING!
SUBSTITUTE TANAKA, WE NEED SOME HERE, TOO!
Coming!
WELL, I GUESS THAT'S MY NEW NAME, NOW...
OH...

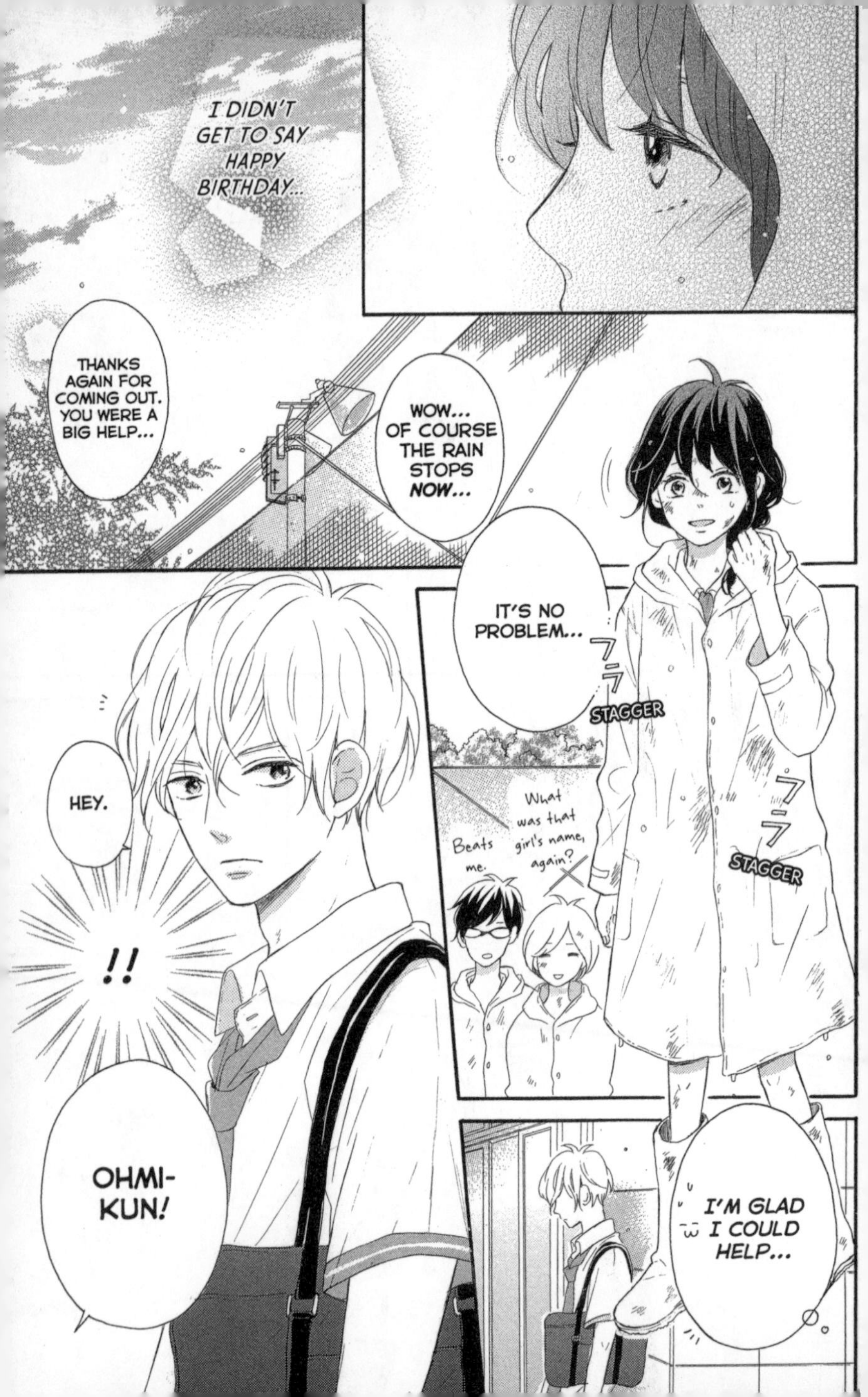

I DIDN'T GET TO SAY HAPPY BIRTHDAY...
WOW... OF COURSE THE RAIN STOPS NOW...
THANKS AGAIN FOR COMING OUT. YOU WERE A BIG HELP...
IT'S NO PROBLEM...
STAGGER
What was that girl's name, again?
Beats me.
STAGGER
I'M GLAD I COULD HELP...
HEY.
!!
OHMI-KUN!

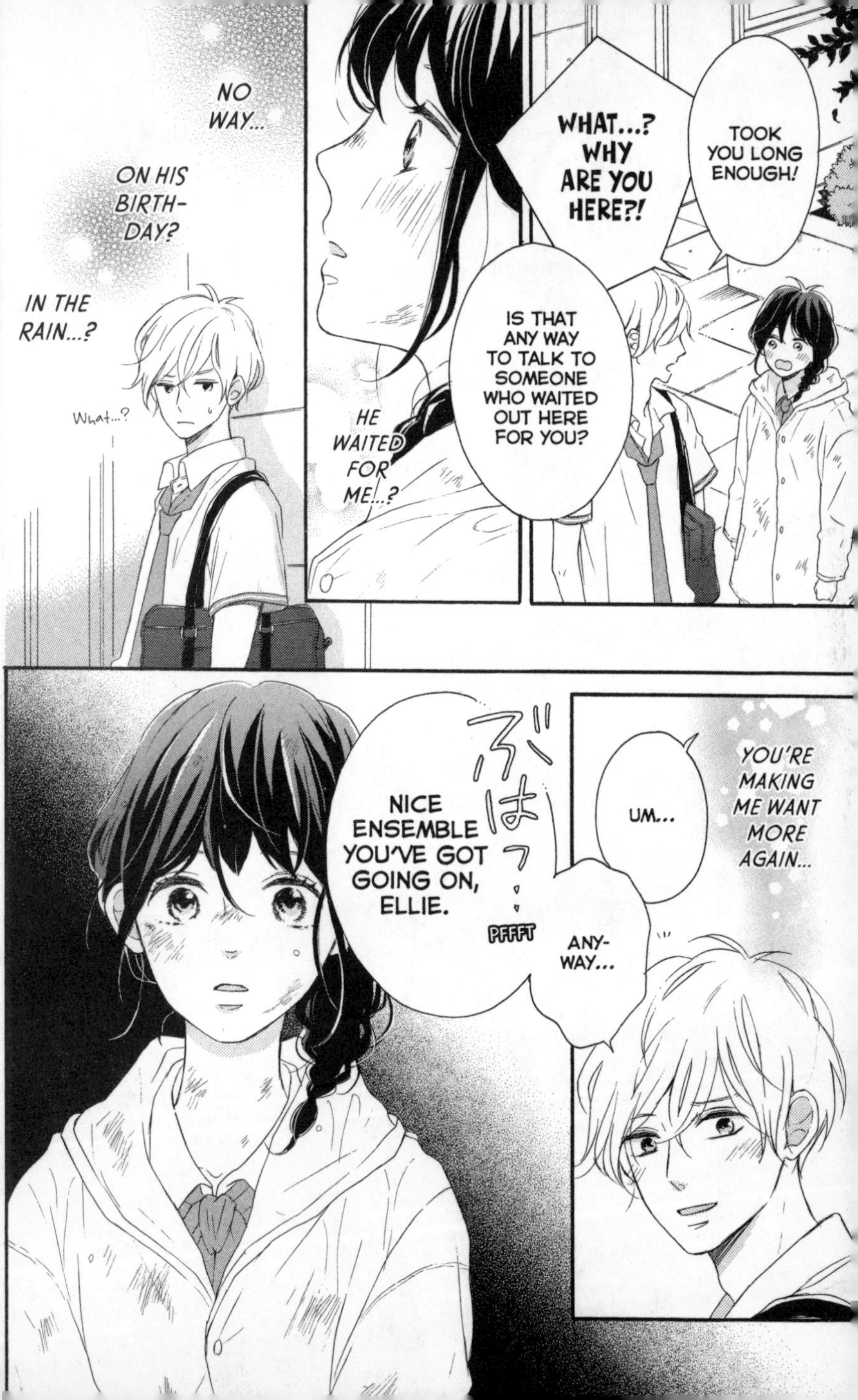
TOOK YOU LONG ENOUGH!
WHAT...? WHY ARE YOU HERE?!
IS THAT ANY WAY TO TALK TO SOMEONE WHO WAITED OUT HERE FOR YOU?
HE WAITED FOR ME...?
NO WAY...
ON HIS BIRTH-DAY?
IN THE RAIN...?
What...?
YOU'RE MAKING ME WANT MORE AGAIN...
UM...
ぶはっ
PFFFT
NICE ENSEMBLE YOU'VE GOT GOING ON, ELLIE.
ANY-WAY...

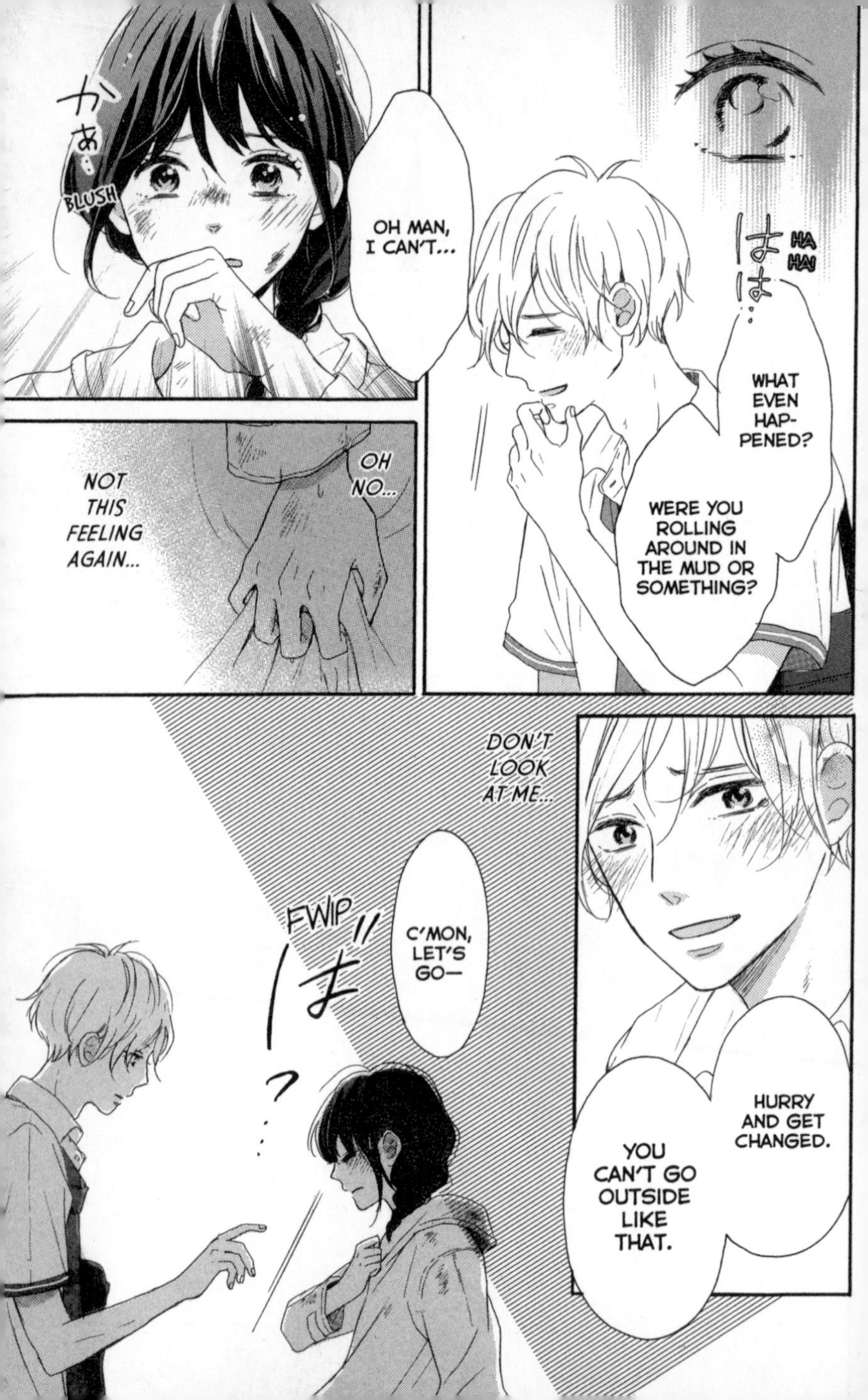
はは…
HA HA
OH MAN, I CAN'T...
WHAT EVEN HAP-PENED?
WERE YOU ROLLING AROUND IN THE MUD OR SOMETHING?
かぁ…
BLUSH
OH NO...
NOT THIS FEELING AGAIN...
DON'T LOOK AT ME...
HURRY AND GET CHANGED.
YOU CAN'T GO OUTSIDE LIKE THAT.
C'MON, LET'S GO—
はっ!!
FWIP
?…

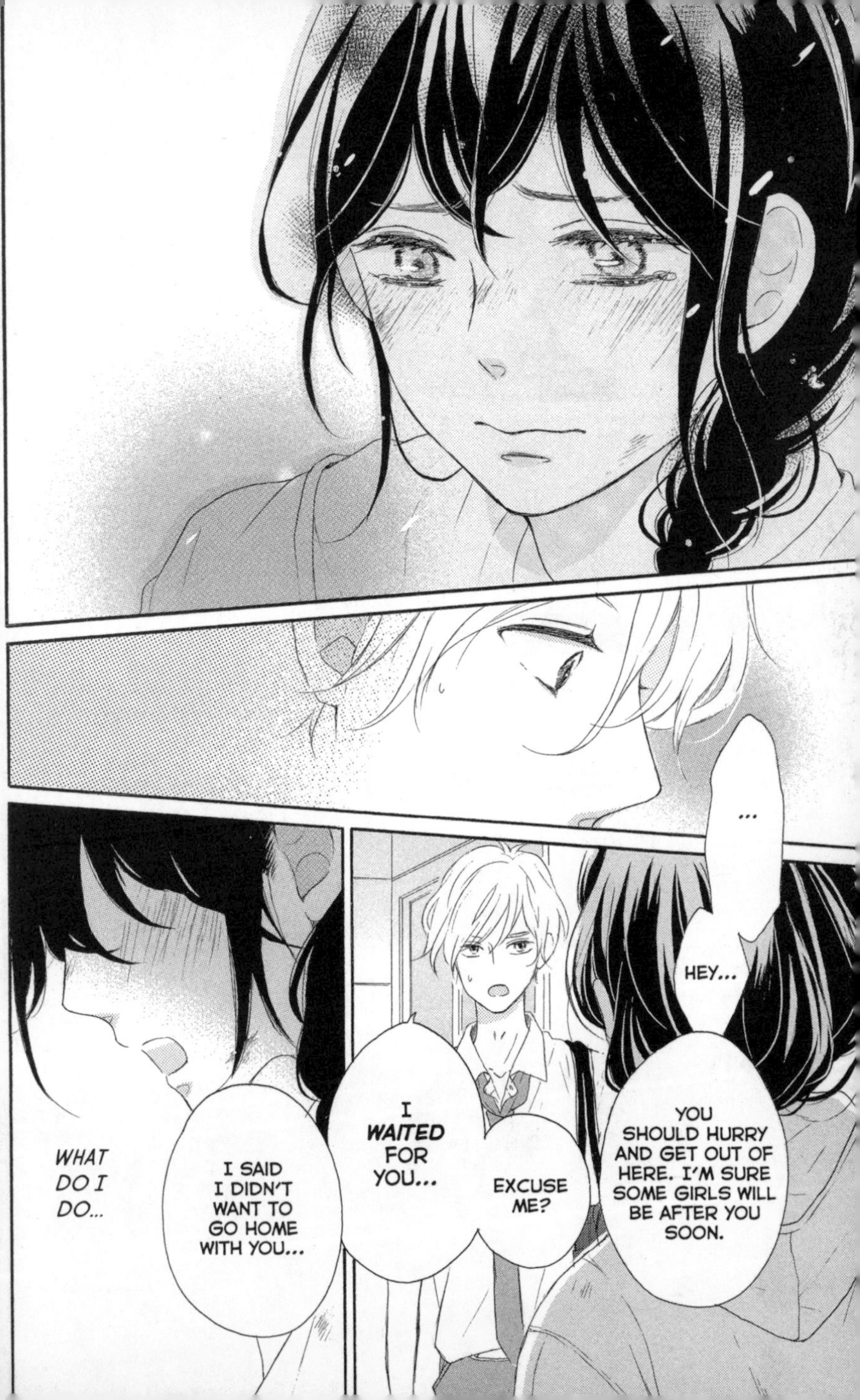
...
HEY...
YOU SHOULD HURRY AND GET OUT OF HERE. I'M SURE SOME GIRLS WILL BE AFTER YOU SOON.
EXCUSE ME?
I *WAITED* FOR YOU...
I SAID I DIDN'T WANT TO GO HOME WITH YOU...
WHAT DO I DO...

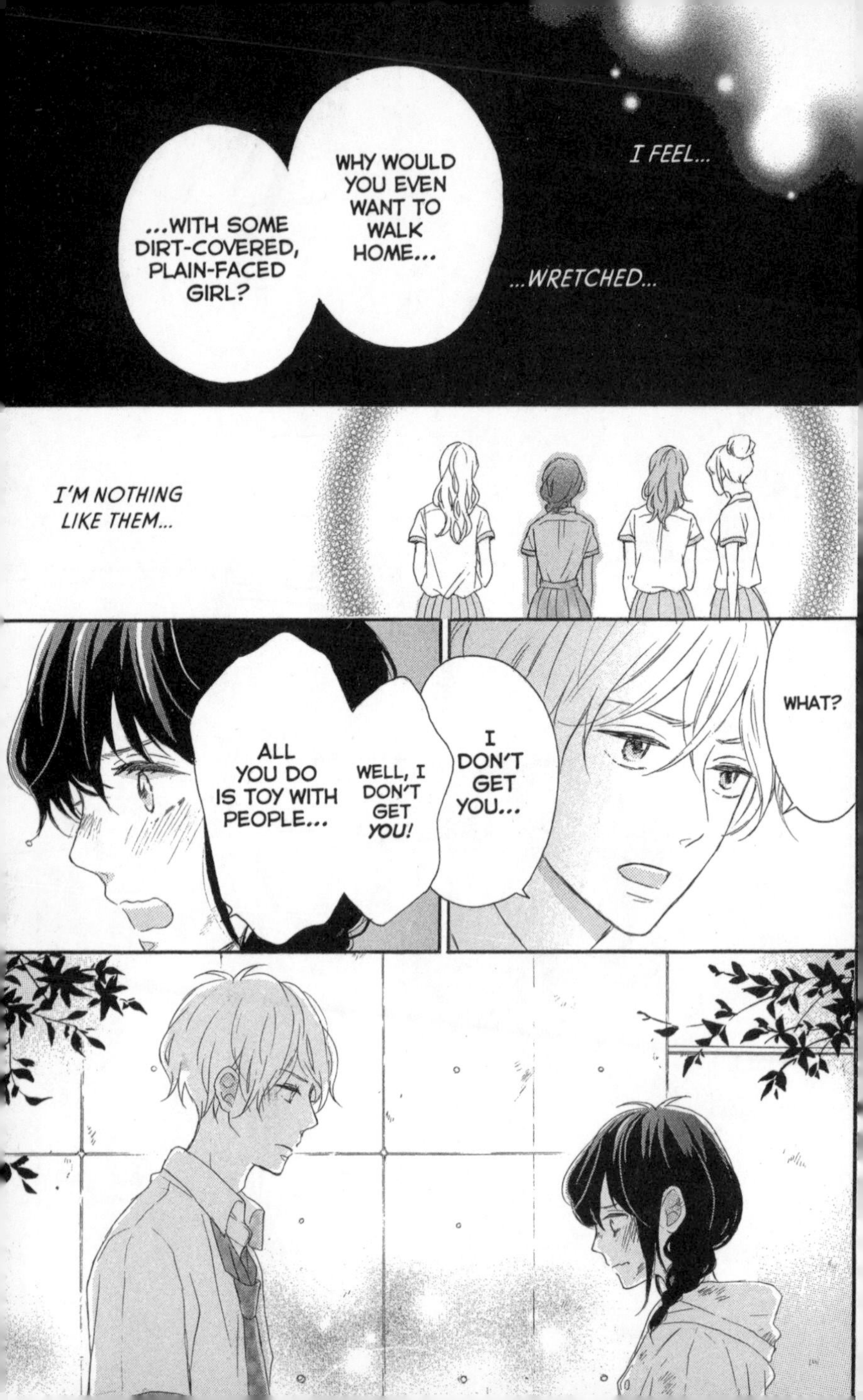
I FEEL...
WHY WOULD YOU EVEN WANT TO WALK HOME...
...WITH SOME DIRT-COVERED, PLAIN-FACED GIRL?
...WRETCHED...
I'M NOTHING LIKE THEM...
WHAT?
I DON'T GET YOU...
WELL, I DON'T GET *YOU!*
ALL YOU DO IS TOY WITH PEOPLE...

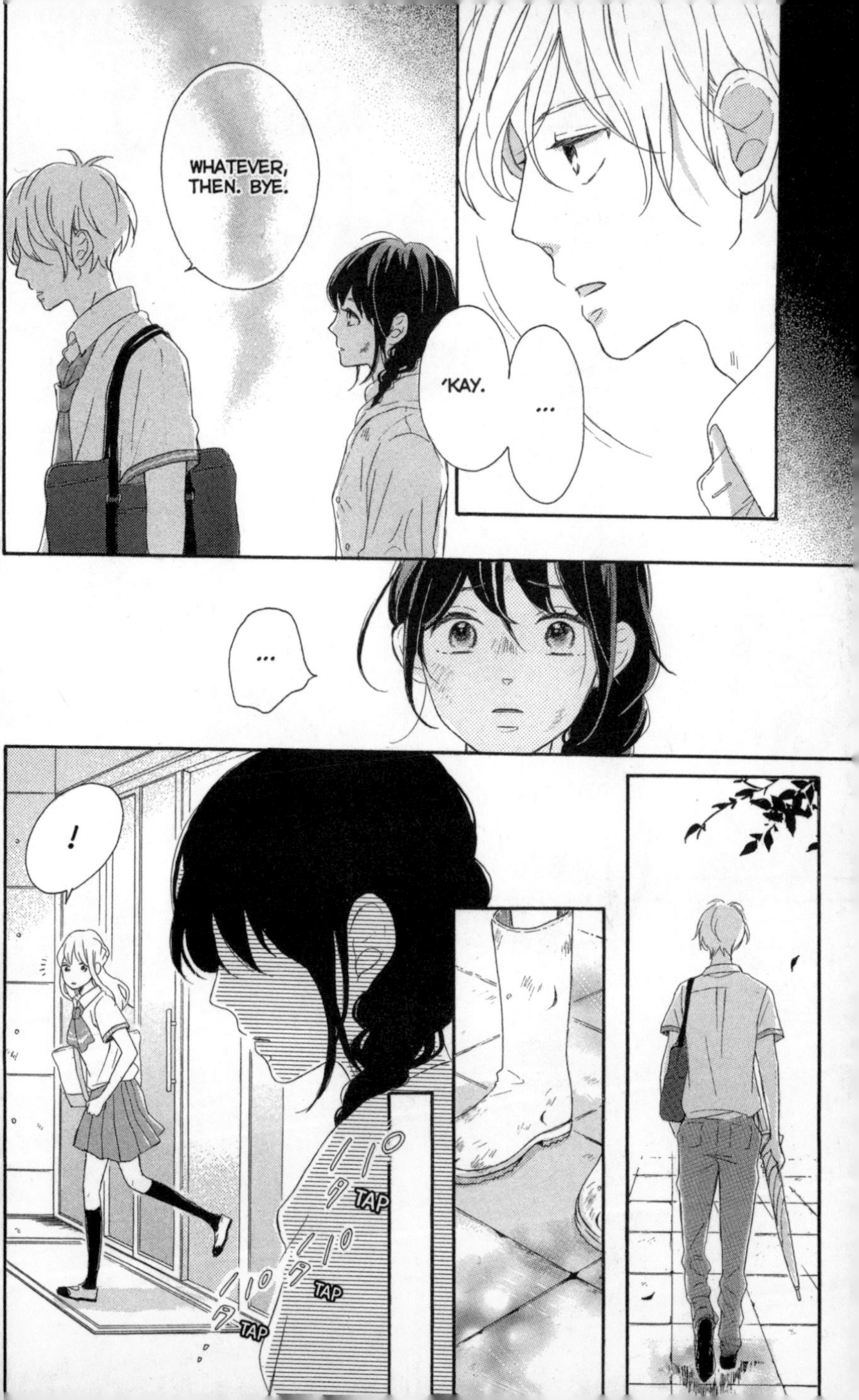
...
'KAY.
WHATEVER, THEN. BYE.
...
TAP
TAP
TAP
!

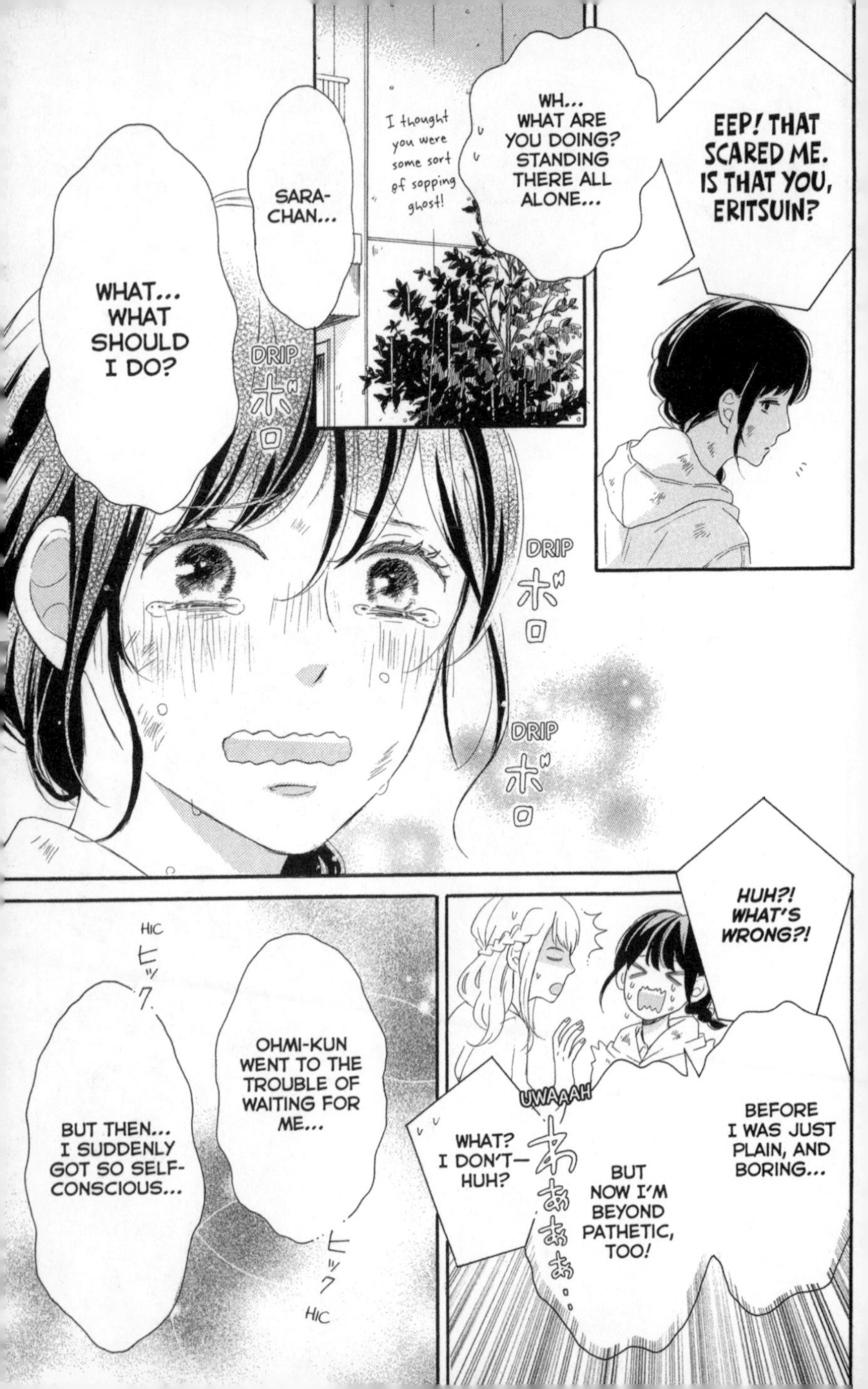
EEP! THAT SCARED ME. IS THAT YOU, ERITSUIN?
WH... WHAT ARE YOU DOING? STANDING THERE ALL ALONE...
I thought you were some sort of sopping ghost!
SARA-CHAN...
WHAT... WHAT SHOULD I DO?
DRIP ポロ
DRIP ポロ
DRIP ポロ
HUH?! WHAT'S WRONG?!
BEFORE I WAS JUST PLAIN, AND BORING...
BUT NOW I'M BEYOND PATHETIC, TOO!
UWAAAH あああ。
WHAT? I DON'T— HUH?
HIC ヒック
OHMI-KUN WENT TO THE TROUBLE OF WAITING FOR ME...
BUT THEN... I SUDDENLY GOT SO SELF-CONSCIOUS...
HIC ヒック

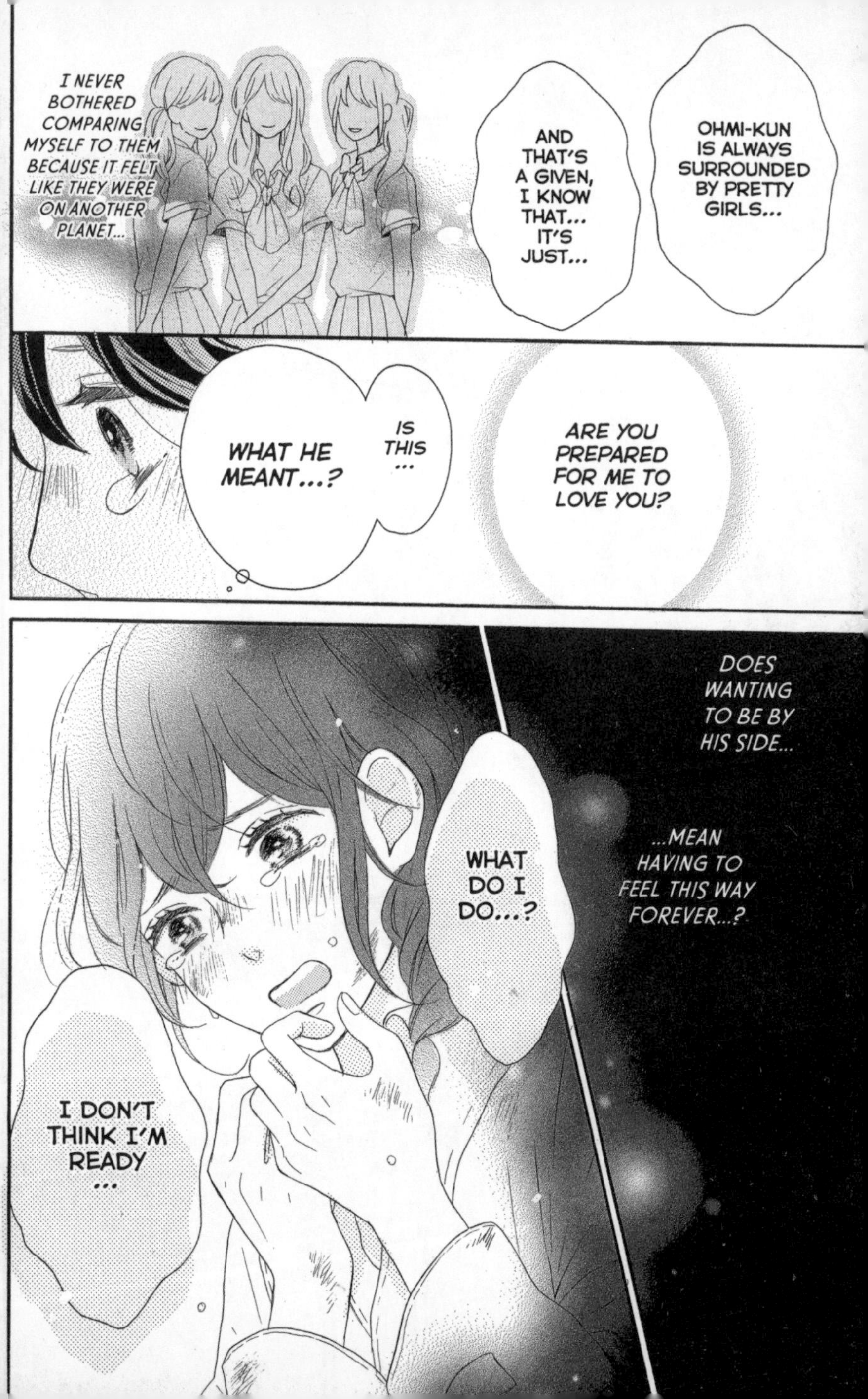
OHMI-KUN IS ALWAYS SURROUNDED BY PRETTY GIRLS...
AND THAT'S A GIVEN, I KNOW THAT... IT'S JUST...
I NEVER BOTHERED COMPARING MYSELF TO THEM BECAUSE IT FELT LIKE THEY WERE ON ANOTHER PLANET...
ARE YOU PREPARED FOR ME TO LOVE YOU?
IS THIS ...
WHAT HE MEANT...?
DOES WANTING TO BE BY HIS SIDE...
...MEAN HAVING TO FEEL THIS WAY FOREVER...?
WHAT DO I DO...?
I DON'T THINK I'M READY ...

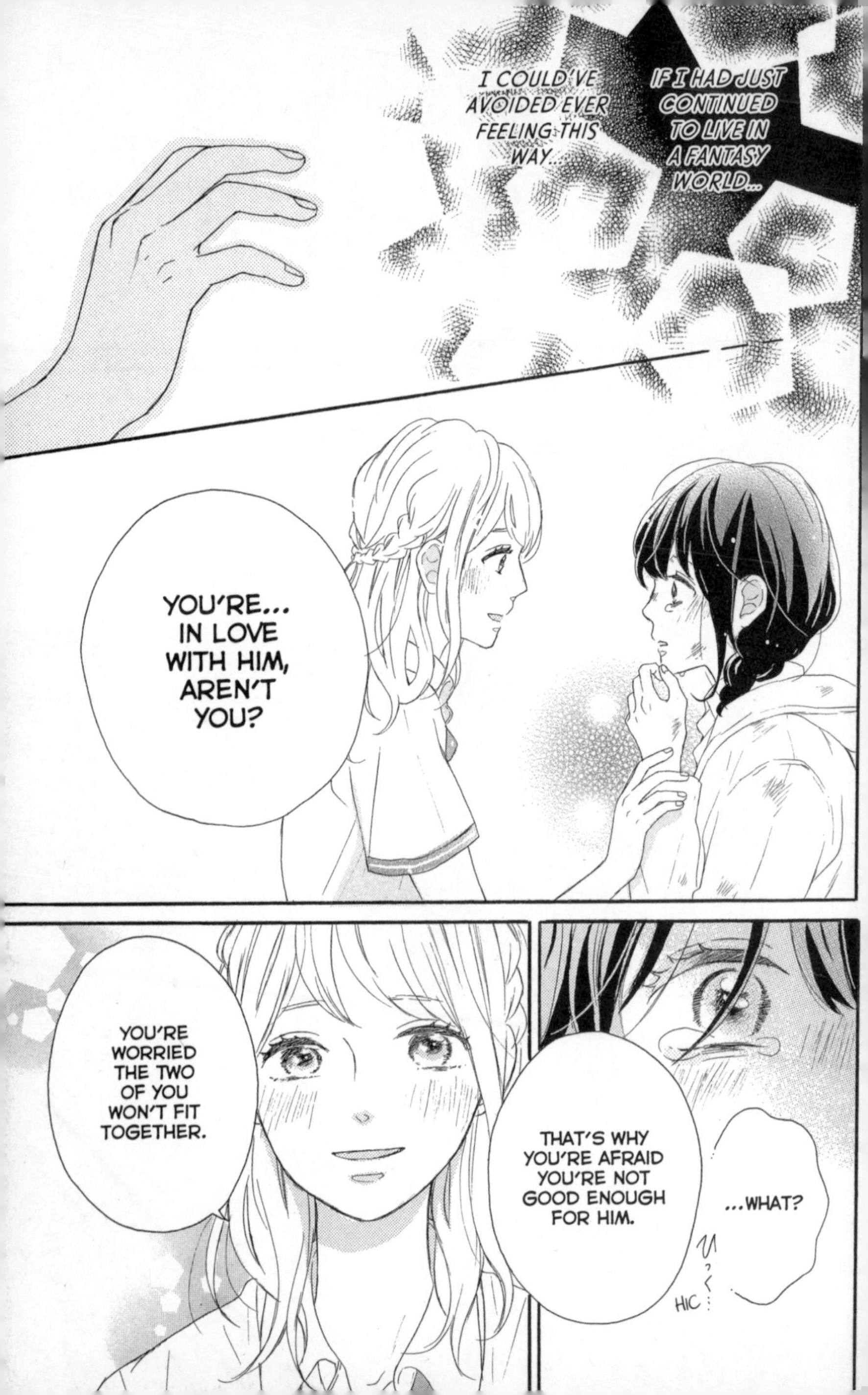
IF I HAD JUST CONTINUED TO LIVE IN A FANTASY WORLD...
I COULD'VE AVOIDED EVER FEELING THIS WAY...
YOU'RE... IN LOVE WITH HIM, AREN'T YOU?
...WHAT?
HIC
YOU'RE WORRIED THE TWO OF YOU WON'T FIT TOGETHER.
THAT'S WHY YOU'RE AFRAID YOU'RE NOT GOOD ENOUGH FOR HIM.

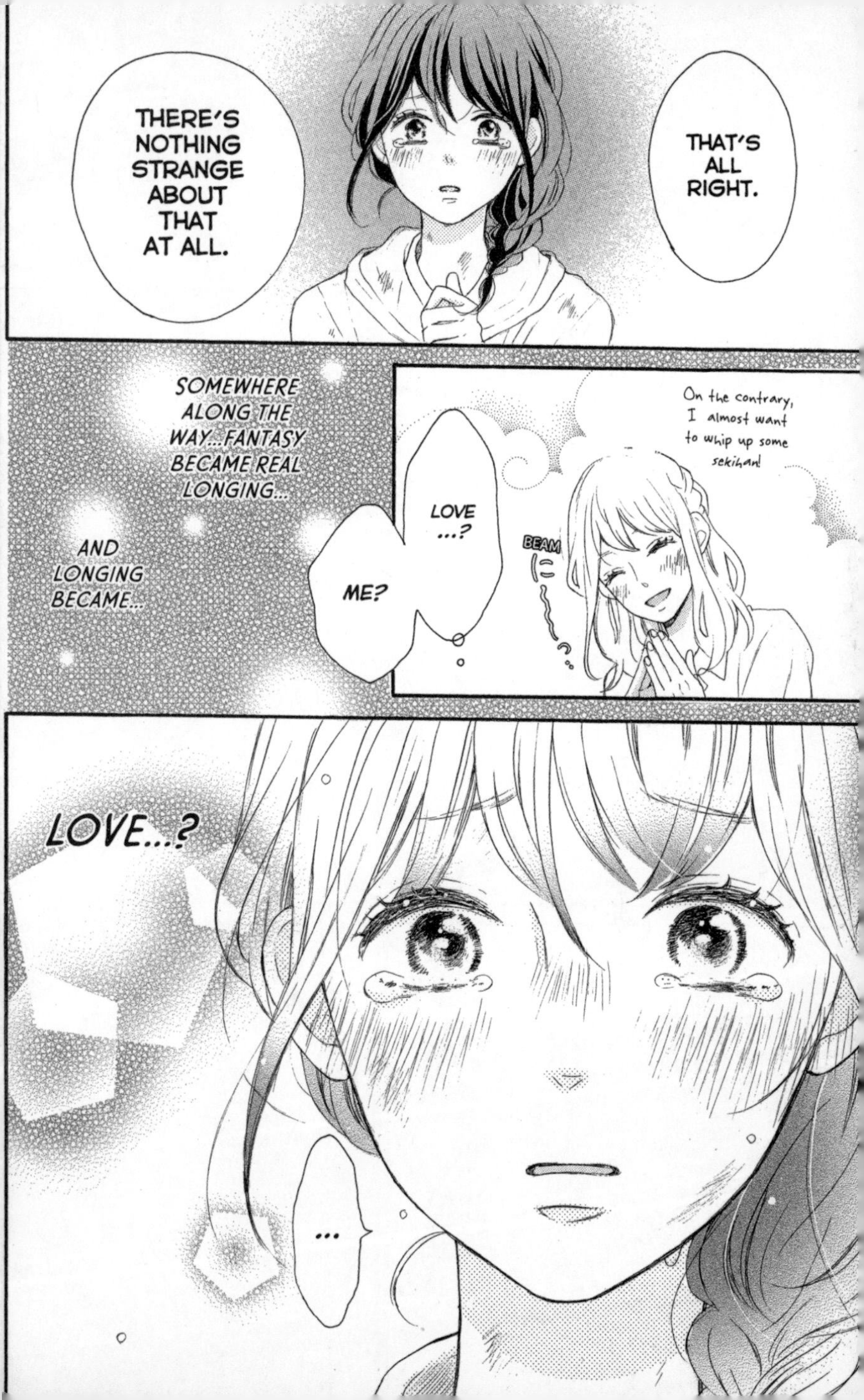
THAT'S ALL RIGHT.
THERE'S NOTHING STRANGE ABOUT THAT AT ALL.
On the contrary, I almost want to whip up some sekihan!
BEAM
LOVE ...?
ME?
SOMEWHERE ALONG THE WAY...FANTASY BECAME REAL LONGING...
AND LONGING BECAME...
LOVE...?
...

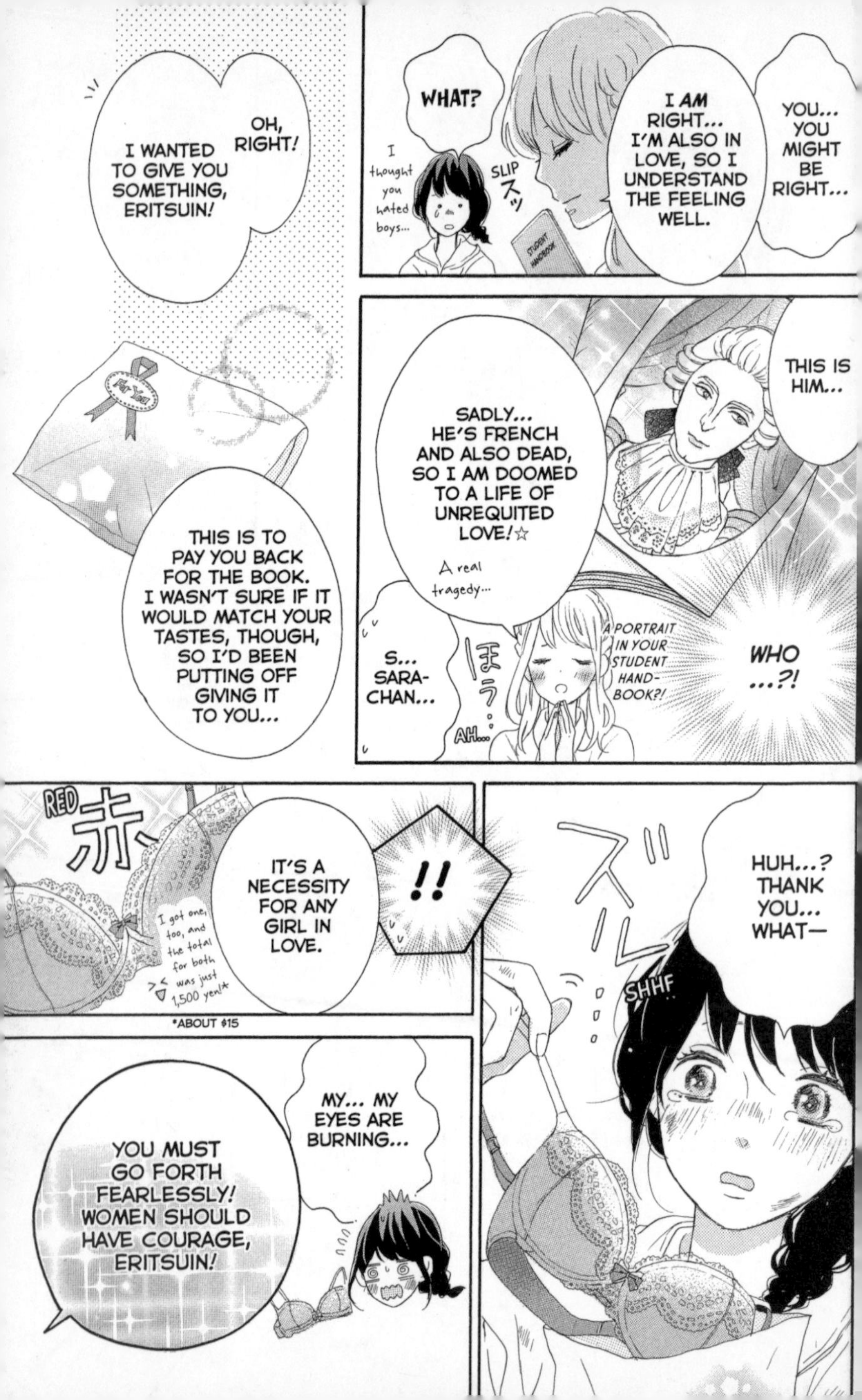
YOU... YOU MIGHT BE RIGHT...
I AM RIGHT... I'M ALSO IN LOVE, SO I UNDERSTAND THE FEELING WELL.
STUDENT HANDBOOK
SLIP スッ
WHAT?
I thought you hated boys...
THIS IS HIM...
WHO ...?!
A PORTRAIT IN YOUR STUDENT HANDBOOK?!
SADLY... HE'S FRENCH AND ALSO DEAD, SO I AM DOOMED TO A LIFE OF UNREQUITED LOVE!☆
A real tragedy...
ほう
AH...
S... SARA-CHAN...
OH, RIGHT!
I WANTED TO GIVE YOU SOMETHING, ERITSUIN!
For You
THIS IS TO PAY YOU BACK FOR THE BOOK. I WASN'T SURE IF IT WOULD MATCH YOUR TASTES, THOUGH, SO I'D BEEN PUTTING OFF GIVING IT TO YOU...
HUH...? THANK YOU... WHAT—
ズル
SHHF
!!
IT'S A NECESSITY FOR ANY GIRL IN LOVE.
RED 赤
I got one, too, and the total for both was just 1,500 yen!*
*ABOUT $15
MY... MY EYES ARE BURNING...
YOU MUST GO FORTH FEARLESSLY! WOMEN SHOULD HAVE COURAGE, ERITSUIN!

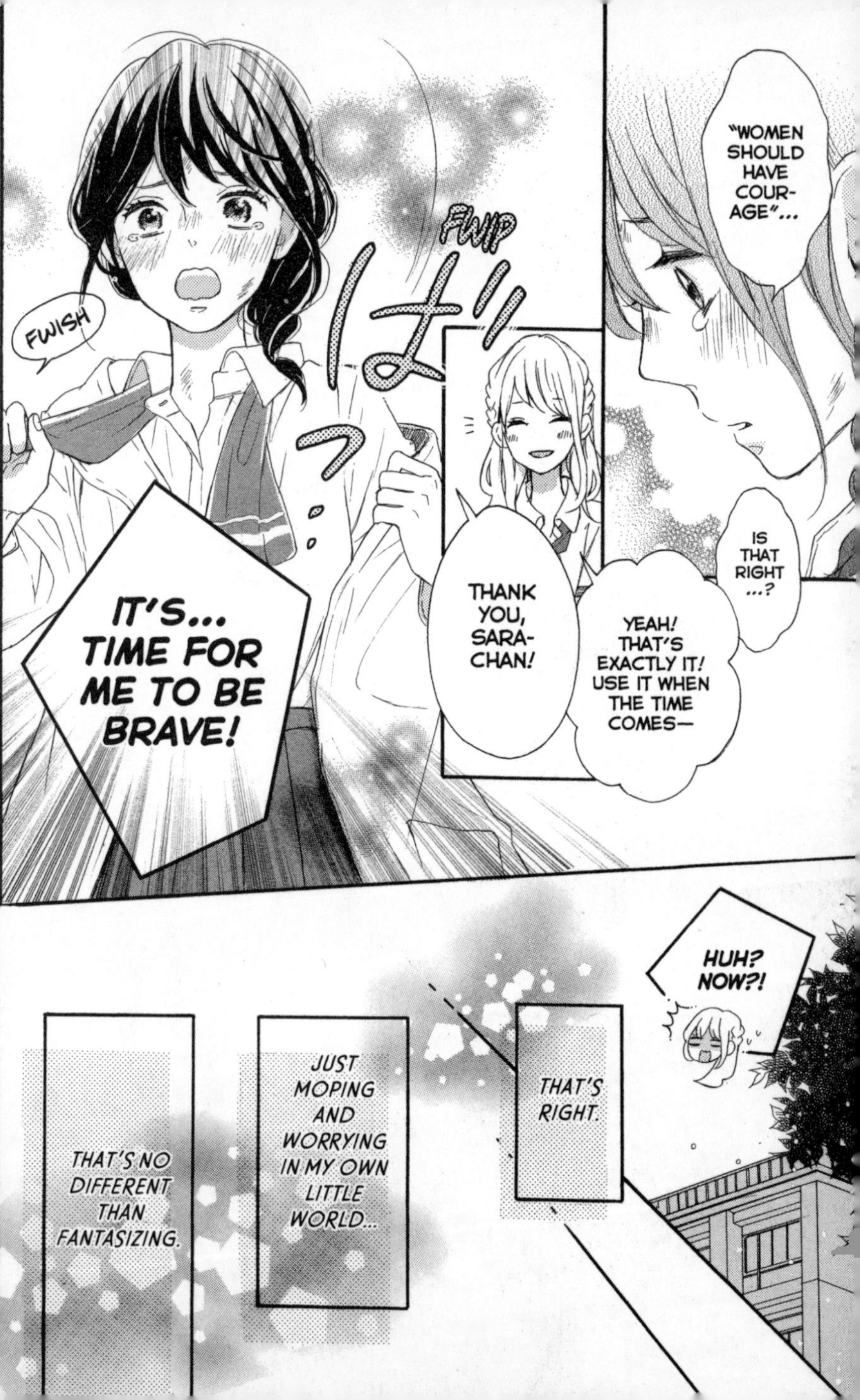
"WOMEN SHOULD HAVE COURAGE"...
IS THAT RIGHT ...?
YEAH! THAT'S EXACTLY IT! USE IT WHEN THE TIME COMES—
THANK YOU, SARA-CHAN!
FWIP
はっ
FWISH
IT'S... TIME FOR ME TO BE BRAVE!
HUH? NOW?!
THAT'S RIGHT.
JUST MOPING AND WORRYING IN MY OWN LITTLE WORLD...
THAT'S NO DIFFERENT THAN FANTASIZING.

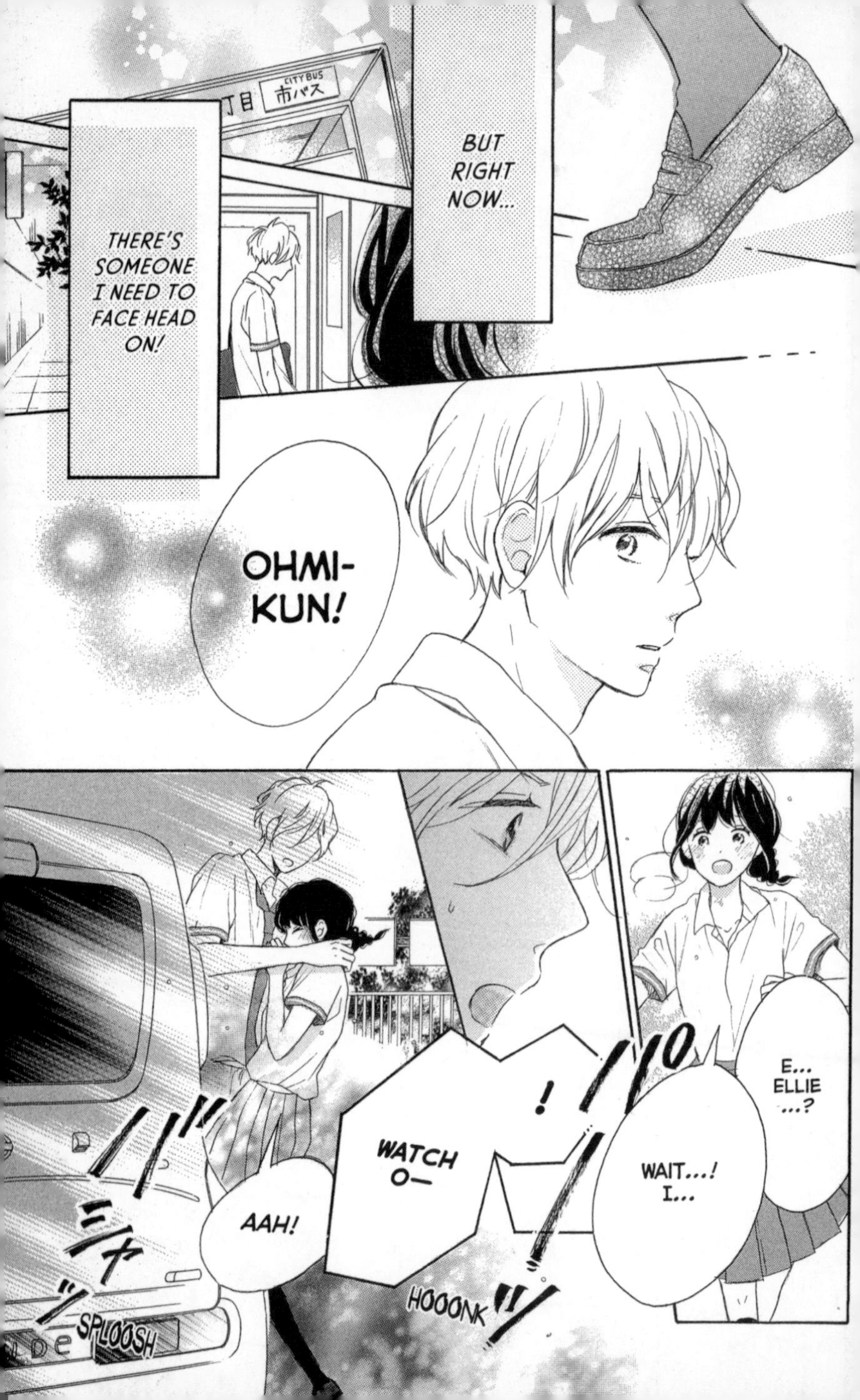
BUT RIGHT NOW...
THERE'S SOMEONE I NEED TO FACE HEAD ON!
CITY BUS
市バス
丁目
OHMI-KUN!
E... ELLIE ...?
WAIT...! I...
!
WATCH O—
HOOONK
AAH!
SPLOOSH

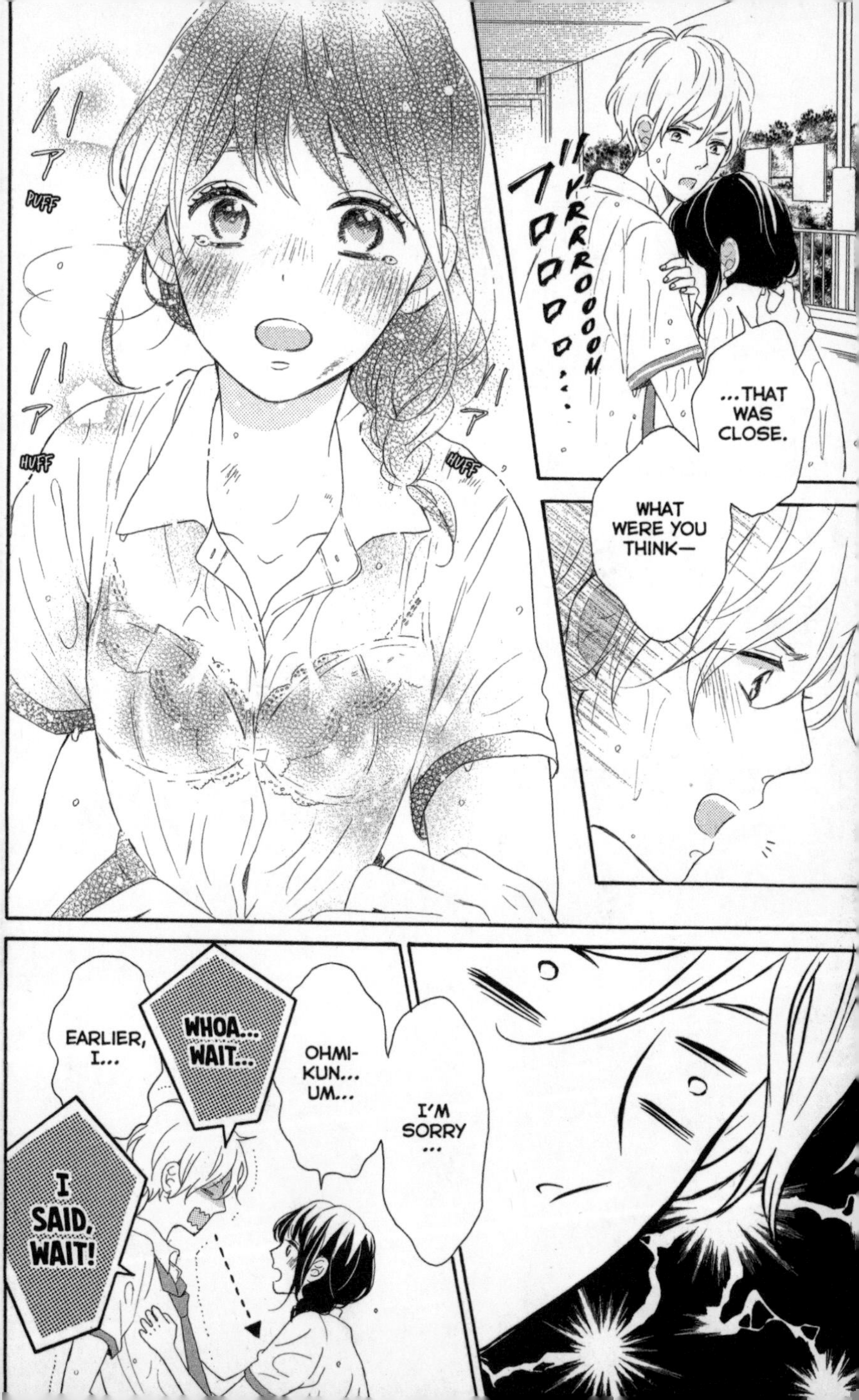
VRRROOOOOM
...THAT WAS CLOSE.
WHAT WERE YOU THINK—
PUFF
HUFF
HUFF
OHMI-KUN... UM...
I'M SORRY...
EARLIER, I...
WHOA... WAIT...
I SAID, WAIT!

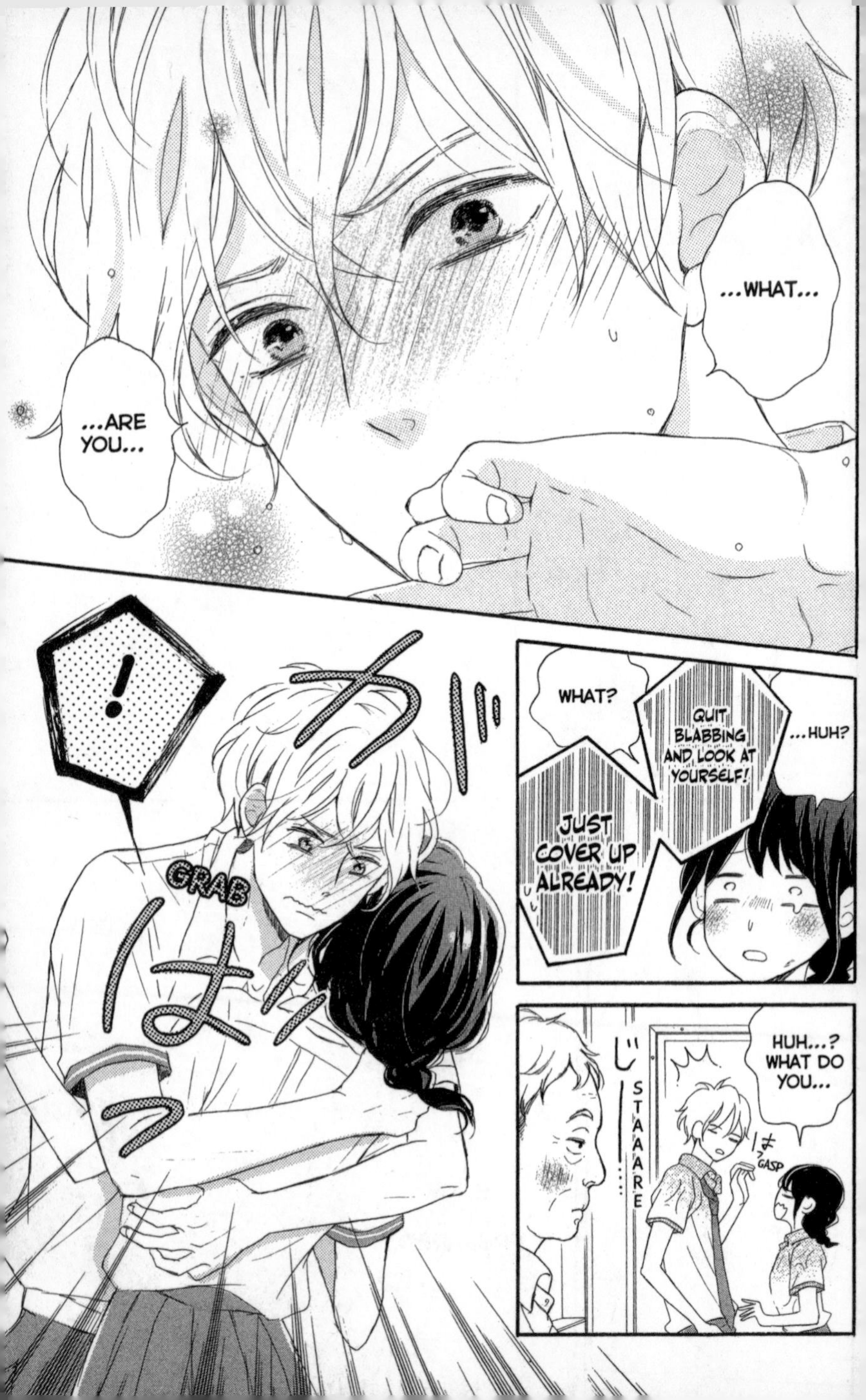

...WHAT...
...ARE YOU...
...HUH?
WHAT?
QUIT BLABBING AND LOOK AT YOURSELF!
JUST COVER UP ALREADY!
HUH...? WHAT DO YOU...
は
GASP
じー
STAAARE
...
!
GRAB
がばっ

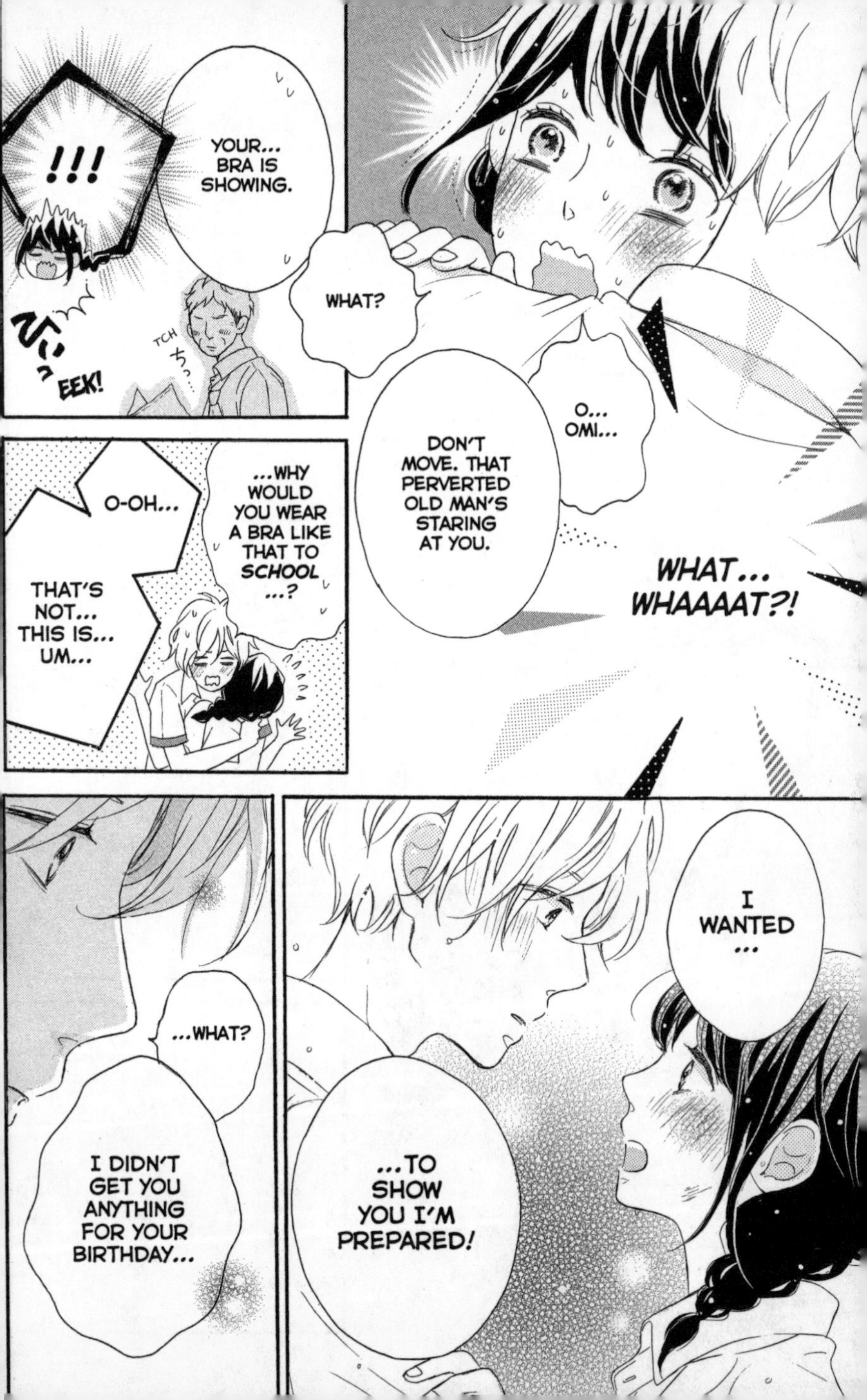
WHAT?
O... OMI...
DON'T MOVE. THAT PERVERTED OLD MAN'S STARING AT YOU.
WHAT... WHAAAAT?!
YOUR... BRA IS SHOWING.
!!!
EEK!
TCH
...WHY WOULD YOU WEAR A BRA LIKE THAT TO *SCHOOL*...?
O-OH...
THAT'S NOT... THIS IS... UM...
I WANTED...
...TO SHOW YOU I'M PREPARED!
...WHAT?
I DIDN'T GET YOU ANYTHING FOR YOUR BIRTHDAY...

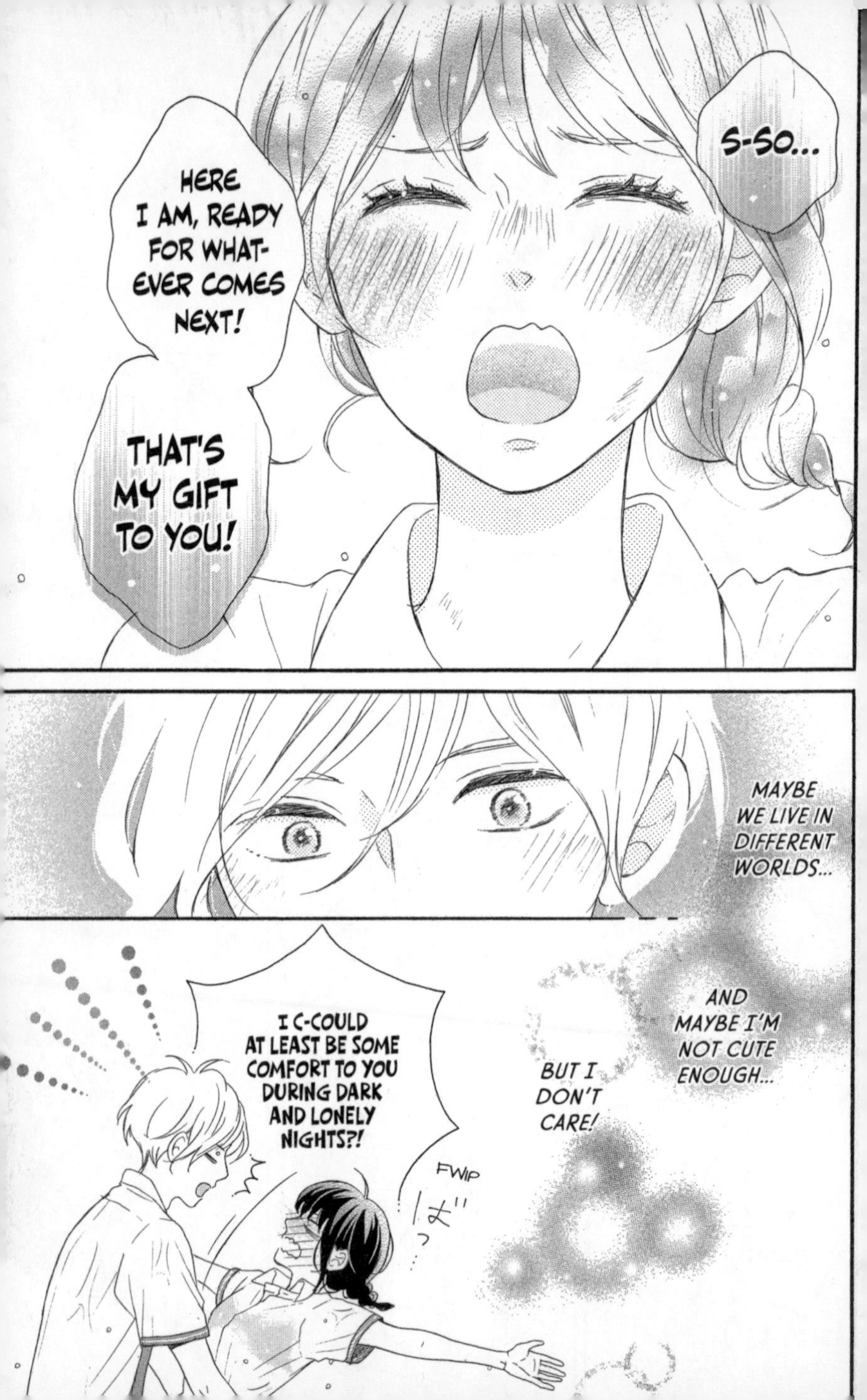
S-SO...
HERE I AM, READY FOR WHAT-EVER COMES NEXT!
THAT'S MY GIFT TO YOU!
MAYBE WE LIVE IN DIFFERENT WORLDS...
AND MAYBE I'M NOT CUTE ENOUGH...
BUT I DON'T CARE!
I C-COULD AT LEAST BE SOME COMFORT TO YOU DURING DARK AND LONELY NIGHTS?!
FWIP

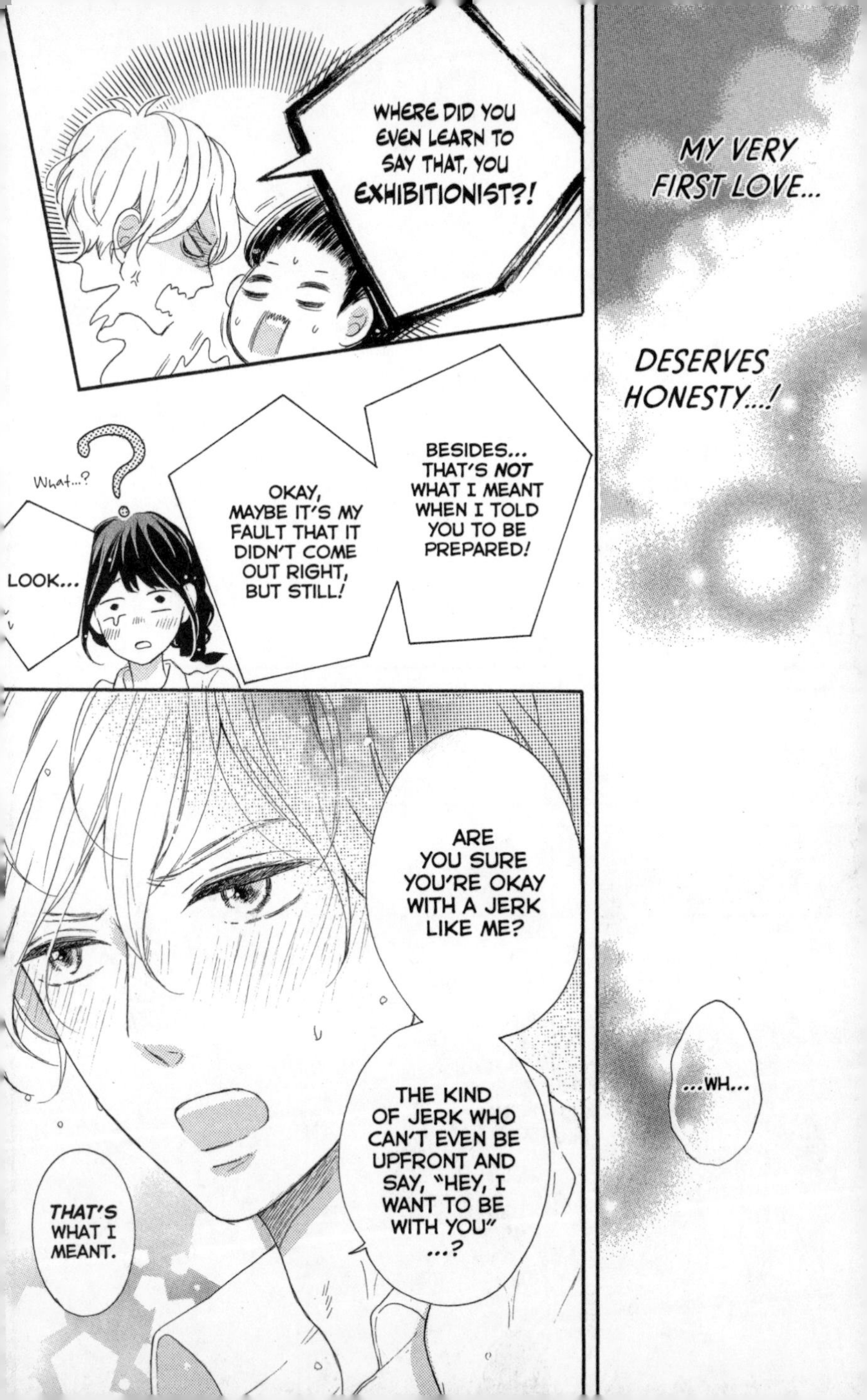
MY VERY FIRST LOVE...
DESERVES HONESTY...!
...WH...
WHERE DID YOU EVEN LEARN TO SAY THAT, YOU EXHIBITIONIST?!
BESIDES... THAT'S *NOT* WHAT I MEANT WHEN I TOLD YOU TO BE PREPARED!
OKAY, MAYBE IT'S MY FAULT THAT IT DIDN'T COME OUT RIGHT, BUT STILL!
LOOK...
What...?
ARE YOU SURE YOU'RE OKAY WITH A JERK LIKE ME?
THE KIND OF JERK WHO CAN'T EVEN BE UPFRONT AND SAY, "HEY, I WANT TO BE WITH YOU" ...?
THAT'S WHAT I MEANT.

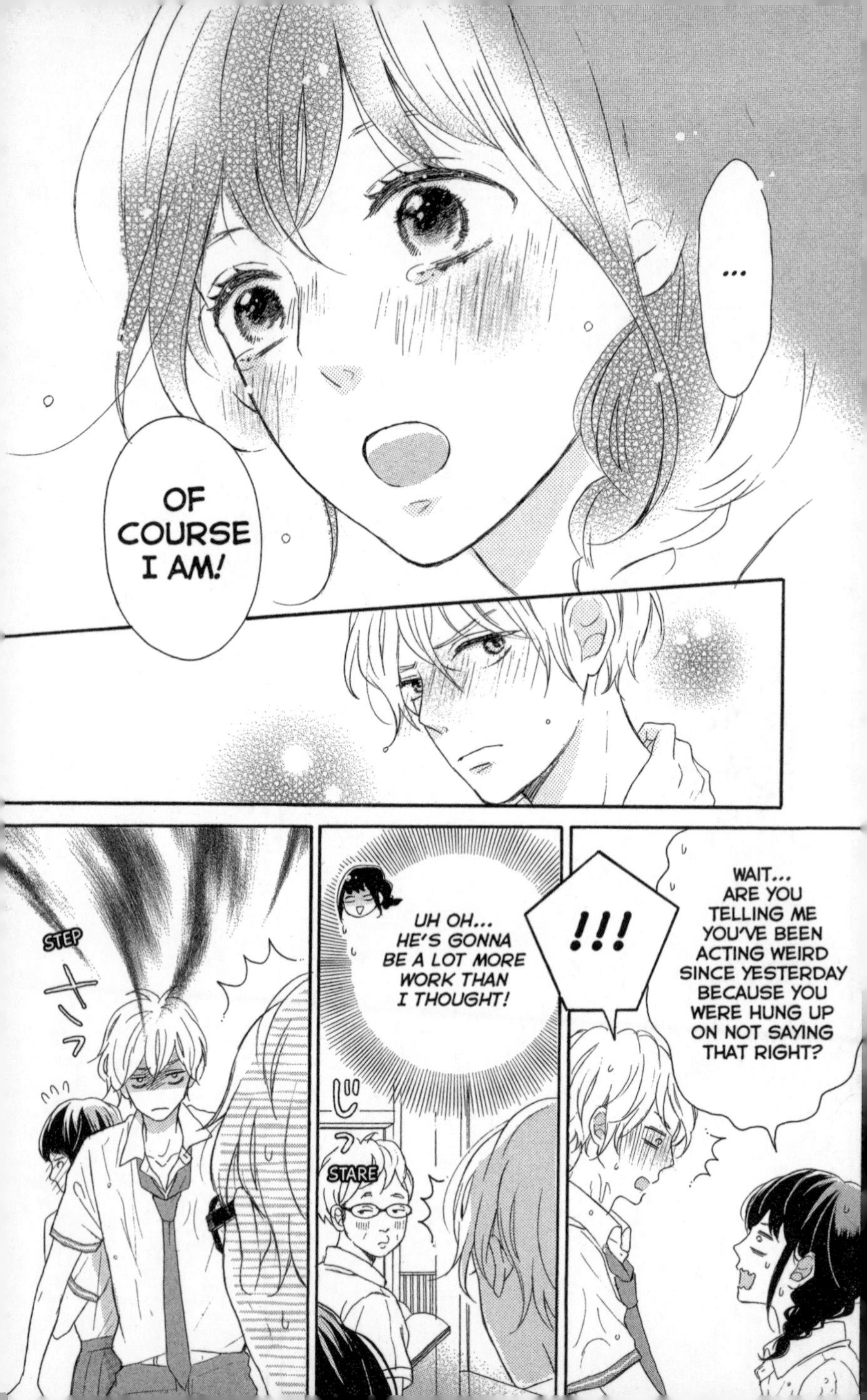
...
OF COURSE I AM!
WAIT... ARE YOU TELLING ME YOU'VE BEEN ACTING WEIRD SINCE YESTERDAY BECAUSE YOU WERE HUNG UP ON NOT SAYING THAT RIGHT?
!!!
UH OH... HE'S GONNA BE A LOT MORE WORK THAN I THOUGHT!
STARE
STEP

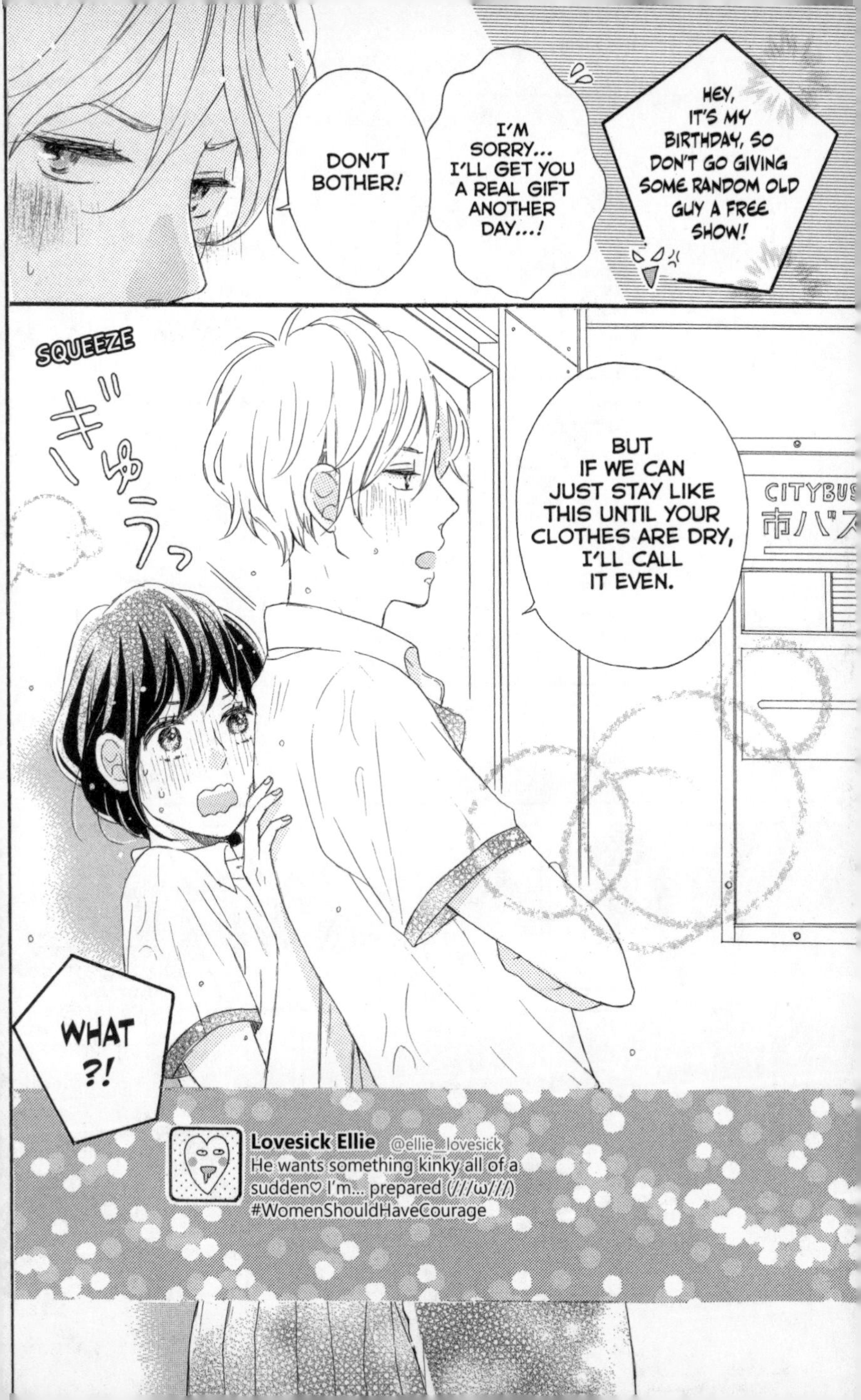
HEY, IT'S MY BIRTHDAY, SO DON'T GO GIVING SOME RANDOM OLD GUY A FREE SHOW!
I'M SORRY... I'LL GET YOU A REAL GIFT ANOTHER DAY...!
DON'T BOTHER!
BUT IF WE CAN JUST STAY LIKE THIS UNTIL YOUR CLOTHES ARE DRY, I'LL CALL IT EVEN.
SQUEEZE
ぎゅうっ
WHAT ?!
Lovesick Ellie @ellie_lovesick
He wants something kinky all of a sudden♡ I'm... prepared (///ω///)
#WomenShouldHaveCourage

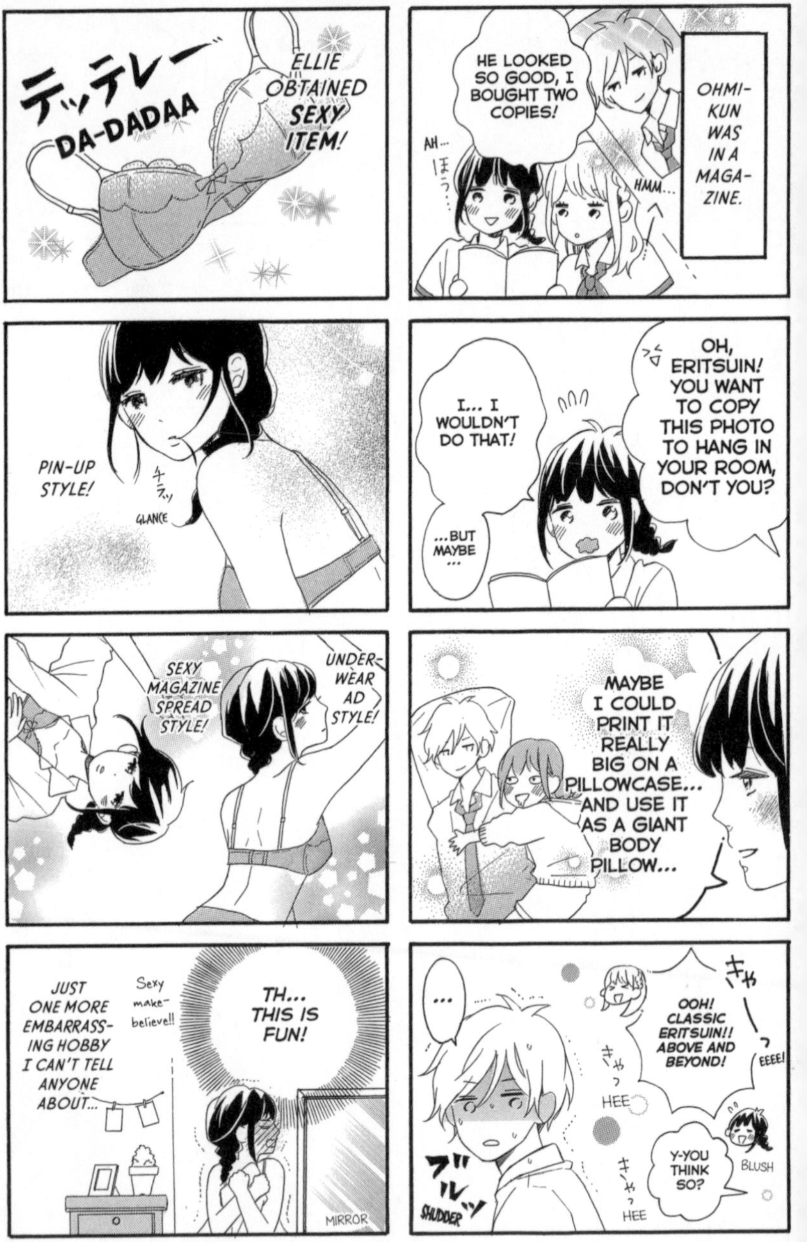
OHMI-KUN WAS IN A MAGAZINE.
HE LOOKED SO GOOD, I BOUGHT TWO COPIES!
HMM...
AH... ほぅ...
OH, ERITSUIN! YOU WANT TO COPY THIS PHOTO TO HANG IN YOUR ROOM, DON'T YOU?
I... I WOULDN'T DO THAT!
...BUT MAYBE ...
MAYBE I COULD PRINT IT REALLY BIG ON A PILLOWCASE... AND USE IT AS A GIANT BODY PILLOW...
きゃーっ EEEE!
OOH! CLASSIC ERITSUIN!! ABOVE AND BEYOND!
...
きゃっ HEE
BLUSH
Y-YOU THINK SO?
きゃっ HEE
ブルッ SHUDDER
ELLIE OBTAINED SEXY ITEM!
テッテレー DA-DADAA
PIN-UP STYLE!
チラッ GLANCE
UNDER-WEAR AD STYLE!
SEXY MAGAZINE SPREAD STYLE!
TH... THIS IS FUN!
Sexy make-believe!!
JUST ONE MORE EMBARRASSING HOBBY I CAN'T TELL ANYONE ABOUT...
MIRROR

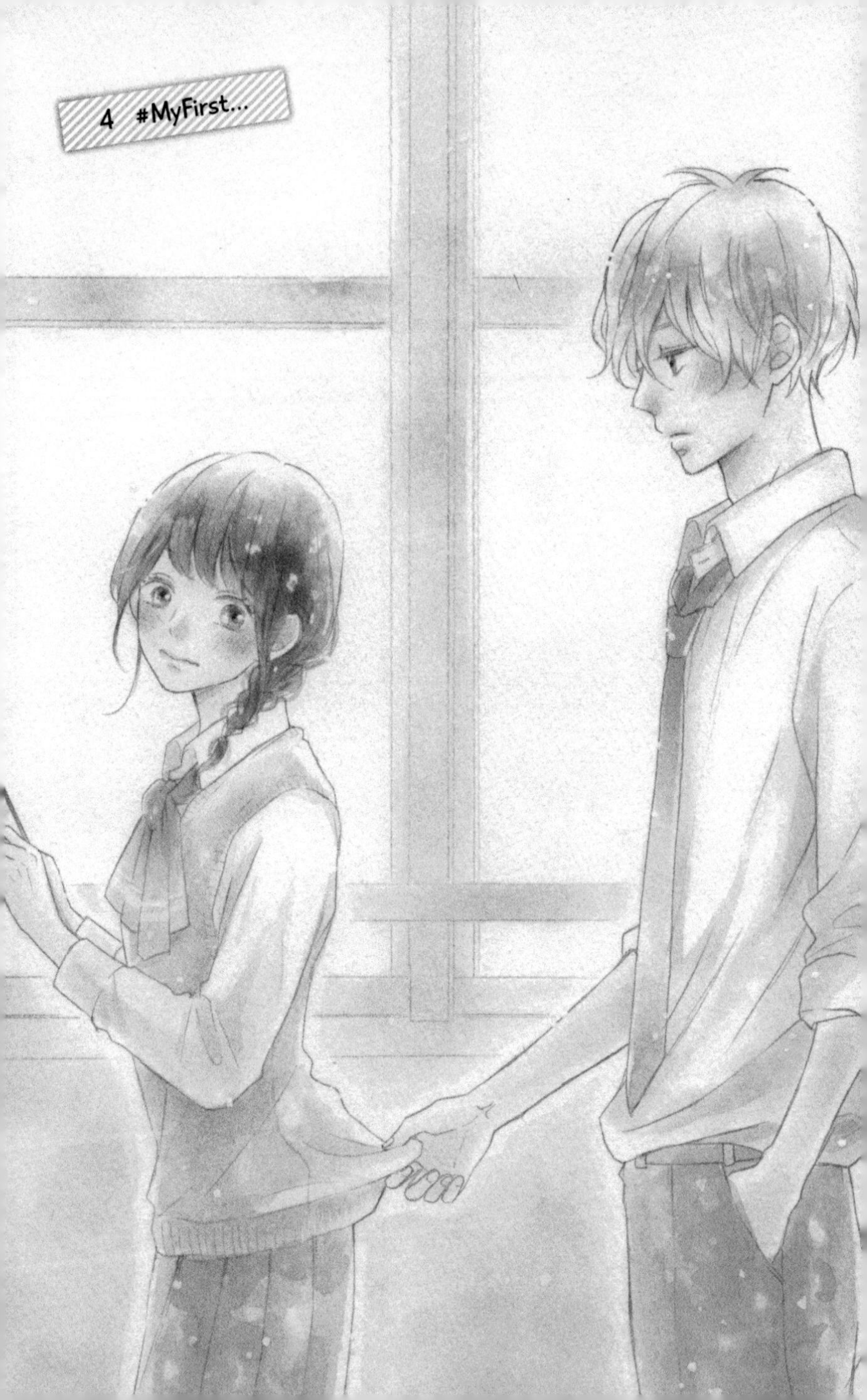
4 #MyFirst...

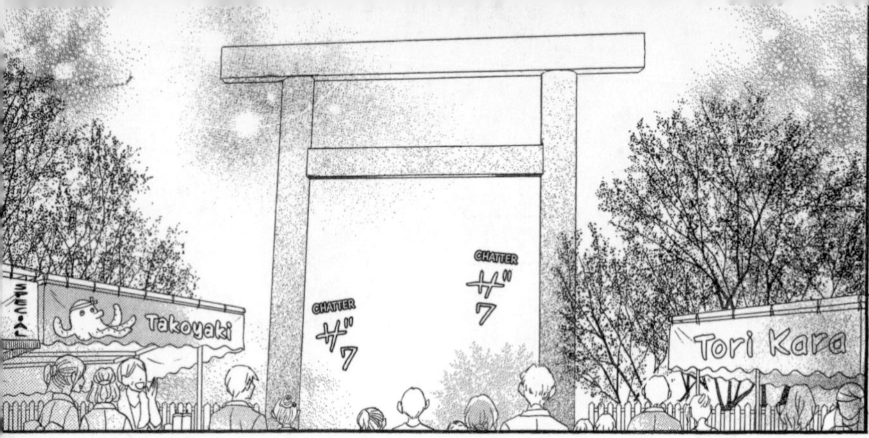
Tori Kara
CHATTER
ザワ
CHATTER
ザワ
Takoyaki

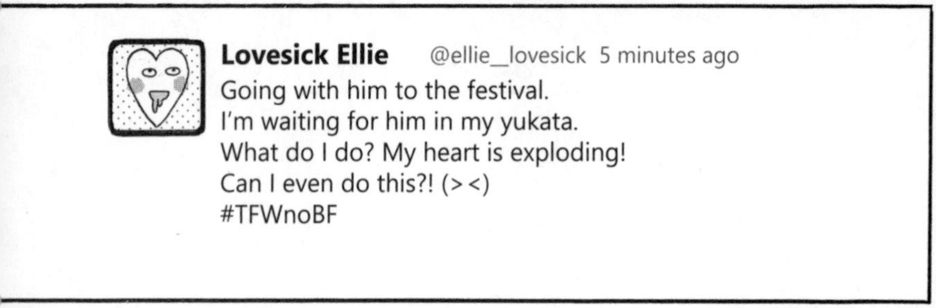
Lovesick Ellie @ellie_lovesick 5 minutes ago
Going with him to the festival.
I'm waiting for him in my yukata.
What do I do? My heart is exploding!
Can I even do this?! (><)
#TFWnoBF

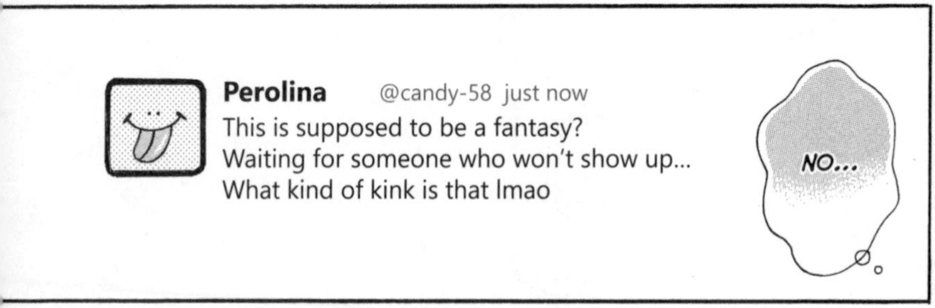
NO...
Perolina @candy-58 just now
This is supposed to be a fantasy?
Waiting for someone who won't show up...
What kind of kink is that lmao

Special Thanks

Kuumii
Editor Minchi
Nagasaki
Designer Osawa
Mecchin (Emotional Supervisor)
Dessert Editorial Department
Everyone involved in the creation of this book
My friends and family

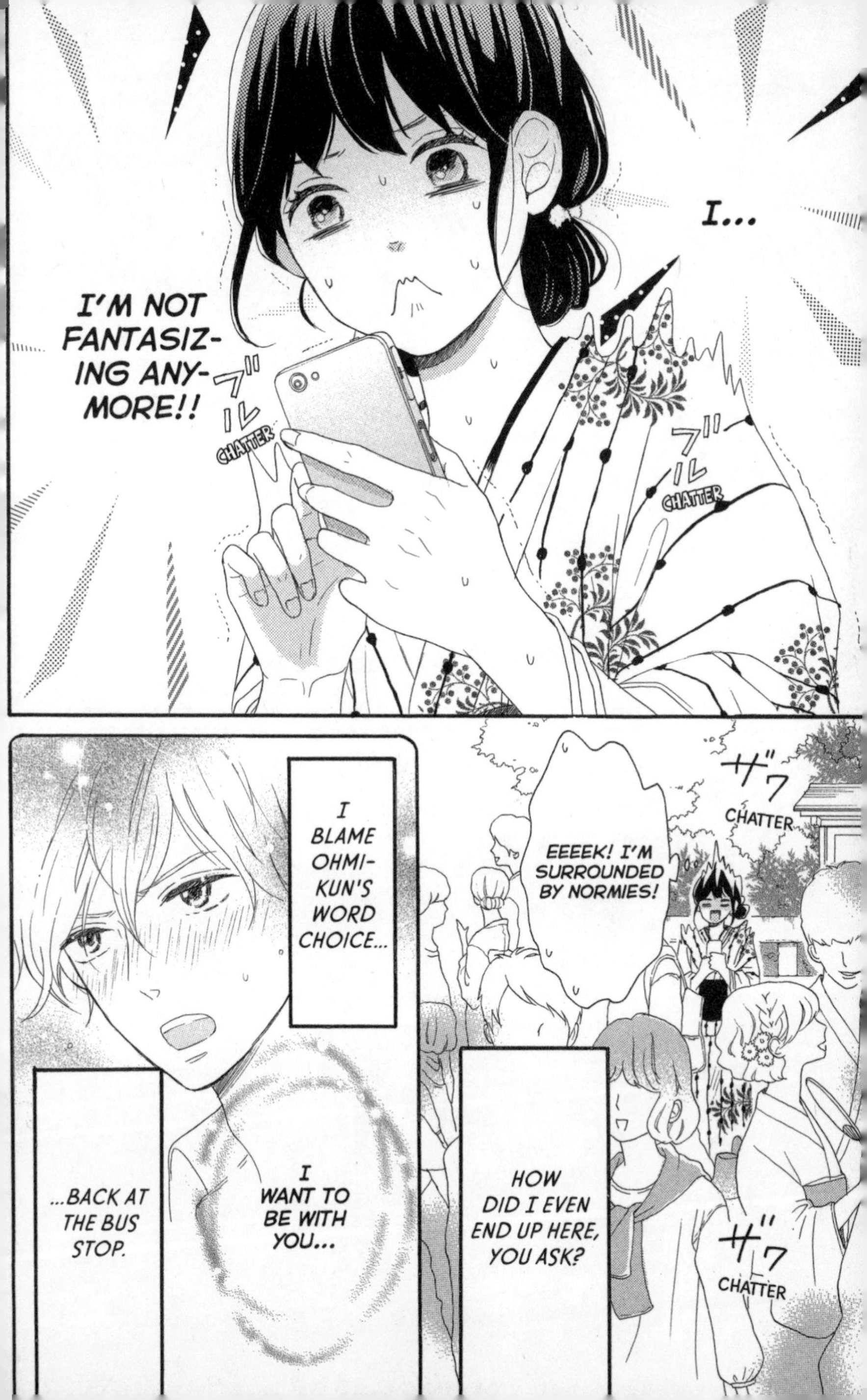
I...
I'M NOT FANTASIZ-ING ANY-MORE!!
ブル
CHATTER
ブル
CHATTER
ザワ
CHATTER
EEEEK! I'M SURROUNDED BY NORMIES!
HOW DID I EVEN END UP HERE, YOU ASK?
ザワ
CHATTER
I BLAME OHMI-KUN'S WORD CHOICE...
I WANT TO BE WITH YOU...
...BACK AT THE BUS STOP.

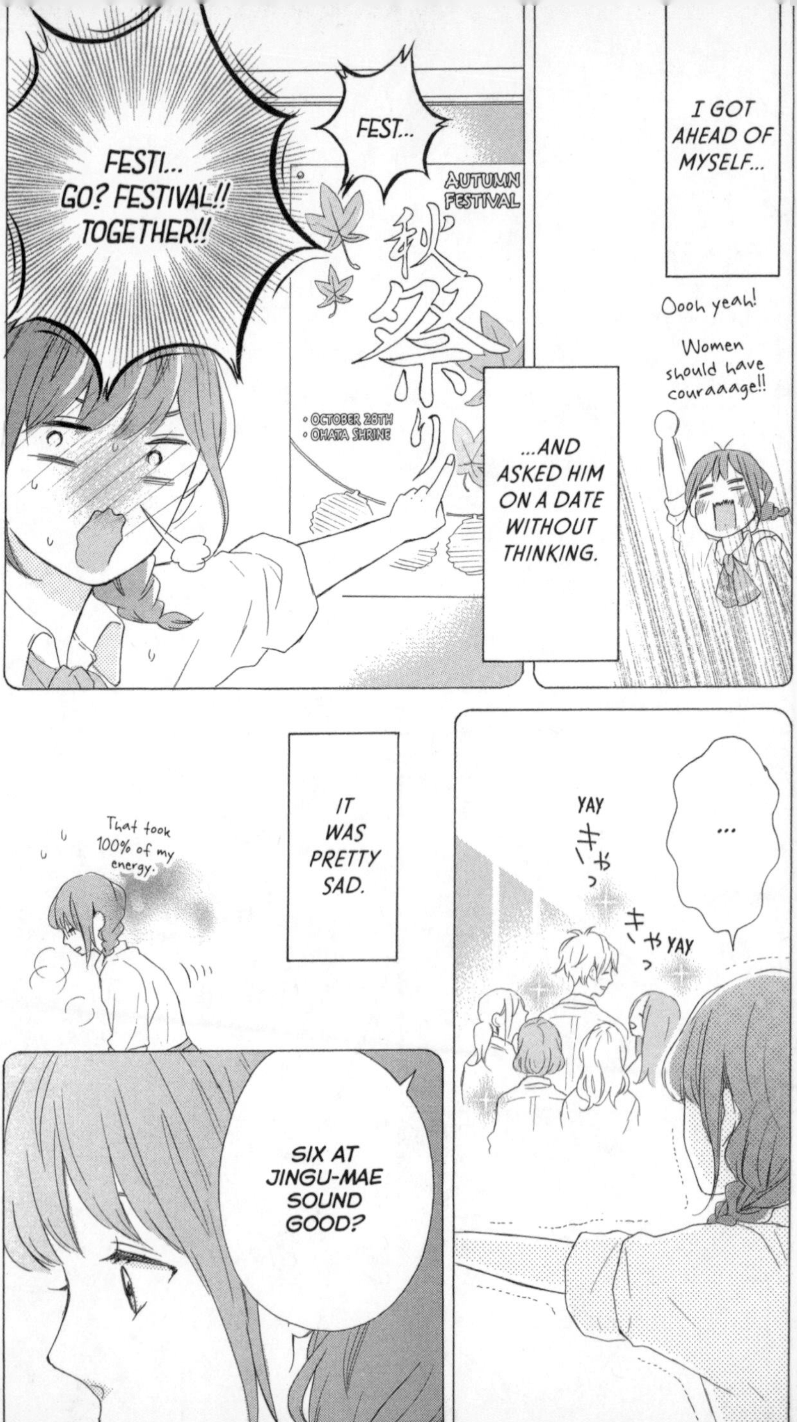
I GOT AHEAD OF MYSELF...
Oooh yeah! Women should have couraaage!!
...AND ASKED HIM ON A DATE WITHOUT THINKING.
FEST...
FESTI... GO? FESTIVAL!! TOGETHER!!
AUTUMN FESTIVAL
秋祭り
• OCTOBER 28TH
• OHATA SHRINE
...
YAY
キャッ
キャッ
YAY
IT WAS PRETTY SAD.
That took 100% of my energy.
SIX AT JINGU-MAE SOUND GOOD?

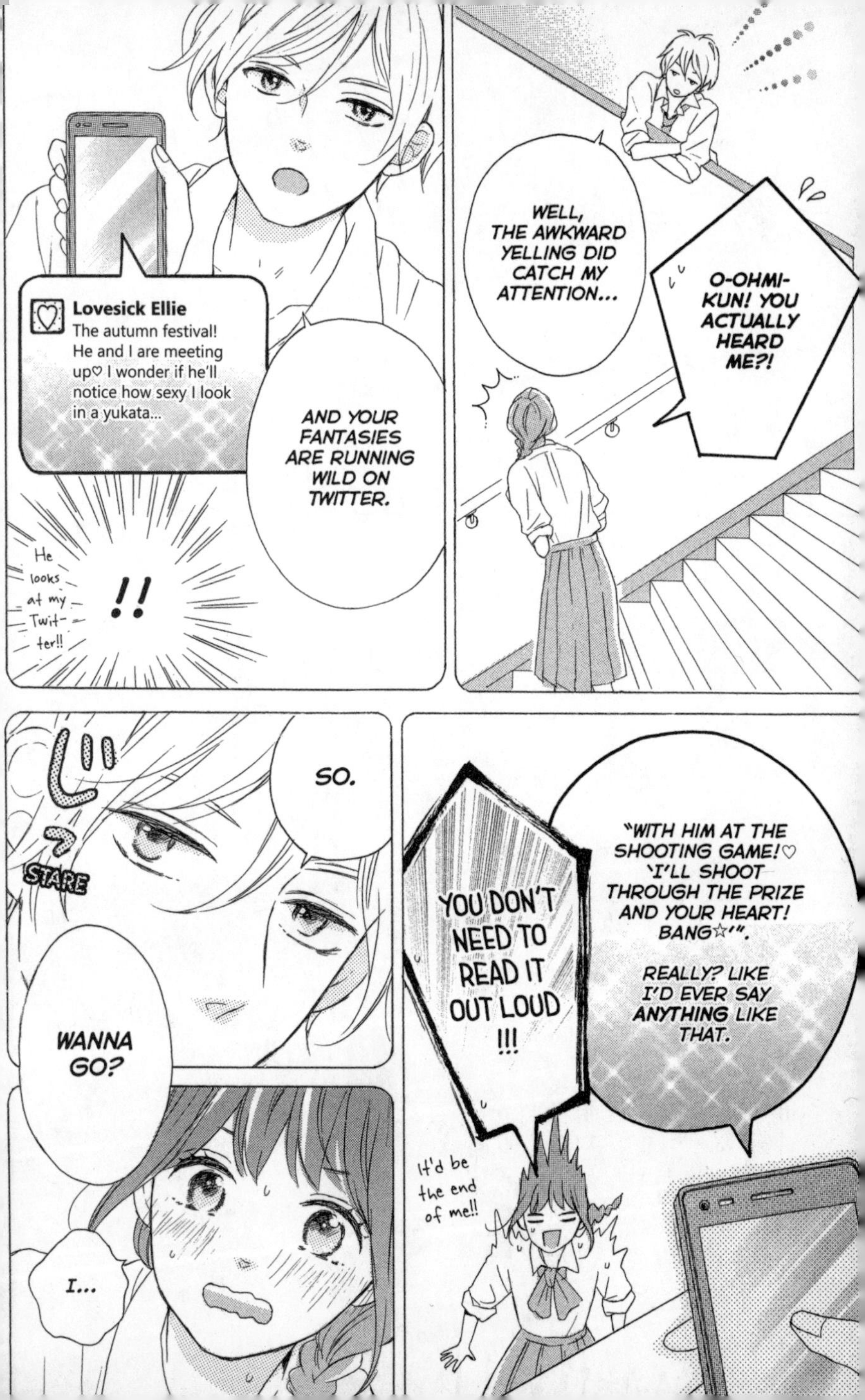
O-OHMI-KUN! YOU ACTUALLY HEARD ME?!
WELL, THE AWKWARD YELLING DID CATCH MY ATTENTION...
AND YOUR FANTASIES ARE RUNNING WILD ON TWITTER.
Lovesick Ellie
The autumn festival! He and I are meeting up♡ I wonder if he'll notice how sexy I look in a yukata...
!!
He looks at my Twit-ter!!
"WITH HIM AT THE SHOOTING GAME!♡ 'I'LL SHOOT THROUGH THE PRIZE AND YOUR HEART! BANG☆'".
REALLY? LIKE I'D EVER SAY ANYTHING LIKE THAT.
YOU DON'T NEED TO READ IT OUT LOUD!!!
It'd be the end of me!!
SO.
STARE
WANNA GO?
I...

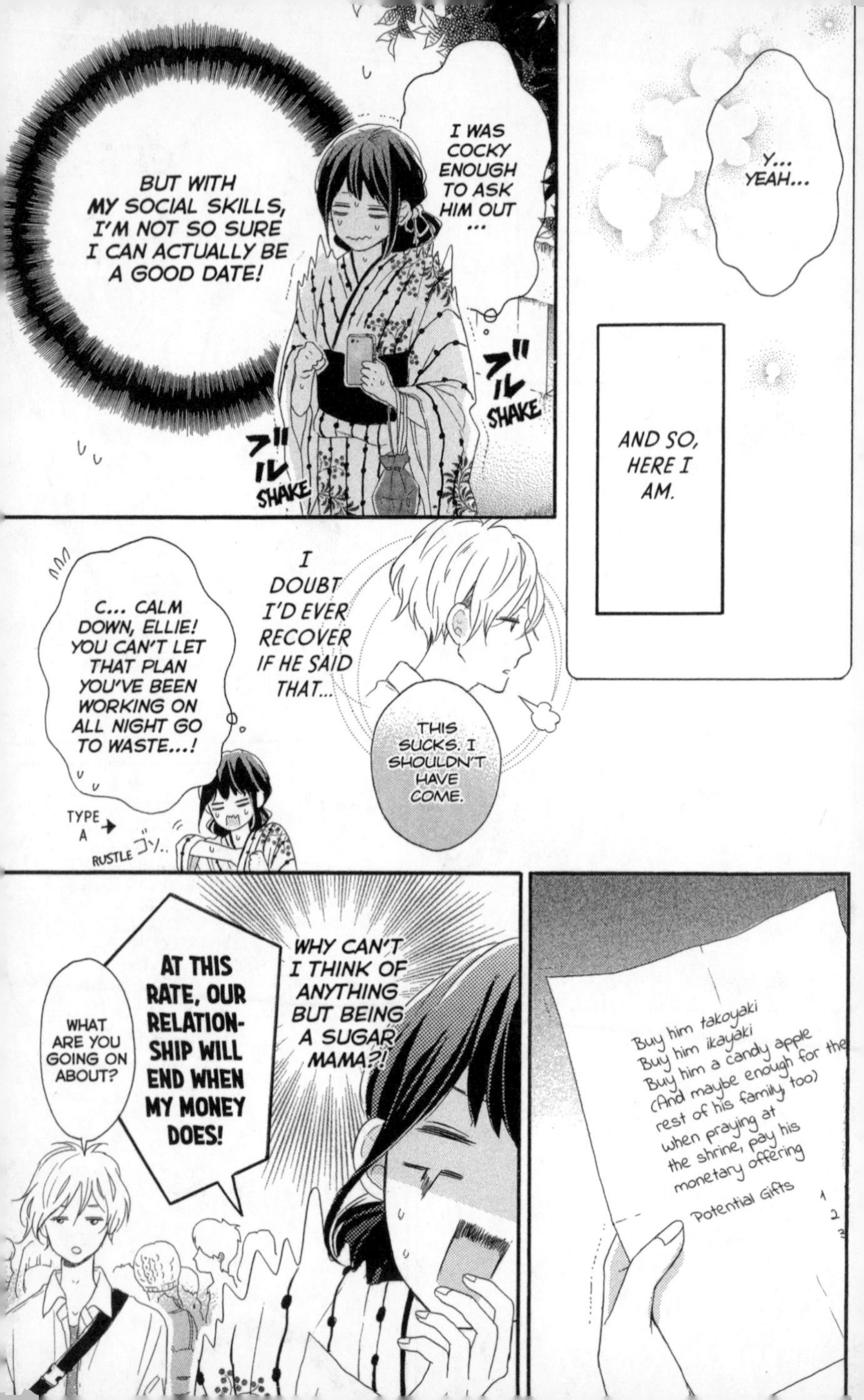
Y... YEAH...
AND SO, HERE I AM.
I WAS COCKY ENOUGH TO ASK HIM OUT...
BUT WITH MY SOCIAL SKILLS, I'M NOT SO SURE I CAN ACTUALLY BE A GOOD DATE!
SHAKE
SHAKE
I DOUBT I'D EVER RECOVER IF HE SAID THAT...
C... CALM DOWN, ELLIE! YOU CAN'T LET THAT PLAN YOU'VE BEEN WORKING ON ALL NIGHT GO TO WASTE...!
THIS SUCKS. I SHOULDN'T HAVE COME.
TYPE A
RUSTLE
Buy him takoyaki
Buy him ikayaki
Buy him a candy apple (And maybe enough for the rest of his family too)
When praying at the shrine, pay his monetary offering
Potential Gifts
1
2
3
WHY CAN'T I THINK OF ANYTHING BUT BEING A SUGAR MAMA?!
AT THIS RATE, OUR RELATIONSHIP WILL END WHEN MY MONEY DOES!
WHAT ARE YOU GOING ON ABOUT?

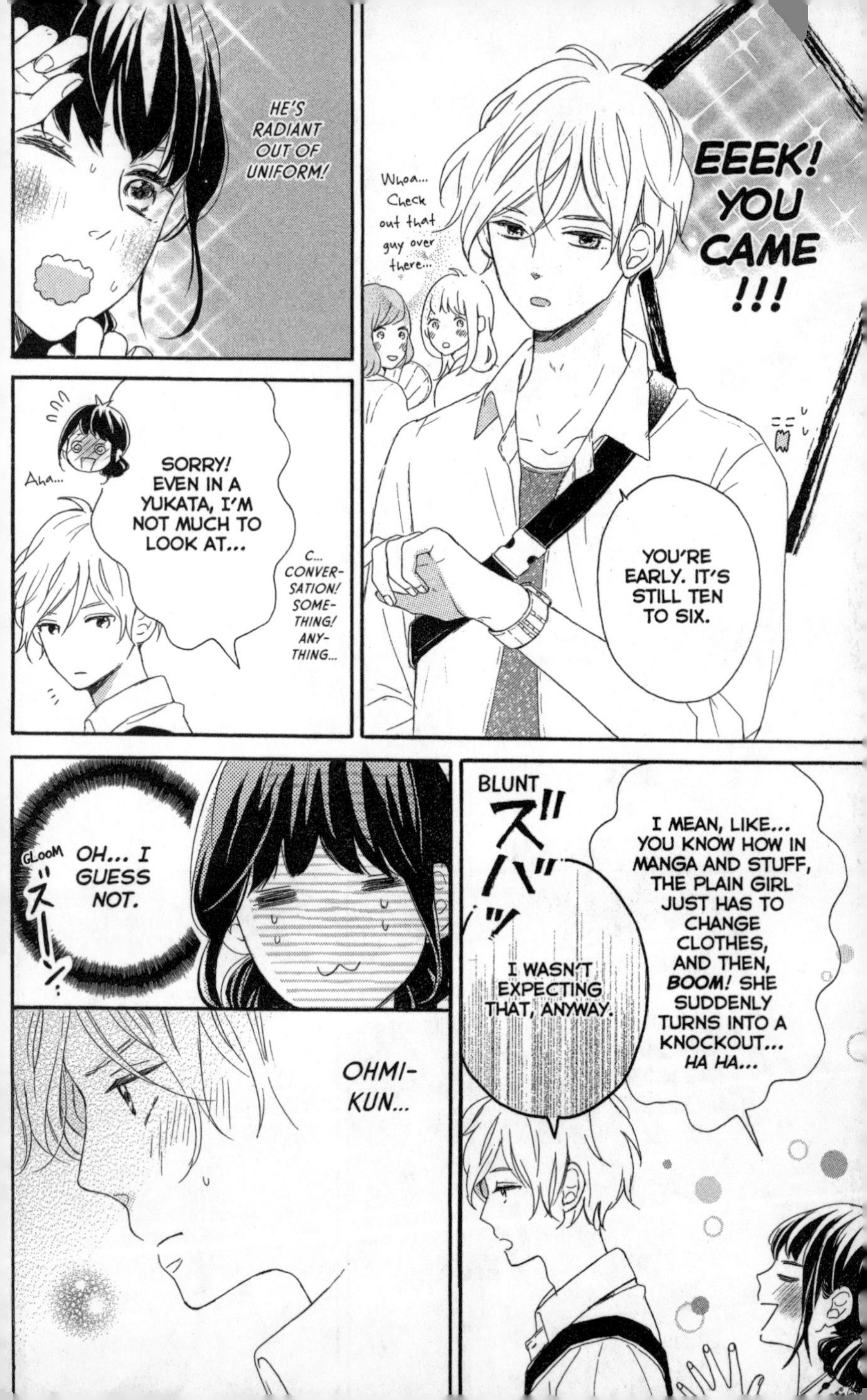
EEEK! YOU CAME!!!
Whoa... Check out that guy over there...
YOU'RE EARLY. IT'S STILL TEN TO SIX.
HE'S RADIANT OUT OF UNIFORM!
SORRY! EVEN IN A YUKATA, I'M NOT MUCH TO LOOK AT...
Aha...
C... CONVERSATION! SOMETHING! ANYTHING...
I MEAN, LIKE... YOU KNOW HOW IN MANGA AND STUFF, THE PLAIN GIRL JUST HAS TO CHANGE CLOTHES, AND THEN, *BOOM!* SHE SUDDENLY TURNS INTO A KNOCKOUT... *HA HA...*
BLUNT
ズバッ
I WASN'T EXPECTING THAT, ANYWAY.
GLOOM
ズーン
OH... I GUESS NOT.
OHMI-KUN...

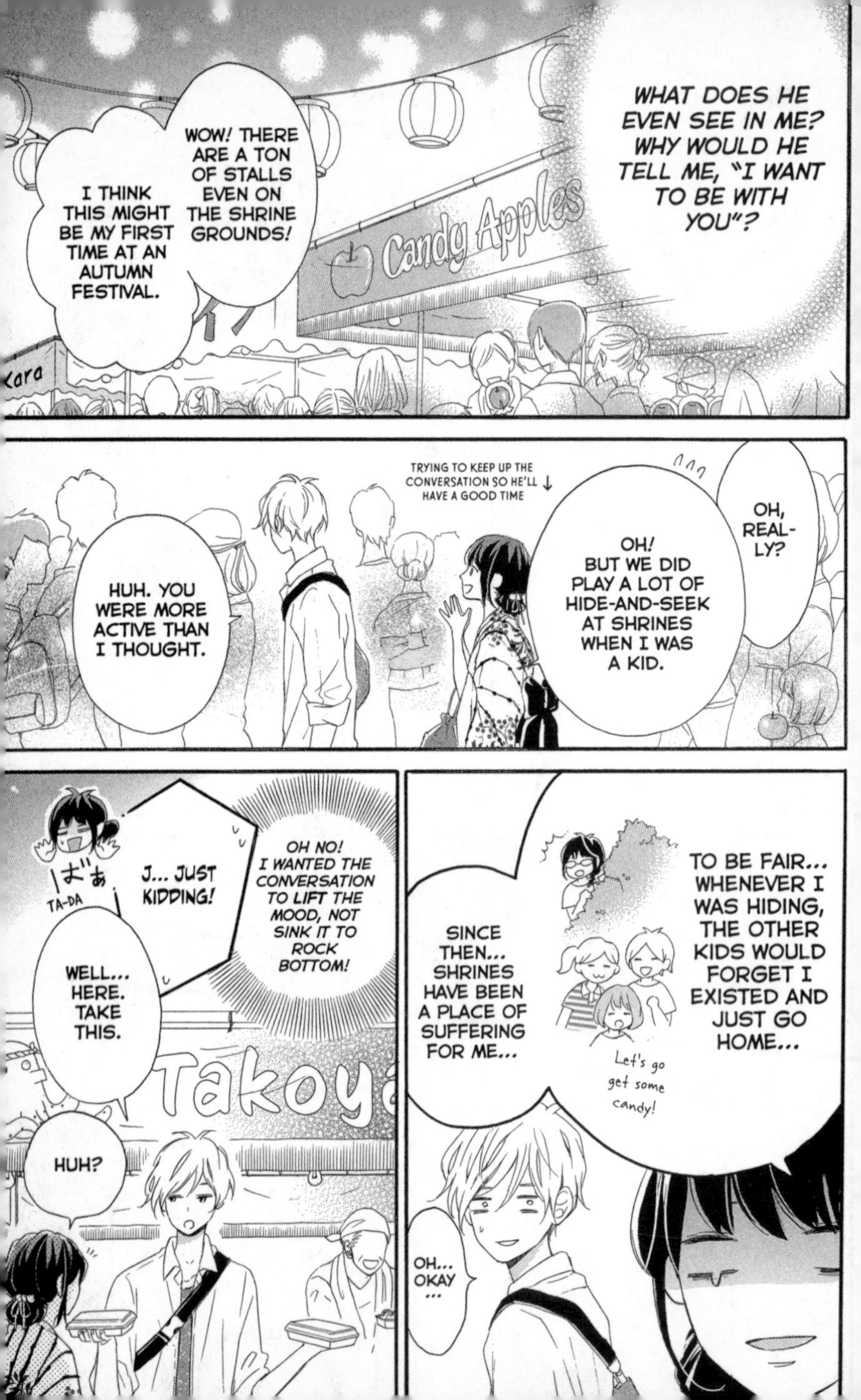
WHAT DOES HE EVEN SEE IN ME? WHY WOULD HE TELL ME, "I WANT TO BE WITH YOU"?
Candy Apples
WOW! THERE ARE A TON OF STALLS EVEN ON THE SHRINE GROUNDS!
I THINK THIS MIGHT BE MY FIRST TIME AT AN AUTUMN FESTIVAL.
Kara
OH, REAL-LY?
TRYING TO KEEP UP THE CONVERSATION SO HE'LL HAVE A GOOD TIME ↓
OH! BUT WE DID PLAY A LOT OF HIDE-AND-SEEK AT SHRINES WHEN I WAS A KID.
HUH. YOU WERE MORE ACTIVE THAN I THOUGHT.
TO BE FAIR... WHENEVER I WAS HIDING, THE OTHER KIDS WOULD FORGET I EXISTED AND JUST GO HOME...
SINCE THEN... SHRINES HAVE BEEN A PLACE OF SUFFERING FOR ME...
Let's go get some candy!
OH... OKAY...
OH NO! I WANTED THE CONVERSATION TO LIFT THE MOOD, NOT SINK IT TO ROCK BOTTOM!
J... JUST KIDDING!
ばぁ
TA-DA
WELL... HERE. TAKE THIS.
Takoya
HUH?

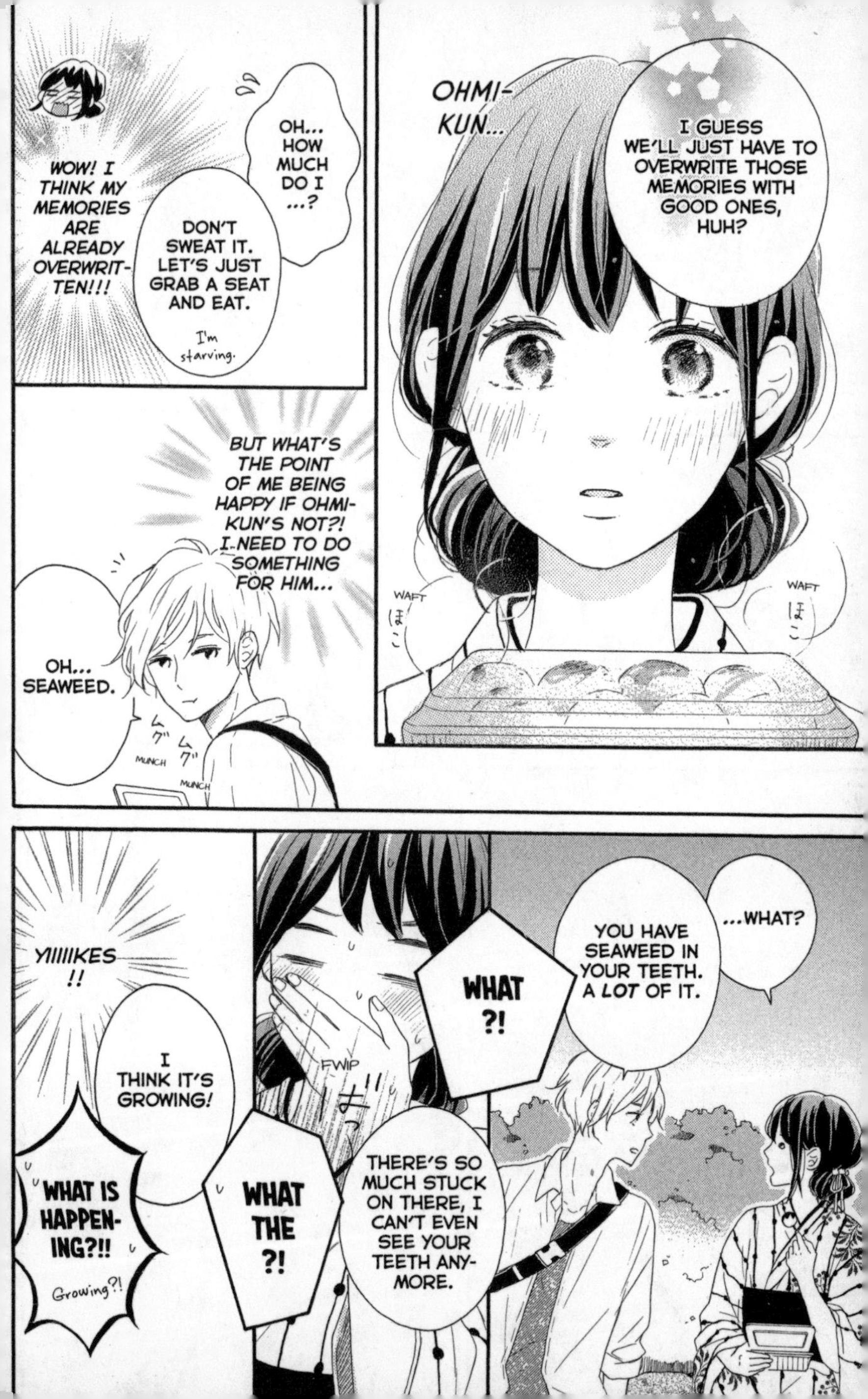
I GUESS WE'LL JUST HAVE TO OVERWRITE THOSE MEMORIES WITH GOOD ONES, HUH?
OHMI-KUN...
WAFT
ほこ
WAFT
ほこ
OH... HOW MUCH DO I ...?
DON'T SWEAT IT. LET'S JUST GRAB A SEAT AND EAT.
I'm starving.
WOW! I THINK MY MEMORIES ARE ALREADY OVERWRIT-TEN!!!
BUT WHAT'S THE POINT OF ME BEING HAPPY IF OHMI-KUN'S NOT?! I NEED TO DO SOMETHING FOR HIM...
OH... SEAWEED.
ムグ
MUNCH
ムグ
MUNCH
...WHAT?
YOU HAVE SEAWEED IN YOUR TEETH. A LOT OF IT.
THERE'S SO MUCH STUCK ON THERE, I CAN'T EVEN SEE YOUR TEETH ANY-MORE.
WHAT ?!
FWIP
はっ
WHAT THE ?!
YIIIIKES !!
I THINK IT'S GROWING!
WHAT IS HAPPEN-ING?!!
Growing?!

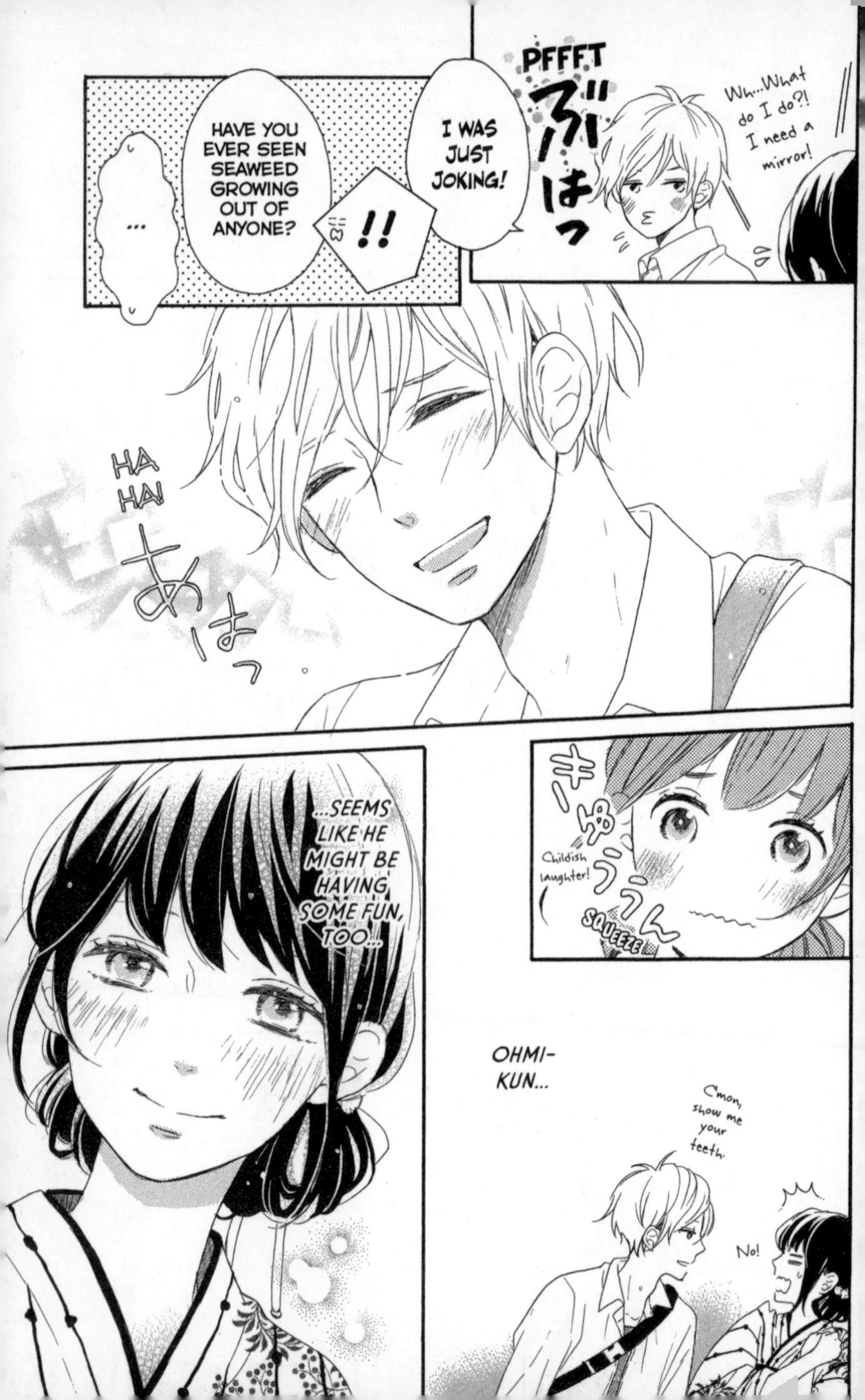
PFFFT
ぶはっ
Wh...What do I do?! I need a mirror!
I WAS JUST JOKING!
HAVE YOU EVER SEEN SEAWEED GROWING OUT OF ANYONE?
!!
...
HA HA!
あはっ
きゅううん
SQUEEZE
Childish laughter!
...SEEMS LIKE HE MIGHT BE HAVING SOME FUN, TOO...
OHMI-KUN...
C'mon, show me your teeth.
No!

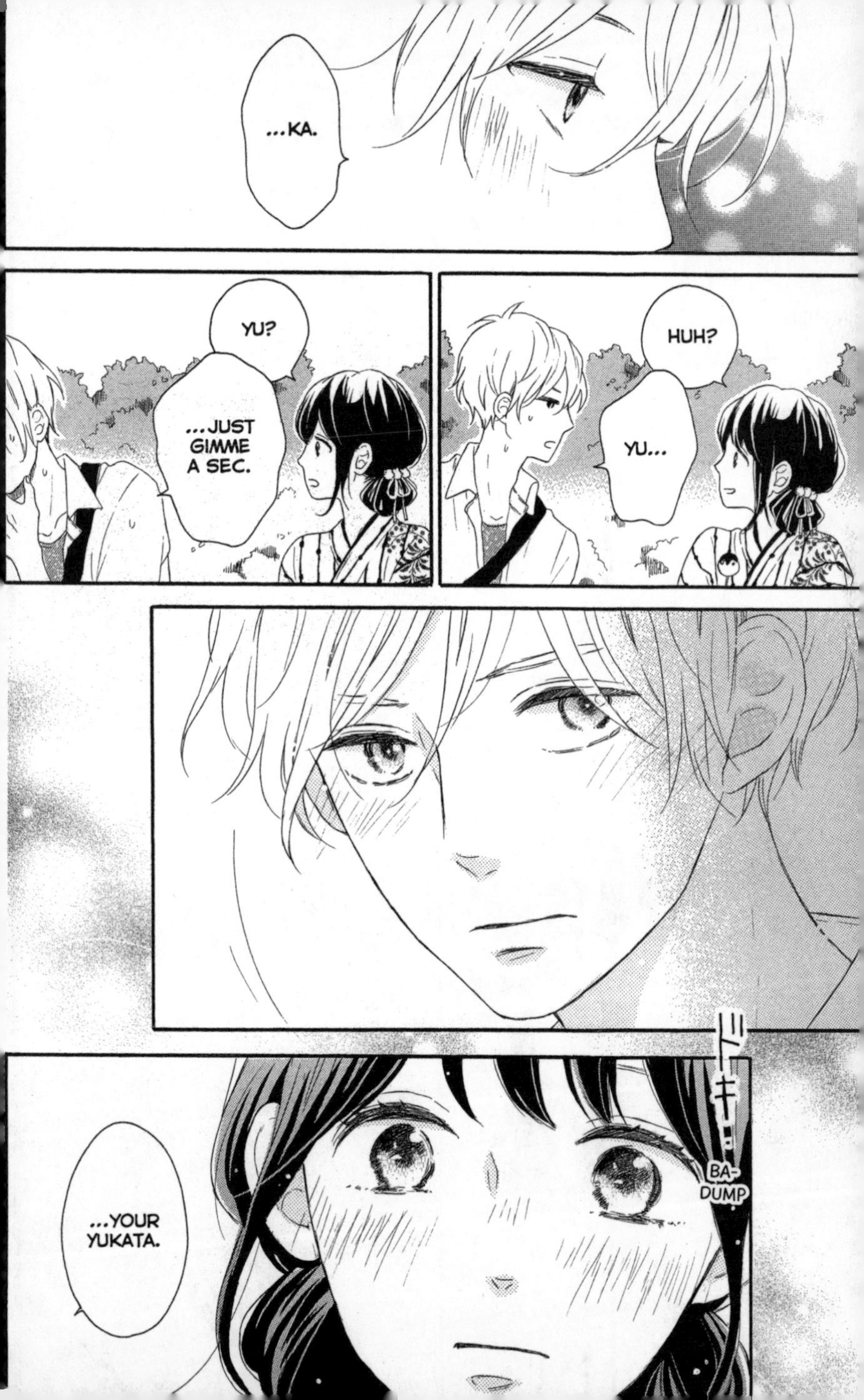
...KA.
HUH?
YU...
YU?
...JUST GIMME A SEC.
ドキ
BA-DUMP
...YOUR YUKATA.

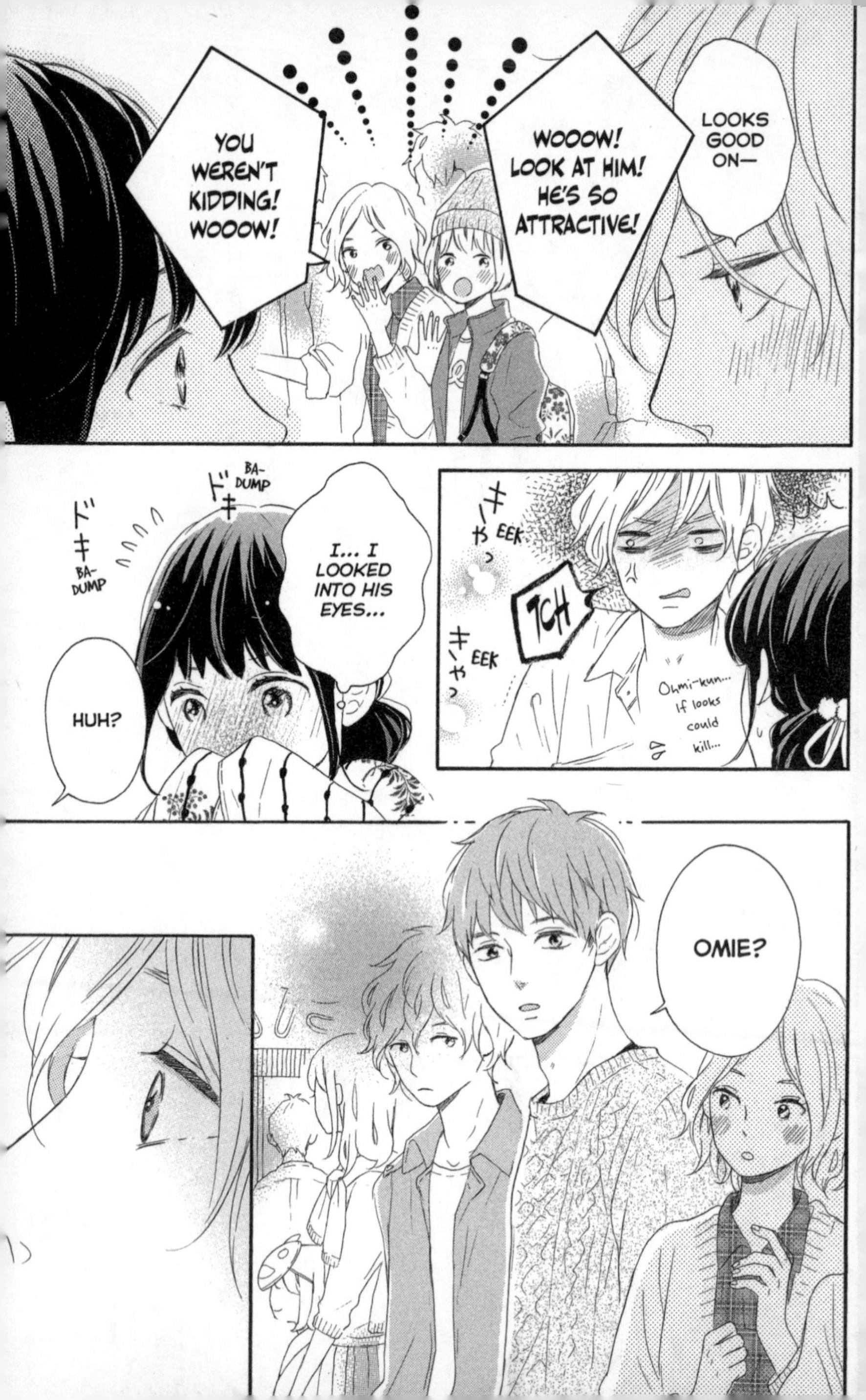
LOOKS GOOD ON—
WOOOW! LOOK AT HIM! HE'S SO ATTRACTIVE!
YOU WEREN'T KIDDING! WOOOW!
キャッ EEK
TCH
キャッ EEK
Ohmi-kun... If looks could kill...
ドキ BA-DUMP
ドキ BA-DUMP
I... I LOOKED INTO HIS EYES...
HUH?
OMIE?

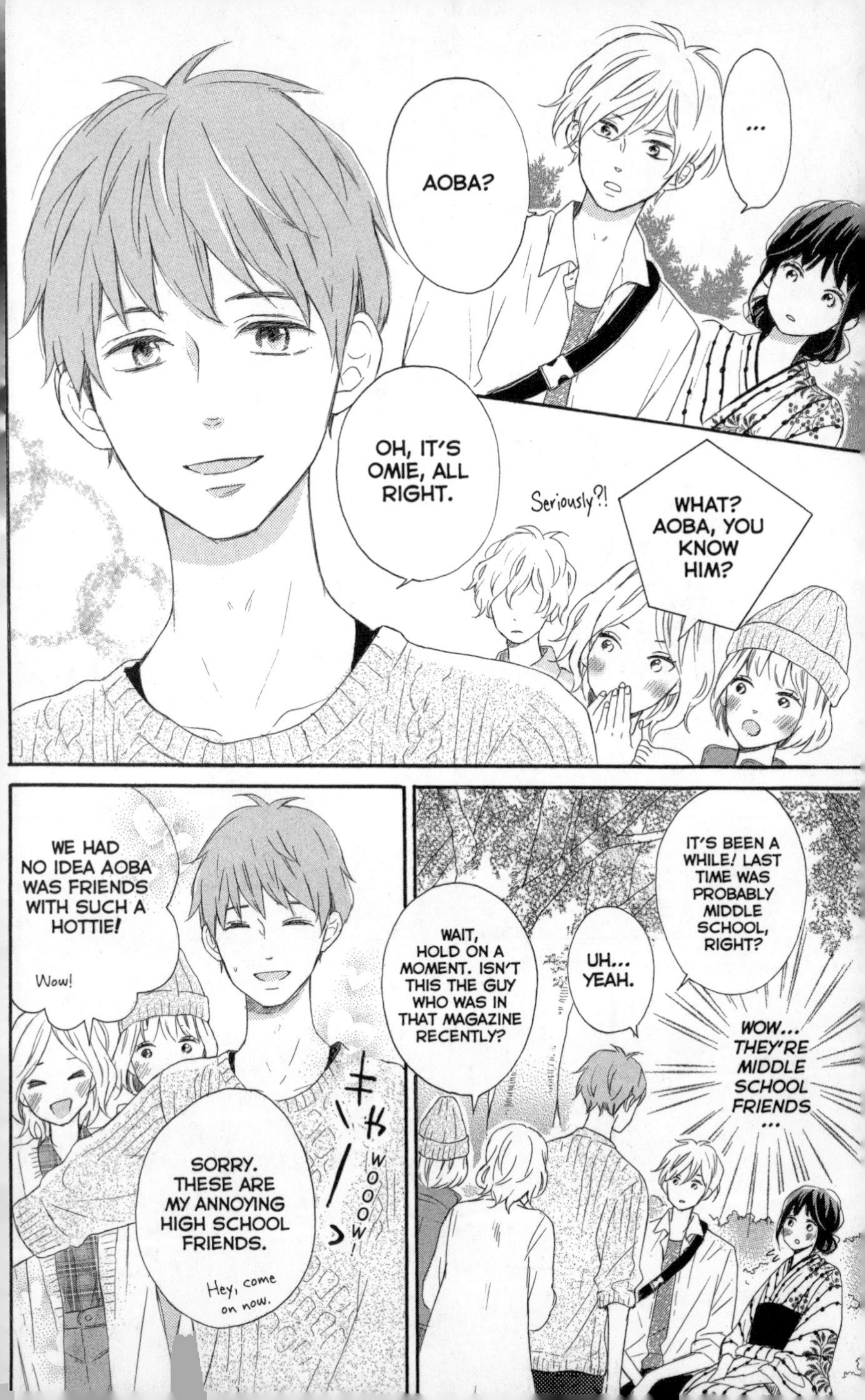
...
AOBA?
WHAT? AOBA, YOU KNOW HIM?
Seriously?!
OH, IT'S OMIE, ALL RIGHT.
IT'S BEEN A WHILE! LAST TIME WAS PROBABLY MIDDLE SCHOOL, RIGHT?
UH... YEAH.
WAIT, HOLD ON A MOMENT. ISN'T THIS THE GUY WHO WAS IN THAT MAGAZINE RECENTLY?
WOW... THEY'RE MIDDLE SCHOOL FRIENDS...
WE HAD NO IDEA AOBA WAS FRIENDS WITH SUCH A HOTTIE!
Wow!
WOOOOW!
SORRY. THESE ARE MY ANNOYING HIGH SCHOOL FRIENDS.
Hey, come on now.

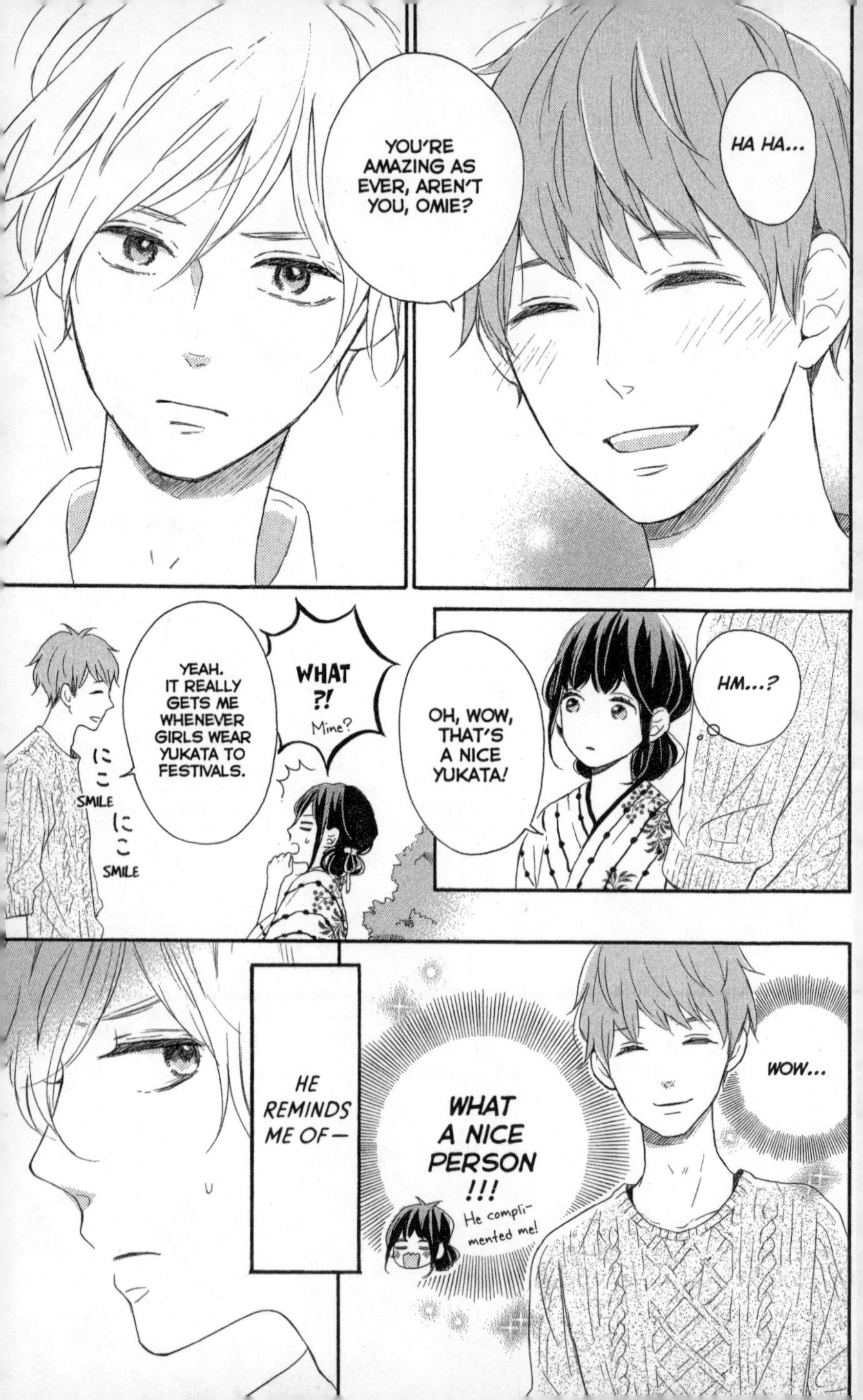
YOU'RE AMAZING AS EVER, AREN'T YOU, OMIE?
HA HA...
HM...?
OH, WOW, THAT'S A NICE YUKATA!
WHAT ?!
Mine?
YEAH. IT REALLY GETS ME WHENEVER GIRLS WEAR YUKATA TO FESTIVALS.
にこ
SMILE
にこ
SMILE
WOW...
WHAT A NICE PERSON !!!
He compli-mented me!
HE REMINDS ME OF—

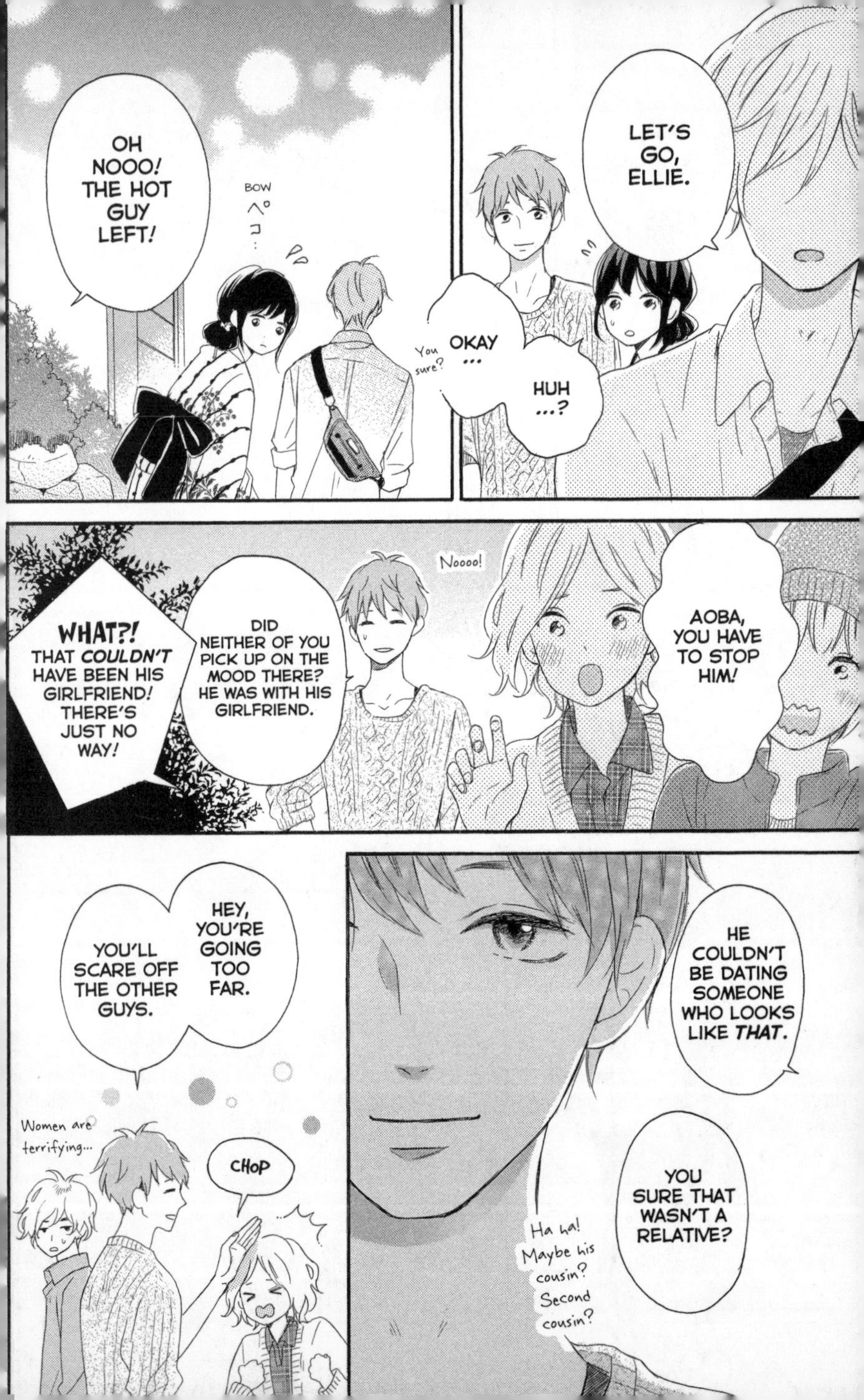
LET'S GO, ELLIE.
OKAY...
HUH...?
You sure?
OH NOOO! THE HOT GUY LEFT!
BOW
ペコ...
AOBA, YOU HAVE TO STOP HIM!
Noooo!
DID NEITHER OF YOU PICK UP ON THE MOOD THERE? HE WAS WITH HIS GIRLFRIEND.
WHAT?! THAT COULDN'T HAVE BEEN HIS GIRLFRIEND! THERE'S JUST NO WAY!
HE COULDN'T BE DATING SOMEONE WHO LOOKS LIKE THAT.
YOU SURE THAT WASN'T A RELATIVE?
Ha ha! Maybe his cousin? Second cousin?
HEY, YOU'RE GOING TOO FAR.
YOU'LL SCARE OFF THE OTHER GUYS.
CHOP
Women are terrifying...

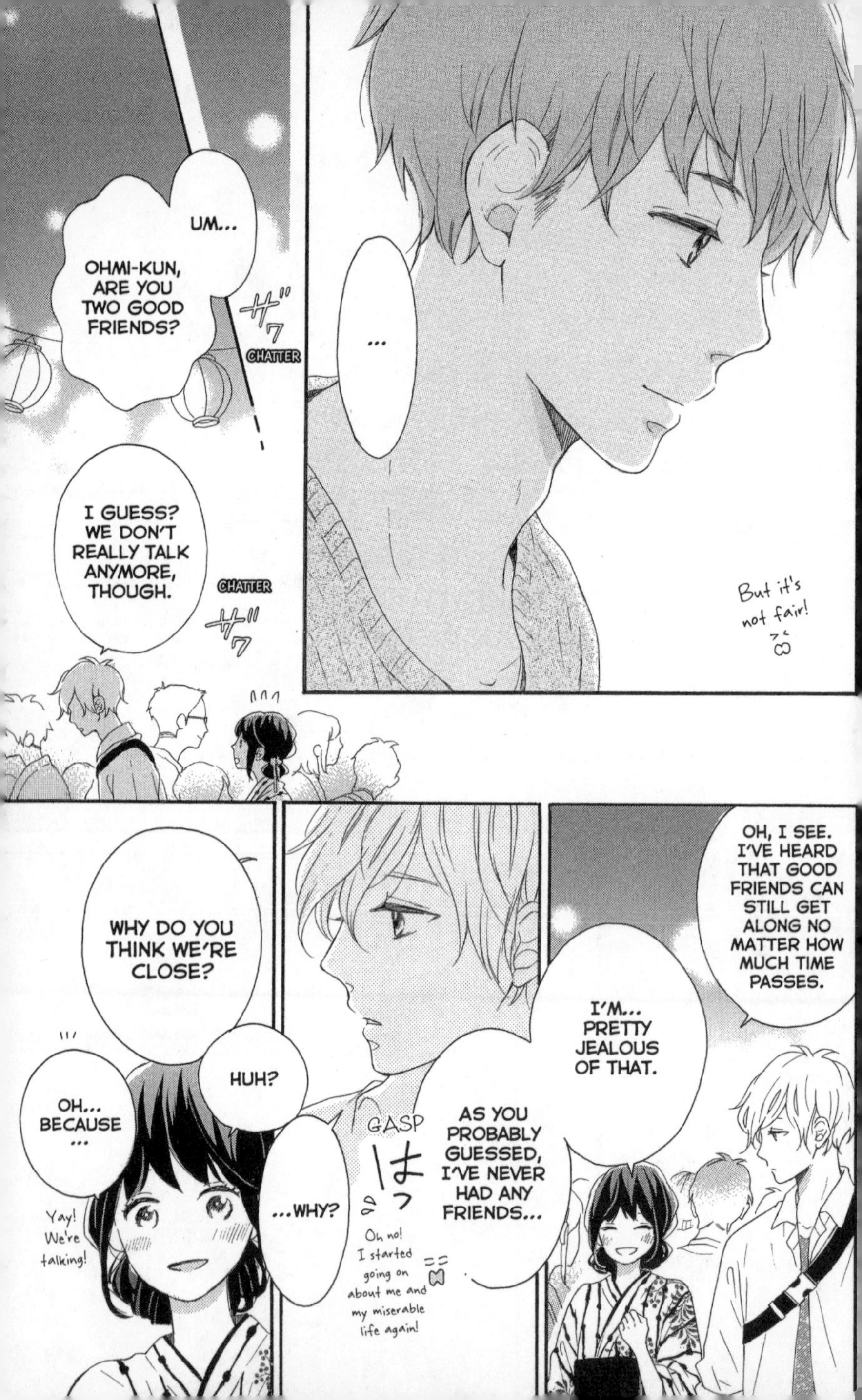
...
But it's not fair!
UM...
OHMI-KUN, ARE YOU TWO GOOD FRIENDS?
CHATTER
I GUESS? WE DON'T REALLY TALK ANYMORE, THOUGH.
CHATTER
OH, I SEE. I'VE HEARD THAT GOOD FRIENDS CAN STILL GET ALONG NO MATTER HOW MUCH TIME PASSES.
I'M... PRETTY JEALOUS OF THAT.
AS YOU PROBABLY GUESSED, I'VE NEVER HAD ANY FRIENDS...
GASP
...WHY?
Oh no! I started going on about me and my miserable life again!
WHY DO YOU THINK WE'RE CLOSE?
HUH?
OH... BECAUSE ...
Yay! We're talking!

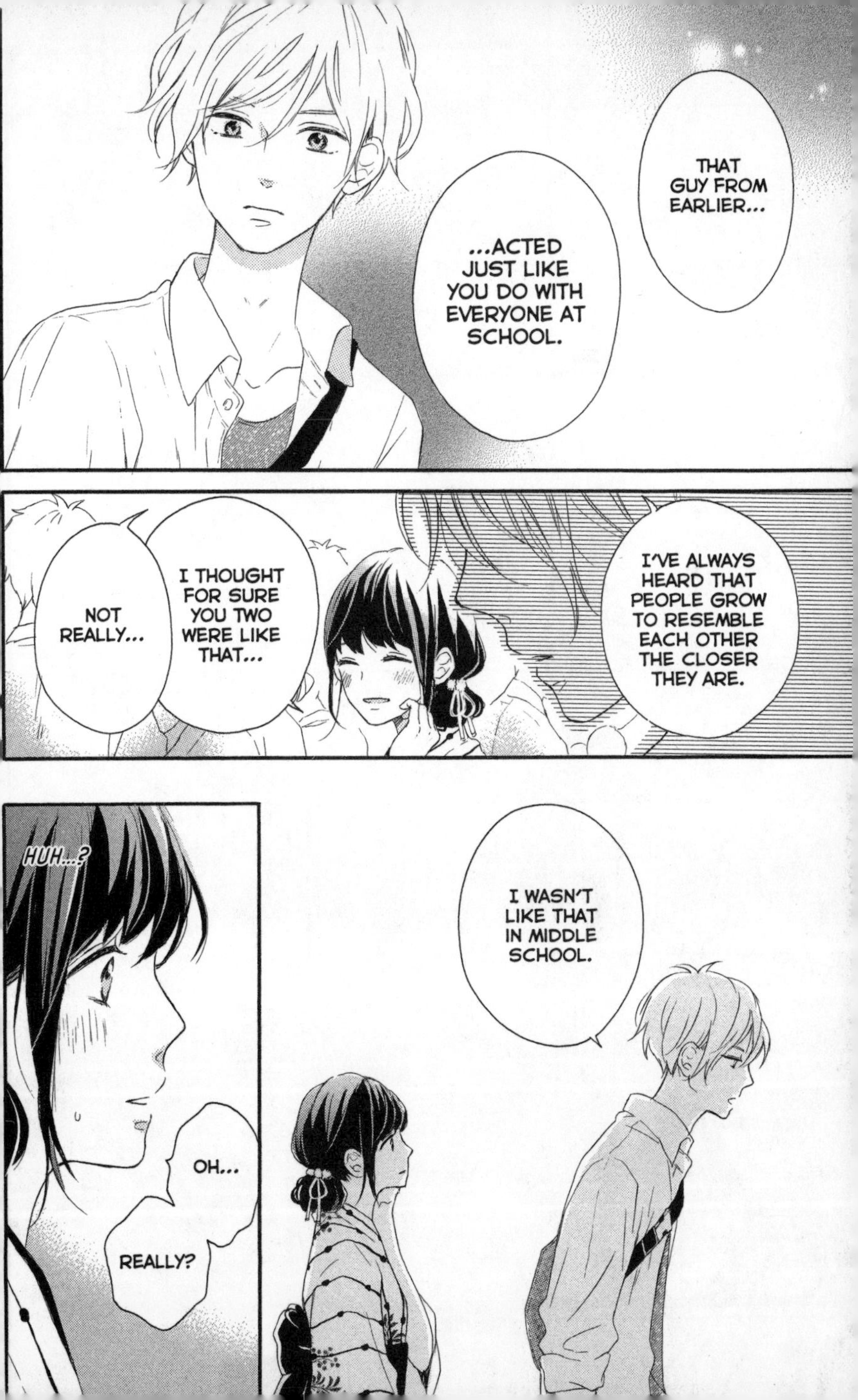
THAT GUY FROM EARLIER...
...ACTED JUST LIKE YOU DO WITH EVERYONE AT SCHOOL.
I'VE ALWAYS HEARD THAT PEOPLE GROW TO RESEMBLE EACH OTHER THE CLOSER THEY ARE.
I THOUGHT FOR SURE YOU TWO WERE LIKE THAT...
NOT REALLY...
I WASN'T LIKE THAT IN MIDDLE SCHOOL.
HUH...?
OH...
REALLY?

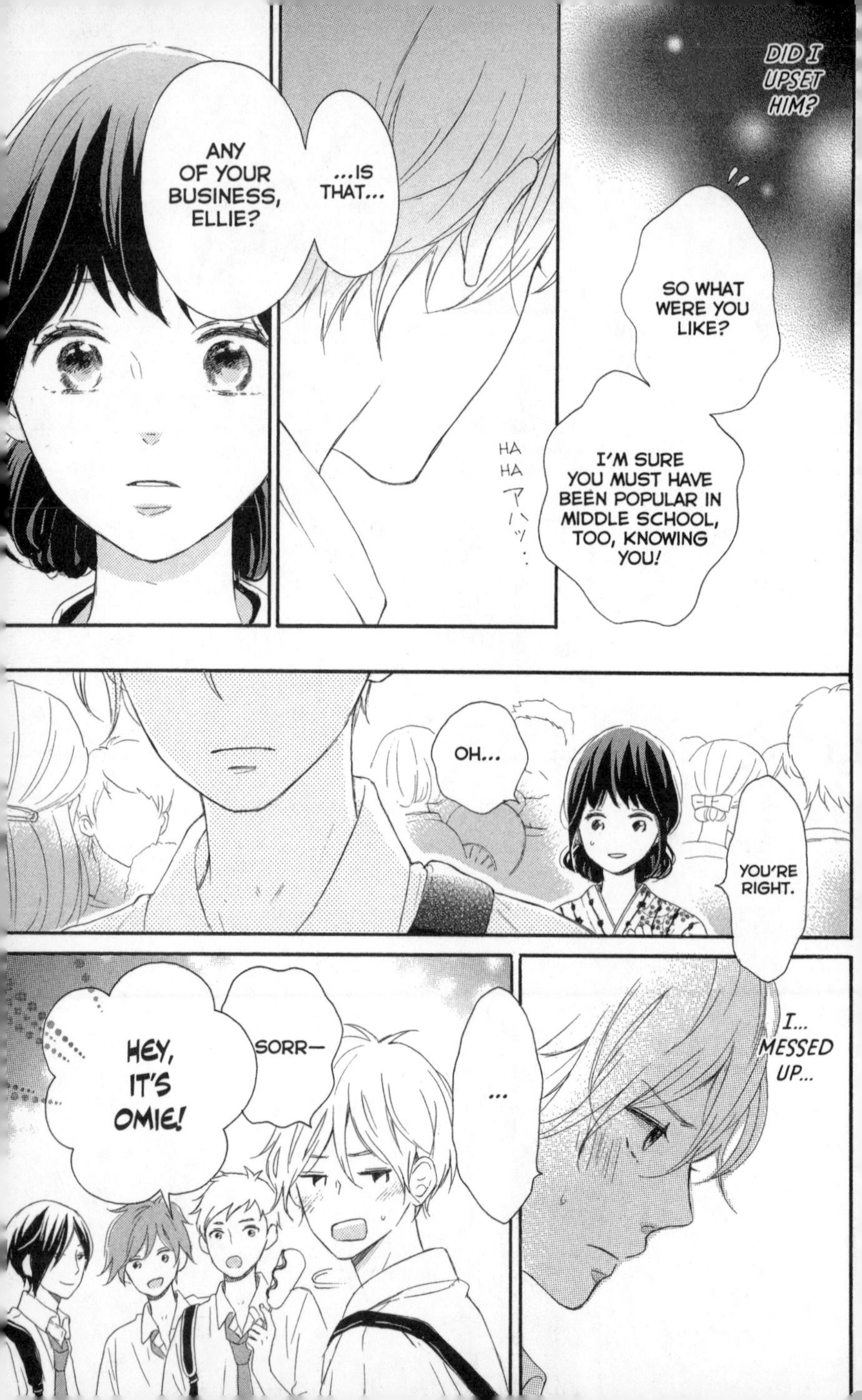
DID I UPSET HIM?
SO WHAT WERE YOU LIKE?
HA HA アハッ・・
I'M SURE YOU MUST HAVE BEEN POPULAR IN MIDDLE SCHOOL, TOO, KNOWING YOU!
...IS THAT...
ANY OF YOUR BUSINESS, ELLIE?
OH...
YOU'RE RIGHT.
I... MESSED UP...
...
SORR—
HEY, IT'S OMIE!

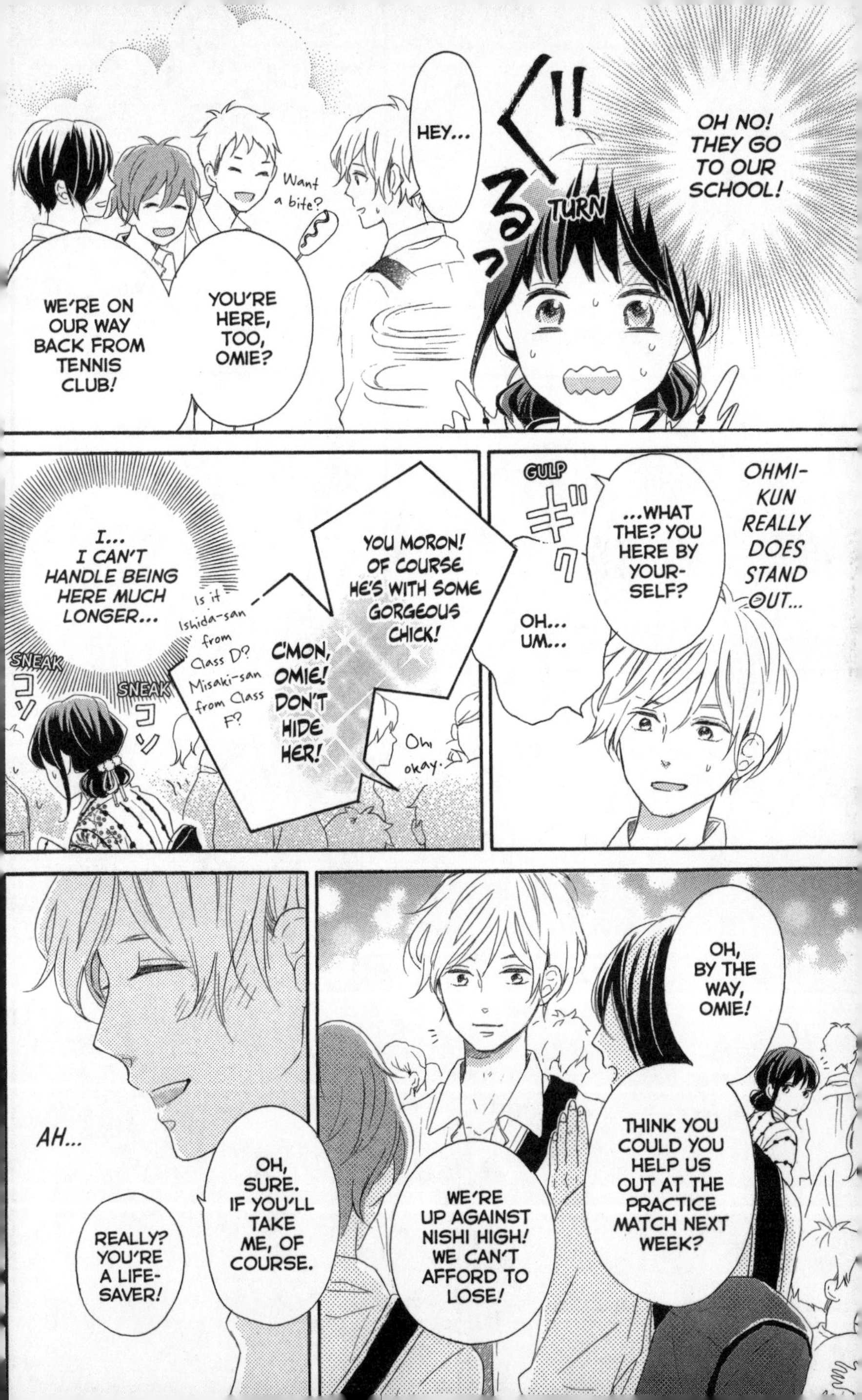
OH NO! THEY GO TO OUR SCHOOL!
TURN
HEY...
Want a bite?
YOU'RE HERE, TOO, OMIE?
WE'RE ON OUR WAY BACK FROM TENNIS CLUB!
OHMI-KUN REALLY DOES STAND OUT...
GULP
...WHAT THE? YOU HERE BY YOURSELF?
OH... UM...
YOU MORON! OF COURSE HE'S WITH SOME GORGEOUS CHICK!
Oh okay.
C'MON, OMIE! DON'T HIDE HER!
Is it Ishida-san from Class D? Misaki-san from Class F?
I... I CAN'T HANDLE BEING HERE MUCH LONGER...
SNEAK
SNEAK
OH, BY THE WAY, OMIE!
THINK YOU COULD YOU HELP US OUT AT THE PRACTICE MATCH NEXT WEEK?
WE'RE UP AGAINST NISHI HIGH! WE CAN'T AFFORD TO LOSE!
OH, SURE. IF YOU'LL TAKE ME, OF COURSE.
REALLY? YOU'RE A LIFE-SAVER!
AH...

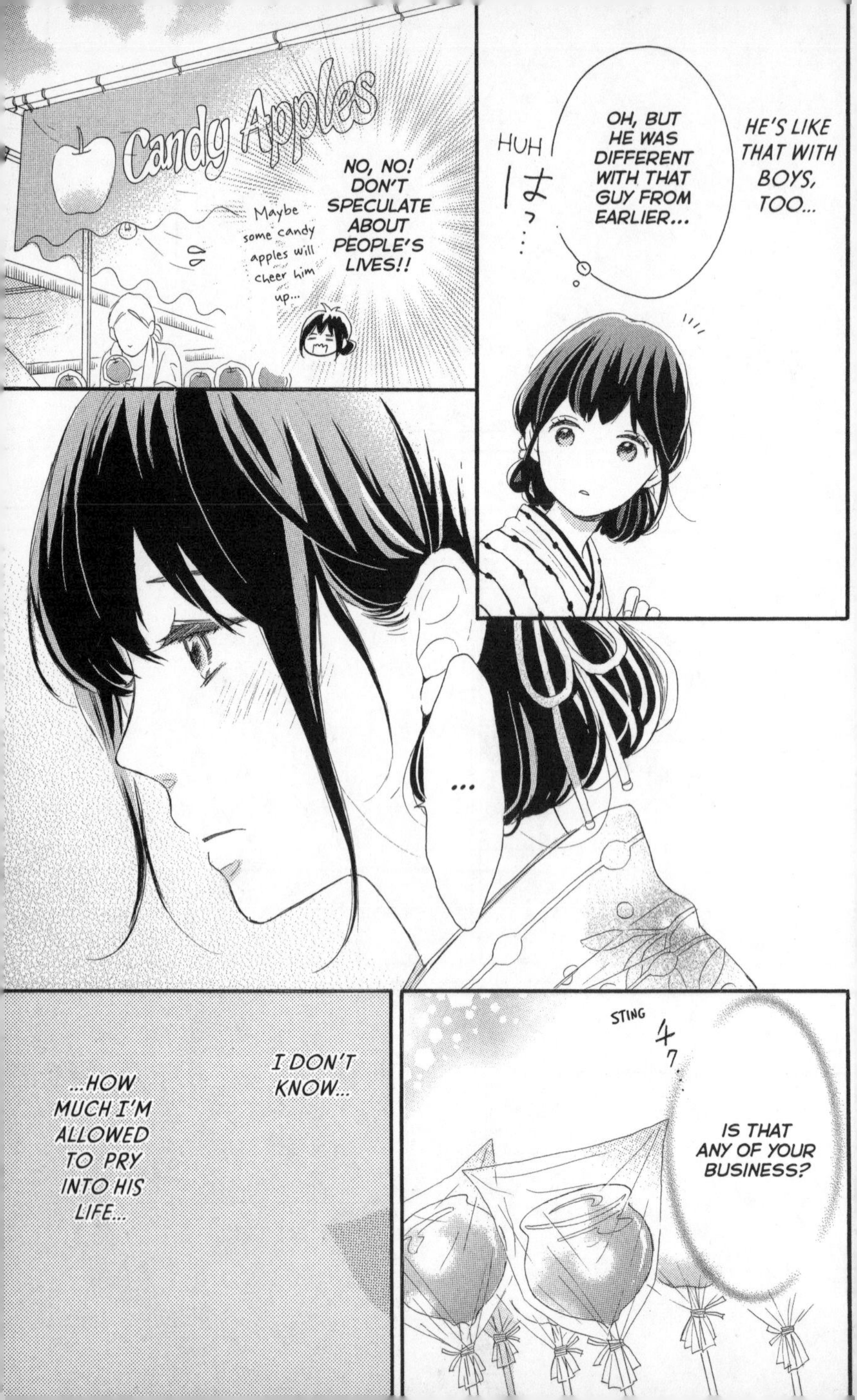
HE'S LIKE THAT WITH BOYS, TOO...
OH, BUT HE WAS DIFFERENT WITH THAT GUY FROM EARLIER...
HUH
はっ…
NO, NO! DON'T SPECULATE ABOUT PEOPLE'S LIVES!!
Maybe some candy apples will cheer him up...
Candy Apples
...
IS THAT ANY OF YOUR BUSINESS?
STING
I DON'T KNOW...
...HOW MUCH I'M ALLOWED TO PRY INTO HIS LIFE...

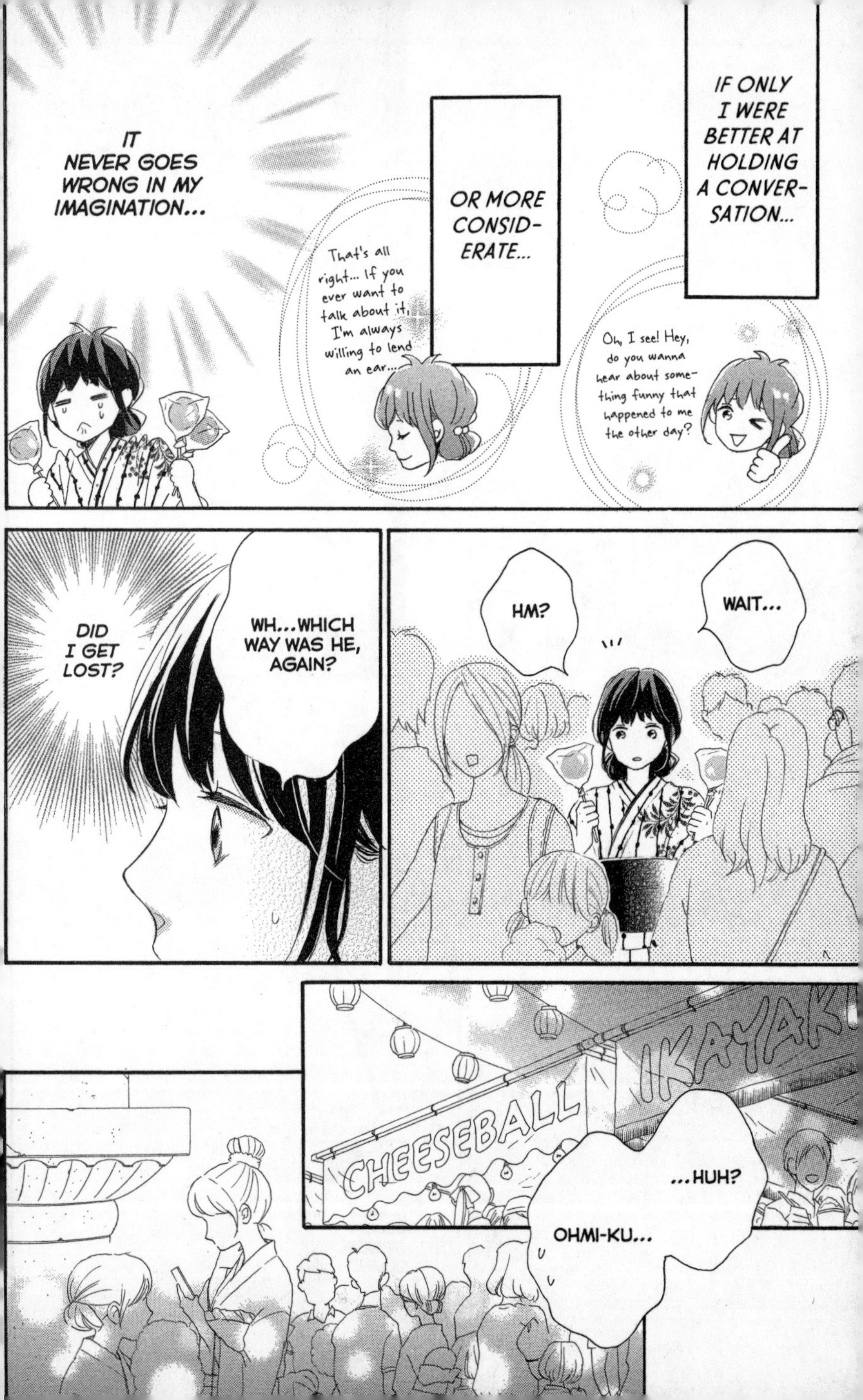
IF ONLY I WERE BETTER AT HOLDING A CONVERSATION...
Oh, I see! Hey, do you wanna hear about something funny that happened to me the other day?
OR MORE CONSIDERATE...
That's all right... If you ever want to talk about it, I'm always willing to lend an ear...
IT NEVER GOES WRONG IN MY IMAGINATION...
WAIT...
HM?
WH...WHICH WAY WAS HE, AGAIN?
DID I GET LOST?
IKAYAK
CHEESEBALL
...HUH?
OHMI-KU...

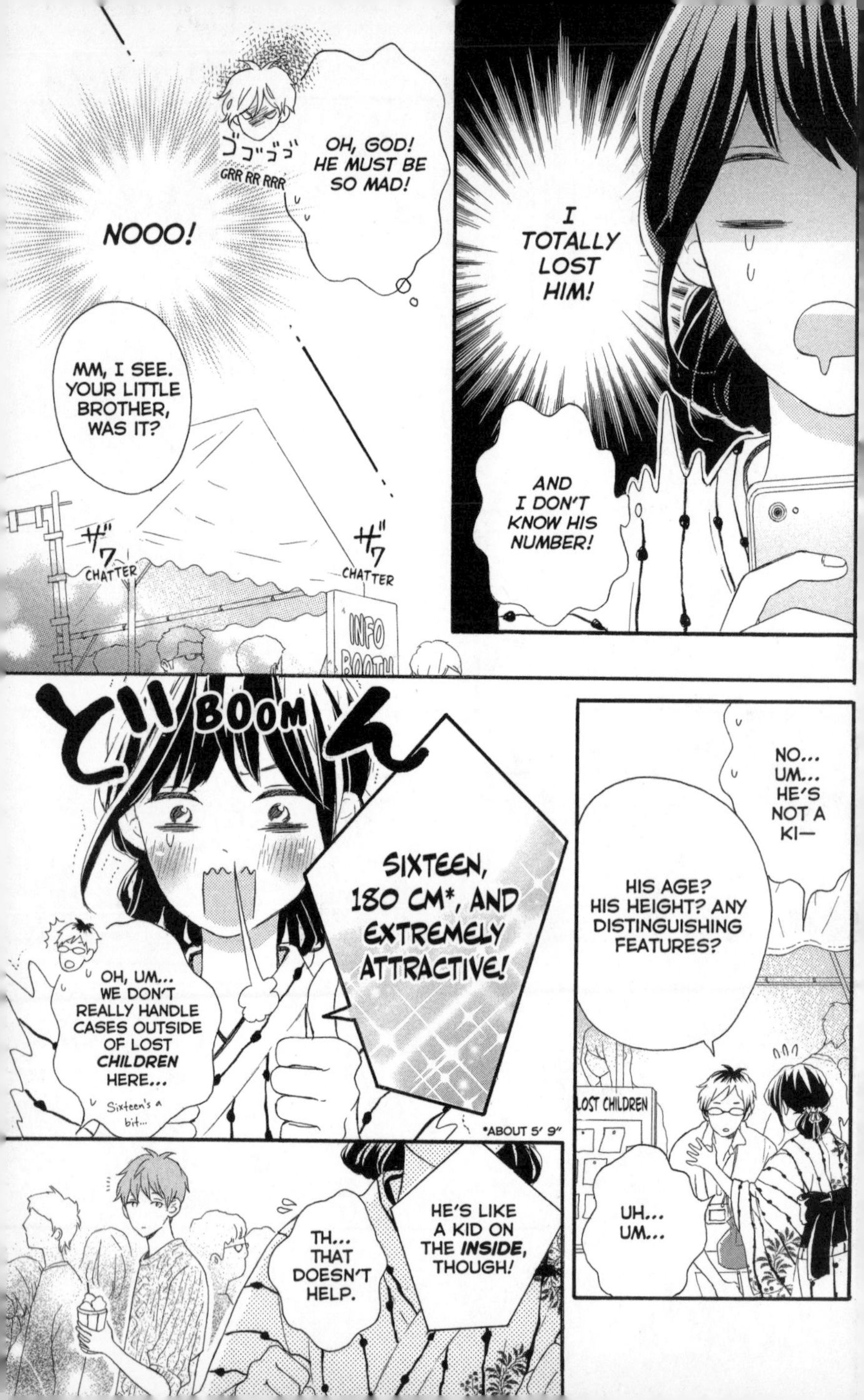
I TOTALLY LOST HIM!
AND I DON'T KNOW HIS NUMBER!
NOOO!
ゴゴゴゴ
GRR RR RRR
OH, GOD! HE MUST BE SO MAD!
MM, I SEE. YOUR LITTLE BROTHER, WAS IT?
ザワ
CHATTER
ザワ
CHATTER
INFO BOOTH
NO... UM... HE'S NOT A KI—
HIS AGE? HIS HEIGHT? ANY DISTINGUISHING FEATURES?
LOST CHILDREN
UH... UM...
BOOM
SIXTEEN, 180 CM*, AND EXTREMELY ATTRACTIVE!
OH, UM... WE DON'T REALLY HANDLE CASES OUTSIDE OF LOST *CHILDREN* HERE...
Sixteen's a bit...
*ABOUT 5' 9"
HE'S LIKE A KID ON THE *INSIDE*, THOUGH!
TH... THAT DOESN'T HELP.

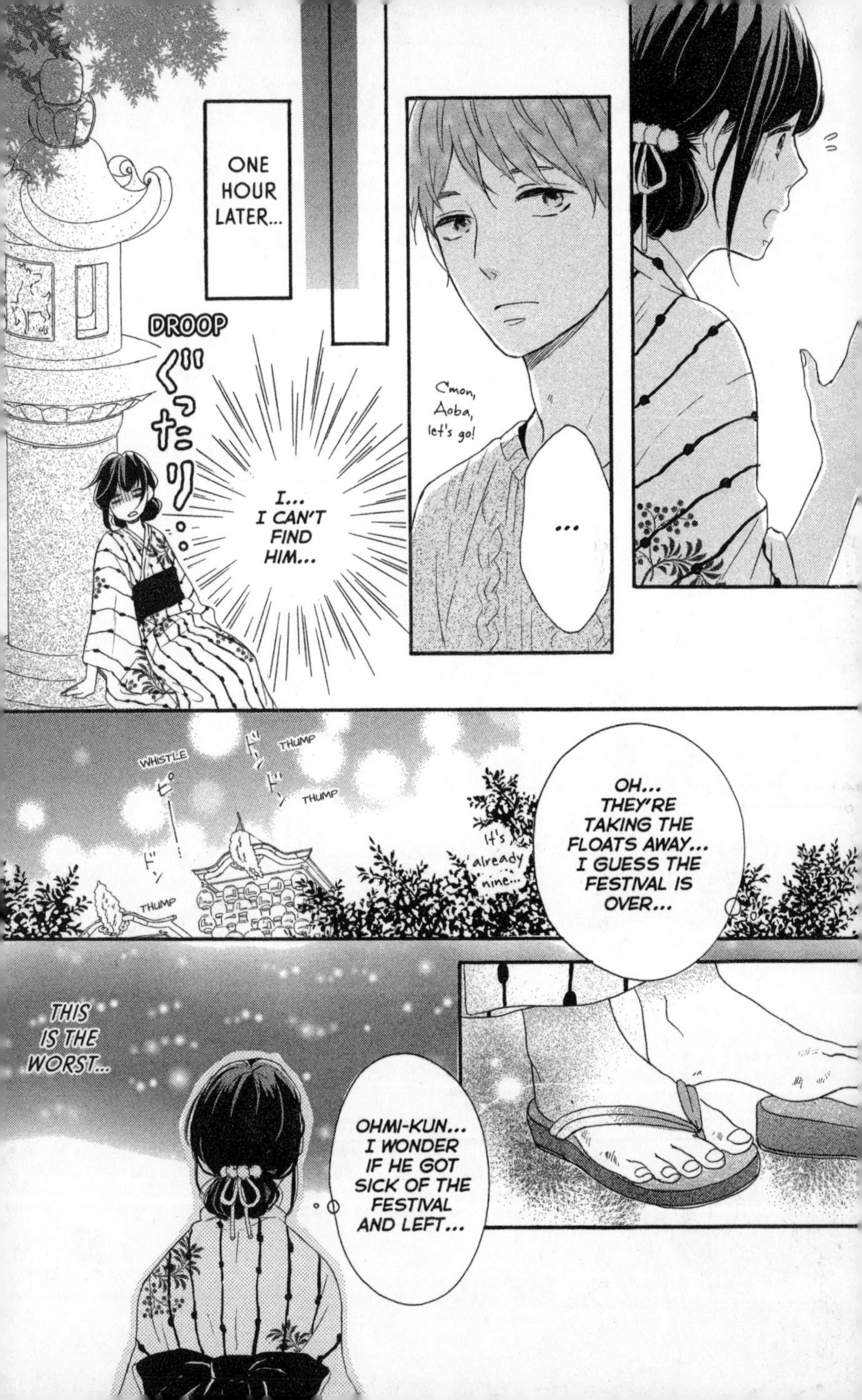
C'mon, Aoba, let's go!
...
ONE HOUR LATER...
DROOP
ぐったり
I... I CAN'T FIND HIM...
OH... THEY'RE TAKING THE FLOATS AWAY... I GUESS THE FESTIVAL IS OVER...
It's already nine...
THUMP
ドン
THUMP
ドン
WHISTLE
ピー
THUMP
ドン
OHMI-KUN... I WONDER IF HE GOT SICK OF THE FESTIVAL AND LEFT...
THIS IS THE WORST...

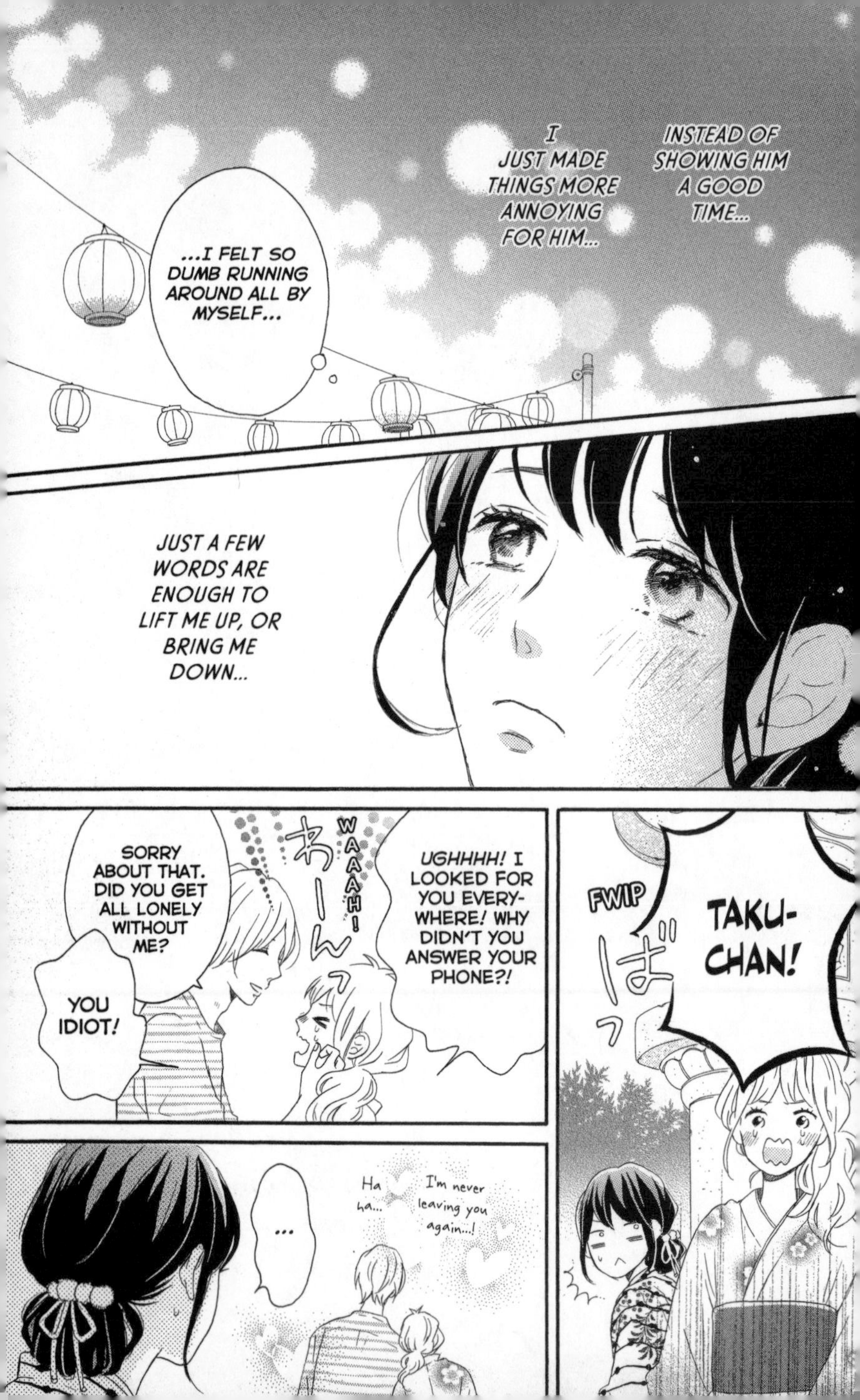
INSTEAD OF SHOWING HIM A GOOD TIME...
I JUST MADE THINGS MORE ANNOYING FOR HIM...
...I FELT SO DUMB RUNNING AROUND ALL BY MYSELF...
JUST A FEW WORDS ARE ENOUGH TO LIFT ME UP, OR BRING ME DOWN...
TAKU-CHAN!
ばっ
FWIP
UGHHHH! I LOOKED FOR YOU EVERY-WHERE! WHY DIDN'T YOU ANSWER YOUR PHONE?!
WAAAAH!
わーんっ
SORRY ABOUT THAT. DID YOU GET ALL LONELY WITHOUT ME?
YOU IDIOT!
I'm never leaving you again...!
Ha ha...
...

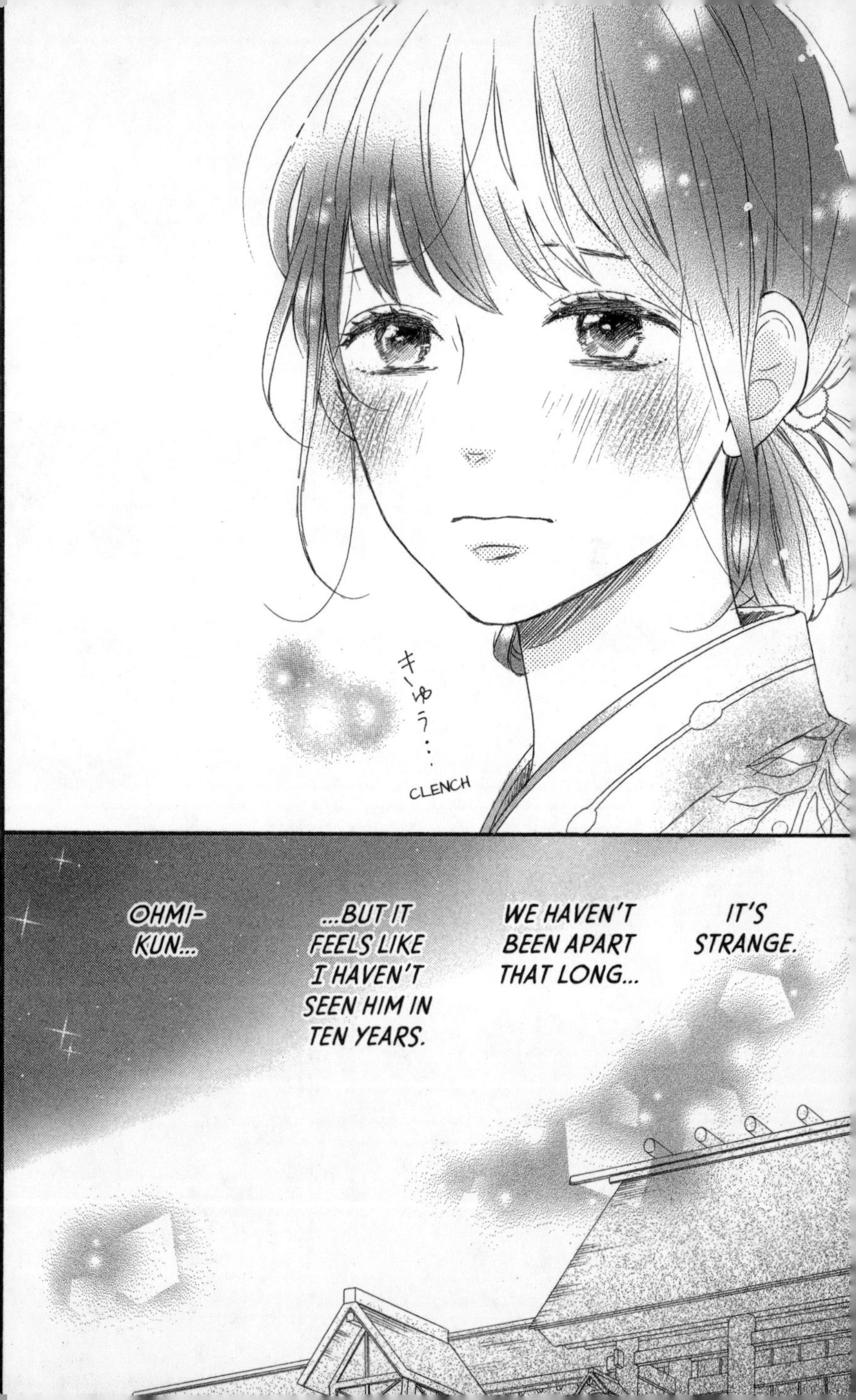
キゅう…
CLENCH
IT'S STRANGE.
WE HAVEN'T BEEN APART THAT LONG...
...BUT IT FEELS LIKE I HAVEN'T SEEN HIM IN TEN YEARS.
OHMI-KUN...

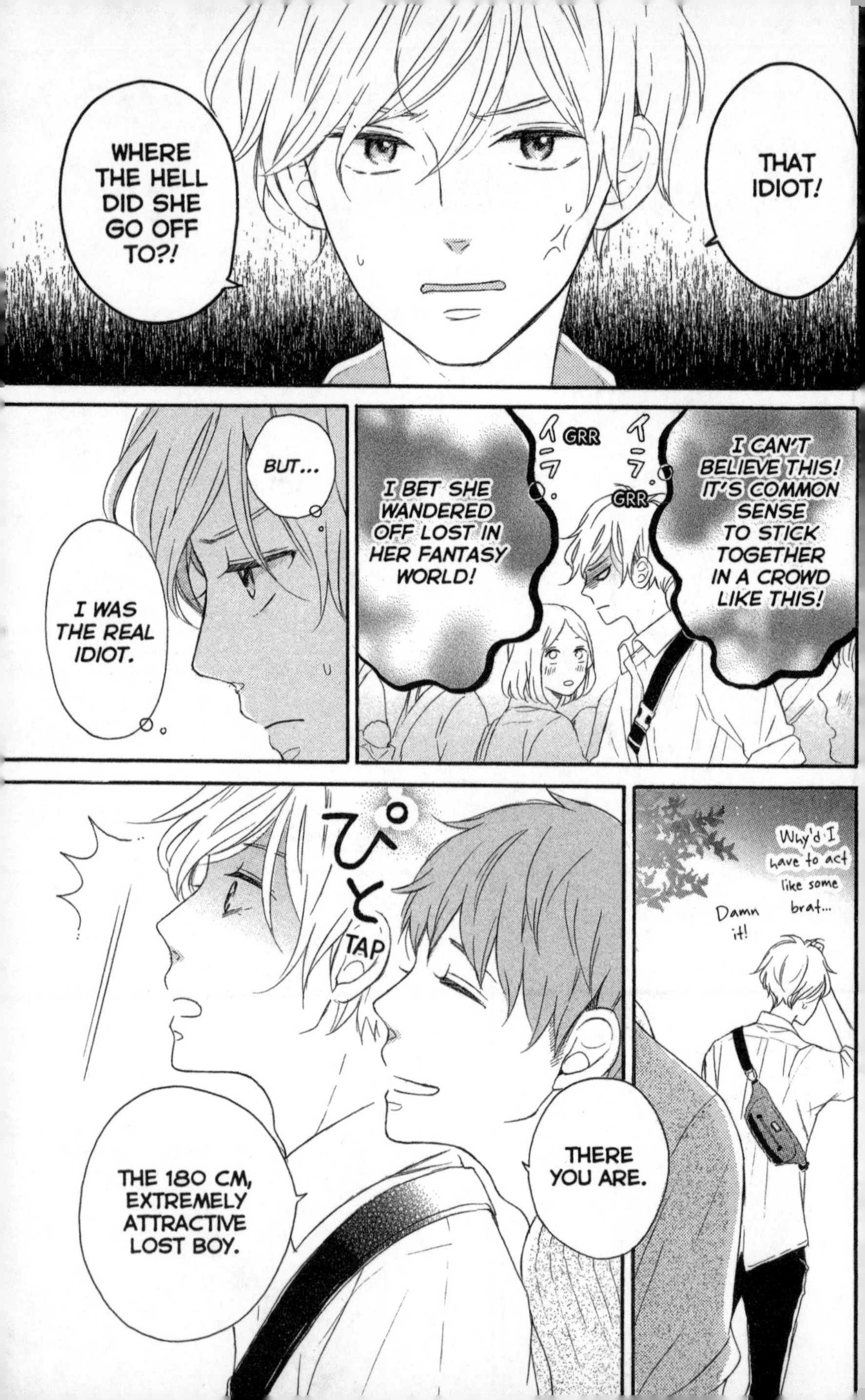
THAT IDIOT!
WHERE THE HELL DID SHE GO OFF TO?!
I CAN'T BELIEVE THIS! IT'S COMMON SENSE TO STICK TOGETHER IN A CROWD LIKE THIS!
イラ GRR
イラ GRR
I BET SHE WANDERED OFF LOST IN HER FANTASY WORLD!
BUT...
I WAS THE REAL IDIOT.
Why'd I have to act like some brat...
Damn it!
ぴと TAP
THERE YOU ARE.
THE 180 CM, EXTREMELY ATTRACTIVE LOST BOY.

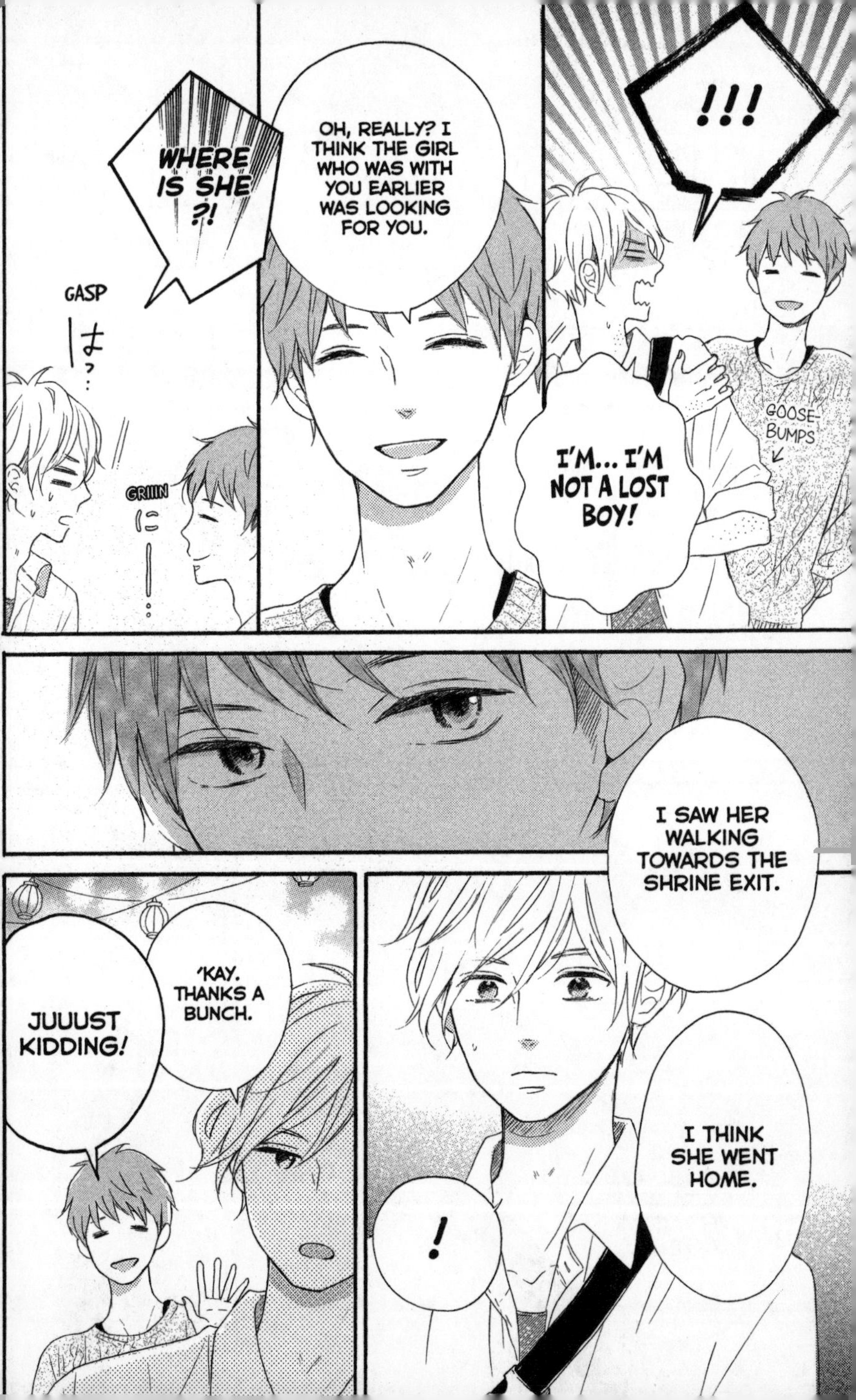
!!!
I'M... I'M NOT A LOST BOY!
GOOSE-BUMPS
OH, REALLY? I THINK THE GIRL WHO WAS WITH YOU EARLIER WAS LOOKING FOR YOU.
WHERE IS SHE ?!
GASP
は
GRIIN
に
I SAW HER WALKING TOWARDS THE SHRINE EXIT.
I THINK SHE WENT HOME.
!
'KAY. THANKS A BUNCH.
JUUUST KIDDING!

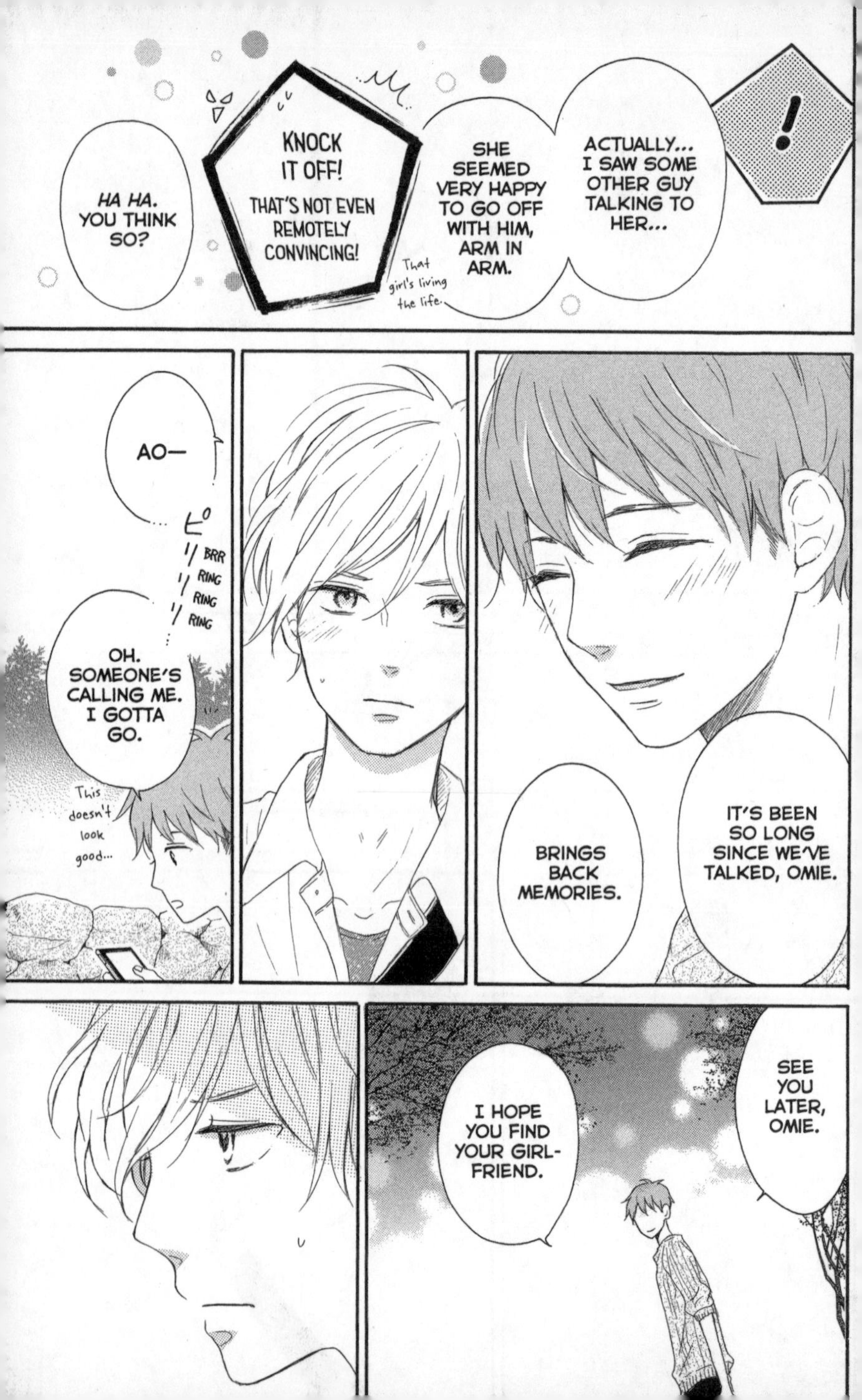
!
ACTUALLY... I SAW SOME OTHER GUY TALKING TO HER...
SHE SEEMED VERY HAPPY TO GO OFF WITH HIM, ARM IN ARM.
That girl's living the life.
KNOCK IT OFF! THAT'S NOT EVEN REMOTELY CONVINCING!
HA HA. YOU THINK SO?
IT'S BEEN SO LONG SINCE WE'VE TALKED, OMIE.
BRINGS BACK MEMORIES.
AO—
ピ
BRR RING RING RING
OH. SOMEONE'S CALLING ME. I GOTTA GO.
This doesn't look good...
SEE YOU LATER, OMIE.
I HOPE YOU FIND YOUR GIRL-FRIEND.

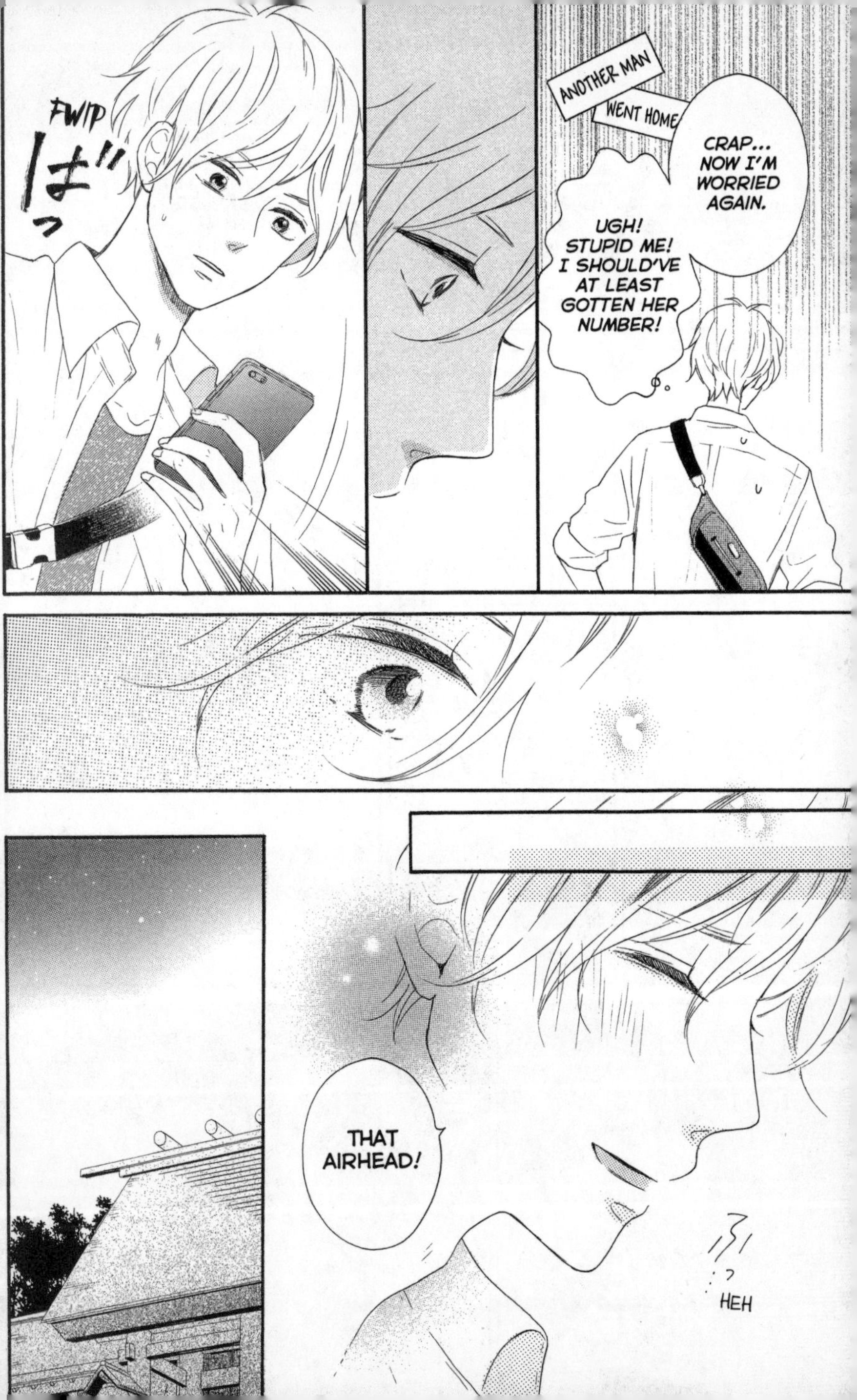
ANOTHER MAN
WENT HOME
CRAP... NOW I'M WORRIED AGAIN.
UGH! STUPID ME! I SHOULD'VE AT LEAST GOTTEN HER NUMBER!
FWIP
ばっ
THAT AIRHEAD!
ふっ
HEH

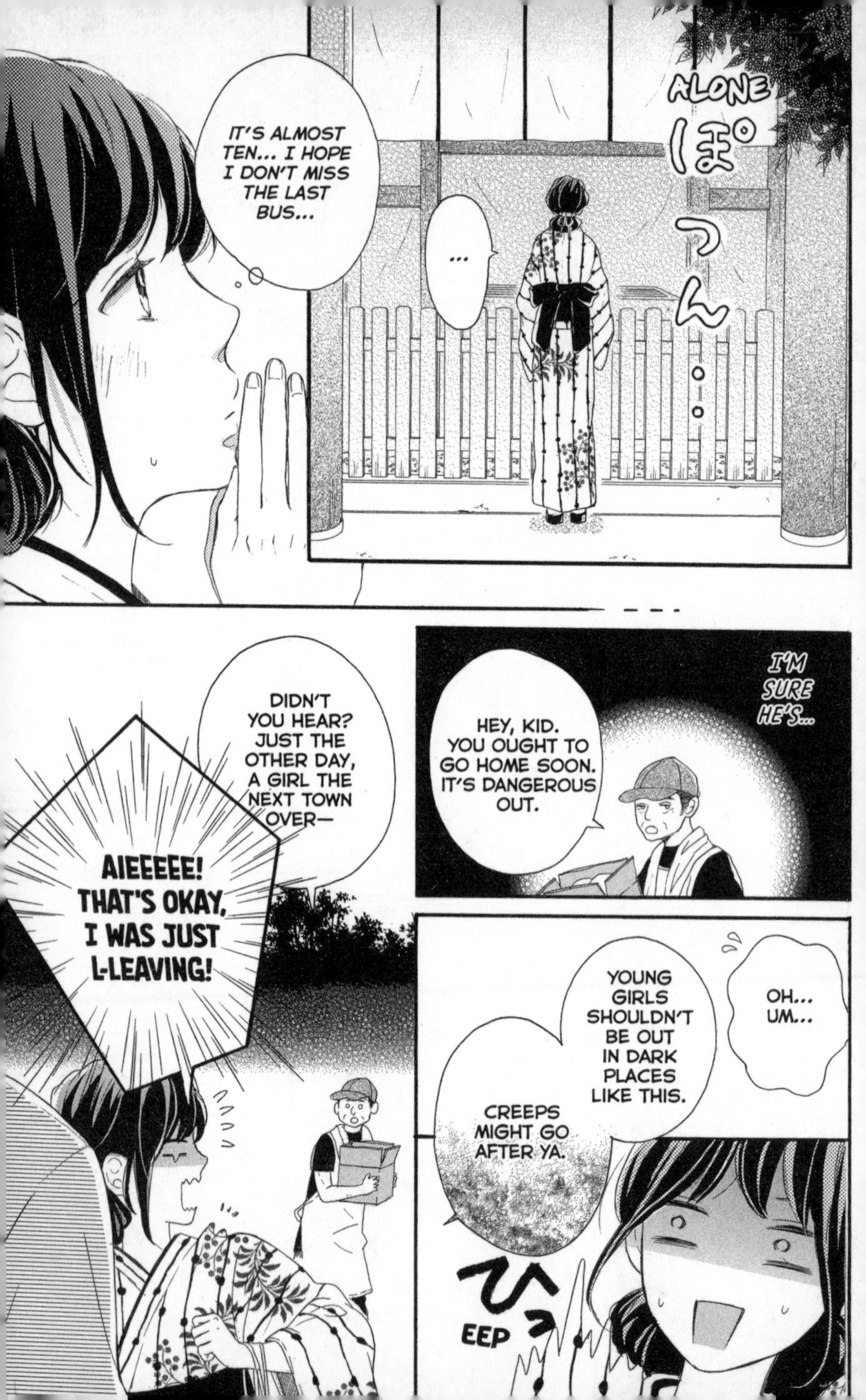
ALONE
ぽつん。。
...
IT'S ALMOST TEN... I HOPE I DON'T MISS THE LAST BUS...
I'M SURE HE'S...
HEY, KID. YOU OUGHT TO GO HOME SOON. IT'S DANGEROUS OUT.
OH... UM...
YOUNG GIRLS SHOULDN'T BE OUT IN DARK PLACES LIKE THIS.
CREEPS MIGHT GO AFTER YA.
ひっ
EEP
DIDN'T YOU HEAR? JUST THE OTHER DAY, A GIRL THE NEXT TOWN OVER—
AIEEEEE! THAT'S OKAY, I WAS JUST L-LEAVING!

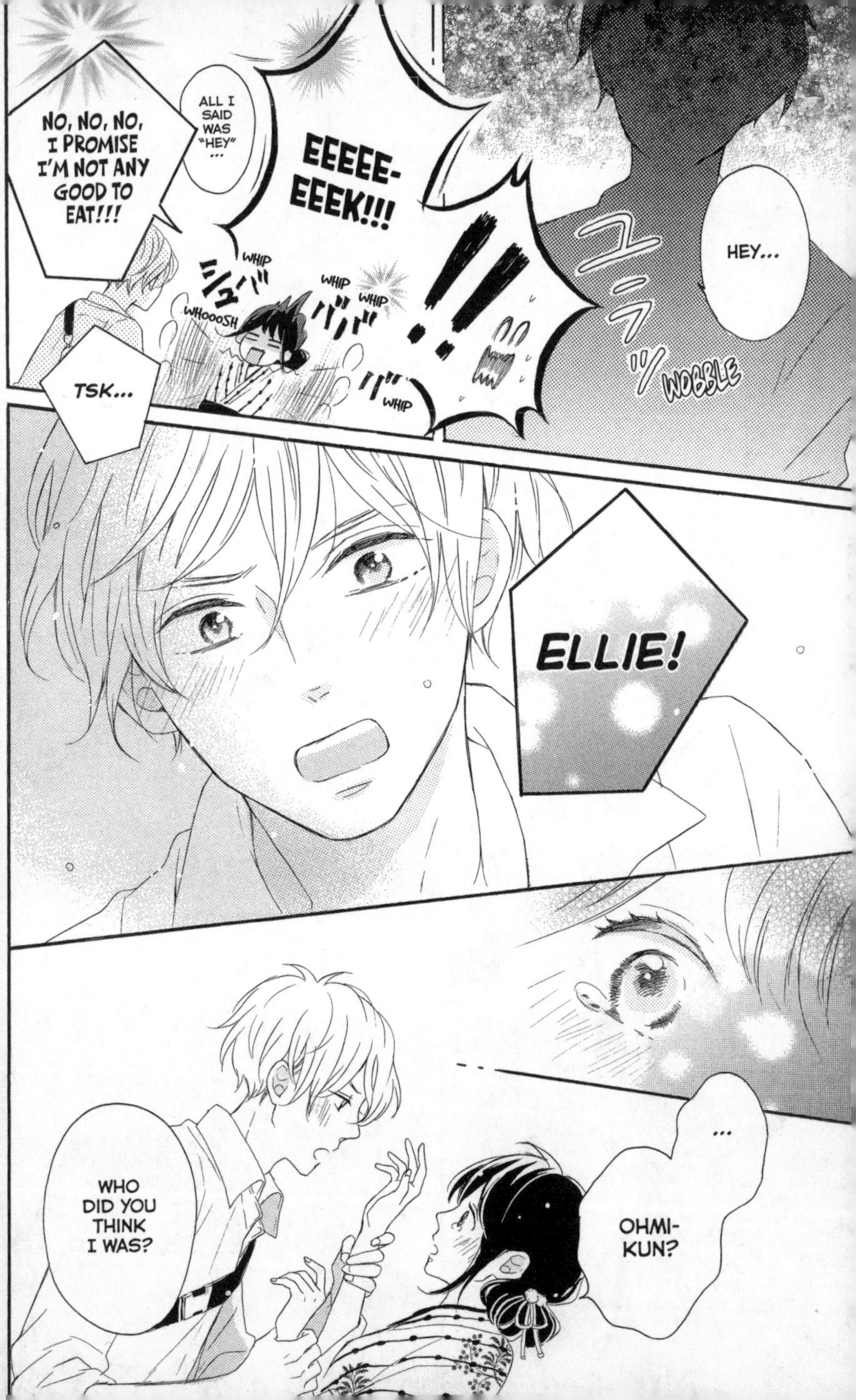
HEY...
WOBBLE
EEEEE-EEEK!!!
ALL I SAID WAS "HEY"...
NO, NO, NO, I PROMISE I'M NOT ANY GOOD TO EAT!!!
WHIP
WHIP
WHIP
WHOOOSH
WHIP
TSK...
ELLIE!
...
OHMI-KUN?
WHO DID YOU THINK I WAS?

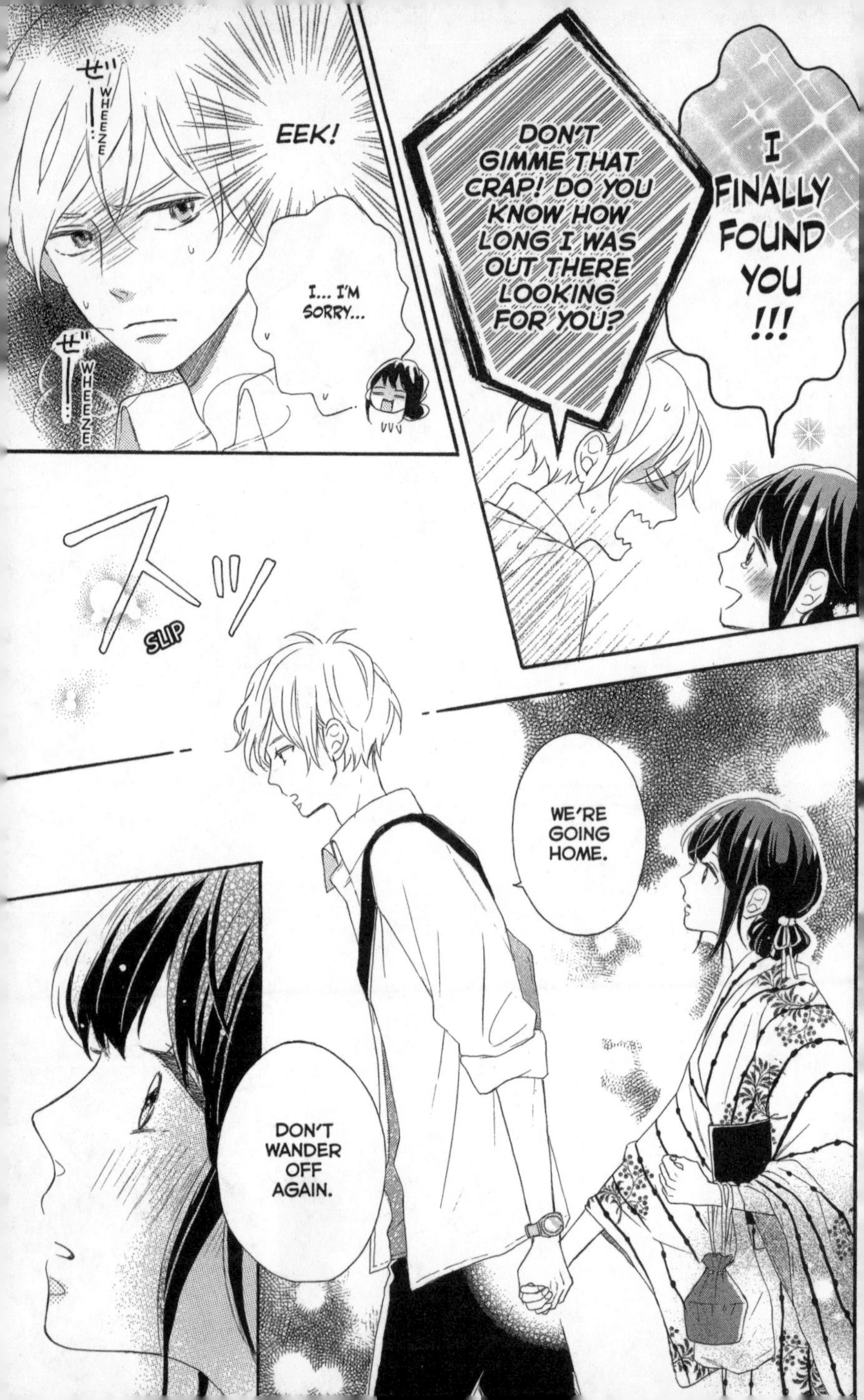
I FINALLY FOUND YOU!!!
DON'T GIMME THAT CRAP! DO YOU KNOW HOW LONG I WAS OUT THERE LOOKING FOR YOU?
EEK!
I... I'M SORRY...
ぜー WHEEZE
ぜー WHEEZE
スッ SLIP
WE'RE GOING HOME.
DON'T WANDER OFF AGAIN.

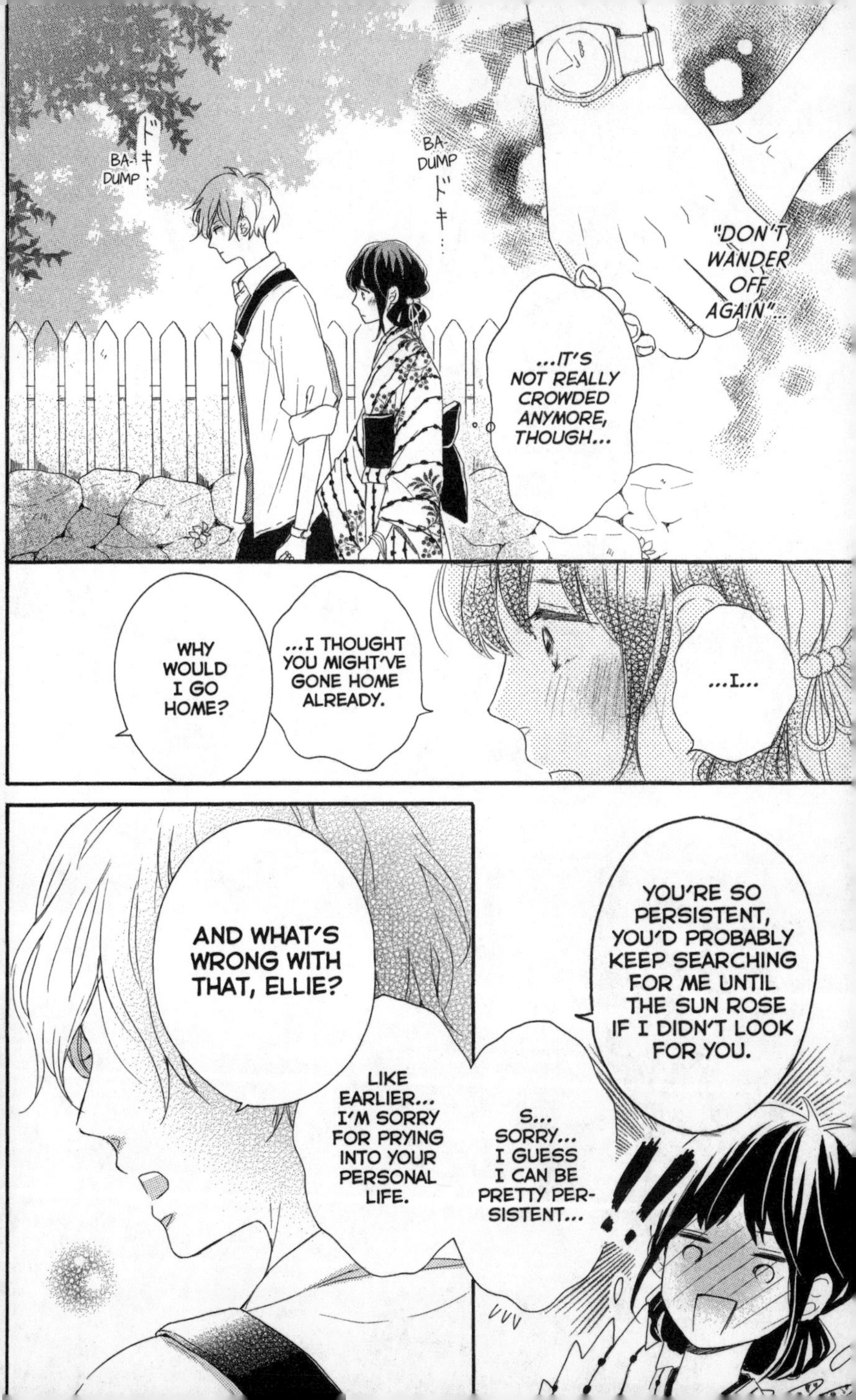
"DON'T WANDER OFF AGAIN"...
...IT'S NOT REALLY CROWDED ANYMORE, THOUGH...
BA-DUMP
ドキ…
BA-DUMP
ドキ…
...I...
...I THOUGHT YOU MIGHT'VE GONE HOME ALREADY.
WHY WOULD I GO HOME?
YOU'RE SO PERSISTENT, YOU'D PROBABLY KEEP SEARCHING FOR ME UNTIL THE SUN ROSE IF I DIDN'T LOOK FOR YOU.
S... SORRY... I GUESS I CAN BE PRETTY PER-SISTENT...
AND WHAT'S WRONG WITH THAT, ELLIE?
LIKE EARLIER... I'M SORRY FOR PRYING INTO YOUR PERSONAL LIFE.

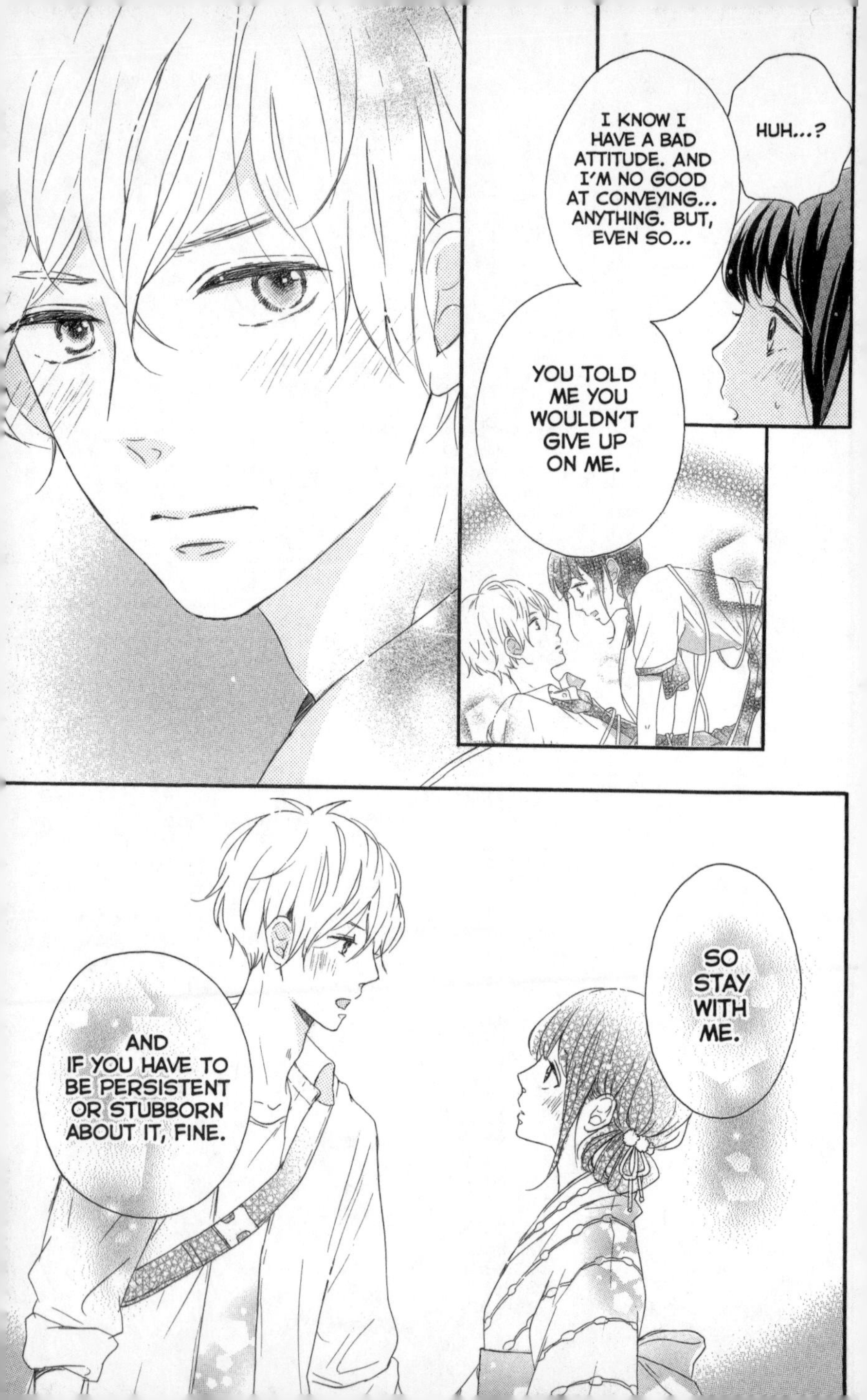
HUH...?
I KNOW I HAVE A BAD ATTITUDE. AND I'M NO GOOD AT CONVEYING... ANYTHING. BUT, EVEN SO...
YOU TOLD ME YOU WOULDN'T GIVE UP ON ME.
SO STAY WITH ME.
AND IF YOU HAVE TO BE PERSISTENT OR STUBBORN ABOUT IT, FINE.

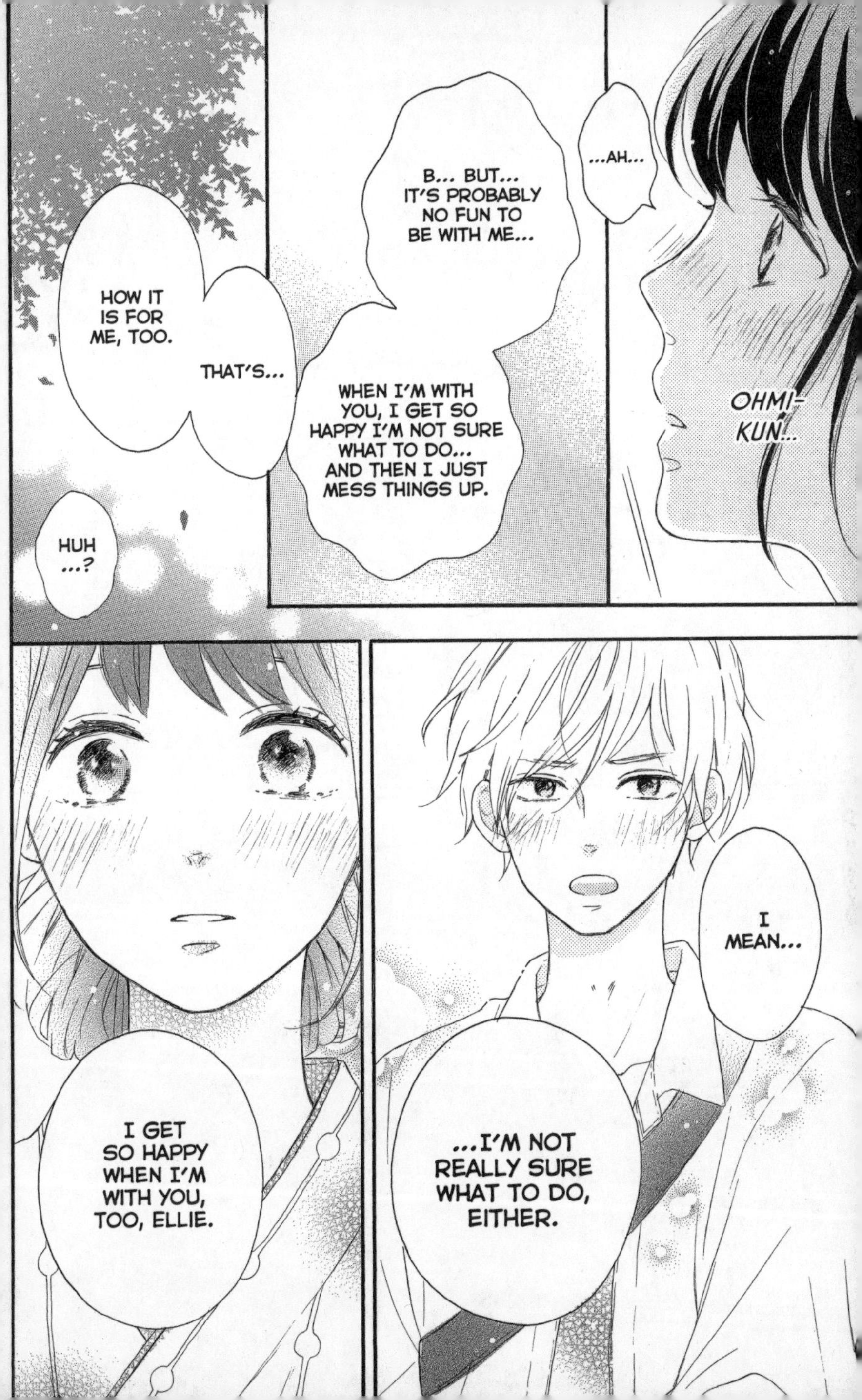
...AH...
OHMI-KUN...
B... BUT... IT'S PROBABLY NO FUN TO BE WITH ME...
WHEN I'M WITH YOU, I GET SO HAPPY I'M NOT SURE WHAT TO DO... AND THEN I JUST MESS THINGS UP.
THAT'S...
HOW IT IS FOR ME, TOO.
HUH ...?
I MEAN...
...I'M NOT REALLY SURE WHAT TO DO, EITHER.
I GET SO HAPPY WHEN I'M WITH YOU, TOO, ELLIE.

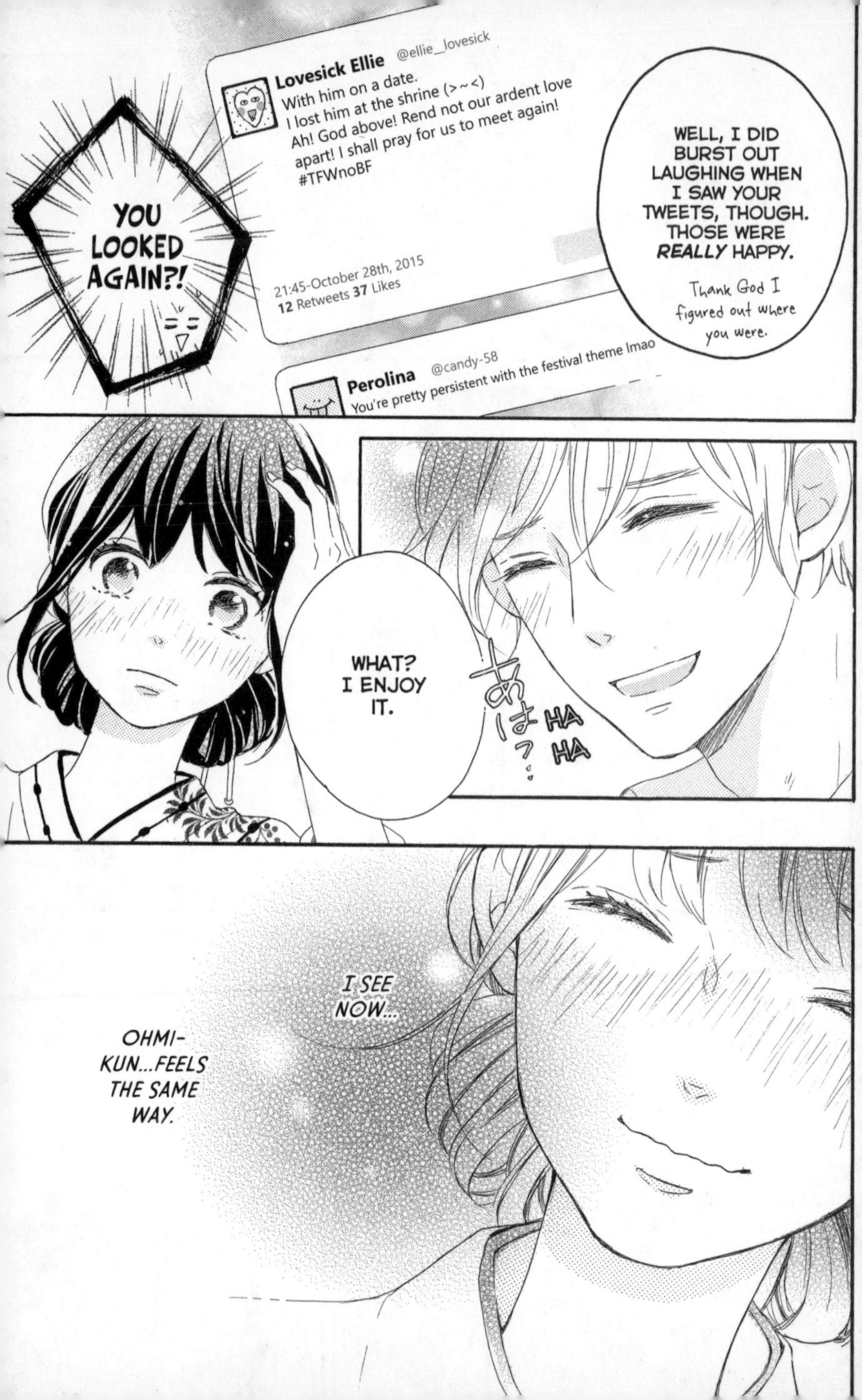

WELL, I DID BURST OUT LAUGHING WHEN I SAW YOUR TWEETS, THOUGH. THOSE WERE *REALLY* HAPPY.
Thank God I figured out where you were.
Lovesick Ellie @ellie__lovesick
With him on a date.
I lost him at the shrine (>~<)
Ah! God above! Rend not our ardent love apart! I shall pray for us to meet again!
#TFWnoBF
21:45-October 28th, 2015
12 Retweets 37 Likes
Perolina @candy-58
You're pretty persistent with the festival theme lmao
YOU LOOKED AGAIN?!
あはっ
HA HA
WHAT? I ENJOY IT.
I SEE NOW...
OHMI-KUN...FEELS THE SAME WAY.

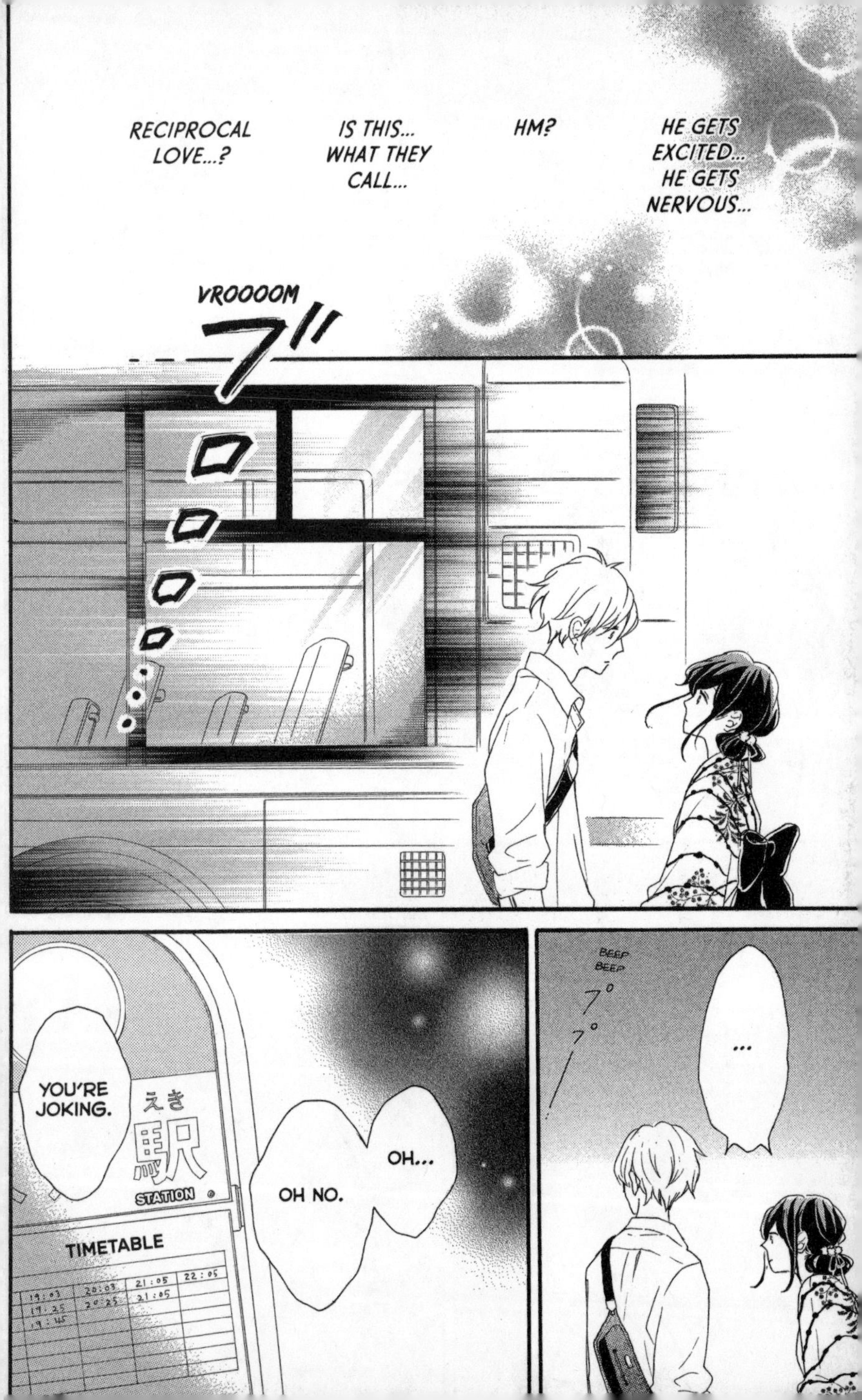
HE GETS EXCITED... HE GETS NERVOUS...
HM?
IS THIS... WHAT THEY CALL...
RECIPROCAL LOVE...?
VROOOOM
BEEP BEEP
...
OH...
OH NO.
YOU'RE JOKING.
えき
駅
STATION
TIMETABLE
19:03 20:03 21:05 22:05
19:25 20:25 21:05
19:45

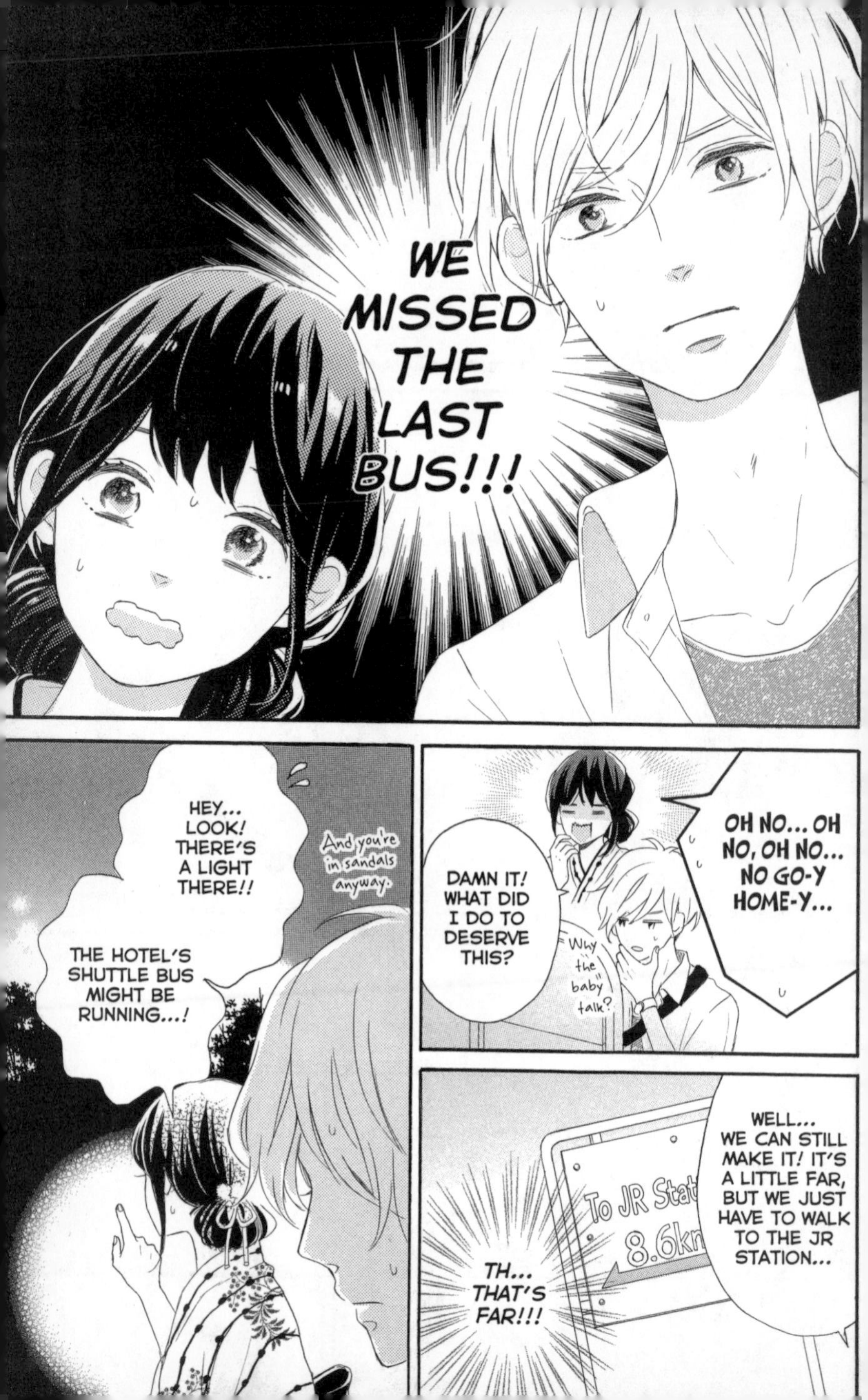

WE MISSED THE LAST BUS!!!
OH NO... OH NO, OH NO... NO GO-Y HOME-Y...
DAMN IT! WHAT DID I DO TO DESERVE THIS?
Why the "baby talk?"
WELL... WE CAN STILL MAKE IT! IT'S A LITTLE FAR, BUT WE JUST HAVE TO WALK TO THE JR STATION...
TH... THAT'S FAR!!!
HEY... LOOK! THERE'S A LIGHT THERE!!
And you're in sandals anyway.
THE HOTEL'S SHUTTLE BUS MIGHT BE RUNNING...!

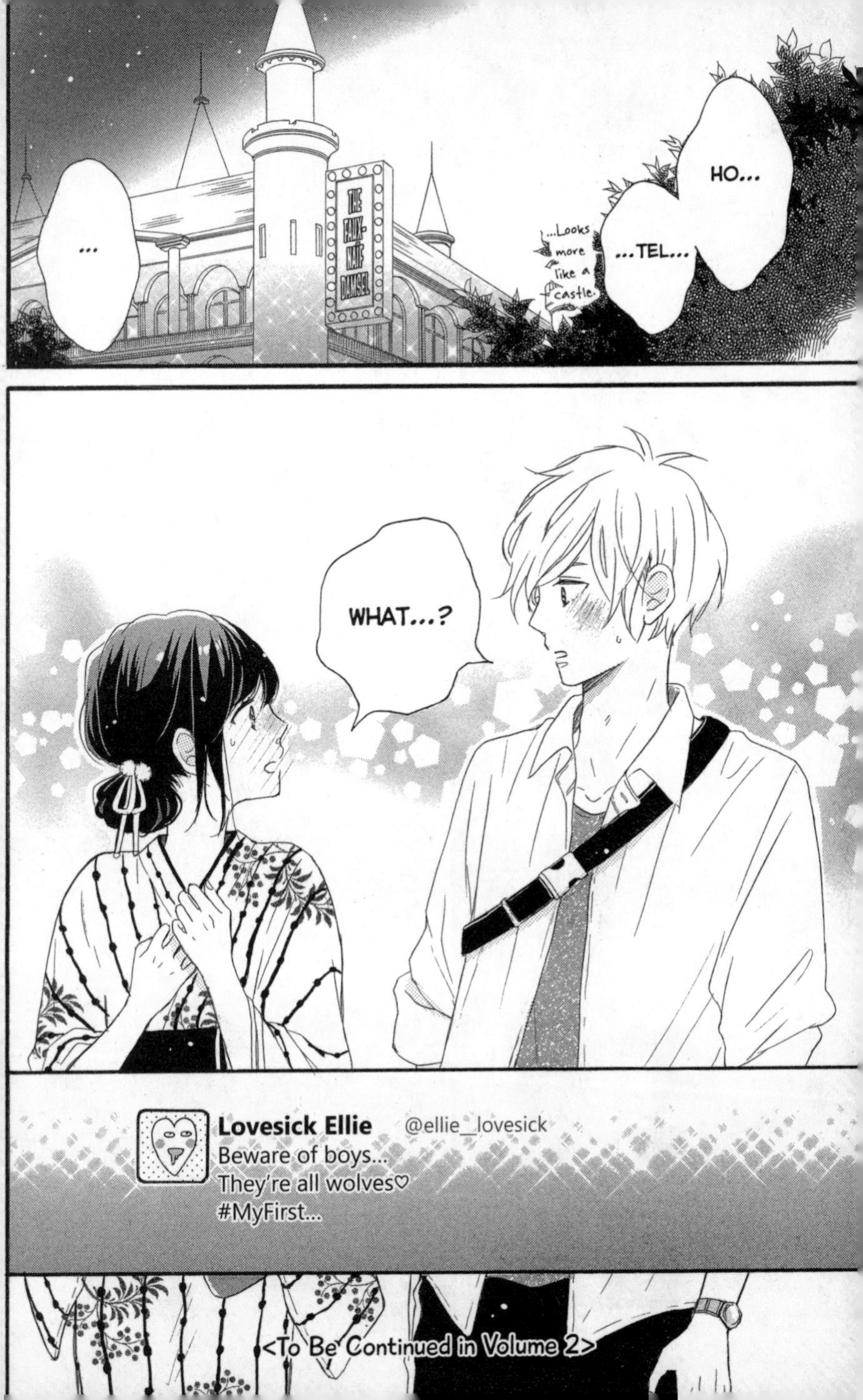
HO...
...TEL...
...Looks more like a castle.
THE FAUX-NAÏF DAMSEL
...
WHAT...?
Lovesick Ellie @ellie_lovesick
Beware of boys...
They're all wolves♡
#MyFirst...
<To Be Continued in Volume 2>

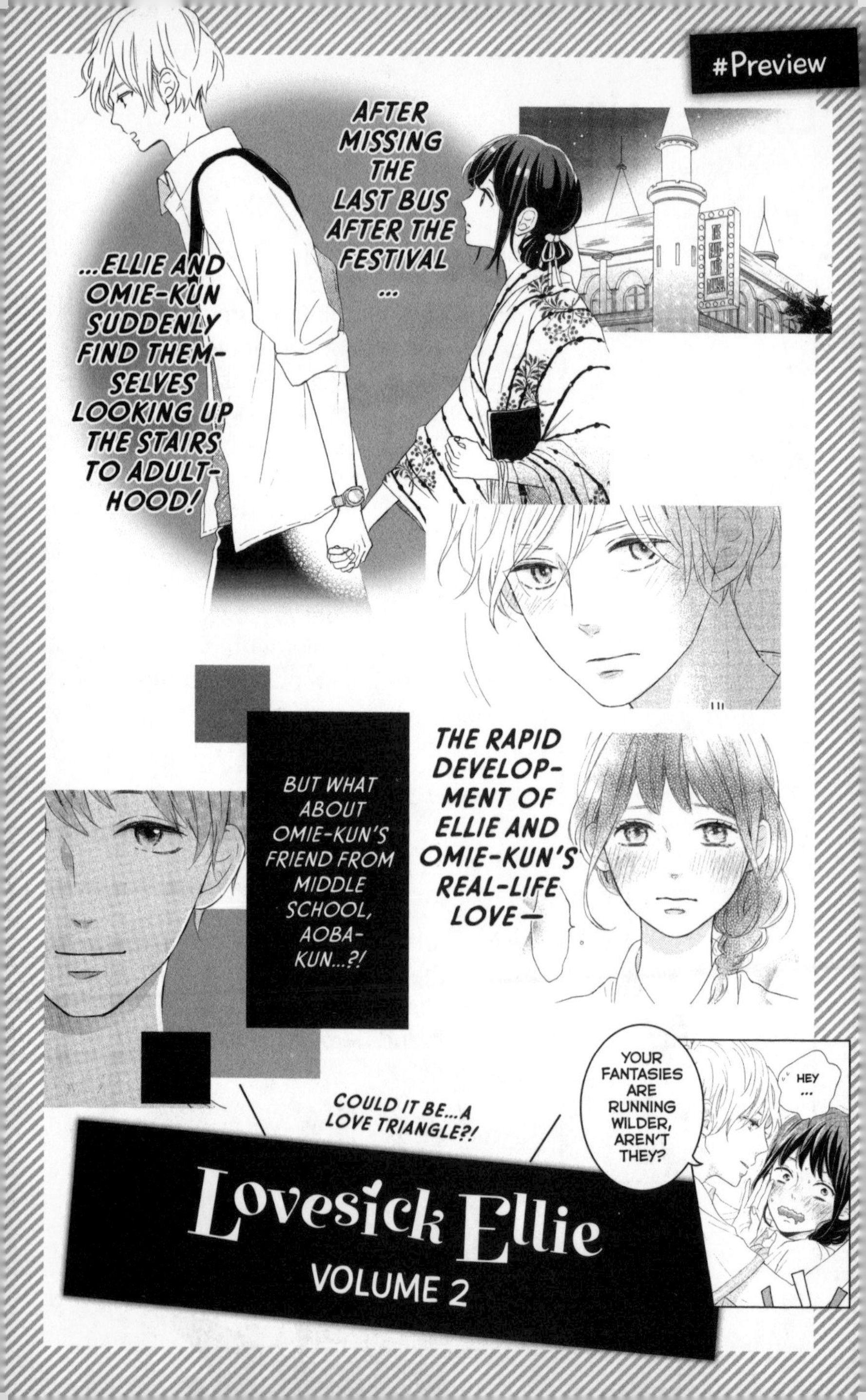
#Preview
AFTER MISSING THE LAST BUS AFTER THE FESTIVAL...
...ELLIE AND OMIE-KUN SUDDENLY FIND THEMSELVES LOOKING UP THE STAIRS TO ADULTHOOD!
THE RAPID DEVELOPMENT OF ELLIE AND OMIE-KUN'S REAL-LIFE LOVE—
BUT WHAT ABOUT OMIE-KUN'S FRIEND FROM MIDDLE SCHOOL, AOBA-KUN...?!
HEY...
YOUR FANTASIES ARE RUNNING WILDER, AREN'T THEY?
COULD IT BE...A LOVE TRIANGLE?!
Lovesick Ellie
VOLUME 2

Lovesick Ellie

@Translation_Notes

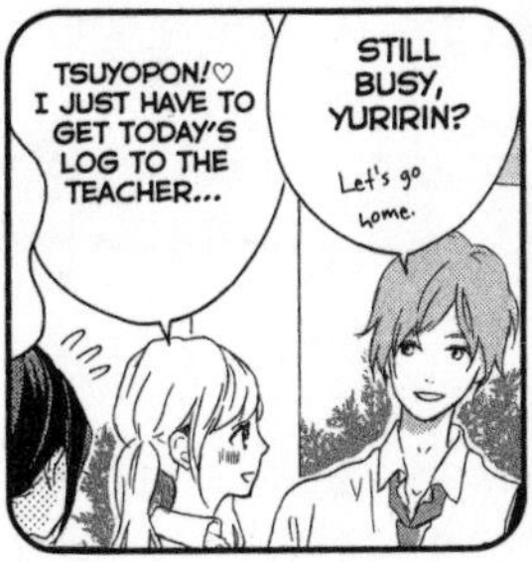
STILL BUSY, YURIRIN?
Let's go home.
TSUYOPON!♡ I JUST HAVE TO GET TODAY'S LOG TO THE TEACHER...

Nicknames @pages 8 and 71
In Japanese, a common way to form a nickname is by adding a cute suffix like *-pon, -rin,* or *-chi* to someone's first or last name. The *-tsuin* in "Eritsuin" is a play on the more common cutesy suffix *-chin.* In the Japanese, Ohmi's name is simply shortened to "Omi" as a nickname, which became "Omie" in English for clarity.

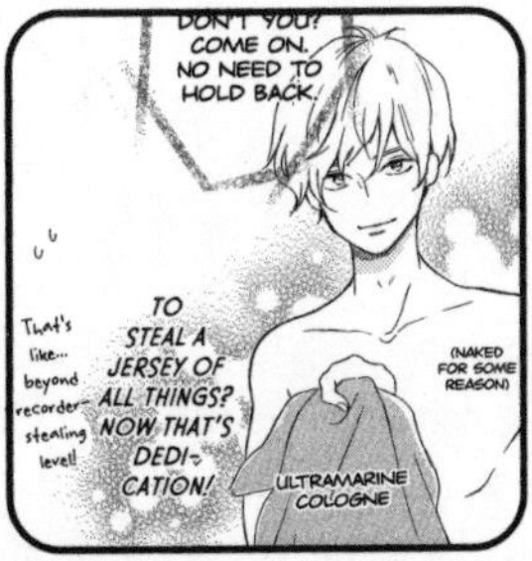
COME ON. NO NEED TO HOLD BACK.
(NAKED FOR SOME REASON)
ULTRAMARINE COLOGNE
TO STEAL A JERSEY OF ALL THINGS? NOW THAT'S DEDI-CATION!
That's like... beyond recorder-stealing level!

Stealing recorders @page 25
Learning the recorder is typically compulsory during elementary and middle school in Japan. Stealing the recorder of your crush is thought to be a sign of affection.

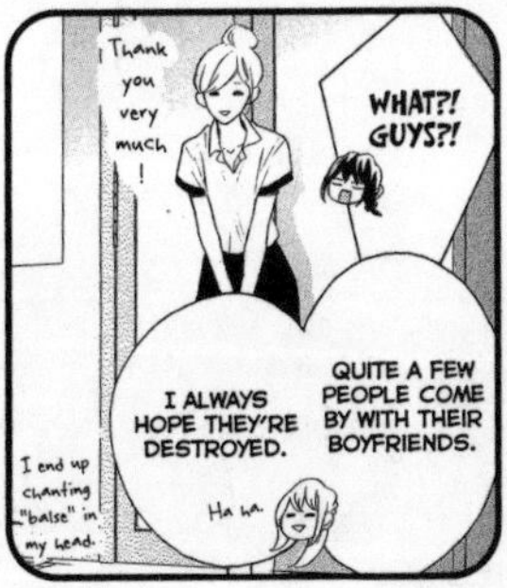
WHAT?! GUYS?!
Thank you very much!
QUITE A FEW PEOPLE COME BY WITH THEIR BOYFRIENDS.
I ALWAYS HOPE THEY'RE DESTROYED.
Ha ha.
I end up chanting "balse" in my head.

Balse @page 104
The incantation used to destroy the castle at the end of the Studio Ghibli film *Castle in the Sky.* It has since become a prominent and beloved meme on 2ch and Twitter.

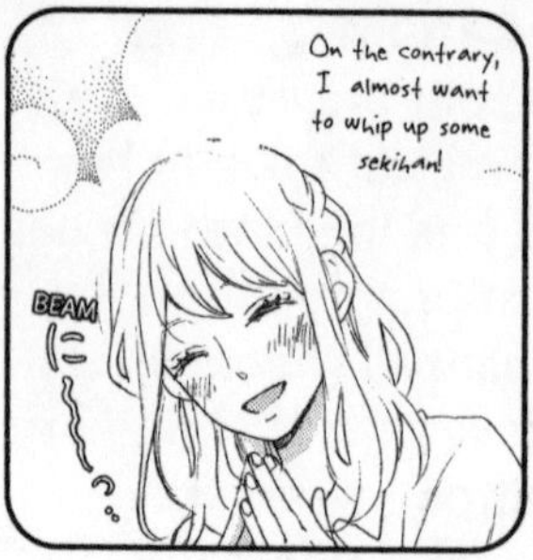
On the contrary, I almost want to whip up some sekihan!
BEAM

Sekihan @page 124

Literally meaning "red rice," this traditional Japanese dish consists of glutinous rice and red beans, and is eaten during auspicious occasions such as birthdays and weddings. In this case, Sara's offer to make *sekihan* is her way of preemptively celebrating Eriko taking the next step in her relationship with Ohmi.

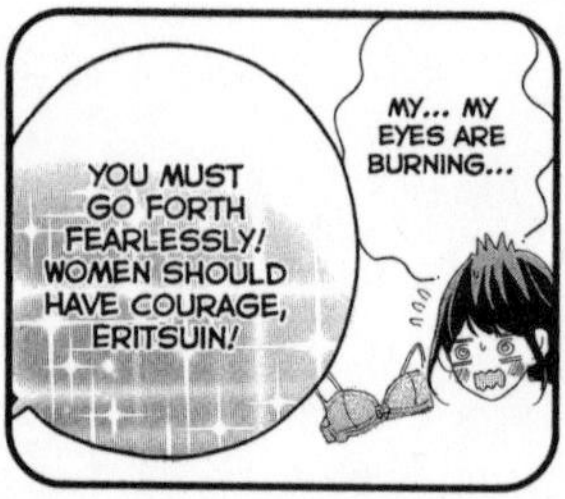
MY... MY EYES ARE BURNING...
YOU MUST GO FORTH FEARLESSLY! WOMEN SHOULD HAVE COURAGE, ERITSUIN!

Women should have courage

@pages 97 and 125

This chapter title is a twist on an old Japanese saying that can be translated as,"Men should have courage, and women charm." As it relates to Eriko, Sara wants to inspire her to be courageous and pursue her feelings for Ohmi proactively, rather than waiting around for him to make a move.

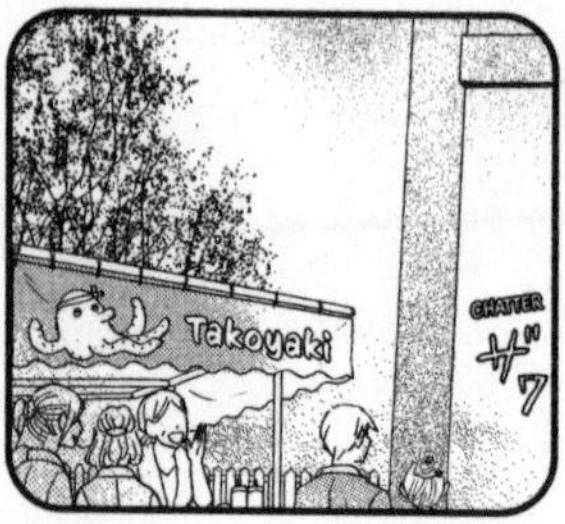
Takoyaki
CHAPTER
7

Festival foods @pages 137 and 141

The festival in chapter four features some common Japanese street foods, including *takoyaki* (fried octopus balls), *ikayaki* (fried squid), and *tori kara* (fried chicken).

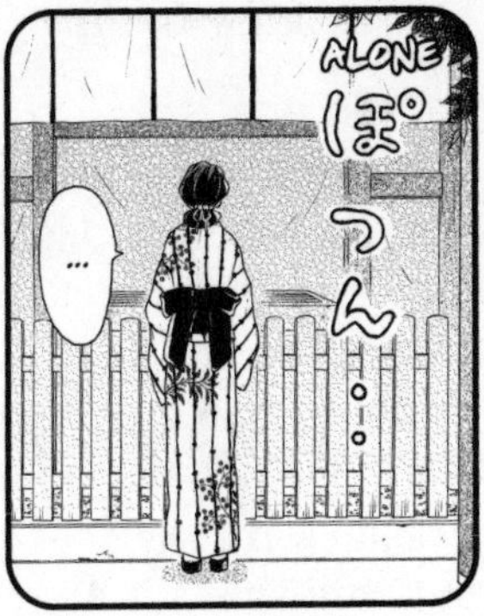
ALONE
ぽつん。。。
...

Pray to meet again @page 171

Eriko's tweet about praying at the shrine gave Ohmi just the hint he needed to find her. In Shinto shrines, the custom is to pray to the shrine deity at the main hall (*honden*). On page 165, Eriko is seen standing in front of the slatted offering box, where visitors make monetary offerings just before beginning their prayers.

Lovesick Ellie

Lovesick Ellie

PERFECT WORLD

Rie Aruga

A TOUCHING
NEW SERIES
ABOUT LOVE AND
COPING WITH
DISABILITY

An office party reunites Tsugumi with her high school crush Itsuki. He's realized his dream of becoming an architect, but along the way, he experienced a spinal injury that put him in a wheelchair. Now Tsugumi's rekindled feelings will butt up against prejudices she never considered — and Itsuki will have to decide if he's ready to let someone into his heart...

"Depicts with great delicacy and courage the difficulties some with disabilities experience getting involved in romantic relationships... Rie Aruga refuses to romanticize, pushing her heroine to face the reality of disability. She invites her readers to the same tasks of empathy, knowledge and recognition."
—Slate.fr

"An important entry [in manga romance]... The emotional core of both plot and characters indicates thoughtfulness... [Aruga's] research is readily apparent in the text and artwork, making this feel like a real story."
—Anime News Network